# BRITISH EXPERIMENTAL JET AIRCRAFT

## BARRIE HYGATE

ARGUS BOOKS

Argus Books
Argus House
Boundary Way
Hemel Hempstead
Hertfordshire HP2 7ST

First published by Argus Books 1990

ISBN 1 85486 010 0

Phototypesetting by GCS, Leighton Buzzard
Printed and bound in Great Britain by William Clowes Ltd, Beccles

# CONTENTS

# ABOUT THE AUTHOR

Barrie Hygate was born in 1938 in Sussex and educated at Collyer's Grammar School in Horsham. His first experience of flying was as a member of the RAF section of the school's Combined Cadet Force, in a Tiger Moth at Redhill Aerodrome, and he also gained a Flying Scholarship, attaining a Private Pilot's Licence shortly after his seventeenth birthday, again in a Tiger Moth flying at Croydon Airport.

He joined the RAF directly from school in September 1956, and trained in Canada on Harvards and T.33's. On completion of training, he completed two operational tours on fighter/ground attack squadrons in England and Singapore, flying Hunters, before attending the Empire Test Pilots School at Farnborough in 1964. He subsequently served at the RAE until leaving the RAF in 1967 to join Handley Page as a development test pilot, primarily on the Jetstream.

On the demise of Handley Page, he started his airline career with Courtline on BAC 1-11's and then with British Caledonian, firstly on the 1-11, then the DC.10. He joined Air Europe at its birth in 1979, firstly commanding the Boeing 737 then the Boeing 757. He is currently flying as an A.320 captain with Cyprus Airways.

His flying career spans some 33 years, on nearly 40 types of aircraft, with to date over 13,000 hours experience.

# ACKNOWLEDGEMENTS

In preparing a book of this nature the task would be impossible without the help and assistance of many individuals and firms. I was very pleased to find that, in the majority of cases, most of my queries and requests for assistance were received with interest and in many cases enthusiasm. Sadly this was not always the case, and it was very frustrating to know that data or information was available but could not be got at for whatever reason.

I would like to make special mention of, and give thanks to, the following individuals to whom I shall always be indebted:— Brian Kervell, RAE Farnborough; Harry Fraser-Mitchell, Handley Page Association; James Goulding, (for Gloster data); Bob Marsh, Hawkers, (for the P.1121 data); Ray Williams, (for A.W.52 data); Eric Morgan, (for Supermarine 545 and TSR.2 data); Mr R Wheeler, Technical Director, Westland Aerospace, (for SR.53. and SR.177 data); Bill Gunston; the RAF Air Historical Branch; The Librarian, A&AEE Boscombe Down; RAF Museum Archives staff; Public Records Office staff; and the Curators of RAF Museum Cosford, RAF Museum Henlow, FAA Museum Yeovilton, IWM Duxford and Midlands Air Museum, who kindly allowed me to crawl all over and around their precious aircraft.

There are many more individuals, but I would need a whole chapter to thank all of them, so, to them, many thanks for their time and patience. Finally, thanks to my wife, Zelma, who at times did not see me for days on end while I was visiting everyone around the country, and who recently has become a 'computer widow' while I was preparing the manuscript – at times she wished she had never bought me a word processor!

The drawings in this book are all to a common 1/72 scale except for those of the SR.A/1 (1/96) and Short SA.4. (1/144), due to reasons of space. Copies of the drawings to 1/72 scale and 1/48 scale are available from the publisher, through the Argus Plans Service.

# Introduction

With the advent of the jet engine as a viable power plant for aircraft, the designers' horizons broadened enormously, with the prospect of developing aircraft which could operate at speeds and altitudes until then only dreamed of. As has always happened in aviation, war accelerated developments, with progress in some countries – especially Germany – being extremely rapid. Much useful research material came to light after the Second World War when Germany capitulated, as it was the indisputable leader in the field of aerodynamics, especially of the swept and delta wing.

With this new potential, however, came problems which until then had only been rarely encountered, such as compressibility at high Mach numbers, and the need to develop new materials and systems to cope with the exceptional heights, speed and temperatures which were encountered. Sadly, many people were to lose their lives in the search for the solutions.

When German research material came to light, some countries, notably America and Russia, welcomed it with open arms, quickly producing such aircraft as the F-86 Sabre and Mig-15, both taking full advantage of the swept-wing research data. For some peculiar reason, in most cases in Britain this material almost seemed to be treated with suspicion. Some designers seemed reluctant to apply the research findings, and it was almost a case of 're-inventing the wheel' before they began most cautiously to develop swept-wing aircraft. Money was also a problem, with all of the cut-backs after the war, as was the lack of qualified engineers. It is a sobering thought that, after the war, Boeing Aircraft employed more aeronautical engineers at Seattle than there were in the whole of the British aircraft industry!

It was not until the last month of 1948 that Britain had two swept-wing fighter prototypes flying, and one of those did not wish to stretch technology too far and have both the wing *and* tail swept: that would have been too adventurous! However, the one area of German data which the British industry really seemed to take to its heart was the delta wing. Of the forty-one designs covered in this book, fifteen of them had variations on this theme, but only two were true deltas with a 60° sweep angle, and one of those never flew. However, after this slow start, it is fair to say that some remarkable aircraft were produced, some leaders in their field, and others well in advance of their time.

Many more aircraft than those selected could have been included in this book and a conscious decision was made at the start to lay down certain criteria for inclusion. Firstly, the subject should not be a re-engined development of an earlier propeller-driven aircraft, thus ruling out some machines which made a valuable research contribution, such as the Avro Ashton, Miles Sparrowjet and the Vickers Tay Viscount, the first British jet airliner. Secondly, each subject must have reached an advanced stage of 'hardware', thus eliminating many projects. In this context, considerable time was spent in trying to assess whether the Miles M.52 should be included. Dependent on who was spoken to, it either did not get past the mock-up stage except for the odd component, or it was well on the way to completion when cancelled. One of its designers categorically stated the latter so, on balance, it was decided that it should be included. Finally, the subject must never have reached the production stage for issue to the Services. However, inevitably there were grey areas in this latter qualification, such as the P.1a which, after virtually an entire redesign, was to become the Lightning, the first British supersonic fighter prototype. Also, there is the Supermarine 525, which after extensive modification was eventually to become the Scimitar. This is included in its guise of the third prototype Supermarine 508.

Although I consulted many reference sources, nothing has been included in the book which could not be authenticated, or which was not source material. This also applies to the accompanying drawings. No areas are 'artists' licence', and any areas that may not be accurate for whatever reason are so noted in the text. I make no claim that the drawings are any more accurate than those which may have been previously published, but most of these were done when the aircraft was new and cloaked in secrecy, so the artists did not have the necessary information. All that can be claimed is that the drawings in this book contain more detail. The amount of coverage given to any subject bears no relationship to its importance, but to the data made available to me.

Problems were also caused by the 'rationalisation' of the aircraft industry, and many famous names have disappeared forever, together with many of their archives. Some, like Handley Page, have ceased trading, others like Fairey, have been taken over, their archives disappearing, being dispersed or even deliberately destroyed, all of which made the task a bit harder. With this happening at what appears to be an accelerating rate, I feel that this might be the last chance to give these unique aircraft a good detailed coverage.

For those who have a long memory, when these aircraft were flying they were most exciting times, the golden era being the early Fifties when it seemed that there was something new in the sky virtually every month, and the annual pilgrimage to Farnborough was a revelation. I hope that I have managed to awaken some of those memories for the older reader, and opened the eyes of some of the younger ones.

B. Hygate.
1 January 1990

The first prototype before receiving its camouflage scheme. Note bands of temperature sensitive paint along aft fuselage to determine the effects on the structure by the new type of power unit. (Pilot Press Ltd.)

# GLOSTER E.28/39

| Manufacturer | Gloster Aircraft Company Ltd |
|---|---|
| Specification | E.28/39 |
| Role | Experimental Fighter |
| First Flight Date | W4041/G — 15th May 1941 |
| | W4046/G — 1st March 1943 |

The specification was raised for a simple airframe to enable the testing of the first flight-capable jet engine. Although destined to be solely a research aircraft, armament was specified but never fitted. In the event, although one of the aircraft was lost, the specification was more than met during the protracted series of flight trials.

## DEVELOPMENT HISTORY

The first British bench-model experimental centrifugal thrust turbojet engine was successfully run on 12th April 1937 and, after extensive development, a flight rated engine was ordered on 7th July 1939.

Attempts were made to find an existing airframe in which to put it, the most suitable being the Gloster F.18/37. This was a single-seat, twin-boom fighter project, the short fuselage allowing a short

jetpipe, contributing to minimum thrust losses. However, this proposed conversion was eventually ruled out because of lack of aerodynamic knowledge regarding the effect of the jet efflux on the tailplane, and the need to keep the all-up weight below 3,500 lbs. due to the very low initial thrust available from the engine.

Therefore, a new Specification, E.28/39, was issued to cover the construction and development of two prototypes specially to accommodate the new engine. Although included in the 1939 batch of specifications, it was actually first issued on 1st January 1940. It called for a design speed of 330 kts., and the aircraft was to be capable of carrying four .303" Browning machine guns, with 500 rpg. (although these were never fitted).

To avoid possible damage from air raids, and to aid security, construction was completed in a garage in Cheltenham! The first prototype, serialed W4041/G (the 'G' signifying that an armed guard was required at all times on the ground) was completed in March 1941, and was taken to Brockworth for initial taxi-ing trials, fitted with a non-flight rated W1X engine. These trials started on 7th April 1941, with the engine limited to 1,300 rpm. Although intended solely to be ground trials, short hops were actually made after the first taxi run. The first landing was tail bumper first, causing the nose-wheel to slam down, and on the second hop (actually the third taxi run) the aircraft was airborne for some 200 yards!

The aircraft was returned to yet another garage in Cheltenham to have its nosewheel modified to allow increased travel. It was then transported by road to Cranwell where the first true flight was to be made. After arrival, and during reassembly, the flight rated W1 engine was fitted, with thrust increased to 860 lbs. It was declared ready for flight on 14th May 1941 but, as the weather was unsuitable, another high-speed taxi-test was made to check the modifications. The first true flight was made successfully on the evening of 15th May 1941, when the aircraft was airborne for 17 minutes, having been loaded with only about 75% fuel due to the low thrust of the engine. Two further flights were made on 16th May. On the third flight on 17th May, it achieved 262 kts. at 5,000 ft. at 16,500 rpm., and on the following day the first climb to height was made, achieving 20,000 ft.

The engine/airframe had been initially cleared for only ten hours flight before inspection and, in the thirteen days from the first flight, this was achieved in fifteen flights. Following this series of flights, therefore, the aircraft was dismantled, and returned to the factory to have a more powerful engine installed, but a full seven months passed before the new W1A engine was ready.

The aircraft was transported by road to Edgehill and was finally ready to continue flight trials on 4th February 1942. For the earlier trials, a 'low-speed' wing had been fitted, with a NACA 23012 section, but this had been replaced by a new 'high-speed' wing of EC1240 section at the root, and EC0940 section at the tip, giving a thickness/chord ratio at the root of 12% and at the tip of 9%. Handling with the new wing proved little different from the previous one, other than in a small increase in the stalling speed.

Some engine problems were encountered after less than 2.5 hours flight, requiring removal and a further ten-day delay. During a flight on 3rd April 1942, engine failure occurred caused by a turbine blade breaking, but a successful forced landing was made at Edgehill, keeping the engine at 10,000 rpm until touchdown. After a repair, a further engine failure occurred at a height of 30,000 ft., but this was due to the engine oil congealing at the very low ambient temperatures. (The advent of the jet engine caused many new aerodynamic problems to be overcome, owing to the vast increase of performance potential, but other attendant problems had also to be solved as the frontiers of knowledge were pushed back. Later in the aircraft's career, problems were encountered with the grease for control surface hinges doing the same thing as the engine oil, again due to inability to cope with very low temperatures.)

The engine oil system was modified, causing further delays and, even when cleared for flight, an emergency landing had to be made due to dropping oil pressure, during which slight damage to the left wingtip was sustained. Testing resumed at Edgehill, but after only four flights the aircraft was transported by road to Farnborough on 30th November 1943, where a further ten hours were spent clearing the modified oil system, before handing the aircraft over for Service evaluation and further trials. The first flight with an RAE pilot took place on 20th December 1943 and, in the short series, the longest flight made was of 54 minutes duration, and the highest altitude reached was 30,000 ft. The aircraft was then taken back to Gloster's factory to have the new Power Jets W2/500 engine installed.

Also at the factory, the second prototype W4046/G had been completed and was, at last and after much delay, having its power plant installed. This was a Rover W2B engine, which was a 'productionised' version of the Power Jets' unit, having nearly a 100% increase in thrust compared to

*The first prototype with the dark earth/dark green camouflage scheme. Note the size of the groundcrew's head in the cockpit, emphasizing the small size of the aircraft.*
*(Royal Aeronautical Society.)*

the first engine. The aircraft was transported by road to Edgehill for flight trials. Some brake-overheat problems were caused by the higher idling thrust of the engine, but a successful first flight was finally made on 1st March 1943.

The aircraft was to be demonstrated at Hatfield on the 19th April, and to get there it successfully completed the first 'cross-country' flight by a jet aircraft in England. The aircraft was flown to Farnborough on 3rd May 1943, and during subsequent trials flew over 50 hours without incident. However, on 30th July a climb was made to 37,000 ft., when aileron control problems were encountered (due to the wrong grease being used on the hinges), causing them to jam. The subsequent manoeuvre, thought to be an inverted spin, was of such violence that the pilot was thrown through the canopy. The aircraft was totally destroyed in the subsequent crash.

The first prototype was now airborne again with its new W2/500 engine, conducting high altitude trials, and the highest altitude achieved by the aircraft was 41,600 ft. A replacement W2/500 engine was installed on completion of this series, for a final 10 hours of stability and control tests, for which small auxiliary 'finlets' were mounted near to the tips of each tailplane surface, to improve directional stability at high speeds. The wing roots were also tufted, and a recording camera fitted at the left wingtip for airflow investigation.

The aircraft was finally grounded, having more than fulfilled the requirements of its original specification and, due to its unique position in British Aviation, was already earmarked for preservation. It still survives in the Science Museum in London, albeit with a spurious colour scheme!

## CONSTRUCTION

The aircraft was intended solely to test the new type of engine, and therefore no additional risks were taken with the use of new techniques or materials. Therefore the overall construction was completely conventional and state of the art, and was of stressed skin, light alloy throughout, except for the rudder which was fabric-covered. The engine, especially early on, had very little power available, and to reduce thrust losses, the intake and jetpipe were kept to the minimum length possible, with a simple, straight-through pitot intake, and the engine exhausting aft of the tail surfaces. The fuselage cross-section was circular over its entire length, with the intake ducting splitting either side of the cockpit, returning to a circular section behind the 81 gallon fuel tank mounted immediately aft of the cockpit, and just forward of the engine bay. The fuel tank and engine were mounted as near to the centre of gravity as possible. Access to the engine was via a large hatch in the upper fuselage skin, and it was mounted parallel to the fuselage datum, the jetpipe also having a 0° thrust-line. A substantial tail-bumper was fitted below the aft fuselage. Several access panels were provided in the lower fuselage skin.

The intake splitter housed the rearward retracting long-stroke nosewheel oleo, its bay being forward, and below, the cockpit. A prominent cooling intake was mounted just aft of the nosewheel bay, to the left of the aircraft centreline. The cockpit had a single-piece moulded windscreen, with an aft-sliding canopy for normal exit and entry. This could be jettisoned in an emergency. The pilot had a conventional seat (ejection seats had still not been developed) and the cockpit was neither pressurised nor heated! The single fuel tank was filled through a panel in the left side of the substantial fairing aft of the canopy.

The tailplane was mounted on a fairing above the main fuselage structure, at an incidence of +1°45',

*The first prototype after being fitted with small auxiliary fins to improve directional stability. The camouflage scheme has now been changed to dark green/dark grey. Note more tail-down attitude with full fuel load (Pilot Press Ltd.)*

with no dihedral and only slight taper to its rounded tips. The elevators were mass balanced but had no trim tabs fitted. Towards the end of the aircraft's career, and only to the first prototype, small auxiliary fins were fitted just outboard of the elevator mass-balances, to improve directional stability.

The relatively small fin and rudder were mounted so that the rudder trailing edge was at about mid-chord on the tailplane. Fin construction was around a single mainspar, to which the rudder was hinged, and a forward auxiliary spar with multiple ribs. As mentioned previously, the rudder was fabric-covered, hinged at three points, and also had no trim tab.

The wings were low-mounted, and were constructed around a single mainspar at about one-third chord, an aft auxiliary spar, to which the ailerons and flaps were hinged, and multiple ribs. For the initial series of trials a conventional, cambered wing, of NACA 23012 section was fitted, but this was soon replaced by a symmetrical section wing, with a root and tip chord of 12% and 9% respectively. The planforms of the two wings were identical. Sweep-back at 30% chord was zero, the overall dihedral angle was 4°12', and the incidence to the fuselage datum +1°. The resultant aspect ratio was 5.75:1. (Note: The second prototype was fitted only with the later wing.)

Split flaps occupied the trailing edge out to approximately half semi-span, outboard of which were the ailerons, each with a spring-balance tab, and outboard mass-balance. All flying control surfaces were manually operated via push/pull rods. A short pitot-head was mounted on the left wing leading edge approximately in line with the aileron's mid span.

The Dowty main undercarriage was fitted with low pressure tyres, and was aft retracting, the oleos turning through 90° during retraction to lie flat in their bays. Despite this, the undercarriage doors had to be bulged, and a streamlined fairing provided on the upper surfaces to give sufficient room for stowage.

An armament of four 0.303" Browning machine guns was specified, mounted in a row across the upper fuselage nose in front of the cockpit and above the intake ducting, but was never fitted.

## POWER PLANT
*First prototype.* For ground tests only, one Power

## DATA

**DIMENSIONS**

| | |
|---|---|
| Span | 29'0" |
| Length | 25'3.75" |
| Height | 9'3" |
| Tailplane Span | 12'0" |

**AREAS**

| | |
|---|---|
| Wing Area (gross) | 146.5 sq ft |
| (net) | 117.0 sq ft |
| Fin and Rudder | 12.8 sq ft |

**WEIGHTS**

| | | |
|---|---|---|
| Loaded weight | 3,604 lbs | (W1X engine) |
| | 3,700 lbs | (W1 engine) |
| | 3,828 lbs | (W1A engine) |
| | 4,180 lbs | (W2/500 engine) |

**PERFORMANCE**
**(W1 engine)**

| | | |
|---|---|---|
| $V_{max}$ | 5,000 ft | 290 kts |
| | 10,000 ft | 291 kts |
| | 20,000 ft | 294 kts |

**(W1A engine)**

| | | |
|---|---|---|
| $V_{max}$ | 330 kts+ | |
| Rate of Climb | 1,700 ft/min | at 1,000 ft |
| | 870 ft/min | at 29,000 ft |

**(W2/500 engine)**

| | |
|---|---|
| $V_{max}$ | 391 kts |
| Ceiling | 42,170 ft |

**(W2B engine)**

| | | |
|---|---|---|
| $V_{max}$ | 10,000 ft | 405 kts |
| Take Off roll | 990 ft | |
| Rate of Climb | 3,000 ft/min plus | at 1,000 ft |

**REFERENCES**

| | |
|---|---|
| 'Aircraft Illustrated' | —November 1969 |
| Science Museum | —The actual aircraft |
| RAE Farnborough | —Library Archives |

Jets W1X centrifugal flow turbojet engine rated at 620 lbs., Static Thrust, but changed for its initial flight trials to one Power Jets W1 centrifugal flow turbojet engine rated at 860 lbs., Static Thrust at 17,750 rpm. Then fitted with a Power Jets W1A centrifugal flow engine rated at 1,160 lbs., Static Thrust at 17,750 rpm. Finally fitted with a Power Jets W2/500 centrifugal flow engine rated initially at 1,620 lbs., Static Thrust, and later 1,700 lbs., thrust both at 16,500 rpm.

*Second prototype.* One Rover W2B centrifugal flow turbojet engine rated at 1,200 lbs., Static Thrust at 15,680 rpm., later 1,526 lbs., thrust at 16,930 rpm.

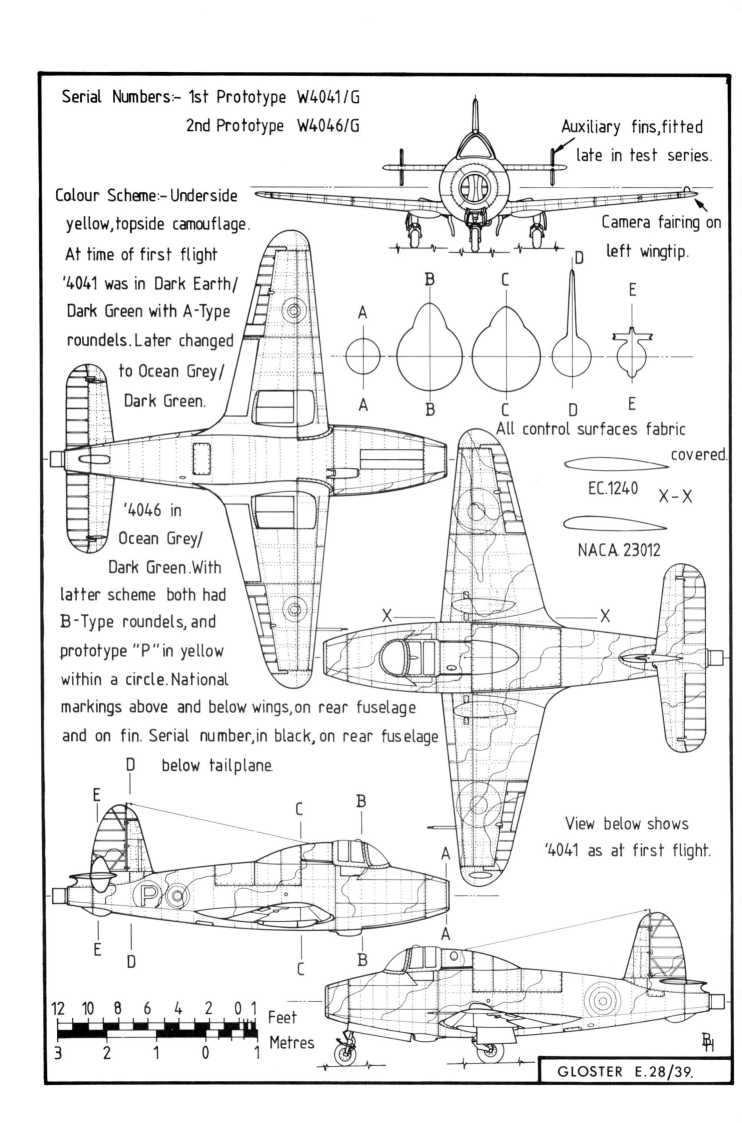

Serial Numbers:– 1st Prototype W4041/G
2nd Prototype W4046/G

Auxiliary fins, fitted late in test series.

Colour Scheme:– Underside yellow, topside camouflage. At time of first flight '4041 was in Dark Earth/ Dark Green with A-Type roundels. Later changed to Ocean Grey/ Dark Green.

Camera fairing on left wingtip.

'4046 in Ocean Grey/ Dark Green. With latter scheme both had B-Type roundels, and prototype "P" in yellow within a circle. National markings above and below wings, on rear fuselage and on fin. Serial number, in black, on rear fuselage below tailplane.

All control surfaces fabric covered.

EC.1240        X – X

NACA 23012

View below shows '4041 as at first flight.

12 10 8 6 4 2 0 1  Feet
3    2    1    0    1  Metres

GLOSTER E.28/39.

*The first prototype just after take-off. A good view of the fixed leading edge slats and the small under wing tip skids.*

# DE HAVILLAND 108

| Manufacturer | de Havilland Aircraft Company Ltd |
|---|---|
| Specification | E.18/45 |
| Role | Experimental Prototype |
| First Flight Date | TG 283 – 15th May 1946 |
| | TG 306 – 21st August 1946 |
| | VW 120 – 24th July 1947 |

Originally planned as a half-scale model of the proposed DH.106 airliner, which when initially conceived was of tail-less layout, events overtook the design while it was under construction. Its career was to be entirely directed to general research into the problems of stability and control of swept-wing aircraft, and it became the first British aircraft to exceed the speed of sound, albeit while totally out of control!

## DEVELOPMENT HISTORY

Immediately after the Second World War, the thoughts of British design teams turned to the resurrection of the civil aircraft industry. Several new designs were started, utilising the new power plants then becoming available and the research completed mainly by the Germans into high speed flight and swept-wing design. The Brabazon Committee was set up to oversee this, and one of the designs to emerge was the world's first all-jet passenger aircraft, eventually to fly as the Comet airliner. However, the DH.106, as it was designated, started life as a tail-less design with sharply swept wings and, due to the radical nature of its layout, it was felt prudent to fly what in effect was a half-scale model to test its aerodynamics. This experimental aircraft was designated the DH.108 and unofficially named 'Swallow'.

The basic design had already been finalised by July 1945, and official authority for the construction of two prototypes to Specification E.18/45 was quickly received by November of the same year. The draft broad specification called for the aircraft to be capable of speeds up to 565 kts., and 0.9 Mach. However, in anticipation of the receipt of official backing, detailed design work had been completed

11

and construction already started by this time.

However, it had already become apparent that the layout was unsuitable for a long-range airliner, and therefore the aircraft was to fulfil purely a research role into high-speed flight characteristics of swept wings, and especially to investigate the load distribution across a swept wing. It was therefore extensively instrumented, and the necessary plumbing was installed for pressure plotting.

Due to the urgency of the programme and the need to keep costs low, it was proposed that standard DH.100 Vampire 1 fuselage nacelles should be used straight from the production lines at Warton. However, it was found necessary to design an entirely new rear fuselage aft of the mainspar mounting frame, which was longer than the original, probably to give the fin and rudder a longer control arm to improve directional stability characteristics. The Ministry also wished to have an ejection seat fitted, but accepted that this would require extensive redesign of the cockpit area and forward fuselage, thereby delaying the completion of the aircraft.

Construction of the two prototypes was well under way: the first, TG 283, intended for the investigation of the low-speed characteristics of the wing, and the second, TG 306, for the high-speed end of the flight envelope. The only real difference, initially, between the two machines were fixed leading-edge slats together with anti-spin para-chutes at the wingtips on the former, and retractable slats and no wingtip fairings on the latter.

The first prototype was completed and ready for ground trials on 28th April 1946, a remarkably short time from inception. However, due to work at Hatfield and the need for secrecy, the aircraft was dismantled and taken by road to Woodbridge, which had a very long runway and was isolated from prying eyes by being situated in the middle of a pine forest. On arrival, reassembly and systems testing were rapidly completed, and taxi-ing trials were started within the short period of six days. There were some initial problems with brake overheating, but the first flight was successfully completed on 15th May 1946. After only four days testing, the aircraft was flown back to Hatfield to continue with the manufacturer's trials. These continued until October 1948, when the aircraft was delivered to RAE Farnborough for further research, particularly into the approach and landing phases of flight. It was modified by the substitution of a long-stroke main undercarriage from a Sea Vampire, to allow higher incidences to be used for landing, speeds being achieved as low as 95 kts. (This new undercarriage required a modified bay to accommodate it when retracted, but it is not clear whether this further modification was made to the airframe.) Thus, the wheels may have been permanently locked down for these trials.

During these trials, on 1st May 1950, the aircraft stalled, entering a spin from which recovery was not possible due to the extremely low altitude, and the aircraft crashed. Without an ejection seat, the pilot could not bail out in the time available, and was killed.

The second prototype, serialed TG 306, joined the test programme just over three months after the first, making its first flight on 21st August 1945. This rapidly started to explore the high speed characteristics and, by its fourth flight, had already climbed to 35,000 ft., achieving 0.89 Mach and, by its seventh flight, had reached an indicated airspeed of 547 kts., at 1,500 ft. Despite dire warnings as a result of wind tunnel tests at the RAE, the aircraft was found relatively pleasant to fly, but already showed characteristics considerably different from those of an aircraft with a normal tail configuration. Approach to land was made at higher speeds than desirable, with flat angles due to the low drag, but larger flaps could not be used due to the resultant trim changes being uncontrollable without a separate tailplane. A marked nose-down trim-change was experienced above 0.88 Mach, together with short period pilot-induced oscillations due to the lack of damping in pitch (very similar to those later to be found on the A.W.52 flying wing design).

*In preparation for a Speed Record attempt from Tangmere*

*The first prototype. Note the fixed leading-edge slats and parachute fairings on the wingtips, both for low-speed trials. (Royal Aeronautical Society)*

It was already apparent that the aircraft was capable of beating the speed record of 535.28 kts. held by a Meteor. After the decision had been taken to make the attempt, a modified cockpit canopy was fitted, with more extensive use of metal and thus reduced window area, plus the external finish of the machine was cleaned up. It had been intended not to exceed 0.87 Mach until powered controls were fitted, but after these modifications it was found that the aircraft was capable of achieving 0.895 Mach.

The actual attempt at the record was to be made from Tangmere, near the south coast, but a final trial was to be made from Hatfield on 27th September before ferrying the aircraft there. This trial, as well as including dives from altitude, was to include high speed runs at low level to simulate the conditions for the actual record attempt. During these trials, severe pitching oscillations were encountered, leading rapidly to loss of control, and the aircraft crashed killing the pilot, who stood no chance under these conditions, especially without an ejection seat. Thus the second prototype's life was only just over one month from first flight.

However, much valuable work had been done, and the design's potential recognised, so that a replacement aircraft was immediately ordered, with several modifications in the light of examination of the wreckage of the crashed machine. These included the overall strengthening of the fuselage,

and all fittings which had failed on the crashed aircraft, no matter for what reason, were also strengthened; however, the wing structure was not changed. The structure was modified to allow the fitting of a tailplane near the tip of the fin at a later date, dependent on further flight and wind tunnel trials. From the pilots' viewpoint, the most significant change was the provision of an ejection seat, necessitating changes to the cockpit and forward fuselage. The overall design was also further cleaned up, with a more pointed nosecone, and much more streamlined cockpit canopy, requiring the seat to be lowered even further in the structure to give the necessary clearances. Powered controls were also at last fitted. The basic fuselage was still based on that of a production Vampire, which at this time was a Mark 5. An uprated engine was also installed to improve performance even further. However, the specification remained unchanged despite the knowledge that the aircraft would more than exceed its requirements.

The third machine, serialed VW 120, was completed and made its first flight on 24th July 1947, and it immediately continued the high speed research programme. Most flights were taken up with pressure plotting, and control and stability trials; however, time was taken out to attempt successfully a new 100 kms., closed-circuit speed record. This was achieved on 12th April 1948, the average speed of the DH.108 being 525.93 kts.

High altitude, high Mach tests continued, and further investigation was made into the pitching oscillation phenomenon, which was hindering the safe achievement of higher speeds than 0.88 Mach. Several solutions were put forward, including the fitting of an autopilot and the removal of the elevon mass-balances. Never-exceed limits were therefore established to avoid problems; these varied dependent on altitude from 0.81 Mach at sea level to 0.97 Mach at 40,000 ft. It was found that pitch control deteriorated to be insufficient at 0.97 Mach, and roll control was totally lost at 0.99 Mach!

On 6th September 1948, a flight test was made from high altitude, when a dive was entered at 45,000 ft. at 0.85 Mach. The initial dive angle was only 30°. Pitching oscillation was experienced at 0.94 Mach and recovery was attempted, but the nose-down pitch became more marked, the aircraft recording -3g. The dive angle increased rapidly to past the vertical, despite the pilot pulling back on the control column with all his strength and both hands. The aircraft hurtled earthwards achieving an indicated 1.04 Mach. As the altitude rapidly reduced, the pitch trim gradually became effective, the dive angle reduced and, with power right off, the aircraft started to decelerate. Controls became effective passing 0.98 Mach, and the aircraft was finally back in level flight at 0.94 Mach at 23,500 ft. Instrument error was calculated, and a true speed of 1.02 Mach had been achieved. The aircraft had thus become the first British aircraft, and the first jet aircraft in the world, to exceed the speed of sound, although completely out of control!

The aircraft exceeded Mach 1 on only one other occasion, this being on 1st March 1949. The characteristics in this dive were completely different. After passing 0.97 Mach, control recovery action was attempted but was unsuccessful. On passing 0.98 Mach severe pitch down was experienced and roll control was totally lost, the bank angle exceeding 90°! At this point the roll virtually stopped, and the nose pitched up. Deceleration and control were achieved during the ensuing climb.

In November of the same year, the aircraft was delivered to Farnborough for trials into the longitudinal stability and control characteristics of the aircraft. During one of these flights, on 15th February 1950, for reasons never fully established, the pilot lost control, did not eject and was killed in the resulting crash.

Despite all three prototypes having crashed, and having killed the pilot on each occasion, much valuable work had been done into the characteristics of the swept wing. The severe limitations of the tail-less layout had been well demonstrated, only to come really into their own many years later with the advent of artificial stability and computer-controlled flight. However, the aircraft had earned its place in history by being the first aircraft to exceed the speed of sound, capable of taking-off and landing under its own power.

# CONSTRUCTION

To speed construction and reduce costs, the forward fuselage aft to the mainspar attachment frame was from a standard production DH.100 Vampire 1 fighter. (The third prototype utilised a Vampire 5 forward fuselage.) This was suitably modified and re-stressed to enable the fitting of the swept wing. The structure was of mixed construction, including a moulded wooden nosecone. The Vampire cockpit canopy was un-modified, and the same fuselage-mounted fuel tank was used. Apart from some additional test instrumentation, the cockpit was also standard, and unpressurised. The radio and instrumentation bays were situated immediately aft of the cockpit, with the whip aerial for the VHF radio being on the top of the fuselage, aft of the canopy rear fairing.

Although the same engine mounts were used, the aft fuselage was completely new, made entirely from light alloy and, compared to the Vampire aft fuselage, was lengthened and streamlined, the jetpipe being installed to give a downthrust angle of 2°. A new, much taller, swept fin and rudder were added, of all light alloy, two-spar construction with multiple ribs. Leading and trailing edge sweep angles were 51°20' and 34° respectively. The rudder was hinged to the aft spar and had a range of movement of ±28°. It was fitted with a spring/ trim tab and was mass balanced at its tip.

The above details also applied to the second prototype, with the exception of the shape of the sliding part of the cockpit canopy which was much strengthened, being made from metal with less transparency area. (This was normal practice for the time, due to the limitations of the normal moulded canopies during high-speed flight tests.) Although it was officially felt desirable, neither aircraft were fitted with ejection seats, due to the urgency of the programme and the necessity for major modification to the fuselage structure to accommodate them.

The third prototype was, however, modified to enable an ejection seat to be fitted, it being mounted much lower in the fuselage to enable its top to clear the shallow, more streamlined, cockpit canopy. The whole canopy was wider and more semi-circular in cross-section than before and, in place of the flat forward windscreen panel and quarter-lights, a moulded, curved windscreen was fitted with a slim, central strengthening frame. The nosecone was lengthened and made more pointed, and the fuselage structure generally strengthened. Another minor improvement was a modified shape to the rudder horn balance.

The swept wing was the aircraft's most radical new feature. All three prototypes possessed basically the same wing planform. Construction was around a mainspar at approximately 33% chord, with fore and aft auxiliary spars, the control surfaces being hinged to the latter. The sweep angles were 43°47', 36°33' and 25°42' measured at the leading edge, mainspar and trailing edge respectively. Although the fuselage mountings for the spars had been modified, the standard Vampire intake and ducting was used, giving the root a thickness/chord ratio of 12.6% measured at the fuselage fairing. Outboard of the ducting and root fillet, the outer panels were of constant 10% thickness/chord ratio from root to tip. The wing was mounted at zero incidence to the fuselage datum, and had no dihedral or washout.

Two additional fuel tanks were fitted inboard on each side between the forward and mainspars and were gravity-filled through panels in the upper wing surface. The standard Vampire mainwheels and oleos were mounted aft of the mainspar, hinged to retract inwards and faired into the wing-root fillet when retracted.

The control surfaces comprised an inboard trim/landing flap out to approximately 50% semi-span of the trailing edge, outboard of which were the elevons which reached right to the wingtips. Directional control was via the rudder, longitudinal and lateral control was by elevons and trim surfaces. (With the exception of the third aircraft, all flying controls were manually operated, but those for VW 120 were powered, apart from the rudder which remained manual.) The elevons had a movement range of ±10° and each had a trim/balance tab at its inboard end. When used in their trimming role, the inboard flaps had a movement range of –15° to +5° and, when used as landing flaps, they could be

| DATA | | |
|---|---|---|
| **DIMENSIONS** | | |
| Span | 39'0" | |
| Length | 25'10" | (TG 283) |
| | 24'6" | (TG 306) |
| | 26'9.5" | (VW 120) |
| Height | 9'8" | |
| Track | 10'10.5" | |
| Wheelbase | 12'8" | |
| **AREAS** | | |
| Wing | 328 sq ft | |
| Fin and rudder (net) | 21 sq ft | |
| **WEIGHTS** | | |
| No Record | | |
| **PERFORMANCE** | | |
| $V_{max}$ | 550 kts | (Sea Level) |
| | 1.02 Mach | (30,000 ft) |
| **REFERENCES** | | |
| 'Aircraft Illustrated' | —October 1971 | |
| 'Aeroplane Monthly' | —August 1973 | |
| Arthur Bentley | —Archives | |
| Argus Books | —Plan Pack 3024 | |
| *The Jet Aircraft of the World* | —Macdonald | |

deflected to +60°, in addition to the +5° for trimming (ie. the maximum deflection angle relative to the fuselage datum was 65°).

The leading-edge slats on the three aircraft differed in operation, although they were virtually identical in size, taking up the outer 50% of the

*The third prototype. Note more streamlined nose profile and re-designed windshield and canopy, also just discernible are the four hinges for the automatic leading-edge slats. (Royal Aeronautical Society.)*

*The third prototype showing details of the wing planform and control surface layout. All three prototypes had an identical wing shape, just the tip profiles being different. (Royal Aeronautical Society.)*

leading edges. As the first aircraft was intended solely for low-speed flight trials, its slats were fixed in the open position, limiting the speed to 305 kts. Those on the second aircraft were made retractable for high-speed trials, and on the third prototype they were fully automatic in operation. The wingtip shape for the first aircraft also differed, the tip fairing being removed and cylindrical fairings fitted, containing anti-spin parachutes. The pitot head on each wing was also re-located on to the front of these fairings. Wing span, however, remained the same. Each wingtip had a small triangular bumper fitted on its lower surface to help prevent damage in the event of a wing-down landing. With the parachute fairings fitted, this was replaced by a skid on each side, attached to the underside of the fairing.

**POWER PLANT**

*First prototype.* One de Havilland Goblin 2 D.Gn.2 centrifugal flow turbojet engine rated at a Sea Level Static Thrust of 3,100 lbs.

*Second prototype.* One de Havilland Goblin 4 D.Gn.4 centrifugal flow turbojet engine rated at a Sea Level Static Thrust of 3,5000 lbs.

*Third prototype.* One de Havilland Goblin 5 D.Gn.5 centrifugal flow turbojet engine rated at a Sea Level Static Thrust of 3,600 lbs.

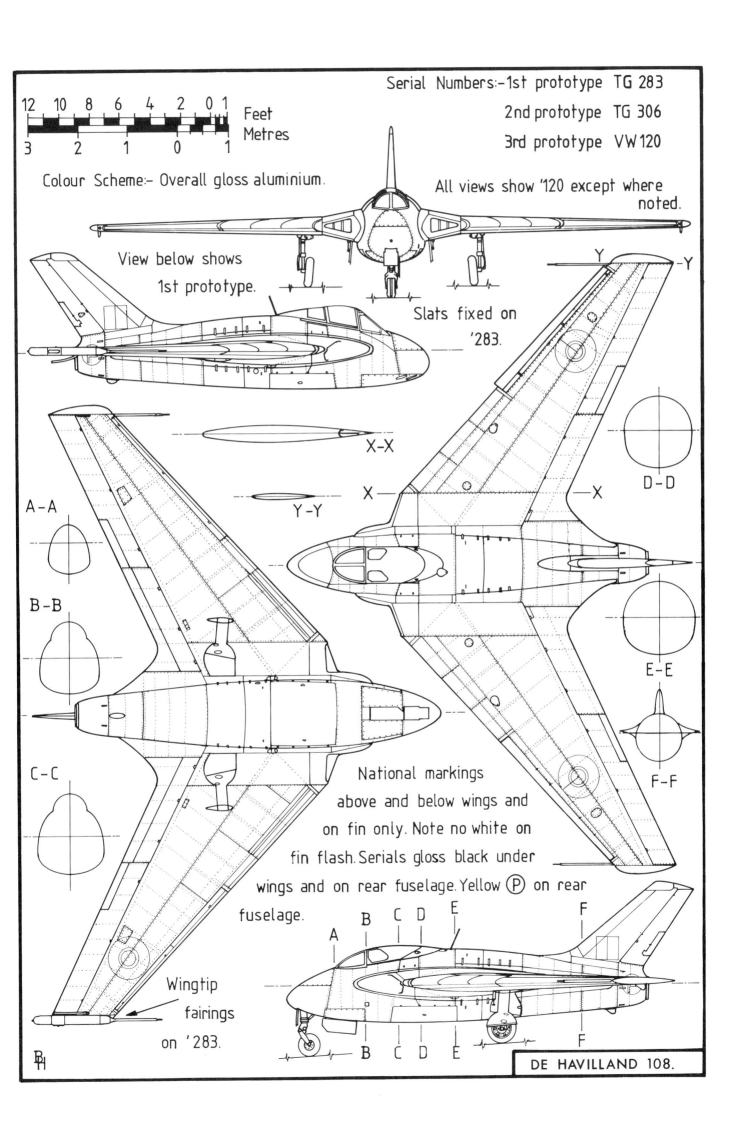

12 10 8 6 4 2 0 1 Feet
Metres
3 2 1 0 1

Serial Numbers:-1st prototype TG 283
2nd prototype TG 306
3rd prototype VW 120

Colour Scheme:- Overall gloss aluminium.

All views show '120 except where noted.

View below shows
1st prototype.

Slats fixed on '283.

X-X

A-A

B-B

Y-Y

X — — X

D-D

E-E

F-F

C-C

National markings
above and below wings and
on fin only. Note no white on
fin flash. Serials gloss black under
wings and on rear fuselage. Yellow Ⓟ on rear
fuselage.

A B C D E F

B C D E F

Wingtip
fairings
on '283.

DE HAVILLAND 108.

*The first prototype just after lift off. Note staggered cannon ports and recently acquired fin/tailplane bullet fairing. Also note the new strengthened cockpit canopy. (Pilot Press Ltd.)*

# SAUNDERS-ROE/A.1

| | |
|---|---|
| **Manufacturer** | Saunders-Roe Ltd |
| **Specification** | E.6/44 |
| **Role** | Experimental Fighter Flying-Boat |
| **First Flight Date** | TG 263 (G–12–1) – 16th July 1947 |
| | TG 267 – 30th April 1948 |
| | TG 271 – 17th August 1948 |

During the closing stages of the Second World War, the design of a jet-powered fighter flying-boat was conceived for use in the Pacific where landing strips were few and far between, and small islands with sheltered lagoons were many, thus providing ideal bases for the aircraft. Plans for sophisticated underground bases were also drawn up for uses in other areas of the world. In the event, the war ended before any of these ideas could bear fruit.

## DEVELOPMENT HISTORY

The idea for the jet-powered flying-boat fighter was first discussed at Saunders-Roe as early as 1943, as the new form of power plant appeared to overcome all the difficulties of designing and building a small, manoeuvrable aircraft, which existed with the use of a normal propeller and piston engine. Detailed design and construction of a mock-up were started at the company's Anglesey works, and Specification E.6/44 was raised to cover the construction of three prototypes, allocated the serials TG 263, 267 and 271. On completion, the first prototype's main assemblies were transported by road and sea to the main factory at Cowes, Isle of Wight, where they were reassembled and, after brief taxi-ing trials on 16th July 1947, the first flight was successfully made on the same day! The take-off run took less than twelve seconds and the lightly-loaded aircraft demonstrated a good climb rate.

The second and third machines were completed and joined the test programme during 1948. Few external modifications were necessary in the light of flight testing, other than the fitting of the bullet fairing at the junction of the fin and tailplane, and the slight reduction in the size of the horn balance on the rudder. There were some modifications to the fuel system.

After the manufacturer's trials, the first and second prototypes went to the Marine Aircraft Experimental Establishment at Felixstowe (the Maritime Boscombe Down!) During a Service pilot's practice in poor visibility for an air display, the aircraft crashed into the sea killing the pilot.

The third aircraft, with its uprated engines, was demonstrated at the 1948 Farnborough display, where the excellent handling and manoeuvrability was dramatically demonstrated by an exceptionally low inverted pass the whole length of the runway, the like of which has never been seen since. The career of this aircraft ended on 6th April 1949 when on landing at Cowes, it hit a baulk of timber half submerged in the water, a large gash was torn in the right side of the planing surface and the right float was ripped off, causing the aircraft to invert in the water. Luckily, the pilot managed to escape, but the aircraft sank without trace.

As hostilities had ended before the aircraft had flown, the research was really only of general interest and, as with the larger passenger-carrying flying boats, emphasis and available facilities had changed. The end of the flying boat era was at hand, except for some very specialist roles. These did not include a fighter and the SR./A.1 remained unique (the later Convair Sea Dart was a hydrofoil craft). It had met its specification and demonstrated admirable manoeuvrability, but it could not match that of its smaller, land-based contemporaries. It had a good range, but the drag from its large hull prevented any real improvement in performance, especially in top speed.

Another problem was that Metrovick had gone back to its pre-war activities and was no longer in the engine world. Its projects were handed over to Armstrong Siddeley but the production of the Beryl engine had stopped after only eleven were built. Thought was briefly given to fitting Rolls-Royce Nene engines, but these were of the centrifugal type and would have required a complete re-design to accommodate them. Therefore, testing ceased in 1949.

Trials resumed briefly in November 1950 and the aircraft made its final public appearance at the Festival of Britain, landing on the Thames at Woolwich Reach and being towed up river to the Festival site. As it no longer had a military connection, before embarking on this last appearance it had lost its original serial of TG 263 and had been given the SBAC number G-12-1.

Luckily, its unique qualities were recognised and it was dismantled and taken by road to the College of Aeronautics, Cranfield, for use as ground instructional airframe. From there it was transferred to the Skyfame Collection and, when this ceased to exist, it was again moved to the Imperial War Museum, Duxford, sporting an all-white colour scheme, where after renovation it is now preserved.

Strangely, the tale of its power plants did not end with that of the aircraft. When it was finally grounded and sent to Cranfield, its engines were removed, and one was installed in another unique machine – the Bluebird jet-powered boat – for an attempt on the water-speed record, which had a tragic ending.

## CONSTRUCTION

The hull was manufactured from light alloy, with a conventional structure consisting of formers and longitudinal stringers. There were 34 frames from bow to stern, with seven additional half-frames in the centre-section. Four deep longerons were joined to the frames from the gun bay at Frame 8 to the jetpipes at Frame 19, two at hip and two at shoulder height. The design of the single-step planing surface was dictated by the best compromise between aerodynamic and hydrodynamic characteristics, and the overall hull length to beam ratio was 6:1. The design was such that the boat rode in a tail-down attitude at low speeds in the water, to enable the intake to stay well clear of the water at all times. As speed increased, the attitude became more level. The engines shared a common oval intake in the extremity of the bow and, as a safeguard against the ingestion of water, it was fitted with an extendable lip, which moved forwards 9", actuated by a hydraulic ram, whenever the floats were extended. It was found to be unnecessary and was never made functional.

The hydraulic ram for the intake extension was mounted in the splitter plate just aft of the intake, where the duct divided into two separate circular ducts which continued back to feed each engine mounted in the centre-section. Access for engine removal was via a large hatch in the fuselage centre-section aft of the mainspar attachment frame. A smaller maintenance hatch was set into the larger one to allow access to the large 'engine room' via a fixed ladder and walkway between the engines! Inlet scoops were fitted either side of the engine hatch at approximately mid-root chord for ventilation of the engine bay. The engines were attached via tubular V-struts to the forward mountings at Frame 12 and directly to lugs at the aft mountings attached to Frame 14. The jetpipes exhausted each side of the fuselage approximately four feet aft of the wing trailing edges, with a downthrust angle of +2° to the hull datum, and toed-out 5° to the centreline. The third prototype differed from the other two by having 'pen-nib' exhaust fairings between the fuselage skin and the jetpipe orifices.

The gun-bay was situated above the intake ducts between Frames 4 and 8, access for re-arming being via two large hatches hinged at their outer edges. Provision was made for mounting four 20 mm., Hispano Mk.5 cannon with 240 r.p.g. The two inner cannon troughs were immediately behind the intake lip, with the outers slightly aft. The expended shell cases and links were retained on-board in containers in the bottom of the hull, below the intake ducting. The cannons were never actually fitted, and auto-observers were mounted in the resulting space for test purposes. At one stage, the cannon ports were faired over, but this resulted in excessively high temperatures in the instrumentation bay, so they were left open purely for ventilation purposes.

The cockpit section was built as a separate cylindrical unit, which was also armour-plated, and installed in the upper fuselage, the pilot sitting in line with the wing root leading edge. He was provided with a Martin-Baker Mk.1 ejection seat. (In fact, that intended for the first prototype was the very first one to be delivered direct to an aircraft manufacturer.) The cockpit was pressurised up to a differential pressure of 3.5 psi., and also heated. The canopy sills were attached to the front gunwales. The sliding hood was jettisonable in an emergency, and initially was a blown bubble-type transparency made from doubled Perspex with dry airspace between. Due to problems, this was later replaced by a strengthened metal hood with four small windows for limited lateral and rearwards vision. The fixed windscreen had three flat panels, the centre being bullet-proof. Protruding from the front of the central panel was a cylindrical fairing for the gun-camera. A gyro gun sight was fitted, despite the lack of cannon. The pilot was provided with float position indicators, much in the style of normal undercarriage position indicators. Two unique controls were the toggle control for the interconnection of the water rudder with the aerodynamic one, and the semi-automatic mooring-hook push-knob control.

The pilot sat on a K-type dinghy, and also had an anti-g suit. An anti-spin parachute was to be fitted in the third prototype, the actual parachute container being housed in the very rear of the tailcone just under the rudder. The pilot's press-to-talk button was mounted on the spade-type control column, connected to a TR1464 VHF radio. An I.F.F.Mk.3 was also fitted.

The electrical system was fed from two 12-volt accumulators mounted below the left engine, with additional ones in a forward compartment when electrical engine starting was provided. (Normally cartridge-starting was used.) Services run from the electrical included the canopy sliding mechanism, fire extinguishers, flap pre-selection gear, gyrogunsight, pitot heater and compass.

The fin was built integrally with the fuselage structure (which was sharply swept up to keep it clear of the water at all times) and was built around a two-spar structure with multiple ribs, the rudder being hinged at the rear spar. The rudder was manually operated from the cockpit via push/pull rods, and had a movement range of +25°. It was horn-balanced and fitted with a geared trim tab at the base of its trailing edge. The horn balance was smaller on the third prototype, and was later reduced to a similar size on the first one.

The horizontal tailplane was mounted approximately halfway up the fin, to provide sufficient clearance from water spray and jet efflux. Similar to the fin, it was of two-spar construction with multiple ribs. It had no dihedral, but it was set at an incidence of +3°30′ to the hull datum. It was of symmetrical section with its maximum thickness at 38% chord. The manually operated elevators were hinged to the rear spar and had a movement range of -25° and +20°. A trim geared tab was fitted to the

## DATA

### DIMENSIONS

| | | |
|---|---|---|
| Span | 46′0″ | |
| Length | 50′0″ | |
| Height | 16′9″ | (measured from base of hull) |
| | 14′5″ | (on beaching trolley) |
| Hull Beam | 6′10″ | |
| Tailplane Span | 16′0″ | |
| Float 'track' | 31′0″ | (extended) |
| | 23′6″ | (retracted) |
| Beaching Trolley | | |
| Track | 8′8″ | |
| Wheelbase | 23′6″ | |

### AREAS

| | |
|---|---|
| Wing (gross) | 415.0 sq ft |
| Ailerons (each) | 13.0 sq ft |
| tabs (each) | 1.1 sq ft |
| Flaps (each) | 12.2 sq ft |
| Dive Brakes (each) | 9.0 sq ft |
| Dive Recovery Flaps (each) | 1.0 sq ft |
| Tailplane | 81.25 sq ft |
| Elevators (total) | 26.37 sq ft |
| tabs (each) | 0.85 sq ft |
| Fin and Rudder | 60.6 sq ft |
| tab | 1.5 sq ft |

### WEIGHTS

| | |
|---|---|
| Empty | 11,262 lbs |
| Loaded | 16,255 lbs |
| Overload | 19,560 lbs |

### PERFORMANCE

| | | |
|---|---|---|
| $V_{max}$ | 448 kts | (TG 271) |
| Climb Rate | 4,000 ft/min.(plus) | |
| Take-Off Time | 11 secs (approx) | |

### REFERENCES

| | |
|---|---|
| Imperial War Museum, Duxford | —The aircraft |
| Public Records Office | —Avia Files |
| 'Aeroplane' | —8th August 1947 |
| 'Aeroplane' | —27th August 1948 |
| 'Flight' | —29th July 1948 |

left elevator, and a spring tab to the right, both of identical size. After initial flights, a bullet fairing was fitted at the junction of the leading edges of the fin and tailplane to eliminate local buffet. This was fitted to the other two aircraft during manufacture.

It was proposed that an anti-spin parachute be fitted in the tailcone of the third prototype, just under the rudder, with two fairing doors. There is no record of whether this was actually fitted.

The wings were manufactured in two sections, and were built around a mainspar at 35% chord and an aft auxiliary spar to which the control surfaces were hinged. The mainspars were manufactured from aluminium alloy, with extruded booms top and bottom, and were attached to the fuselage centre-section at Frame 14 (the principal hull frame) and the auxiliary spar at Frame 18. In addition, a series of 'boundary bolts' around the root skin took torsional loads. The wing had a high-speed symmetrical section designed specially by the company, which had a thickness/chord ratio at Rib 1 of 14%, with a chord of 11'8", reducing to 12% at the tip Rib 30, (whose chord was 5'6"). The maximum thickness was at a constant 38% chord and the leading edge sweep was 10°, and the aft 9° (forwards). The wing was set at an incidence of +4°30' to the hull datum, and had a dihedral angle measured along the top surface of 3°15'. (Dihedral was less on the third machine, but the exact figure is not known.) A long yaw vane boom was fitted to the right wingtip, and a pitot head in a similar place on the left.

All internal fuel was carried in four integral tanks, two in each wing leading edge, forward of the mainspar, situated between the root and float-strut attachment ribs. They were divided into sections separated by non-return valves, and the ribs served as baffles. Total capacity was 426 gallons. This could be supplemented by additional fuel carried in two 140 gallon, flush-fitted magnesium drop tanks under the wing inboard sections. These were never actually carried on any of the aircraft.

Streamlined floats were fitted on each wing at the end of hinged struts to enable them to retract inboard. The retraction sequence was such that the float itself rotated 90° inwards whilst the strut was folding inwards so that, when completed, the float lay with its upper surface exposed and its planing surface within the wing structure. The attachment rib was reinforced and, while normal operation was hydraulic, a pneumatic bottle allowed emergency lowering.

Dive recovery flaps, with a movement of 80°, were fitted aft of the mainspar on the inboard undersurfaces, supported on struts and operated via a torque tube. They were electrically signalled and hydraulically operated. Inboard of the float bay, the trailing edge of the wing was occupied by the split flap surfaces. The lower part of the flaps acted in the normal fashion, with a maximum deflection of 75°. They were electrically preselectable in four positions – up/take-off/three-quarters down/down – and were hydraulically operated. The upper part of the flap, identical in size, was interconnected to the lower surface, but acted as airbrakes with an upwards deflection of 30°. If the flaps were selected down while the airbrakes were deployed, the angle of the lower surface was increased to compensate.

Outboard of the float bay, the trailing edge to the tip was occupied by the ailerons. They were hinged to the aft auxiliary spar and had a movement range of ±16°. Each was fitted with two tabs, the inner being a spring tab, and the outer a geared trim tab.

For water-borne operation, the hull was divided into watertight compartments by means of fire-proof canvas partitions mounted at Frames 4, 8, 10, 20 and 23. These partitions unzipped to allow access along the walkway in the centre-section. A mooring point was provided right in the bow and slightly

*The aircraft banking away to show a good view of the planing surface shape. Note unusually long yaw vane probe on right wingtip. (Royal Aeronautical Society.)*

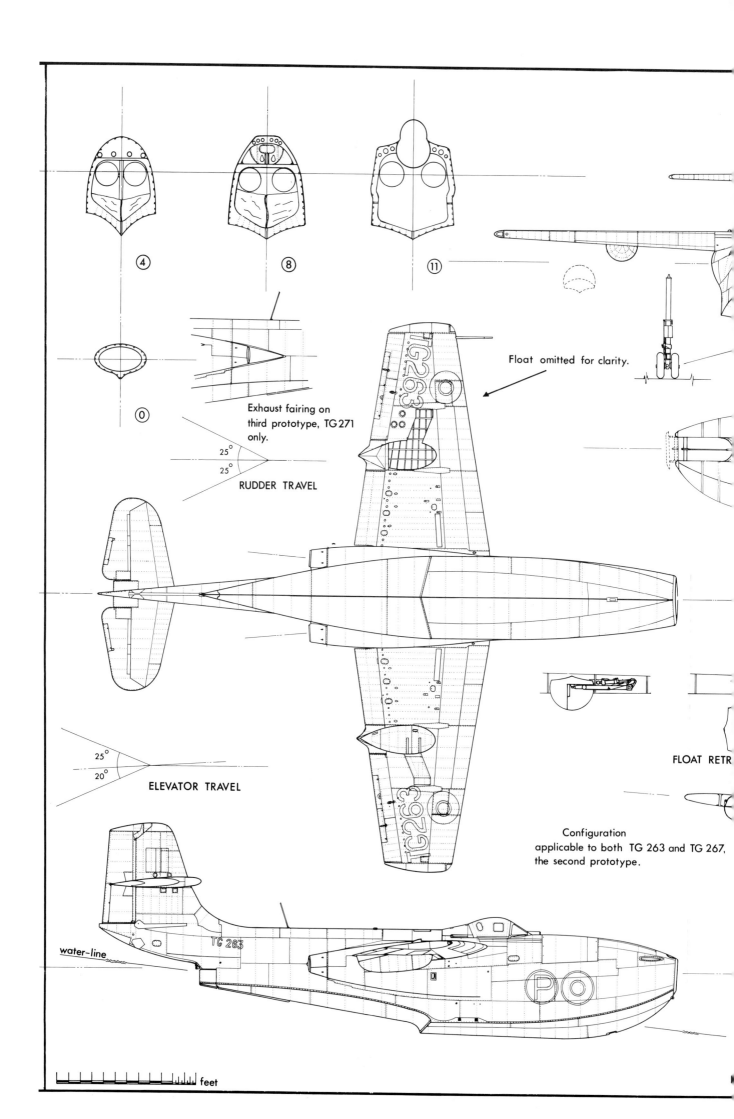

④

⑧

⑪

Float omitted for clarity.

○

Exhaust fairing on
third prototype, TG 271
only.

25°
25°
RUDDER TRAVEL

TG 263

TG 263

25°
20°
ELEVATOR TRAVEL

FLOAT RETR

Configuration
applicable to both TG 263 and TG 267,
the second prototype.

water-line

TG 263

P O

feet

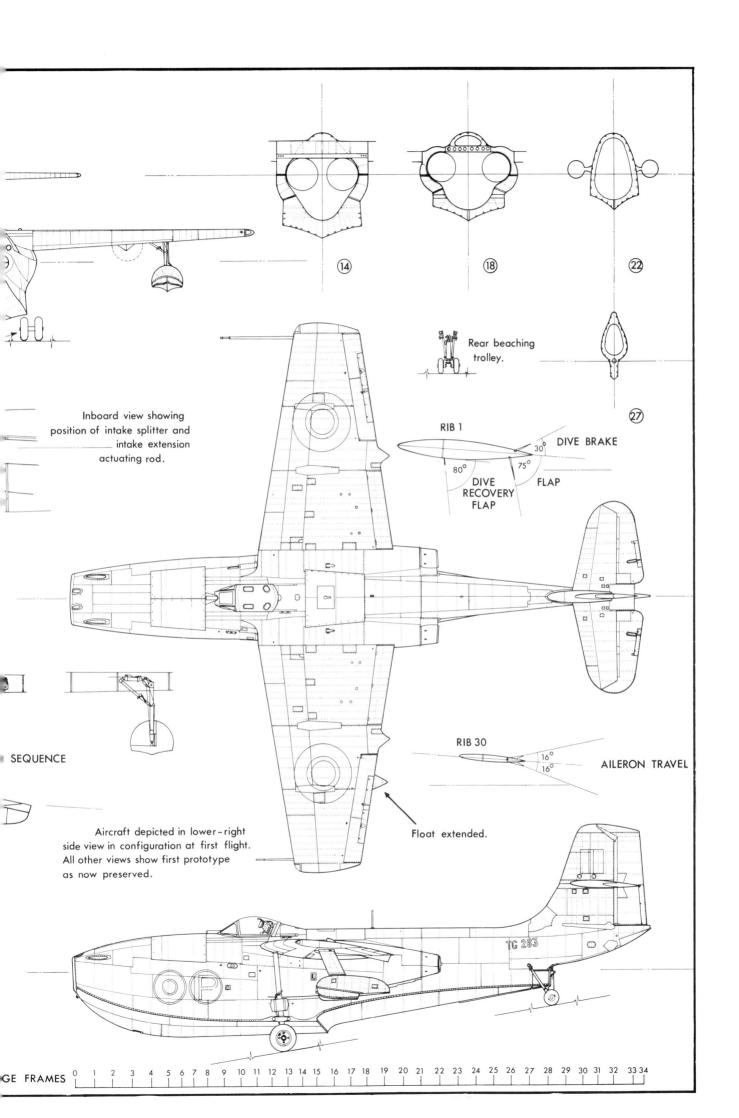

⑭  ⑱  ㉒

Rear beaching trolley.

㉗

Inboard view showing position of intake splitter and intake extension actuating rod.

RIB 1

DIVE BRAKE

30°

80°

75°

DIVE RECOVERY FLAP

FLAP

RIB 30

16°

16°

AILERON TRAVEL

SEQUENCE

Aircraft depicted in lower-right side view in configuration at first flight. All other views show first prototype as now preserved.

Float extended.

TG 263

GE FRAMES  0 1 2 3 4 5 6 7 8 9 10 11 12 13 14 15 16 17 18 19 20 21 22 23 24 25 26 27 28 29 30 31 32 33 34

*The first prototype. Note original canopy, and good view of planing surface, sea rudder and retracted float. Also visible are mounting points for the beaching trolley. For some reason the top half of the fuselage roundel appears to be missing, its outline just being discernible. (Pilot Press Ltd.)*

further aft, on the keel was an automatic pick-up hook for the mooring line which was releasable by the pilot from the cockpit. For manoeuvring in the water, and during the initial stages of the take-off run, before the aerodynamic rudder became effective, a water-rudder was fitted at the aft end of the planing surface. This was connected to the rudder pedals and was cable-operated from the tie-rods of the main controls. It could be connected/disconnected from a cockpit control, and was locked central for flight. Just forward of the step in the lower hull just above the chines, at Frames 12 and 13, pick-up points for the main beaching trolleys were provided which, in conjunction with a socket in each wing root undersurface, allowed the attachment of the trolleys while the aircraft was in the water. The trolleys were designed to float vertically in the water, at the correct depth for ease of attachment, the correct buoyancy being ensured by pouring up to six gallons of water into each of the twin-tyre units. A further three-point pick-up attachment was provided at the aft end of the planing surface, for the small auxiliary twin-

wheeled trolley. With these all in place the aircraft could either be winched ashore, or could taxi under its own power.

Armament was never carried, but, in addition to the internally mounted cannon, several different underwing loads could be carried. These comprised either: two 1,000 lbs. bombs; two 500 lbs. bombs; two 250 lbs. bombs; two 200 lbs. smoke floats; two practice bombs carriers; two drop tanks; eight rocket projectiles; or four rocket projectiles with semi-filled tanks.

**POWER PLANT**
*First Prototype* Two Metropolitan Vickers Beryl M.V.B.1 axial flow turbojets, each with a Sea Level Static Thrust of 3,250 lbs.
*Second Prototype* Two Metropolitan Vickers Beryl M.V.B.2 axial flow turbojets, each with a Sea Level Static Thrust of 3,500 lbs.
*Third Prototype* Two Metropolitan Vickers Beryl 1 M.V.B.2 axial flow turbojets, each with a Sea Level Static Thrust of 3,850 lbs.

*This view emphasises the elegant fuselage lines. Note original unframed windscreen and fin shape, together with the rectangular shape of the fairing aft of the jetpipe orifice. Compare with view below of P.1040 with framed screen and pen-nib eflux fairings as flown by Sqn. Ldr. Neville Duke to win the Kemsley Challenge Trophy at Elmdon on 30 July 1949 at 508 m.p.h.*

# HAWKER P.1040/1072

| Manufacturer | Hawker Aircraft Company Ltd |
|---|---|
| Specification | Naval Specification – N.7/46 |
| Role | Single-Seat Research Prototype |
| First Flight Date | P.1040 (VP 401) |
| | 2nd September 1947 |
| | P.1072 (VP 401) |
| | 16th November 1950 |

The P.1040 was Hawker Aircraft's first jet-engined design actually to be built and, after its initial flight test career, following modification, and re-designation to P.1072, it also became the first British mixed-power plant experimental prototype to fly. The P.1040, after some refinement, went into production as the Sea Hawk, but initially was very different aerodynamically and therefore warrants inclusion in this book.

## DEVELOPMENT HISTORY
Design of the first Hawker jet aircraft started in late 1944, initially as a modified Fury with the engine in

*Rear three-quarters view of the P.1040. Note shape of original fairing aft of jetpipe orifice. Compare fin and rudder shape to that when in its other guise as the P.1072.*

the centre-section of the fuselage, designated P.1035. This crystallised in December of that year into the P.1040, with its distinctive bifurcated jet

## DATA

### DIMENSIONS
| | |
|---|---|
| Span | 36'6" |
| Length | 37'7" |
| Height | 8'9" |
| Track | 7'11.5" |
| Wheelbase | 12'9" |

### AREAS
| | | |
|---|---|---|
| Wing (gross) | 256 sq ft | |
| Fin and Rudder | 33.1 sq ft | (as first flown on P.1040) |
| Tailplane and Elevator | 40.1 sq ft | |
| Total Flap | 50 sq ft | |

### WEIGHTS
| | |
|---|---|
| **P.1040** | |
| normal loaded | 10,000 lbs |
| max. overload | 11,200 lbs |
| **P.1072** | |
| empty | 11,050 lbs |
| normal loaded | 14,050 lbs |
| Rocket motor weight in P.1072 | 215lbs. |

### PERFORMANCE
| | | |
|---|---|---|
| $V_{max}$ | 522 kts IAS | (Mach 0.85) at 36,000 ft |
| $V_{max}$ at Sea Level P.1072 | 505 kts IAS | |
| Time to 35,000 ft | 10mins 30secs | |
| Service Ceiling | 44,500 ft | |

### REFERENCES
| | |
|---|---|
| RAE Farnborough | —Library |
| British Aerospace (Kingston) | —Archives |
| British Aerospace (Kingston) | —Photographic Archives |
| P.1052 (drawings reference) | —The Aircraft |

exhausts. Although lacking any official support, design work continued until October 1945 when the company authorised construction of a prototype. As it was felt that the aircraft showed little or no performance increase over that of the Meteor then in service, the Royal Air Force did not wish to order it. Luckily the Navy still continued its support, resulting in the issuing of Specification N.7/46, which eventually, after considerable modification, resulted in the Sea Hawk.

The aircraft first flew at Boscombe Down on 2nd September 1947, and three days later moved to Farnborough to continue its test programme, as the firm's airfield at Langley was not suitable for this purpose (although late in its career it was damaged at Langley on 16th January 1948).

Even before the P.1040 had flown, and before any rocket motors existed in Britain except for captured German examples, proposals were made to install one in the tail to improve performance. Armstrong Siddeley started work on their rocket motor in 1947, and the plans were resurrected with the suggestion that a second prototype P.1040 be built. However, as the motor would not be ready for fitment until the first prototype P.1040 had completed its development trials, it was decided to install the engine in this machine.

The motor was installed in the modified airframe on 20th June 1950, and the first flight, ferrying the aircraft to Bitteswell, was made on turbojet power alone on 16th November 1950. Four days later, the rocket motor was ignited for the first time in the air, providing a spectacular performance increase, especially during the climb.

After only six flights using rocket power, on 19th January 1951 there was an explosion while in flight during an attempt to restart the motor, resulting in a fire which damaged the tail section. Luckily, the pilot was able to make a safe landing. The aircraft was repaired barely one month later but was never flown again due to an Air Ministry policy change.

The aircraft was finally struck off charge on 10th August 1954, and scrapped.

# CONSTRUCTION

## P.1040

The aircraft was of all-metal stressed skin construction, the fuselage featuring wing-root engine intakes within the integral stub wings. The unpressurised cockpit was placed well forward to give the pilot excellent forward visibility, and he was provided with a Malcolm type ejection seat. When first flown, the canopy featured a curved, one-piece windscreen with no framing, but later in the trials this was replaced with a more conventional three-piece windscreen with an optically flat centre panel, and curved quarter-lights on each side. As with other jet aircraft of that era, due to the lack of any attitude reference in the absence of a long nose housing a piston engine, a small horizon reference bead was mounted on a short mast directly in front of the windscreen.

The nosewheel oleo retracted forwards to lie right in the forward end of the nosecone when retracted. The P.1040 was unarmed, but provision was made in the fuselage directly beneath the cockpit for four 20 mm.cannon.

The engine was mounted in the fuselage centre-section, exhausting through a bifurcated jetpipe either side of the fuselage aft of the wing roots. The fairings aft of each exhaust were initially rectangular in shape, but were later modified to a more streamlined, pointed profile. Fuel was carried in three fuselage tanks, with a total capacity of 370 gallons.

The fuselage ended in an elegant, curved fin and rudder, with a mid-mounted tailplane carrying conventional elevators. Both the rudder and elevators were fitted with small trim tabs.

The wing was mid-mounted, and constructed around a main forward spar, multiple ribs, and an aft auxiliary spar, to which were hinged the ailerons and flaps. The wing had a symmetrical aerofoil section with a thickness/chord ratio of 9.5% and an Aspect Ratio of 5.0. Dihedral angle was 4°30′ and incidence to the aircraft datum of +0°30′.

*The aircraft in flight, still in its original configuration, a beautiful study by Hawker Aircraft Photographer, Cyril Peckham.*

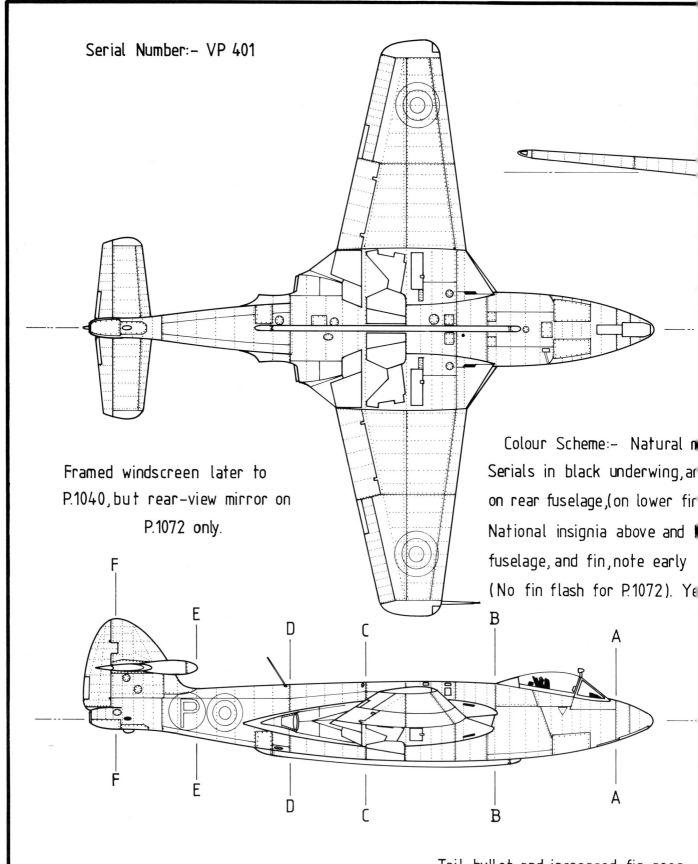

Serial Number:- VP 401

Framed windscreen later to
P.1040, but rear-view mirror on
P.1072 only.

Colour Scheme:- Natural m
Serials in black underwing, an
on rear fuselage,(on lower fir
National insignia above and
fuselage, and fin, note early
(No fin flash for P.1072). Ye

F

E

D

C

B

A

F

E

D

C

B

A

Tail bullet and increased fin area
on P.1072 only.

12  10  8  6  4  2  0 1
Feet
Metres
3    2    1    0    1

BH

A-A   B-B   C-C   D-D   E-E

F-F

Sections identical for
P.1040 except for ventral
fuel pipe and rocket motor
fairing.

ews show P.1072 configuration
ept bottom right which
s P.1040 as at first flight.

erall.

072).

ings,on rear

or P.1040.

"and circle on rear
uselage. Logo,white on black
isc on nose.

Hawker Siddeley Logo

View above as for P.1072, but
illustrating P.1040 frameless windscreen,
fin/tailplane and upper surface roundels.

Note exhaust fairing, changed
to later type early in P.1040 flight testing.

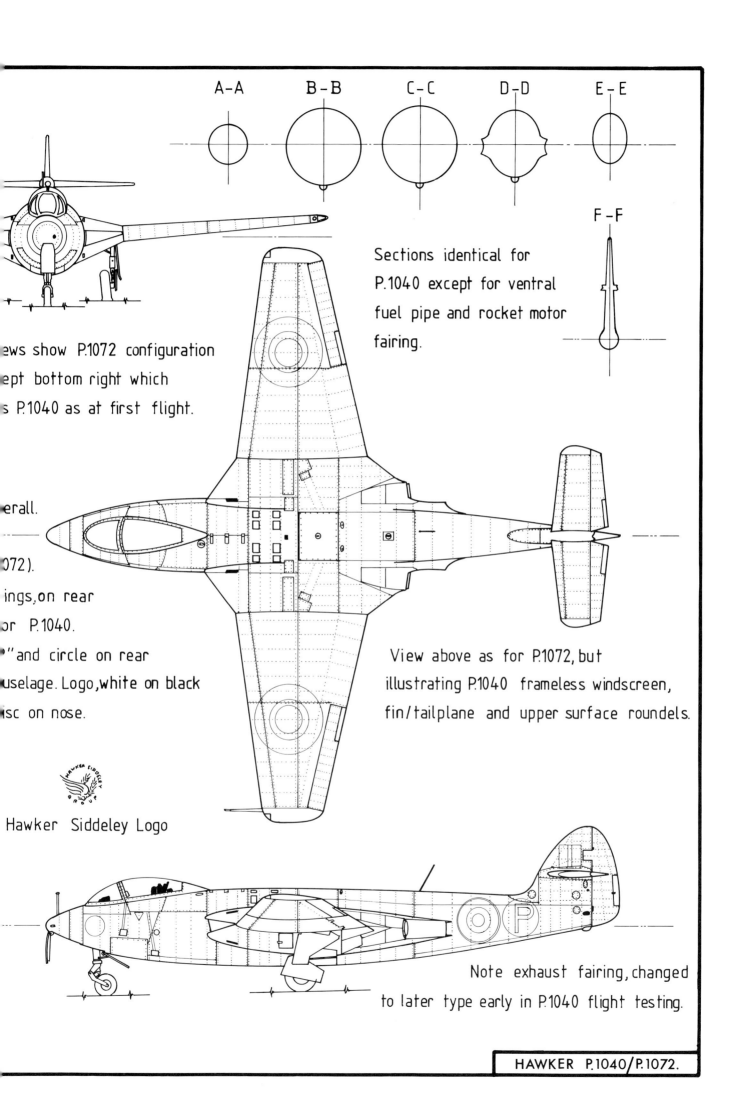

HAWKER P.1040/P.1072.

*Compared to its earlier guise as the P.1040, note new framed windscreen, external rear-view mirror to enable the pilot to monitor the rocket plume, under-belly duct fairing and revised fin shape. (British Aerospace.)*

# P.1072

Being a straight development of the earlier aircraft, construction of the P.1072 was the same, embodying all of the modifications made to that airframe. Externally, the primary difference to the P.1040 was in the tail section. The base of the rudder was cut off just below the bottom of the trim tab, and the aft fuselage modified to a circular section to accommodate the Armstrong Siddeley Snarler rocket engine, which exhausted in line with the trailing edge of the rudder to eliminate the possibility of any acoustic effects on the fin and rudder. The tailcone housing the rocket nozzle was split horizontally to allow easy access to the motor.

The leading edge, and tip, of the fin were altered in shape, very slightly increasing the area, and a large bullet fairing was added at the leading edge junction of the fin and tailplane to eliminate turbulent flow.

Substantial changes were made internally within the fuselage to accommodate the new fuel system for the rocket motor. Tankage for the jet engine's kerosene was still housed in three tanks, in the forward, mid and aft sections, but its capacity was drastically reduced to a mere 175 gallons. For the rocket motor, a spherical tank was installed in the forward fuselage containing 75 gallons of liquid oxygen and, aft of the rear kerosene tank, one containing 120 gallons of water-methanol was added. The liquid oxygen supply pipes to the motor were routed outside the fuselage and covered by a removable ventral fairing. A separate pneumatic system was provided to actuate the rocket fuel system's jacks and valves. This fuel capacity gave an endurance of only 2 mins. 45 secs. at full power.

*Rear view illustrating the changes to the rear fuselage and the cut-back rudder. Also shown well is the fairing under the belly covering the delivery pipe from the liquid oxygen tank in the forward fuselage. (British Aerospace.)*

## POWER PLANT

*P.1040* – One Rolls-Royce Nene 1 R.N.1 centrifugal flow turbojet developing a Sea Level Static Thrust of 4,500 lbs, later replaced with a Rolls-Royce Nene 2 R.N.2 turbojet developing a Sea Level Static Thrust of 5,000 lbs.

*P.1072* – One Rolls-Royce Nene 2 R.N.2 centrifugal flow turbojet developing a Sea Level Static Thrust of 5,000 lbs, plus one Armstrong Siddeley Snarler ASSn.1 liquid-fuel rocket motor, with 2.75 minutes endurance, Sea Level Static Thrust 2,000 lbs.

*The first prototype just after first rollout at Bagington (via Ray Williams).*

# ARMSTRONG WHITWORTH
# A.W. 52

| | |
|---|---|
| Manufacturer | Sir W G Armstrong Whitworth Aircraft Ltd |
| Specification | E.9/44 |
| Role | Research Prototype |
| First Flight Date | TS 363 – 13th November 1947 |
| | TS 368 – 1st September 1948 |

During the War years, much work had been done on the characteristics of the laminar flow wing and its promised large reduction in drag, which would therefore be of immense benefit for greater range and speed for a given power output. Several examples had been tested with varying degrees of success, one being on the North American Mustang fighter. Armstrong Whitworth submitted such a design as early as 1942 and, to optimise the benefit from the laminar flow sections, they selected an all-wing design with only the cockpit canopy spoiling the lines. Their work was eventually to result in Britain's only flying wing design to get off the drawing board – the A.W.52.

## DEVELOPMENT HISTORY

Although initially aimed at a bomber project, after the War had ended, Armstrong Whitworth proposed the all-wing design as a basis for a six-engined airliner. In view of the radical nature of the design and the many unknowns, it was felt prudent to build a $\frac{1}{3}$ scale glider version to investigate the low speed end of the flight envelope; this was allocated the firm's designation of A.W.51. After some revision of the overall design, the glider's designation was changed to A.W.52G. This was of all-wood construction and had a fixed under-carriage, and on completion was flown for the first time in February 1945.

Although it produced useful data regarding low-speed handling, there were obvious restrictions to its use as a research tool due to its very limited flight time per sortie, which varied anywhere between 5 and 35 minutes, dependent on the particular profile flown and the launch height. Having been towed to altitude by the last production Whitley bomber, maximum release height was 20,000 ft. and the maximum permitted speed was 217 kts. The Whitley was replaced as tow-aircraft by a Lancaster, and trials continued until March 1950. It was transferred to the Airborne Forces Experimental Establishment at Beaulieu for brief trials, towed to launch height by a Valetta. It was returned to Armstrong Whitworth, and was put on static display. Sadly, the wooden structure deteriorated rapidly in the open air and it was eventually scrapped in the late 50s.

As the limitations of the glider as a research tool were recognised early on, a powered version was projected in 1944 to explore the high speed end of the flight envelope. Specification E.9/44 was raised, covering the manufacture of two prototypes, the first to be powered by two Rolls-Royce Nene engines and the second by two Derwents. (The use

*A rear three-quarters view showing jet orifices, control surfacesx and landing flap profiles. Note also subtle shape of wingtip profile due to washout angle. (via Ray Williams)*

of axial flow turbojets, which due to their smaller diameter, could have been accommodated entirely within the wing without the nacelle bulges, had been considered. However, it was thought that they would not be available in time and so they were rejected.) Although primarily a pure research vehicle, provision was made for the aircraft to carry up to 4,000 lbs. of mail.

As the design was further refined, the pure wing 'sprouted' a central fuselage nacelle which projected ahead of the wing leading edge; otherwise, the overall shape followed very closely that of the earlier machine.

Construction of the first prototype, TS 363, was completed, and initial taxi-ing trials started on 1st April 1947. The aircraft was dismantled and taken by road to be reassembled for static display at the 1947 Farnborough Air Display, before being taken apart again and transported to Boscombe Down, where taxi-ing trials recommenced on 28th October. It was found that, at high speed, the nose rose uncontrollably and could only be made to drop by cutting power to the engines. Adjustments to the control settings finally solved the problems but, even at this early stage, it was apparent that the aircraft was extremely sensitive in pitch. These taxi-ing trials resulted in two short 'hops', the first being unintentional as the nose could not be lowered in time! The first flight was finally made on 13th November 1947. The flight lasted only 20 minutes and the landing proved to be difficult. There was little drag and, despite the use of landing flap, the aircraft floated a long way before touching down, and during this stage no movement of the control column was made in pitch, as the slightest elevator movement set up a rapid pitch oscillation.

The second flight was not made until the 17th November, and ended in an emergency when the nosewheel could not be locked down. Surprisingly, after landing the aircraft was much easier to manoeuvre due to the nosewheel jack not being fully extended and the oleo having less rake. So this emergency actually helped the programme by pointing the way to modification of the nosewheel oleo geometry!

Flight testing continued, and the phenomenon of over-sensitivity in pitch continued to cause problems. The rapid pitching oscillations were triggered in all but the smoothest air. The aircraft was ferried back to the firm's factory for minor modifications on 14th December, after which trials continued. Under certain conditions, marked airframe buffet was also experienced, which was caused by wing flexure, but the main problem still remained the pitch control and the general lack of harmonisation between the pitch and roll controls. Modifications to the control surfaces were made during November 1948, separate spring and trim tabs being fitted, and the control hinges were stiffened.

Meanwhile, having flown on 1st September 1948, the second prototype, TS 368, had joined the flight test programme, its primary task being the investigation of airframe and control vibration.

On 26th May 1949, during a test flight in TS 363, very rough air was experienced whilst descending at 320 kts. at 5,000 ft. The rapid pitch oscillation started and became dangerously divergent, such that after only 15 seconds the pilot had to abandon the aircraft. He thus became the first British pilot to use the Martin-Baker ejection seat in an emergency. The aircraft eventually stabilised, possibly due to the change of trim and airflow after the pilot had departed, but crashed tearing off its engines. No repair was attempted and the airframe was scrapped.

Just before this incident, similar violent pitch oscillations were experienced in TS 368, producing accelerations in the order of +12g and –5g; however, the aircraft was luckily in a climb and, after throttling back and decelerating, they ceased and a very careful recovery and landing was made! Following the crash of TS 363 under similar circumstances, and after a delay for structural check, trials continued, but with a limiting maximum speed of 250 kts. being imposed. These trials concerned detailed pressure plotting of the wing and attempts at determining the actual position of the transition of the boundary from laminar to normal flow.

The aircraft was ferried to Farnborough on 25th October 1950, for continuation of laminar flow trials and general research into the airflow over swept wings. To enable the airflow to be visualised, a thin chemical film was sprayed over the wings outboard of the engines and, to enable it to be seen, the wings had to be painted black over the test area.

Tests results were disappointing in that laminar flow was achieved over a very small percentage of the wing chord. Due to surface irregularities, especially in the region of the nose spar and skin joint, and the problem of dust particles and insects adhering to the wing skin, laminar flow was limited to as little as 5% of the chord!

All spanwise joints on upper and lower surfaces were practically obliterated by filling and paint and, to prevent adherence of the dust and insects, the leading edges were even covered with sheets of paper, removed at the last minute before take-off. But even these measures produced little improvement. Transition from laminar flow was achieved at the following points during these tests:

On the top surface: 5% chord at 120 kts.
15% chord at 180 kts.
5% chord at 210 kts.

On the lower surface: 5% to 6% at all speeds from 120 – 240 kts.

The programme was terminated in September 1953 and, after languishing at Farnborough, the aircraft

## DATA

### DIMENSIONS

| | | |
|---|---|---|
| Span | 90'11" | (overall) |
| | 90'0" | (between fin centrelines) |
| Length | 37'3.5" | |
| Height | 14'4.6" | |
| Track | 21'7" | (23'7" to outer tyre centres) |
| Wheelbase | 15'2.3" | |

### AREAS

| | |
|---|---|
| Wing (gross) | 1,314.0 sq ft |
| Flap | 148.75 sq ft |
| Fin and Rudder (total) | 75.06 sq ft |
| Rudder (each) | 12.68 sq ft |
| tab (each) | 1.46 sq ft |
| Controller (each) | 57.7 sq ft |
| tab (each) | 6.65 sq ft |
| Corrector (each) | 48.2 sq ft |

### WEIGHTS

| | TS 363 | TS 368 |
|---|---|---|
| empty | 19,662 lbs | 19,185 lbs |
| loaded | 34,154 lbs | 33,305 lbs |
| wing loading | 25.1 lbs/sq ft. | 24.7 lbs/sq ft |

### PERFORMANCE

| | TS 363 | TS 368 |
|---|---|---|
| $V_{max}$ | | |
| Sea Level | 434 kts | 390 kts |
| 20,000 ft | 434 kts | |
| 36,000 ft | 417 kts | |
| Rate of Climb | | |
| Sea Level | 4,800 ft/min | 2,500 ft/min |
| 20,000 ft | 3,000 ft/min | |
| 36,000 ft | 1,600 ft/min | |

| | TS 363 | TS 368 |
|---|---|---|
| Ceiling | 50,000 ft | 45,000 ft |
| Range (20,000 ft) | 980 miles at 243 kts (true) | |
| or | 880 miles at 347 kts (true) | |
| Range (36,000 ft) | 1,500 miles at 287 kts (true) | |
| or | 1,420 miles at 347 kts (true) | |
| Maximum | 2,130 miles | |
| Take-Off Run | 600 yds | (approximately) |
| Landing Roll | 800 yds | (approximately) |
| Max Lift Coefficient | 1.6 | (flaps down) |

### REFERENCES

| | |
|---|---|
| Armstrong Whitworth | —Drawing No 96665 |
| Armstrong Whitworth | —A.W.52 Manual Vol 1 |
| Public Records Office | —Avia Files |
| RAE Farnborough | —Library |
| Ray Williams | —Archives |
| Ray Williams | —Photographic Archives |
| 'Flight' | —19th December 1946 |
| | —15th January 1948 |
| 'Aeroplane' | —16th January 1948 |
| Hawker Siddeley Group Data Sheet | —A.W.52 |

was struck off charge on 10th March 1954 and was allocated to Shoeburyness to act as a gunnery target to where it was transported by road on 29th May.

As with all tail-less designs, the maximum value of the Coefficient of Lift was low, even with full flap, the primary reason being the short moment arm between the control surfaces and the centre of gravity, resulting in high down-load on the surfaces to correct the pitching moment at low speeds. The problems of the aircraft's stability and control could not be solved with the facilities and knowledge available at that time, and only now with artificial stability is this being achieved. But even now the problems of achieving satisfactory laminar flow have yet to be resolved due to contamination of the wing surface by foreign bodies.

# CONSTRUCTION

The entire airframe was constructed from light alloy, with a stressed skin. In the attempt to achieve laminar flow, the contour accuracy was kept to within 1/2000". This was done by using a thick (16 to 18 gauge) sheet for the skin, and the wing was constructed in the jig from the skin inwards, the structure being based around two spars. This meant that the ribs had to be split longitudinally, allowing the top and bottom surfaces to be made separately. The closely spaced spanwise stiffeners formed a corrugated inner skin to attempt to limit local distortion.

The wing was built in three major sections, the centre-section and the two outer wing panels. The centre-section span was 36'4" and its leading edge sweep angle was 17°33'48"; there was no sweep on the trailing edge. The high lift wing sections were developed by the National Physical Laboratory, designed to maintain laminar flow back to 55%

chord. That at the centreline was NPL Section 655-3-218, with a chord of 21'4", and thickness/chord ratio of 18%. The section at Rib 4, to which the outer wing panels attached, was NPL 655-3-118, also with an 18% thickness/chord ratio, the chord being 15'7" at this point. The fuselage 'nacelle' projected 5'9" in front of the theoretical apex of the wing. Its maximum diameter was 5'4" and it faired into the wing top surface at approximately 1/3 chord, and continued aft right to the trailing edge of the wing on the underside.

The constant 5'2" chord Fowler-type slotted flap extended across the centre of the trailing edge, spanning 28'4". It was hinged at six points, with a maximum deflection of 40° for landing, with 25°-30° being used for take-off. The underslung engine nacelles were situated with their centrelines 7'0" out from the wing centreline. The engines were fed from a flat oval intake, the engine being mounted at approximately mid-chord, with the jet-pipe orifices exhausting over the flap upper surfaces within semi-circular fairing ducts. Large side-hinged engine access doors were provided in the undersurfaces of the nacelles between the spars, for maintenance and for engine removal. This was achieved via two holes in the upper surface, through which cables from a standard 2,000 lbs. bomb winch could be passed to support the engine when being removed or installed. Two rectangular flaps were fitted in the intake for the control of the boundary layer suction system. Two massive spars stretched right across the whole centre-section, to the ends of which were bolted the outer wing sections.

Just outboard of the engine nacelles on each side, between the spars, were the main undercarriage bays. Long travel oleos were fitted to allow for non-flare landings, each having a pair of wheels with 30" diameter low pressure tyres. The Dowty under-

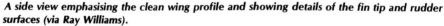
*A side view emphasising the clean wing profile and showing details of the fin tip and rudder surfaces (via Ray Williams).*

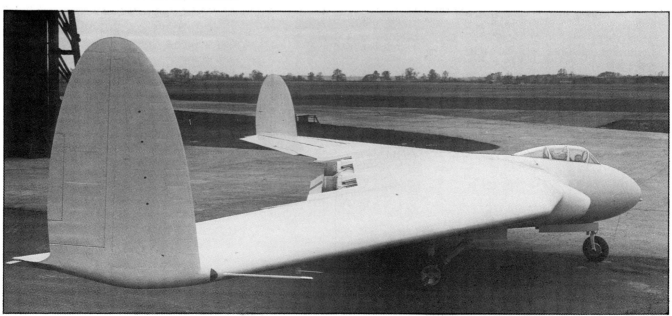

34

carriage retracted upwards and rearwards into the wing. Each oleo had a central main shock absorber, with a Y-shaped retraction link and two radius arms leading forwards. Two fuel tanks occupied the remainder of the wing between the spars outboard of each undercarriage bay. The fore tank capacity was 178 gallons and the aft 228 gallons.

The outer wing panels were attached to the centre-section by a series of high-tensile bolts at Rib 4, this junction being referred to as the wing 'knuckle'. The wing inboard of Rib 4 had no dihedral, but outboard to the tip it was 1° measured at 45% chord. Leading and trailing edge sweep angles were 34°6′ and 22°44′43″ respectively, the wing tapering to an extended tip chord of 8′8″, with a thickness/chord ratio of 15%, the section changing to NPL 645–3–015.

For the total wing planform this gave a quarter chord sweep of 24°45′18″, but measured outboard of the knuckle only, this reduced to 13°21′14″. Compared to the airframe fore and aft datum, the wing had an incidence of +1°20′ at the centreline, 0° at the knuckle, and –2° at the tips.

The inboard end of the wing outer panels between the spars housed two more fuel tanks each side, the capacities being 204 gallons in the forward tank and 240 gallons in the aft. These brought total fuel capacity to 1,702 gallons.

The elliptical fins were mounted at the very tips of the wings, with a root chord of 5′6″. The rudders were each fitted with servo/trim tabs, and their movement was biased to give a range of 30° outward and 10° inward. For low-speed trials, cylindrical anti-spin parachute containers were mounted below the base of the rudders, on the outboard surfaces of the fins. A yaw vane boom and a pitot head were fitted to the wingtip leading edges on the right and left respectively.

The fuselage nacelle contained the cockpit at its forward end, which accommodated two crew members, the pilot sitting in line with the root leading edge, under a long glazed canopy which was offset 3″ to the left of the centreline. This could be jettisoned in an emergency and, at the same time, a system locked the control column forwards against the instrument panel to allow clearance for the pilot's legs during ejection. Only the pilot was provided with an ejection seat, a Martin-Baker Mk.1; the observer, who sat behind and below the pilot, had to bale out manually through the normal crew entry hatch on the lower right side of the nacelle, which was also jettisoned. The cockpit was heated and pressurised by engine bleed-air to a maximum differential of 5.5 psi. The 300 cu.ft. freight compartment was situated immediately behind the aft pressure bulkhead of the cockpit, but was neither heated nor pressurised. Access was

via a door in the lower left side of the fuselage nacelle at approximately mid chord.

The cockpit windscreen consisted of a flat centre panel which was both heated and de-iced, and curved quarter-lights, the left-hand one of which had an openable direct vision panel. Cockpit control layout was conventional, with a normal 'bomber-type' spectacle control column, to the centre of which was mounted an additional wheel for control of the nosewheel steering. The nose-wheel oleo retracted rearwards into a bay under the forward end of the cockpit and, like the cockpit, this was offset 3″ to the left of the centreline. (Note: no record can be found for the reason for this rather unusual layout for the nosewheel.)

In addition to the specialist instrumentation and recording cameras, provision was made for the carriage of a 'Gee' indicator type ARI.5083 and a TR.1464 VHF radio, whip aerials for which were mounted below the fuselage in front of the nosewheel bay and on the upper fuselage behind the cockpit canopy.

Hydraulically-operated dive recovery flaps were fitted to the undersurfaces of the centre-section, beneath the fuel tanks. These were rectangular surfaces each with a length of 5′3″ and chord of 10″, and they could be selected to one of two positions by the cockpit push-button control, either 30° or 45°.

The outer part of the wing trailing edge was occupied by the large 20′2″ span elevons, which were divided over their entire length, at approximately 50% chord, into 'correctors' forward, and 'controllers' aft. Spring and trim tabs were fitted at the inboard end of each controller. The 'controller' was the actual elevon for roll and pitch control; the function of the 'corrector', to which the controller was hinged, was to provide a powerful longitudinal trimmer to counteract the pitching moment caused by lowering and raising the flap but, in so doing, would not impair the lightness of the controls, stick-free stability being a requirement. The correctors were each operated by three screw jacks with a chain interconnection, these in turn being operated by a single hydraulic jack. When 20° flap was lowered, the correctors were raised 4°, at 40° flap they were raised another 2°, with an override control allowing another 6° if required, total movement available thus being 12°. The elevon movement was –24° and +20°.

Two different, but important, services to try to ensure laminar flow under all circumstances, were the wing anti-icing and boundary layer control systems. Both were run from air bled off from the engines.

The boundary layer removal system was fitted to try to overcome the tendency that all swept wings

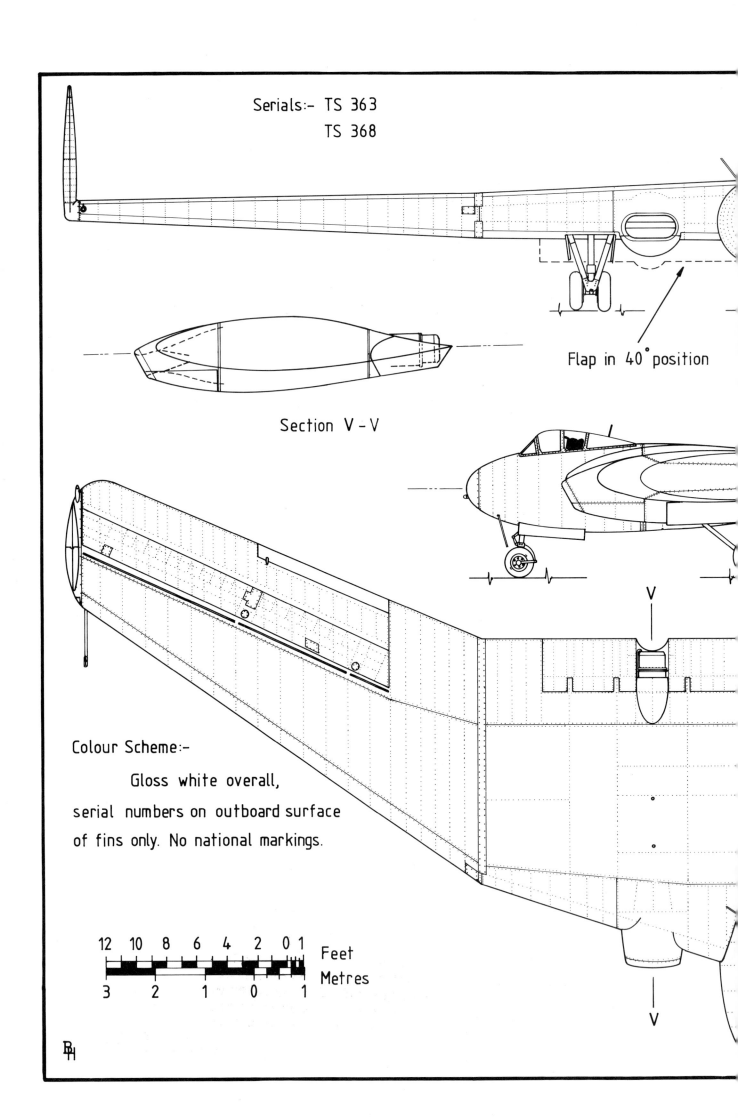

Serials:- TS 363
TS 368

Section V - V

Flap in 40° position

V

V

Colour Scheme:-

Gloss white overall,
serial numbers on outboard surface
of fins only. No national markings.

12  10  8  6  4  2  0 1    Feet
                           Metres
3      2      1      0    1

B.H.

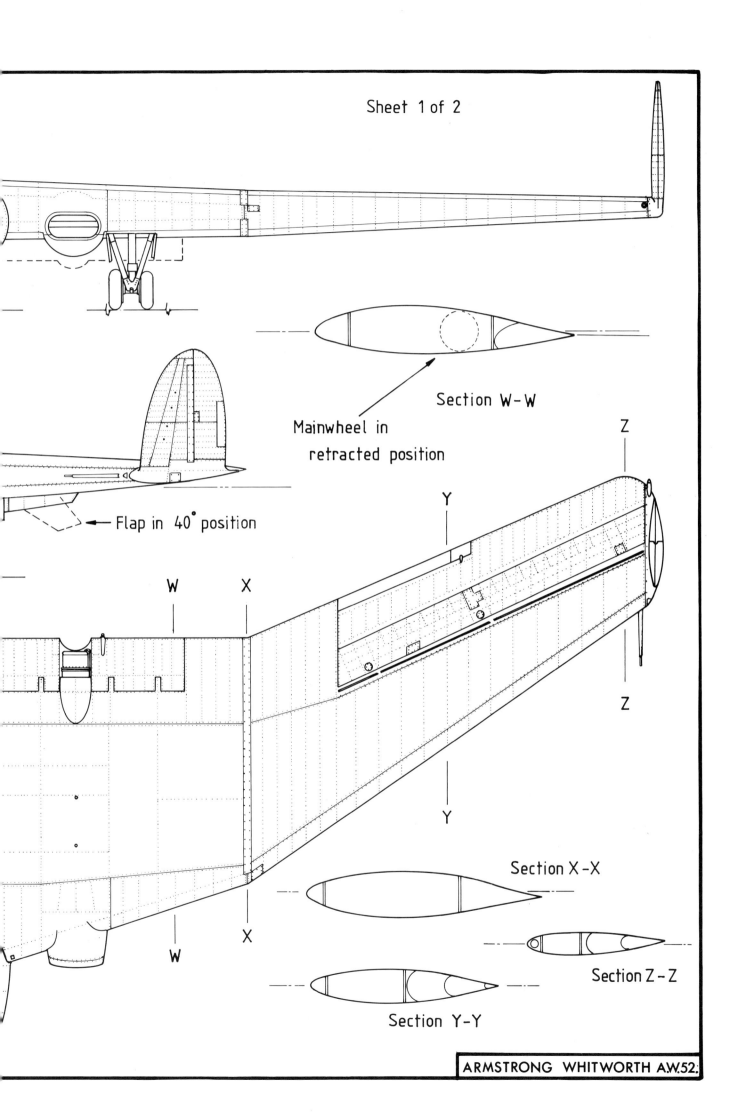

Sheet 1 of 2

Section W-W

Mainwheel in
retracted position

Flap in 40° position

W        X

W        X

Y

Y

Z

Z

Section X-X

Section Z-Z

Section Y-Y

ARMSTRONG WHITWORTH A.W.52.

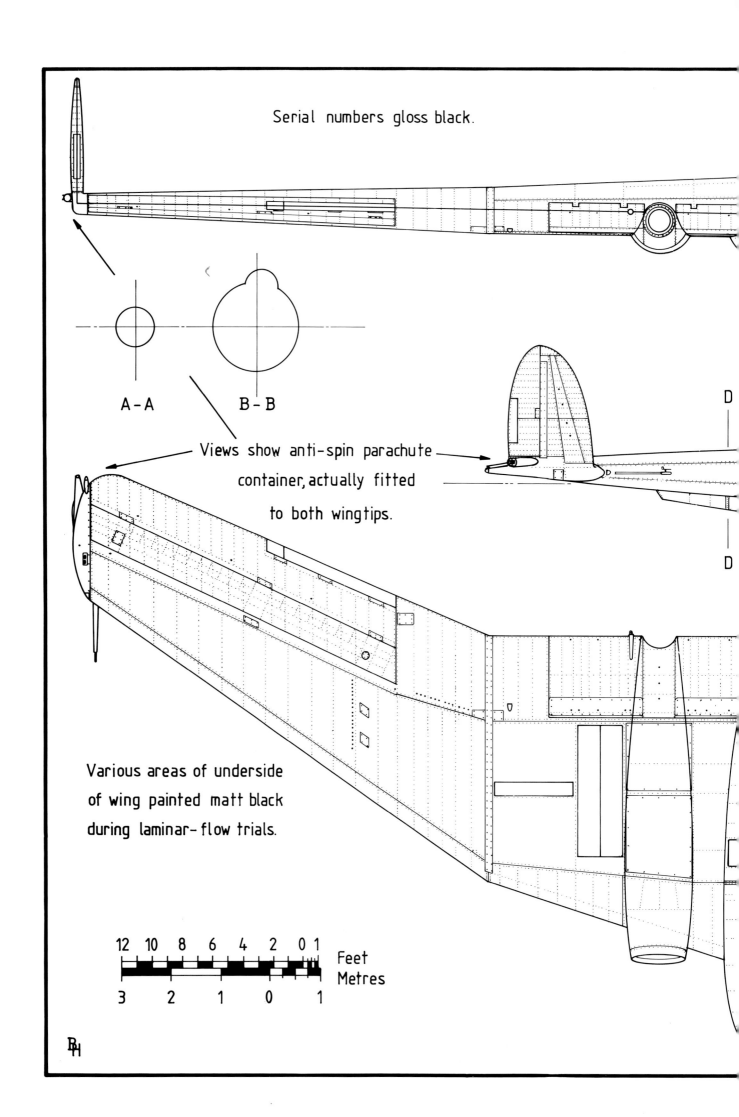

Serial numbers gloss black.

A - A

B - B

D

D

Views show anti-spin parachute
container, actually fitted
to both wingtips.

Various areas of underside
of wing painted matt black
during laminar-flow trials.

12 10 8 6 4 2 0 1  Feet
                   Metres
3     2    1   0   1

B͞H

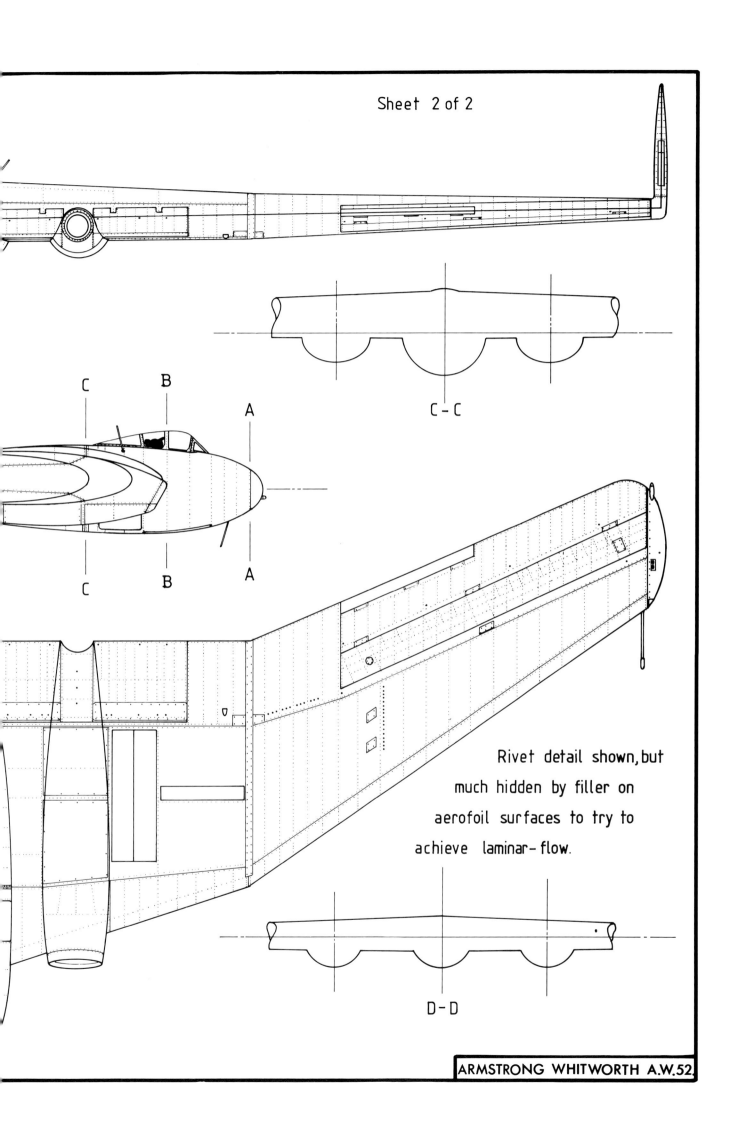

C B A

A

C - C

C B

C B A

Rivet detail shown, but
much hidden by filler on
aerofoil surfaces to try to
achieve laminar-flow.

D-D

ARMSTRONG WHITWORTH A.W.52.

had of stalling at the tips first, and to prevent stick force reversal. This was to be achieved by suction through one-quarter inch wide slots cut in the wing along the whole leading edge of the correctors at approximately 55% chord on the upper surfaces, which was the point at which laminar flow was designed to break down. The resultant flow was forwards between the wing spars to partially sealed chambers in the wing leading edges, which were in turn connected to the engine intake ducts. The air flow was achieved by opening a pair of rectangular flaps in each engine intake duct. These flaps were automaticaly controlled from both the throttles and elevons. The idea was to increase suction whenever the throttle was retarded below 8,000 rpm. and/or the control column was pulled back. The resultant loss of thrust from the engines was approximately 300 lbs. at maximum suction bleed and, to help compensate, the engines' flight idling speed had to be increased by some 2,000 rpm. The suction air ducts were connected by a balance pipe between each engine intake. The suction control flaps were opened 40% travel with the engines at flight idle, and 30% with the control column fully back and the engines at high power settings. In the situation of the column fully back and the engines also at idle, the flaps were 80% open.

The anti-icing system consisted of the outer wing leading edges being heated by using hot air bled directly from the engines' jetpipes. Just aft of each jetpipe orifice was mounted a curved pipe, which could be moved into the hot exhaust-gas stream whenever anti-icing was required. These hot gases were then mixed with cold air to give the correct temperature to the wing ducts, circulation being solely by ram effect. Part of the hot air was taken along the wing leading edges, to exhaust eventually through outlet ducts under each wingtip, the remainder recirculated back through corrugations between the outer and inner wing skins, over an area varying from 13% chord at the knuckle end to 20% at the tip. This then exhausted into the wing structure between the ribs, eventually being dumped overboard through a row of twelve circular holes behind the aft spar in the area of the fuel tanks.

**POWER PLANT**
*First prototype* Two Rolls-Royce Nene 2 R.N.2 centrifugal flow turbojets with a Sea Level Static Thrust of 5,000 lbs., each.
*Second prototype* Two Rolls-Royce Derwent 5 R.D.7 centrifugal flow turbojets with a Sea Level Static Thrust of 3,500 lbs., each.

*Underside and undercarriage details. Uneven skinning of underside aft of the rear spar and on control surfaces resulted despite special care during manufacture (via Ray Williams).*

*An artist's impression of the aircraft in flight. The shortened fuselage aft of the rudder illustrates the aircraft in its configuration with an afterburner fitted with the 37" diameter jetpipe.*

# MILES M.52

| Manufacturer | Miles Aircraft |
|---|---|
| Specification | E.24/43 |
| Role | Research Prototype |
| First Flight Date | Not Flown – Planned for 1947 |

This aircraft was the first attempt in Britain to design and develop an aircraft whose sole purpose was to fly faster than the speed of sound. As it transpired, the aerodynamics proved to be correct but the whole project was sadly let down by the totally inadequate power units at that time available. When it became obvious that the aircraft performance would be little better than more conventional designs then becoming available, the project was cancelled.

## DEVELOPMENT HISTORY

To realise the full potential offered by the new form of propulsion from the jet engine, the Ministry of Aircraft Production (later the Ministry of Supply) formulated a requirement for an experimental aircraft capable of flying at the unprecedented speed of 1000 mph (870 kts. /Mach 1.5).

After the Specification E.24/43 had been raised, the contract for the construction of the aircraft was placed with Miles Aircraft without seeking tenders from any other companies, partly due to their history of producing unusual and unique designs and, being a small company, a highly secret project could be undertaken with the minimum of security problems. Also, Miles was chosen so as not to sidetrack the larger companies and disrupt the design and production of operational aircraft desperately needed for the war effort. (Interestingly, the same logic was used in the choice of Bell Aircraft for the X–1 project.) The design received the firm's designation of M.52.

The location of the firm's works was also ideally suited to enable close co-operation with both the RAE at Farnborough, and with what was to become known as the National Gas Turbine Establishment at Pyestock. Work started on 3rd October 1943, and the contract was signed on 13th December 1943,

*View of a large scale stainless steel wind tunnel model. Just visible is the slab tailplane pivot point, also the lighting illustrates well the conical camber section of the fin. Note also the very sharp intake lips and relatively shallow intake profile.*

initially covering two prototypes and parts for a third. An additional contract, covering a further airframe for structural testing, was placed on 17th April 1944 and, a day later, the whole project was downgraded from Top Secret to Secret.

As with the 'rival' X–1, it was established early on that a design with minimum drag and cross-sectional area was required, and that the best shape was similar to that of a bullet to enable it to attain the same sort of velocity. Also, surfaces of minimal thickness were needed to reduce drag and, as the German research findings regarding swept wings, with their advantage of delaying the onset of compressibility effects and their associated drag-rise, were not available, a straight wing with bi-convex section was chosen, its planform ensuring that it stayed at all times within the angle of the shock-cone produced by the aircraft's nose.

There was no precedent to follow with such a thin wing planform, and therefore it was decided to build and fly a wooden full-scale model of the proposed wing design, and fit it to a Miles M.3B Falcon. The aircraft also had a similar, but unswept, tailplane to that proposed for the M.52. A new main undercarriage was also fitted to the aircraft to keep the wing clean, as on the final design. The very thin wing had extremely sharp leading and trailing edges, requiring the fitting of fibre matting to protect the ground-crew whilst working on and manoeuvring the aircraft. So sharp were the

aerofoils that the aircraft was nicknamed 'Gillette Falcon' (Gillette being the brand-name of a famous type of razor blade).

As was to be expected with such a thin wing, the take-off performance was worse compared to the normal Falcon; it was longitudinally unstable and neutrally stable in roll. Surprisingly, the stalling behaviour was quite innocuous. It was felt, however, that, although proving the basic aerodynamics of the wing shape, there was little relevance in the control characteristics to those of the M.52 as the latter was to have fully powered surfaces.

The requirement for a minimum cross-sectional area also meant the smallest diameter fuselage around the pilot and engine. The fuselage size was determined by the size of the chosen engine and, as the wings were too thin, the fuel also had to be carried within the fuselage, in a tank wrapped around the engine bay and exhaust duct close to the aircraft's centre of gravity to reduce trim changes due to fuel usage.

A normal 'stepped' cockpit canopy would have also added too much drag, but the pilot needed adequate vision for take-off and landing. The cockpit was therefore faired completely into the relatively small intake centre-body, with the pilot having to lie almost horizontal, its greatest diameter being a maximum of 3'9". His feet were almost on a level with his shoulders, and the nosewheel retracting into a bay between his feet and behind the instrument panel. The very shallow angle of his eye-line to the canopy transparencies, together with the shallow view available above the instrument panel shroud, would have provided a very marginal field of view, especially under anything less than perfect flight conditions. Recovery to land in any adverse weather conditions, with no real navigational aids, would have been, to say the least, difficult. (While I was discussing the project with Mr G. Miles, he stated that, contrary to some previously published accounts, the cockpit was designed around the Miles Chief Test Pilot who was 6'0" tall, and could accommodate a person of this stature, and it was intended that he should make the first flights. Short pilots were not a prerequisite!)

By April 1944, the design was already beginning to suffer from weight growth, the original estimates of 5,140 lbs., and 6,500 lbs for the normal and overload case having risen to 7,754 and 8,654 lbs. respectively. This was partly due to the need for an additional 70 gallons of fuel to cater for the higher specific consumption of the engine, but primarily due to the engine itself having increased in weight by nearly 90% since the original calculations.

Initial flights were to be made with a non-afterburning version of the basic engine, which was a direct development of the original Whittle design first flown in the E.28/39., with an exhaust duct diameter of 18.5" but, when the augmentor fan and afterburner were fitted, two larger ducts were proposed of 37" and 44" diameter. Initial flights were also to be made with a normal tailplane and elevator, pending solution of some problems with the all-flying version, tests of it to be made fitted to a Spitfire.

To highlight other areas of uncertainty, and illustrate attempts to reduce drag to a minimum, a retractable 21.25" aerial was designed for the four-channel TR 1464 VHF radio. This was also to avoid the possibility of aerial damage at maximum speed. It was proposed to place it under the cockpit nacelle but, as can be seen from the drawings, it was eventually fitted, non-retractable, just aft of the right main undercarriage bay.

Wind tunnel tests and calculations were already showing that the aircraft's maximum speed in level flight would be no greater than 0.95 Mach and, for it to achieve anywhere near its design performance, it would require greater thrust or a steep dive, or both. A further problem was a considerable loss of longitudinal stability with increased Mach. no. With the centre of gravity at 0.26 mean aerodynamic chord, this became neutral at 0.82M.

There was no prospect of any vast increase in thrust from the engine, the redesign of the original Whittle engine proving a more complicated task than at first envisaged. The basic engine had been flown in the tail of a Wellington bomber test-bed, but much work was still left to be done on the augmentor fan and afterburner. The design risked being caught in the designer's nightmare spiral of more thrust, needing more fuel, thus more weight and less performance, thus more thrust, etc., etc. There was also the much disliked situation of having a new engine, in a new airframe, operating at speeds and altitudes about which there was little knowledge. (It must be remembered that, at that time, few jet engines could be reliably operated above 35,000 ft., let alone at nearly twice that height!)

Several avenues were explored, such as the fitting of a new engine (the axial flow Metrovick F.2 having already flown) to provide extra thrust; the fitting of an auxiliary rocket engine to boost the aircraft through the transonic region; and the substitution of a rocket engine alone. The subsequent glide recovery to base would have proved operationally impossible in the normal UK weather, even if airfields with large enough runways were available. A plan was also put forward to carry the aircraft aloft suspended under a Lancaster bomber in a cut-away bomb bay to save fuel, but this was also rejected.

The possibility was investigated of reducing the thickness/chord ratio to as little as 4% in the attempt to further reduce drag, but this was not pursued. (The root and tip thickness were already as little as 6" and 2" respectively, and construction of any thinner section would have been beyond the state of the art at that time.) It was obvious, therefore, that the original idea of sustained supersonic speed in level flight would never be possible, and even in a steep dive, starting at a maximum level speed of 0.94M, and 50,000 ft., only 1.03M would be achieved, far short of the planned 1.5M. Wind tunnel tests had shown that climb to altitude was quicker, and an increase in ceiling of approximately 6,000 ft. was possible, with a conventional aerofoil section. The actual wing section appeared to have little effect on the drag coefficient at supersonic speeds, the thickness/chord ratio being the predominant factor. The subsequent dive from the greater height allowed a slightly better top speed of 1.07 M being achieved at a higher altitude, therefore giving more height for recovery.

However, there was another area causing concern – that of pilot escape in the event of an emergency. Ejection seats were in their infancy, and anyway there was insufficient room in the cockpit to accommodate one. Plans were in hand to have the entire cockpit ejected as a capsule separated from the rest of the airframe by explosive bolts, and a parachute stowed behind the cockpit rear bulkhead would be deployed for slowing down and descent to a safe altitude. The pilot would then jettison the canopy and manually bail out, using his personal parachute for the final descent in the normal way. This form of escape was also untried, and no trials had been successfully completed with mock-ups of the system.

Blower tunnel tests had shown that the canopy could be jettisoned successfully, as it was carried well clear of the fin at all speeds. Two forms of canopy were tested, one with the canopy alone and the other with the main instrument panel integral with it. Both were equally successful.

The pilot, however, was less lucky. If he was able to force himself out into the airstream, he would probably break his neck or back by the force of the airflow. This was also pre-supposing that he had previously been able to shut down the engine and not be sucked towards the sharp edge of the intake. Escape when not inverted was virtually impossible; however, there was a chance of successful escape if the aircraft was inverted, provided that the speed was not below approximately 295 kts., when the pilot was liable to hit the wing, and when not above 355 kts., when he was in danger of hitting the fin!

Emergencies never happen under 'ideal' conditions, allowing him to invert the aircraft and achieve a given very narrow speed bracket, therefore there was little prospect of the pilot being able to survive.

By now, the results of German research were becoming available, and their jet aircraft being assessed. The swept wing was showing itself to be superior to the straight wing in the transonic region (although the M.52 aerodynamic design was proved right for the supersonic regime). The prospect of never achieving its design objectives, and the entirely inadequate thrust available from the engine, together with the pilot's escape problems, sounded the death-knell for the project.

The project was officially cancelled on 13th March 1946 but work had, in fact, ceased the previous month. Several attempts to revive it were made by the company, even to the extent of fitting a German rocket engine and flying it by remote control, but all were unsuccessful.

Trials of the basic aerodynamics shape continued with approximately $3/10$ scale models of the M.52, conducted by Vickers-Armstrong, unmanned and powered by rockets. They were air-launched from a Mosquito bomber and, after two unsuccessful attempts, on 10th October 1948, the model achieved 1.38M before being lost at sea. Thus the aerodynamics of the basic design were proved right for supersonic flight.

Over the years the blame for the cancellation, and the subsequent setback to the British aircraft industry in the achievement of supersonic flight, has been laid on the Ministry of Supply who stated that "...in the light of the limited knowledge then available, the risk of attempting supersonic flight in manned aircraft was unacceptably great..."

However, the true situation was that the M.52, although aerodynamically sound, would never have achieved its design performance due to totally inadequate thrust from its planned engine. Despite its exotic lines, in fact it would have been little faster in level flight than the 'ordinary' Supermarine Attacker then under construction. It was, therefore, pointless continuing with the project. There was also the matter of the pilot's safety, not from supersonic flight, but purely from the limitations of the design and his negligible chances of escaping in the event of any emergency. Possibly the Ministry statement should have said ... "the risk of attempting supersonic flight in *this particular* manned aircraft was unacceptably great."

The parts of the prototype completed at that stage, jigs and tools, and the mock-up, were scrapped, and all research data, including wind tunnel results and calculations for the project, were sent to the United States. It is not known whether they had any direct bearing on the final design of the Bell X–1, or whether, despite its eventual similarity in layout, it had already reached an advanced stage of development for the results to not be relevant. (It is also of interest to note that the X–1 needed a four-barrel rocket motor producing a total of 6,000 lbs. of thrust to achieve supersonic speed in level flight. Britain had to wait another ten years before it had an aircraft which achieved the performance required from the M.52, and that was the Fairey Delta 2, which achieved the magic 1,000 mph on 10th March 1956, with an afterburning thrust of just over 9,500 lbs.)

# CONSTRUCTION

The airframe was of light alloy construction except for certain high stress components which were made from steel. The fuselage structure was conventional, consisting of closely spaced frames and longitudinal stringers covered by a stressed light alloy skin. Frontal area was kept to a minimum consistent with accommodating the engine and pilot. All cross-sections were circular, the pilot being accommodated in a pointed nacelle which formed the centre-body of the annular engine intake.

Except for the nosewheel bay beneath the cockpit, the entire nacelle was pressurised to a differential pressure of 2.5 psi. to give an equivalent cabin altitude of 35,000 ft., when the true aircraft altitude was 60,000 ft.

Maximum diameter of the nacelle was only 3'9", and therefore the pilot lay almost horizontal, with the nosewheel oleo retracting forwards into its bay between his feet. The canopy transparencies were in two parts. The forward one was fixed and was made from a single piece of curved plate glass, and the aft one consisted of three panels, and was detachable for normal entry and exit. It could be jettisoned in an emergency to allow the pilot to bail out manually. No ejection seat was provided. The windows were hot air de-misted from engine bleed-air, which first de-misted the left, then the right, lower panel, before passing to the gallery around the forward end of the plate glass windscreen, flowing between the nosewheel shroud and the canopy. A clear vertical glass panel prevented flow directly into the pilot's face. The cockpit was provided with a ventilator to provide some airflow during gliding flight. The windscreen also had an alcohol spray de-icing system.

It was intended that eventually the entire nacelle would be jettisoned in any emergency, separating from the main fuselage by means of explosive bolts.

A parachute, in the nacelle aft end behind the cockpit rear pressure bulkhead, would automatically deploy slowing the capsule and, after descent to a safe altitude, the pilot could then jettison the canopy and bail out manually, using his own personal parachute for the final descent and landing.

The nosecone forward of the nosewheel bay and transparencies was detachable to give access to the automatic observer and its associated camera. An

## OUTLINE SPECIFICATION

| | |
|---|---|
| $V_{max}$ | 870 kts/1.5 Mach |
| Stress Limits | +6.7g to –3.4g |
| Horizontal acceleration 1.3g | |

## DATA

### DIMENSIONS

Span 26'10.5"
Length 39'0.5" (duct diameter 18.5"; duct length 28'10.6"
37'0.25" (duct diameter 37"; duct length 26'10.25")
36'4.75" (duct diameter 44"; duct length 26'0.75")

(Note the above lengths include the pitot head)

| | |
|---|---|
| Height (static) | 11'7" |
| Length of nosecone | 6'8" |
| Maximum Fuselage Diameter | 5'0" |
| Wheelbase | 9'0" |
| Track | 4'6" |
| Tailplane Span | 14'6.3" |

### AREAS

Wing
| | |
|---|---|
| Wing (gross) | 141.4 sq ft (bi-convex section) |
| Wing (net) | 108.1 sq ft (bi-convex section) |
| Aileron | 4.86 sq ft (each) |
| Flap | 17.2 sq ft |
| Span/side | 6'9.5" |

Tailplane
| | |
|---|---|
| Gross | 49.8 sq ft |
| Net | 31.2 sq ft |

Fin and Rudder
| | |
|---|---|
| Gross | 19.1 sq ft |
| rudder only | 6.3 sq ft |

Weights
| | |
|---|---|
| Zero Fuel Weight | 5,954 lbs |
| Pilot | 200 lbs |
| Fuel (200 gall) | 1,600 lbs |
| All Up Weight | 7,754 lbs |
| Overload | 8,654 lbs |
| Wing loading | 54.5 lbs/sq ft |

### PERFORMANCE

Take-Off (with bi-convex section wing, 30° flap)

| | auw | T/O speed | Distance |
|---|---|---|---|
| W2/700 engine | | | |
| (150 gall fuel) | 5,955 lbs | 114 kts | 4,560 ft |
| W2/700 plus afterburner | | | |
| (200 gall fuel) | 7,493 | 128 | 4,650 |
| (320 gall fuel, with drop tank) | 8,553 | 136 | 6,120 |
| Take-Off (with conventional section wing, 30° flap) | | | |
| (200 gall fuel) | 7,493 | 114 | 3,240 |

### Climb

Best climb speed 504–530 kts (varying with altitude)
Time to 36,000 ft 1.5 mins

Fuel required in Climb

| | to 40,000 ft | to 50,000 ft |
|---|---|---|
| W2/700 | 56 gallons | |
| W2/700 (with afterburner) | — | 120 gallons |
| | | 148 gallons (with drop tank) |

Maximum Speed
Wind tunnel results show max Mach No.
attainable in level flight      0.95M

| Height (x1,000 ft) | SL | 10 | 20 | 30 | 40 | 50 |
|---|---|---|---|---|---|---|
| W2/700 (70 galls—at 5,315 lbs) | 447 kts | 478 | 495 | 508 | 491 | — |
| W2/700 (200 galls—7,493 lbs) (afterburner) | 613* | — | 582 | 556 | 543 | 539 |

*limited to 560 kts due to duct pressure restriction.

Diving (45° angle, with a 3g pullout)
Start dive at 56,000 ft with conventional wing
$V_{max}$ at 42,500 ft—1.07M in 32 secs
Start dive at 50,000 ft with conventional wing
$V_{max}$ at 36,000 ft—870 kts (1000 mph sounds better!)
Start dive at 50,000 ft with bi-convex wing
$V_{max}$ at 40,000 ft—1.03M in 27 secs

Landing
| | |
|---|---|
| Landing speed | 140 kts |
| Distance from 50' | 4560 ft |

### REFERENCES

| | |
|---|---|
| Public Record Office | —Avia Files |
| RAE Farnborough | —Library |
| | —NGTE Report R.4 |
| Miles Drawing | —D.5200000 |
| W2/700 Drawing | —A10249 |

Note. During research for this aircraft, it was very difficult to determine whether it met the criteria of actually having reached an advanced stage of construction, for inclusion in this book. Some sources stated that it had reached only an advanced, detailed, design stage, with only a mock-up completed, and some smaller components manufactured. Other sources, including Mr G. Miles himself, and others employed by his firm at the time, stated that construction of the actual prototype was well advanced at the time of cancellation. On balance, it was therefore decided to give the aircraft the benefit of the doubt and include it in this collection of subjects.

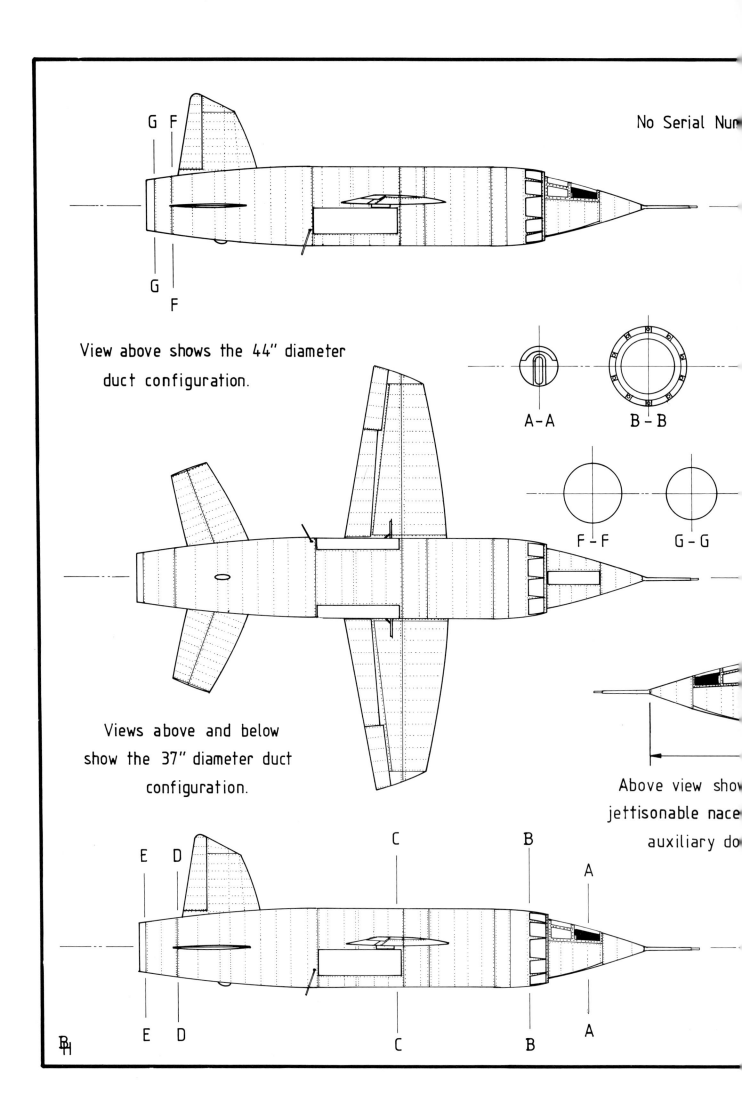

G F

No Serial Num

View above shows the 44" diameter
duct configuration.

A-A          B-B

F-F          G-G

Views above and below
show the 37" diameter duct
configuration.

Above view sho
jettisonable nace
auxiliary do

E D          C          B

A

E D          C          B          A

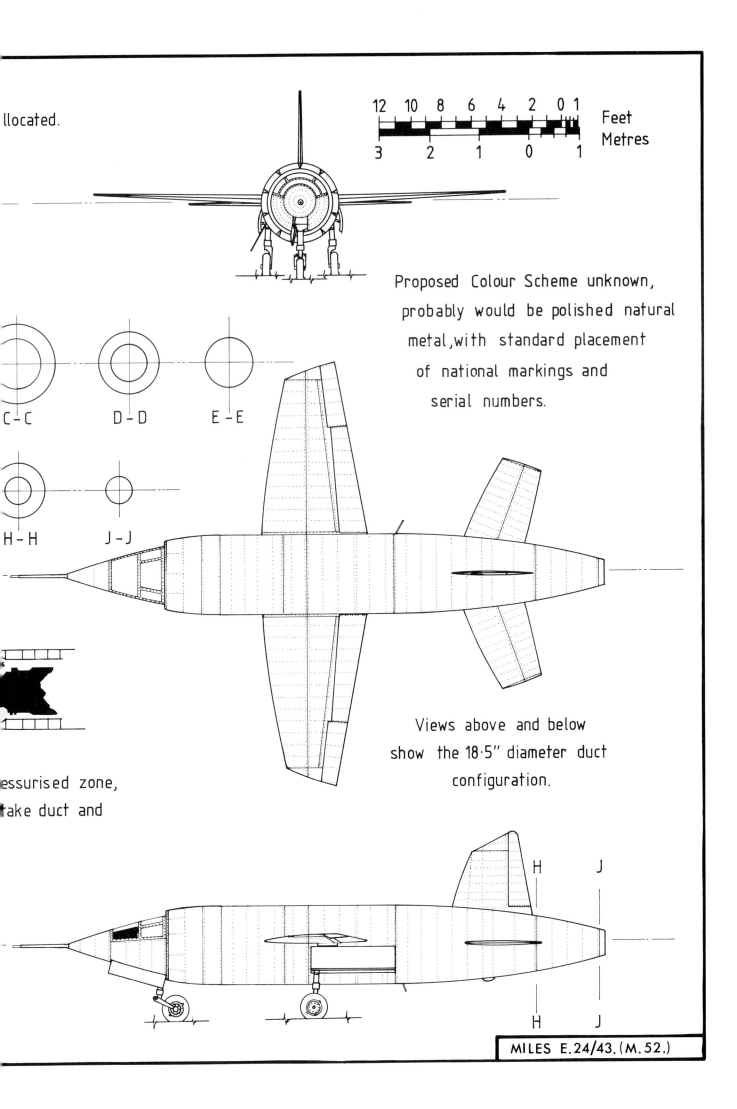

llocated.

12  10  8  6  4  2  0 1    Feet
3     2     1     0     1    Metres

Proposed Colour Scheme unknown,
probably would be polished natural
metal, with standard placement
of national markings and
serial numbers.

C-C          D-D          E-E

H-H          J-J

essurised zone,
take duct and

Views above and below
show the 18·5" diameter duct
configuration.

H          J

H          J

MILES E.24/43.(M.52.)

*The fuselage mock-up showing details of construction, also location of slot in the structure for the tubular wing mainspar to pass right through. Clearly visible are the cut-outs for the intake suction relief doors, 'gills'. An engine mock-up can also be seen mounted in the forward part of the fuselage.*

electrically-heated pitot static boom was fitted to the extreme tip of the nosecone.

The external power supply socket was mounted on the side of the right keel member within the nosewheel bay. The electrical control box was also on the right side of the cockpit, as were the two accumulators. All electrical connectors through the rear cockpit pressure bulkhead were pressure-tight and were pull-out quick release for easy disconnection in the event that the cockpit capsule was jettisoned.

The engine was mounted in the forward end of the main fuselage as near to the aircraft's centre of gravity as possible, and was fed via a sharp-edged annular intake. As there was no space in the wings, the fuel was also housed in the fuselage, in an annular tank around the engine bay to minimise centre of gravity movement with fuel usage. A fuel filler cap was in the top of the fuselage. Provision was made for a 100 gallon ventral drop tank, which increased the total fuel capacity up to 320 gallons.

The main electrical supply was from a 500 watt generator mounted centrally on the lower rear face of the cockpit aft bulkhead.

As the main fuselage consisted entirely of a narrow walled duct, to keep sufficient rigidity access panel cut-outs were kept to a minimum. Several items of internal equipment were situated within the main undercarriage bay with easy access through the two large fairing doors. The TR 1464 radio was mounted on the keel member on the right side, with the compass transmitter unit mounted just aft of this, and on the left side. The radio's whip aerial was fitted just aft of the right mainwheel bay door.

The initial configuration, with the non-afterburning engine, had an 18.5" diameter duct, which extended in a tailcone well aft of the fin. There were two other planned configurations, with much shorter modified aft ends, with duct diameters of

37" and 44" respectively, the last having its orifice just aft of the fin. These accommodated the afterburner and augmentor fan of the developed engine. To cope with the required increase in mass flow, a series of ten, spring-loaded, auxiliary doors were fitted around the lip of the main intake. These were not fitted for the original non-afterburning configuration. They were referred to as 'gills' in contemporary documents.

The entire fuselage aft of the mainspar attachment frames was detachable for engine, afterburner and jetpipe removal. This operation was to be done with the aircraft in a *vertical* position, requiring a pit to be dug of 10' depth. Suitable strong-points for slinging the aircraft were to be provided. (This very complicated procedure made logistical support very difficult except from the aircraft's home base.)

The main undercarriage retracted aft to lie either side of the jetpipe duct, and gave the aircraft a ground angle of 1.5° when static.

The wing was mounted just above the central longitudinal datum of the aircraft, and was unusual in having a tubular mainspar bolted to reinforced fuselage frames. It had a fore and aft auxiliary spar and closely spaced ribs, with a relatively thick skin to provide torsional stiffness. The leading and trailing edges were very sharp, the former being curved and the latter straight, the wing planform ending in stream-wise tips to keep the entire surface within the shock-cone formed by the aircraft's nose. The outboard ailerons, without trim tabs, and the inboard plain flaps were hinged to the aft auxiliary spar. Maximum deflection of the flaps was 65°.

The wing had an incidence to the aircraft datum of +0°33' and a dihedral angle of 2°. The aspect ratio was 5.1:1, with a root and tip chord of 6'8" and 3'7" respectively, which with the thickness/chord ratios of 7.5% and 4.9%, made the physical thickness at the root only 6" and 2" at the tip. Originally the wing section was symmetrical bi-convex, but later an ordinary symmetrical section was used.

The tailplane, also of symmetrical biconvex section, was constructed around a single mainspar at approximately mid-chord, which passed right through the fuselage duct, joining the two surfaces. It was planned to be a slab surfaced, all-flying tailplane, with no trim tabs. Early problems may have required the aircraft to fly initially with conventional elevators, pending successful trials with a similar tail fitted to a Spitfire.

The tailplane had a quarter-chord sweep of 24°, and no dihedral. Its thickness/chord ratio varied from 6% at the root to 4.25% at the tip.

The fin was constructed around main and auxiliary spars, the rudder being hinged to the aft spar. The section was symmetrical bi-convex, with thickness/chord ratios at the root and tip of 7.5% and 4.4% respectively.

All flying controls were power operated.

Small dive recovery flaps were fitted to hinge out from the fuselage just aft of the wing's mid-chord, between the wing undersurface and the top of the mainwheel bay doors. They each measured only 12"x3" and extended perpendicular to the airflow, producing a nose-up pitch to aid dive recovery when deployed.

## POWER PLANT
W2/700 centrifugal flow turbojet with augmentor fan and afterburner, developing a Sea Level Static Thrust of 3,175 lbs. and a thrust of 4,725 lbs., at 508 kts. at SL. limited by a 1,500°C turbine temperature at 16,750 rpm.

(Note: It is difficult at this distance in time to determine the actual maximum thrust rating achieved in the test chamber. The NGTE report states tests were made simulating conditions at 50,000 ft./478 kts., 36,000 ft./870 kts., and Sea Level/434 kts., and the highest thrust achieved was "5,250 lbs", but not under which of these conditions.)

(Author's Note: The undercarriage shown in the accompanying drawing is conjectural, no authentic information being available for the shape of the oleos. The wheelbase and track is correct, as is the 2°33' angle of the mainwheels when viewed from the front. The shape of the oleos has been arrived at from the geometry of the wheels and their relation to their respective bays in the fuselage.)

*The second prototype, showing original shaped fin and rudder and tail-mounted parachute container. This side view illustrates the 'portly' fuselage shape of the aircraft, the design looking almost nose heavy!*

# GLOSTER E.1/44

| Manufacturer | Gloster Aircraft |
|---|---|
| Specification | E.1/44 |
| Role | Experimental Fighter Prototype |
| First Flight Date | SM 809 – Not flown |
| | TX 145 – 9th March 1948 |
| | TX 148 – 1949 |
| | TX 150 – Not Flown |

The Specification E.1/44 was raised to design an operational aircraft which in effect was an attempt to produce the smallest, most efficient airframe capable of accommodating a single engine, with sufficient fuel and ancillary equipment, plus pilot and an internal armament of four cannon. Although it achieved this aim, it was felt that the development potential was not as flexible as that of its stablemate, the Meteor, and thus further development was abandoned.

## DEVELOPMENT HISTORY

Having been awarded the contract for the design and construction of prototypes and pre-production series aircraft, work at Gloster's factory started in late 1944, the design being allocated the company designation of P.190, and later the G.42. It bore some superficial resemblance to the earlier E.5/42 but was a completely new design. Priority was given to the production of the twin-engined Meteor, and thus labour, materials and design effort were concentrated on this, causing progress on the E.1/44 to be very slow.

Therefore, it was not until August of 1947 that the first prototype, SM 809, was completed and ready to fly. It was transported to Boscombe Down, but the vehicle on which it was being carried jack-knifed and the aircraft was irreparably damaged. Therefore, flight trials had to be delayed even further until the second prototype, TX 145, was ready. This was successfully transported to Boscombe Down where it made its first flight on 9th March 1948. After brief trials, it was returned to the Gloster factory for minor modifications.

Continuing wind tunnel tests of its longitudinal and directional stability characteristics showed that the basic design was suitable for the carriage of external underwing stores. However, handling trials with the original low set tailplane revealed less than ideal characteristics. Model tests at Farnborough proved the effectiveness of a revised tail layout to keep the tailplane clear of turbulence at high speeds, so a new tail layout was designed and adopted for the second aircraft to fly, actually the third prototype, TX 148, which flew successfully from Boscombe Down in 1949. (The layout was identical externally and became very familiar on the Meteor F.8 and later variants, and it has sometimes been thought that this was therefore fitted to the E.1/44, but in fact the reverse was the case. It was designed for the E.1/44 and was so successful that it was adopted for the Meteor, replacing the original design on that aircraft.) The fin did, in fact, differ from that on the Meteor, in that the part of the fin above the tailplane was of wooden construction and housed a VHF aerial in its leading edge.

Meanwhile, TX 145 had arrived at Farnborough on 2nd December 1949, to be joined by TX 148 on 14th February 1950. They were both then used at Farnborough for various research projects, not associated directly with the original design, including braking parachute trials and research into flying control systems. TX 145 survived a crash landing after engine failure on 2nd November 1950 but suffered no damage. It also experienced violent nosewheel shimmy whilst taxi-ing on 10th January 1951.

Both aircraft were disposed of on 24th September 1951, and went to Shoeburyness to act as ground targets for research into the effects of various armament on contemporary airframes.

The fourth prototype, TX 150, was destined never to fly, being used for ground trials only, and commenced structural tests to proof load on 8th November 1949. It was eventually to prove the longest surviving example of the aircraft, being sold to the College of Aeronautics, Cranfield on 14th April 1956. At the end of its career as an instructional airframe it was finally scrapped at Cranfield.

The design proved basically successful and fulfilled all the requirements of the original Specification but, due to the slowness of construction and the long delays following the unfortunate accident and damage to the first prototype, it was overtaken by events, and was bypassed by many other, more capable designs. (Including the much more advanced, all-swept, and transonic, North American F.86 Sabre, which made the E.1/44, and several other current designs obsolescent overnight.)

In addition to the four prototypes, several pre-production machines had also been partially completed. A projected swept-wing variant had also been allocated the Specification E.23/46, but was not developed.

The aircraft was too late and had too little development potential compared to the Meteor, which was to soldier on in front line service for many more years, until later, higher-performance, aircraft were produced.

## CONSTRUCTION

Apart from the upper half of the fin, the structure was primarily of light alloy with a stressed skin, although certain parts of the wing were from steel. The broad fuselage was divided into five sections for ease of manufacture by sub-contractors, comprising the nose, front, centre and rear portions and the tailcone. The nose contained the cockpit, nosewheel bay and internal armament, and was built around two fore and aft webs with light alloy formers. The upper part of the nose forward of the windscreen formed an equipment bay, accommodating two electrical accumulators at its forward end and the VHF radio aft. The aft retracting nosewheel was housed in the very forward part of

*View showing the second prototype during ground-running tests illustrating well the details of the nose and cockpit.*

*The third prototype from the rear illustrating well the changed tail design. Note also the flat oval fuselage cross-section and open semi-circular suction relief doors on the top of the fuselage*

the nosecone, the bay giving access for charging of the pneumatic reservoir. The main electrical panel was accessible through a panel in the lower fuselage, aft of the wheelbay.

The internal armament of four Hispano 20 mm. cannon was housed in the very bottom of the nose, two cannon on each side of the wheelbay. The ammunition, 180 rpg., was housed in two large bays either side of the cockpit, accessible through two large hatches for quick re-arming.

The cockpit had an optically flat, three panel 'fighter' windscreen, which had provision for both de-icing and de-misting. The pilot had an electrically-operated, aft sliding canopy for normal entry and exit, which could be jettisoned in an emergency – he did not, however, have an ejection seat. Ventilation of the cockpit was via a pipe whose inlet was in the tip of the nosecone. A second 'hole' immediately below this housed a gun camera. The two semi-circular intakes were situated on each side of the fuselage, with their associated prominent boundary layer bleed slots, intake ducting passing each side of the main fuel tank, which was situated just aft of the cockpit.

Access to the tank was obtained via a large circular hatch, which could be reached after

removal of the aft fairing of the cockpit canopy. The nose and forward section of the fuselage was bolted to the centre-section at four pick-up points, which was built around reinforced frames, with heavy double-channel frames at the mainspar and engine mounting points. This section contained the engine which was provided with a large hatch in the top of the fuselage for servicing and removal, its auxiliary gearbox and ancillaries being accessible through another hatch just forward of that for the main bay. The rear fuselage and tailcone were of semi-monocoque construction, and were riveted to the centre-section, and contained a further two fuel tanks and the jetpipe.

The tailplane and fin were primarily of light alloy construction around a single mainspar with multiple ribs. However, the upper part of the fin was made from wood, and contained a VHF aerial in its leading edge. Projecting aft from its base almost to the tip of the tailcone, was a long fairing which contained an anti-spin parachute. The rudder was mass-balanced, and had a single balance/trim tab. The tailplane was mid-set on the fuselage and had no dihedral, and its elevators were fitted with a spring tab on each surface. All the controls were manually operated via push/pull rods. The fin on TX

148 was taller, and the anti-spin parachute container projected aft from its base to overhang the jet orifice. The tailplane was fitted approximately halfway up, dividing the rudder into two sections.

The fuel system comprised a total of five tanks, three in the centre-section, and one each side of the jetpipe in the aft fuselage. Total internal capacity was 428 gallons. This could be supplemented by two 100 gallon drop tanks fitted under each outer wing panel, 12'4.5" from the centreline.

The mid-mounted, symmetrical section wings were built in four parts, two inner and two outer panels, and were of exceptional strength, being built around a steel mainspar and a light alloy aft auxiliary spar. Adding further to the strength, the wing had very closely spaced ribs, with a stainless steel skin back to the web aft of the central mainspar. (This added considerably to the problems of manufacture.) The remainder of the structure and skin was from light alloy.

The wing had no sweep, but had marked taper on both the leading and trailing edges, and had a chord at the centreline of 11'3", and tip chord of 3'0". The hydraulically-operated wide track, inward retracting, main undercarriage was housed in bays in each inner wing section, immediately aft of the mainspar.

Plain flaps inboard, and ailerons outboard, were hinged to the aft auxiliary spar. Each aileron had a single spring tab fitted, and was manually operated. Rectangular dive recovery flaps were fitted underwing, forward of the mainspar. Vented forward-hinged airbrakes were fitted at approximately mid-semi-span on each wing approximately in line with the aileron/flap junction. These were in eight sections, four above the wing, and four below.

# DATA
## DIMENSIONS
| | |
|---|---|
| Span | 36'0" |
| Length | 38'0" (TX 148 38'11") |
| Height | 11'8" |
| Track | 17'6" |
| Wheelbase | 15'4" |
| Tailplane Span | 14'6" |

## AREAS
| | |
|---|---|
| Wing (gross) | 266 sq ft |
| Wing Loading | 44 lbs/sq ft |

## WEIGHTS
| | |
|---|---|
| Loaded | 11,470 lbs |
| Empty | 8,260 lbs |

## PERFORMANCE
| | | |
|---|---|---|
| Maximum Speed | 550 kts | at Sea Level |
| Initial Climb Rate | 5,000 (plus) ft/min | |
| Time to 40,000 ft | 12 mins 30 secs | |
| Service Ceiling | 44,000 ft | |
| Absolute Ceiling | 48,000 ft | |
| Range (internal fuel) | 650 n m | (approximately) |

## REFERENCES
| | |
|---|---|
| Public Records Office | —Avia Files |
| RAE Farnborough | —Library |
| Gloster Drawings | —P.190 G.A. |

## ARMAMENT
The internal armament comprised four 20mm. Hispano cannon with 180 rpg., with provision for underwing stores of either two 1,000 lbs. bombs, or eight 90 lbs. rocket projectiles.

## POWER PLANT
One Rolls-Royce Nene R.N.2 centrifugal flow turbojet developing a Sea Level Static Thrust of 5,000 lbs.

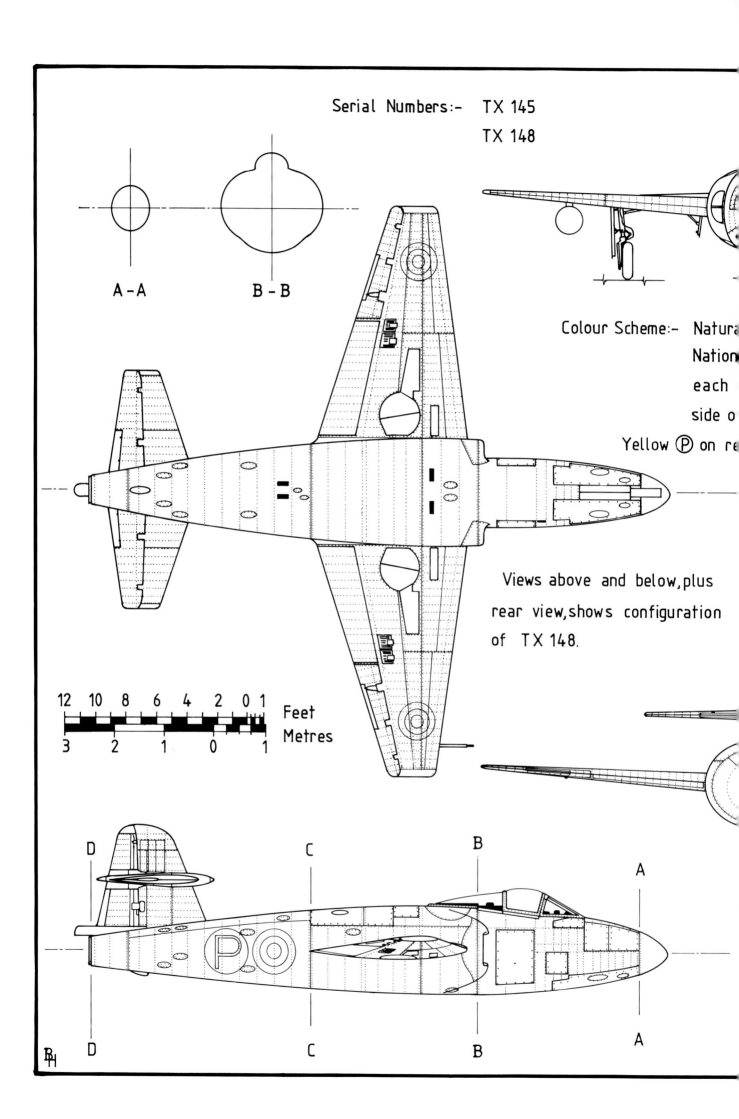

Serial Numbers:- TX 145
TX 148

A – A    B – B

Colour Scheme:- Natur...
Nation...
each
side o...
Yellow Ⓟ on re...

Views above and below, plus
rear view, shows configuration
of TX 148.

12  10  8  6  4  2  0  1    Feet
3      2      1      0   1    Metres

D    C    B    A

D    C    B    A

ᴮₕ

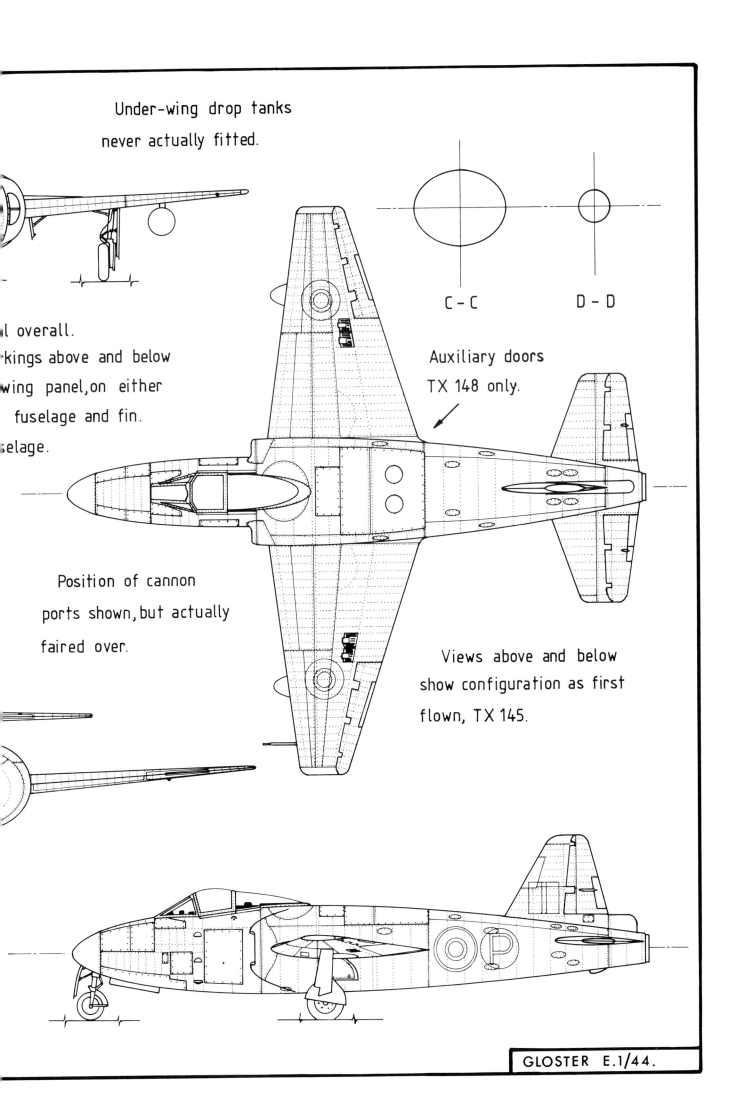

Under-wing drop tanks
never actually fitted.

C – C          D – D

l overall.
kings above and below
wing panel, on either
fuselage and fin.
selage.

Auxiliary doors
TX 148 only.

Position of cannon
ports shown, but actually
faired over.

Views above and below
show configuration as first
flown, TX 145.

GLOSTER E.1/44.

*In its original configuration with unswept tailplane. The natural metal unpainted finish emphasizes the simple, elegant lines of this aircraft. (Pilot Press Ltd.)*

# HAWKER P. 1052

| Manufacturer | Hawker Aircraft Company Ltd |
|---|---|
| Specification | E.38/46 |
| Role | Single-Seat Research Prototype |
| First Flight Date | VX 272 – 19th November 1948 |
| | VX 279 – 13th April 1949 |

The P.1052 was a progressive development of the P.1040, incorporating a swept wing, and later a swept tailplane, in the long development of the RAF's eventual replacement for the Meteor day-fighter, the Hawker Hunter.

## DEVELOPMENT HISTORY

Late in 1945, Hawker Aircraft proposed a development of the P.1040, with a swept wing and rocket motor, designated the P.1047. This was still-born, but a requirement was raised for a research aircraft to investigate the aerodynamics of the swept wing, resulting in the issue of Specification E.38/46 in November 1946. Hawker's submission to meet this specification was accepted and a contract covering the construction of two prototypes, plus a structural test specimen, was issued in May 1947.

The resulting design was basically that of the P.1040, but with swept wings. The anticipated performance increase over current in-service types was such that a proposal to put the aircraft into production was made, even before the first prototype had flown, but this was rejected.

After completion at Kingston, the first prototype, VX272, was transported by road to Boscombe Down and, after brief taxi-ing trials, flew for the first time on 19th November 1948. The second prototype, VX279, followed five months later, with a first flight on 13th April 1949.

The idea of the rocket-engined P.1047 was again raised, but with a new designation, the P.1078, but as the P.1072 was already under development, this idea was again abandoned. An assessment at Boscombe Down on behalf of the Australian Government was made, but resulted in no further interest.

The wing of the P.1052 was one of the first to be instrumented for pressure plotting. Trials continued to investigate the behaviour of the swept wing, especially looking at its characteristics in the transonic region. Although delaying the onset of the shock-waves, handling qualities, as with many early jets, were less than desirable, with marked trim changes above approximately 0.86 Mach, with the maximum nose-up change being at 0.89 Mach. However, the Mach limit was set at 0.93 with an uncontrollable wing-drop, which could not be held with the manually-controlled ailerons. Low speed and stalling characteristics were found to be quite normal. Trials also highlighted a lack of elevator control under certain circumstances, possibly due to the swept wing but unswept tailplane. Plans were therefore drawn up for the fitting of a swept, variable incidence tailplane.

VX 272 made a forced landing after the failure of its fuel pump drive and, while the repairs were being made, tests on the third airframe, the structural test specimen, resulted in the decision to reinforce the wing spars and fuselage mounting frames to allow an increased all-up weight above 12,500 lbs. Because of this, and the resulting delay incurred in incorporating these modifications, the planned variable incidence tail was not fitted until much later.

Repairs were completed by March 1950, and VX 272 continued with the trials alone, VX 279 having been returned to Kingston in April for modification to become the P.1081. Its original rear fuselage was strengthened and modified to have an arrester hook, for carrier trials, for fitting to VX 272, but the latter again crashed on 24th July due to a partial undercarriage failure, resulting in a landing on the left mainwheel and damage to the right wing. Sadly, its first flight after repair, in September, resulted in another crash landing due to undercarriage retraction problems, although this time damage was slight. During the resulting repairs, the replacement rear fuselage was fitted.

A similar modification as on the P.1040 was made early in 1952, with the fitting of a large bullet fairing to the leading edge intersection of the fin and tailplane together with a similar change to the fin tip profile, slightly increasing the area, improving the airflow in this area, and consequently the high Mach number characteristics. After the fitting of long-stroke Sea Hawk oleos, the deck-landing trials were made during May 1952.

The final modification was made the following month, when the long-planned pressure-plotting, variable incidence, swept tailplane was at last fitted. Trials recommenced at RAE Farnborough, until a final forced landing in September 1953.

Having come to the end of its useful life, the aircraft was struck off charge on 3rd December 1953. Despite still carrying its Naval colour scheme, it was repaired and allocated as an Instructional Airframe, serialed 7174M. It was displayed outside at RAF Cardington, together with its contemporary, the Supermarine 510/517, both with a 'RAF ground-equipment blue' colour scheme, before being transferred to the collection at RAF Colerne.

When this closed, the aircraft, now returned to its earlier Naval colour scheme, was again transferred to the museum collection at RAF Cosford, where it still survives although minus its arrester hook.

# CONSTRUCTION

The basic fuselage, fin and tailplane were identical to those used in the P.1040, the external differences being in the fitting of the swept wing and modification to the engine intakes and stub wing trailing edge fairing.

The wing-root engine intakes were made deeper, but 6" shorter, than those fitted to the P.1040, thus retaining the same cross-section area. The wing's

## DATA
### DIMENSIONS

| | | |
|---|---|---|
| Span | 31'6" | |
| Length (minus hook) | 37'7" | (original tail) |
| | 38'0" | (swept tail) |
| Height | 10'6" | |
| Track | 8'8" | |
| Wheelbase | 12'11" | |
| Tailplane Span | 11'6" | (unswept tail) |
| | 9'10" | (swept tail) |

(Note the dimensions for length differ from those previously published, but have been confirmed on the actual airframe.)

### AREAS

| | |
|---|---|
| Wing | 258 sq ft |

### WEIGHTS

| | |
|---|---|
| Empty | 9,450 lbs |
| Loaded | 13,488 lbs |

### PERFORMANCE

| | |
|---|---|
| $V_{max}$ | 0.87 Mach at 36,000 ft (swept tail) |
| $V_{max}$ | 593 kts at Sea Level |
| Service Ceiling | 45,500 ft |

### REFERENCES

| | |
|---|---|
| RAF Museum Cosford | —The Aircraft |
| RAE Farnborough | —Library |
| British Aerospace (Kingston) | —Photographic Archives |

actual leading edge root started 6" further inboard, but its trailing edge root was 3" further outboard, requiring a modification to the shape of the stub wing trailing edge fairing.

The wing's construction was around a forward mainspar and rear auxiliary spar, to which were hinged the flaps and ailerons, with multiple spars parallel to the fuselage datum. The mainspar fuselage mountings were identical, and in fact the spar was unswept out to Wing Station 96. (Measured in inches from the centreline.) Sweep angles were 40° on the leading edge, 35° at quarter-chord and 15°30' on the trailing edge. Thickness/Chord Ratio was 10%, and the dihedral angle was reduced to 1°45'. Despite the swept wing, and thus the slightly further aft centre of gravity, the mainwheel location gave the same wheelbase dimensions as on the P.1040. The track, however, was some 8.5" greater, increasing the already good ground manoeuvre stability. The oleos were the same, but the wheel-well cut-out and fairing doors were modified.

The manual ailerons each had a spring/trim tab fitted, plus on the right aileron was a small fixed, ground-adjustable only, aerodynamic tab. The trailing-edge split flaps, although still in three sections under each wing panel, were modified in layout. Small dive recovery flaps were mounted at approximately mid chord under the stub wings. Late on in the development programme, airbrakes were fitted to the trailing edge of the wings. These were mounted just inboard of the ailerons, and formed a 'cut-out' in the outer flap surfaces. Being single surface units, they were pivoted at approxi-

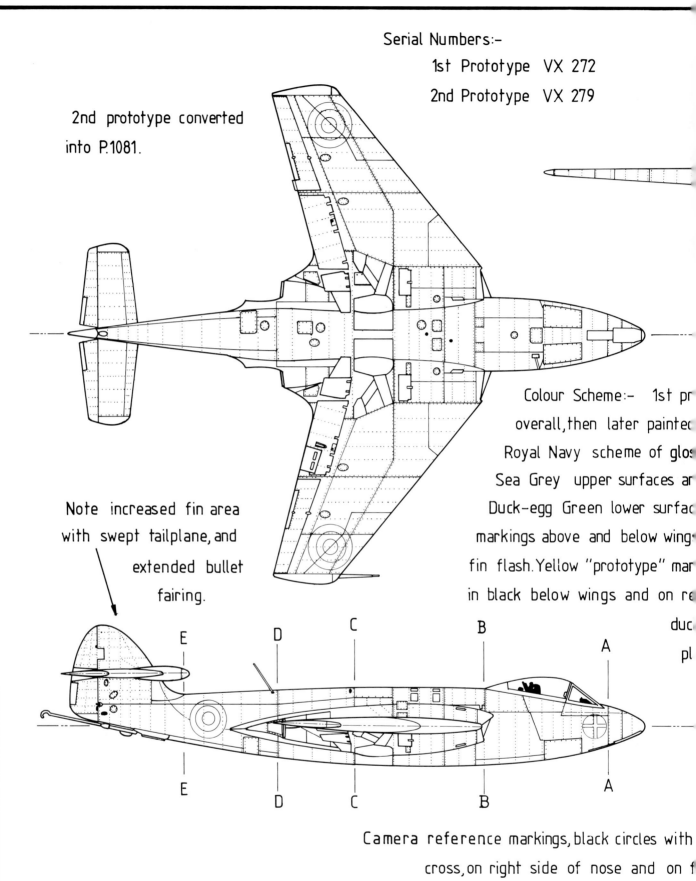

Serial Numbers:-
1st Prototype  VX 272
2nd Prototype  VX 279

2nd prototype converted
into P.1081.

Colour Scheme:-   1st pr
overall, then later painted
Royal Navy  scheme of glos
Sea Grey  upper surfaces an
Duck-egg Green lower surfac
markings above and below wing
fin flash. Yellow "prototype" mar
in black below wings and on re
duc
pl

Note increased fin area
with swept tailplane, and
extended bullet
fairing.

E    D    C    B    A

E    D    C    B    A

Camera reference markings, black circles with
cross, on right side of nose and on f
during parts of test programme.

12  10  8  6  4  2  0 1
Feet
Metres
3      2      1      0      1

B
H

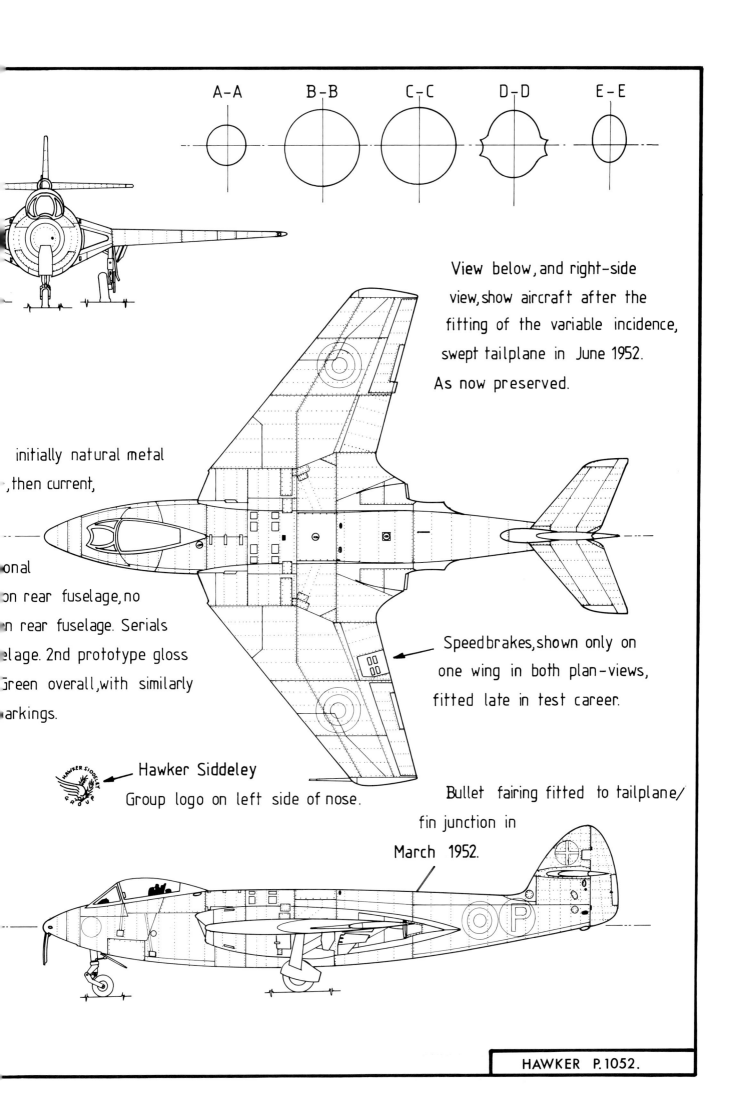

A-A  B-B  C-C  D-D  E-E

View below, and right-side
view, show aircraft after the
fitting of the variable incidence,
swept tailplane in June 1952.
As now preserved.

initially natural metal
, then current,

onal
on rear fuselage, no
n rear fuselage. Serials
elage. 2nd prototype gloss
Green overall, with similarly
arkings.

Speedbrakes, shown only on
one wing in both plan-views,
fitted late in test career.

Hawker Siddeley
Group logo on left side of nose.

Bullet fairing fitted to tailplane/
fin junction in
March 1952.

HAWKER P.1052.

*Banking away showing underside details. No detailed photographs of this aircraft could be found of it flying in its swept tailplane configuration. (Pilot Press Ltd.)*

mately mid-flap chord, opening upwards and backwards relative to the upper surfaces and downwards and forwards underneath. Four vents were provided on their upper surface and two below.

As the development programme proceeded, various other modifications were made to the airframe to cure problems associated with the design, rather than those encountered due to the characteristics of the swept wing. The fin tip shape forward of the rudder hinge was subtly altered in outline, slightly increasing the area, and a large bullet fairing added at the junction of the fin and tailplane leading edges. Late in the programme, the unswept tailplane was changed to a variable incidence, swept surface, with no separate elevators. (No records could be found of its movement range.)

Although provision was made in the underside of the nose section, armament was never fitted, as the four gun ports were permanently faired over. Fuel capacity was 395 gallons housed in three fuselage tanks.

For the deck-landing trials, long-stroke 'Sea Hawk' oleos were substituted for the earlier type, and a 'Sea Hawk' arrester hook was mounted under the strengthened rear fuselage. This increased the overall length by 2'0".

*An almost true planform view of the aircraft. (Royal Aeronautical Society.)*

## POWER PLANT
One Rolls-Royce Nene 2 R.N.2 centrifugal flow turbojet developing a Sea Level Static Thrust of 5,000 lbs.

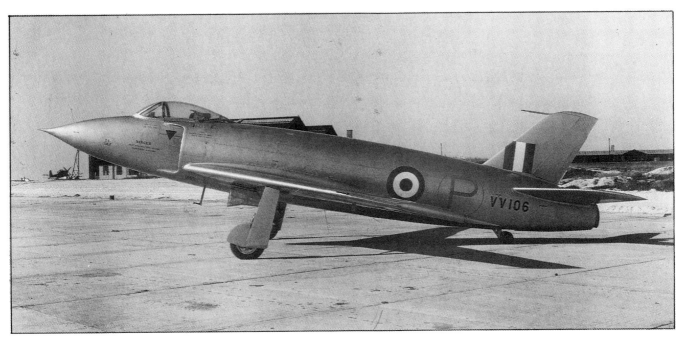

*The aircraft in its original configuration with pointed nose and unframed cockpit canopy. Note original flush boundary layer bleeds. (Crown Copyright)*

# SUPERMARINE TYPE 510/517

| | |
|---|---|
| **Manufacturer** | **Vickers Armstrong (Aircraft) Ltd., Supermarine Division** |
| **Specification** | **E.41/46** |
| **Role** | **Experimental Research Prototype** |
| **First Flight Date** | **VV 106 – 29th December 1948** |
| | **VV 119 – 27th March 1950** |

It is hard to believe that it was as late as 1948 before Britain's first all-swept experimental fighter actually flew, and even then it was only a very conservative development using standard Attacker components for all but the new flying surfaces, and well after the all-new F-86 Sabre in America. The Hawker P.1052 had flown only ten days beforehand, but this still had a standard Sea Hawk-type tail unit. However, one advantage it did have was a nosewheel undercarriage, something which did not appear on a Supermarine jet for some time. This aircraft was to be the first tentative step in the long development story of the only post-war fighter from the Supermarine stable to enter Royal Air Force service – the ill-fated Swift.

## DEVELOPMENT HISTORY

The research work carried out in Germany during the Second World War demonstrated the delay of drag rise at high subsonic speeds by sweeping the wings. After some apparent initial scepticism, a requirement was drawn up to apply swept wings to two existing types, the Hawker P.1040 and the Supermarine Attacker, and some preliminary design work had been done back in 1945. The official Specifications E.38/46 and E.41/46 were raised, the latter applying to the Supermarine design. Broadly, it called for an aircraft suitable for the investigation of the flight characteristics of swept wings at high subsonic speeds, with a maximum design speed of 610 kts. The contract for both companies covered the construction of two machines each.

The design received the manufacturer's designation of Type 510 and work progressed slowly at the Supermarine works, but it was not until late in 1948 that the first prototype was completed, then transported by road to Boscombe Down where it eventually made its first flight on 29th December 1948.

As the flight envelope was extended, it soon became apparent that there were handling problems at both the low and high speed ends. Tip stalling was experienced at low speed causing longitudinal instability (ie. pitch-up). Provision had been made for leading-edge slats on the outboard end of the wing leading edges but these were never used and were permanently locked in the up position. These were in fact completely removed during July 1949.

*A three-quarters rear view showing extraordinarily large flap deflection in the landing configuration for maximum drag rather than increased lift. (Crown Copyright)*

At the high end, it was found that a very strong lateral trim change required full right control column deflection to hold wings level. Lateral control was lost at 0.93 Mach, which thus became the limiting Mach number. A servodyne gave power assistance to the ailerons, but it was already apparent that fully powered controls would be needed to maintain lateral and longitudinal control at any higher speeds. The aircraft actually flew on 10th May with the servodyne disconnected, pending modification to the system. This was done by re-positioning the servodyne, the work being done at the same time included removing the leading-edge slats but, despite this, control at high speed remained much the same.

Engine problems were also encountered, with a forced landing at Boscombe Down on 17th March 1949. It was found that severe engine vibration and intake rumbling was experienced when power was reduced past 6,000 rpm. This also had a serious effect on directional stability, with the power back at 4,000 rpm., causing the aircraft to yaw randomly left or right through approximately 5°, these were described as 'random darts'. These symptoms disappeared (in reverse order) on opening up past 6,000 rpm. again. Most disconcerting for a pilot! The cause was found to be a function of both airspeed and engine speed, and originated from turbulent flow in the intakes. The problem was cured by raising and redesigning the boundary layer bleed louvres above and below each intake lip, and fitting an Attacker-type front engine mount. At the same time, the cabin ventilator was

removed, which could also have caused some turbulent flow into the right intake.

Preliminary handling trials were done by Service pilots whilst the aircraft was still at Boscombe Down. They assessed that the F-86 Sabre handling was better at low level than the Type 510, but their performance was about the same at 25,000 ft. However, above that height, and at high speed, the American aircraft was far superior, primarily due to its variable incidence tailplane and the use of fully powered controls. Other comments showed a dislike for the cramped cockpit, although it was felt that the aircraft possessed better ground handling characteristics than the Attacker.

During 1950, the aircraft was ferried to Farnborough where flight tests covered drag and maximum Coefficient of Lift research at high subsonic speeds. Also at this time, thoughts were turning to trials relating to the use of swept-wing fighters on aircraft carriers, following on from the success of its predecessor, the Attacker. The normal 13.5 ft/sec. main oleos were replaced by uprated 16 ft/sec. oleos, and an 'A'-type arrester hook fitted, both standard Attacker equipment. The aircraft was also cleared to carry four RATO units, one below and one above each wing root trailing edge for take-off boost from the carrier, allowing an increase in all-up weight to 12,790 lbs. After being thus modified, the aircraft first flew on 14th September 1950. Practice dummy deck landing trials were made at Farnborough, until the end of the year when, on 29th December, the Type 510 became the first swept-wing aircraft to land on an aircraft carrier. These trials were generally successful, except for during one take-off when one of the RATO units failed to fire, causing the aircraft to yaw badly. Luckily the pilot was just able to retain control and get airborne, but not before causing some damage to the left wingtip by striking the top of a gun turret. On the completion of this series of deck trials, all Naval equipment was removed from the aircraft.

(The second prototype, serialed VV 119, had by now been completed and taken to Boscombe Down where it completed its first flight on 27th March 1950. It was highly modified, especially around the intakes and aft fuselage, which had been redesigned to accommodate an afterburner. During manufacture, these modifications had caused it to be re-designated Type 528, and further description of the aircraft will be found later under the heading Supermarine Type 528/535.)

General high Mach number trials continued at Farnborough throughout the remainder of 1951 and 1952, not without incident when, on 14th December 1952, the main wheels failed to come down and a wheels-up landing had to be made. For some while, proposals had been considered to modify the aircraft to make it capable of maintaining full control at high speeds, including the removal of the elevator spring tab (thought to be a possible flutter source), the reduction of elevator chord and provision of a fully powered elevator (but retaining the original trim tab). However, Supermarine had instead come up with the design with the whole of the rear fuselage and jetpipe being hinged at the fuselage frame just aft of the rudder hinge fitment, adjustable through a range of 4°, but retaining the fixed tailplane. The aircraft returned to the factory on 10th July 1953 to have this fitted. As it was considered to be a major modification to the original design, the aircraft received a new designation – Type 517. Although a radical solution, it worked, and proved to be a powerful and effective trimmer but was initially too fast acting. When the rate had been reduced to a more acceptable level, it was generally liked by the pilots.

The aircraft was finally struck off charge on 14th January 1955 after a long and valuable testing career, adding much to the knowledge of problems at high subsonic speeds. Three days later it was dismantled and transported by road to Halton to act as an instructional airframe. However, to my certain knowledge it was acting as a 'gate-guardian' at Cardington, together with its contemporary the Hawker P.1052, both in spurious blue colour schemes, in September 1956.

Subsequently, still in its odd colour scheme, it became part of the collection at RAF Colerne, before going to its present resting place at the RAF Museum, Cosford. It has now been returned to a more representative colour scheme but, despite still being in its final configuration of Type 517, it is still labelled and catalogued as the Type 510!

Although designed purely as a research vehicle, an operational version was proposed, with four wing-mounted 20mm cannon and outboard wing leading-edge slats, designated Type 520. Also, an export version, retaining the same wing but with an extended pointed nose, designated the 'Swift' Type 510 'Australian' version, was proposed, powered either by a Nene or Tay engine, with a much larger diameter jetpipe and rear fuselage. This was to have a nosewheel undercarriage, as was another variant, the 'Swift' Type 510 'RAF' version, which had an identical configuration to what was to become the Type 535. (Supermarine drawings identify both of these variants as the Type 535, (Sheets 1 and 4), as well as 'Australian' and 'RAF' Type 510, to add to the confusion!). However none were proceeded with, apart from the eventual development into what was to become the experimental prototypes Type 535 and Type 541.

## CONSTRUCTION

### TYPE 510
The fuselage was basically identical to that of a

**DATA**

**DIMENSIONS**
| | |
|---|---|
| Span | 31'8.5" |
| Length | 38'1" |
| | 39'10" (with pointed nosecone) |
| Height | 8'9.75" (tail down) |
| Ground angle | 9°42' |
| Tailplane span | 12'7.2" |
| Track | 14'2.5" |
| Wheelbase | 16'7.5" |

**AREAS**
| | |
|---|---|
| Wing (gross) | 273 sq ft |
| Tailplane | 61.1 sq ft |
| Elevators | 15.6 sq ft |
| Fin and Rudder | 40.5 sq ft |

**WEIGHTS**
| | |
|---|---|
| loaded | 12,177 lbs |
| | 12,790 lbs (with RATO fitted) |

**PERFORMANCE**
$V_{max}$ 570 kts IAS
$V_{max}$ 0.93 Mach (true). (Uncontrollable at 0.94 with roll to left)

**REFERENCES**
| | |
|---|---|
| Public Records Office | —Avia Files |
| RAF Museum | —Supermarine Archives |
| RAF Museum, Cosford | —The aircraft |
| 'Flight' | —2nd March 1950 |
| 'Aeroplane' | —16th December 1949 |
| Aviation Bookshop | —Photographic Archives |
| Veron Models | —Truscale range |

*The aircraft with blunt nosed configuration, but still with its original unframed canopy.*

standard production Attacker, except for those minimal modifications to allow a swept wing to be attached to the normal wing-mounting frames, and was manufactured from light alloy with a stressed skin. The rear fuselage was also re-stressed to enable the swept tail surfaces to be mounted, again using the same pick-up points. Equipment layout was also the same, with the whole nosecone occupied by an equipment bay, forward of the cockpit front pressure bulkhead. During the aircraft's career, the cockpit canopy and nosecone went through the most changes. When first flown, a standard 'blunt' Attacker nosecone and blown canopy were fitted. Then the nosecone was changed by the fitting of one with a long pointed fairing, which increased the aircraft's overall length by 1'9", still with the same cockpit canopy. Finally, the nosecone reverted to its original form but the canopy was changed for a heavily strengthened one with smaller windows and heavy framing. This was retained throughout the rest of its life, both as the Type 510 and 517. The main windscreen consisted of an optically flat centre panel with curved quarter lights, the flat panel having a curved glass fairing fixed in front of it for streamlining purposes.

The intakes were the 'Supermarine trade-mark elephant ears' with prominent boundary layer bleed ducts exhausting above and below each intake. As described previously, these were originally flush louvres but were modified by raising them above the fuselage skinning. Aft of the intakes, right to the end of the tailcone, the fuselage cross-section was circular. The fuel was carried in bag-tanks around the intake ducts, and immediately behind the cockpit, capacity being 312 gallons. No fuel was carried in the wings.

The engine compartment occupied the entire centre-section, accessible through a large, stressed hatch in the upper fuselage skin, with the strengthened wing mainspar mounting frame at its forward end. Four oval spring-loaded suction relief doors were fitted in this hatch for increasing the airflow available to the engine at high power settings at low speed.

The aft fuselage was of normal semi-monocoque construction, retaining the Attacker's twin-tail-wheel layout, which retracted rearwards into the fuselage beneath the jetpipe, the bay being faired by two small doors. The swept fin and rudder were attached at their spar roots to reinforced fuselage Frames 23 and 24. The fin was built around a forward mainspar and aft auxiliary spar with multiple ribs. The rudder was hinged to the auxiliary spar, with a small horn balance at its tip. Leading and trailing edge sweeps were 45° and 24°, giving a quarter chord sweep of 40°. Thickness/chord ratio was 10%. A long pitot boom extended forwards from the tip leading edge. The rudder was manually operated and had a spring/trim tab at approximately mid length. For a short period whilst engaged in low speed trials, an anti-spin parachute was carried housed in a large 'blister' fairing mounted on the fuselage just aft of the rudder root trailing edge.

The tailplane was mounted on the tailcone with a dihedral angle of 10°, a thickness/chord ratio of 9%, and its incidence being adjustable through ±2°, adjustable on the ground only. Its leading and trailing edge sweep angles were 43° and 21°40', giving a quarter-chord sweep of 40°. The elevators each had long slim trim tabs over 75% of their inner trailing edges.

The low-set wing was attached to the fuselage at

# SUPERMARINE TYPE 510/517

the same mounting points as the straight-wing Attacker's. It had a mainspar at approximately mid-root chord, which was 'cranked' at Wing Station 96", with an aft auxiliary spar to which the control surfaces were hinged. It had a straight leading and trailing edge, whose sweep angles were 44°25' and 27° respectively. This gave an identical quarter-chord sweep as on the fin and tailplane, being 40°. It was of symmetrical, laminar flow section, had a constant thickness/chord ratio from root to tip of 10%. Chord at the centreline was 12'1" and at the extended tip 5'5", giving an aspect ratio of 3.68:1. It was mounted at an incidence of +2°30' to the fuselage datum and had a 2° dihedral angle.

The main undercarriage oleos were the same as those on the land-based version of the Attacker, allowing a 13.5 ft./sec. touchdown rate; however their pivots had been modified to allow for the swept configuration. They retracted into bays forward of the mainspar whose outboard ends were just inboard of the mainspar 'kink'. Just aft of the outboard end of the bays were small triangular-shaped dive recovery flaps. The split trailing edge flaps occupied the inner trailing edge of the wing, between Stn. 96 and the root fillet. They were multi-position surfaces, selectable from the cockpit, with a 75° maximum opening angle. Outboard of Stn.102 the large slotted ailerons occupied the whole trailing edge to the tips. Each were power-assisted, via a servodyne, and had a large spring tab along the inboard 50% of their trailing edges, and on the left ailerons only midway between the outboard end of the spring tab and the tip was a small trim tab. The size of the ailerons imparted exceptional roll rate to the aircraft.

## TYPE 517

The construction of the airframe was identical to that earlier, with the exception of the fuselage tailcone and the tail surfaces. The fuselage was split at Frame 24 and the structure modified to hinge about a point in line with the tailplane which was this time rigidly attached to the fuselage structure. Movement of the tailcone through ±4° was electrically signalled and hydraulically actuated by a single ram positioned below the jetpipe and just to the right of the tailwheel retraction bay, being anchored at Frame 23, at the forward end of the undercarriage bay. A spherical, or 'bellows' type, joint was fitted in the, now, split jetpipe to allow its movement with the tailcone. Thus, longitudinal trimming was by aerodynamic means via the tailplane and also by thrust deflection (this latter being well ahead of its time in view of current research projects some 40 years later!). The fin was attached to the structure in front of Frame 24 and therefore was fixed.

The tailplane and elevators had the same overall shape and area, but the elevators had been reduced in chord, having two very small trim tabs at approximately mid-semi span, in place of the original larger ones. To allow for the up movement of the tailcone without fouling the rudder, the base of the rudder was cut back at its base with a rounded junction with its trailing edge, otherwise the fin and rudder structure remained as before.

## POWER PLANT

One Rolls-Royce Nene 2 R.N.2 centrifugal flow turbojet with a Sea Level Static Thurst of 5,000 lbs.

*The aircraft as preserved at Cosford. Note framed canopy and, just discernible, the modified base to the rudder to clear the all-moving tailcone. The type of roundels and fin flash are dubious, this style only being applied early in the aircraft's career as the Type 510. (Ron Moulton)*

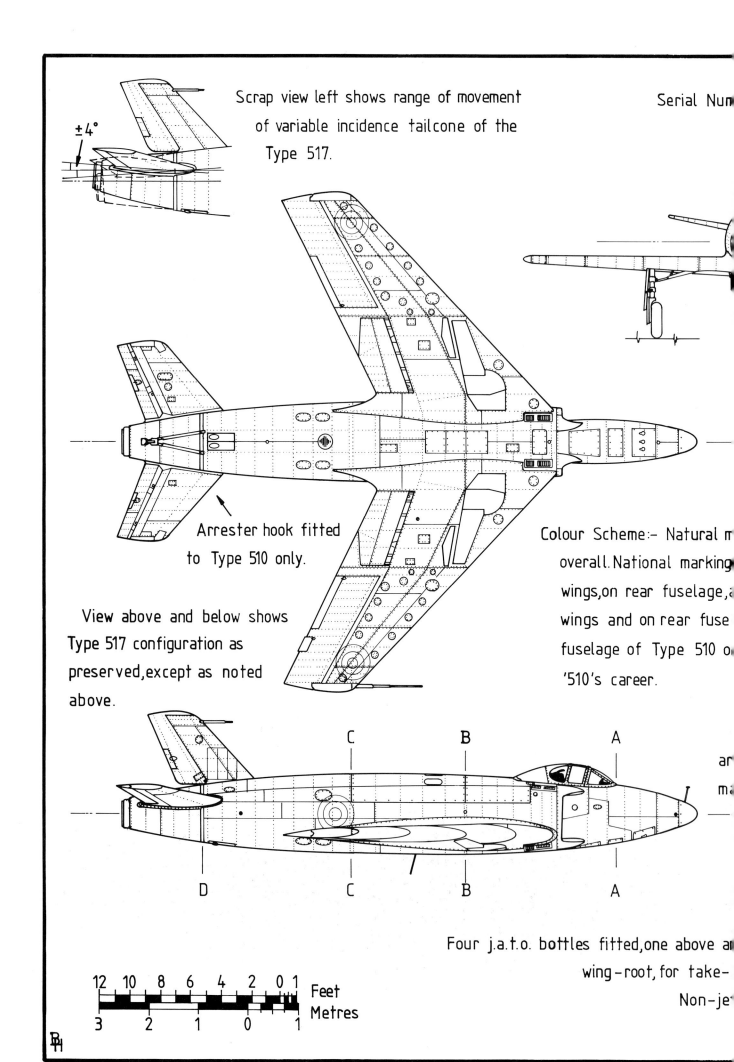

Scrap view left shows range of movement
of variable incidence tailcone of the
Type 517.

±4°

Serial Nun

Arrester hook fitted
to Type 510 only.

View above and below shows
Type 517 configuration as
preserved,except as noted
above.

Colour Scheme:– Natural m
overall. National marking
wings,on rear fuselage,a
wings and on rear fuse
fuselage of Type 510 o
'510's career.

C          B          A

ar
m

D          C          B          A

Four j.a.t.o. bottles fitted,one above a
wing-root, for take-
Non-je

12 10  8   6   4   2   0 1
3    2    1    0    1

Feet
Metres

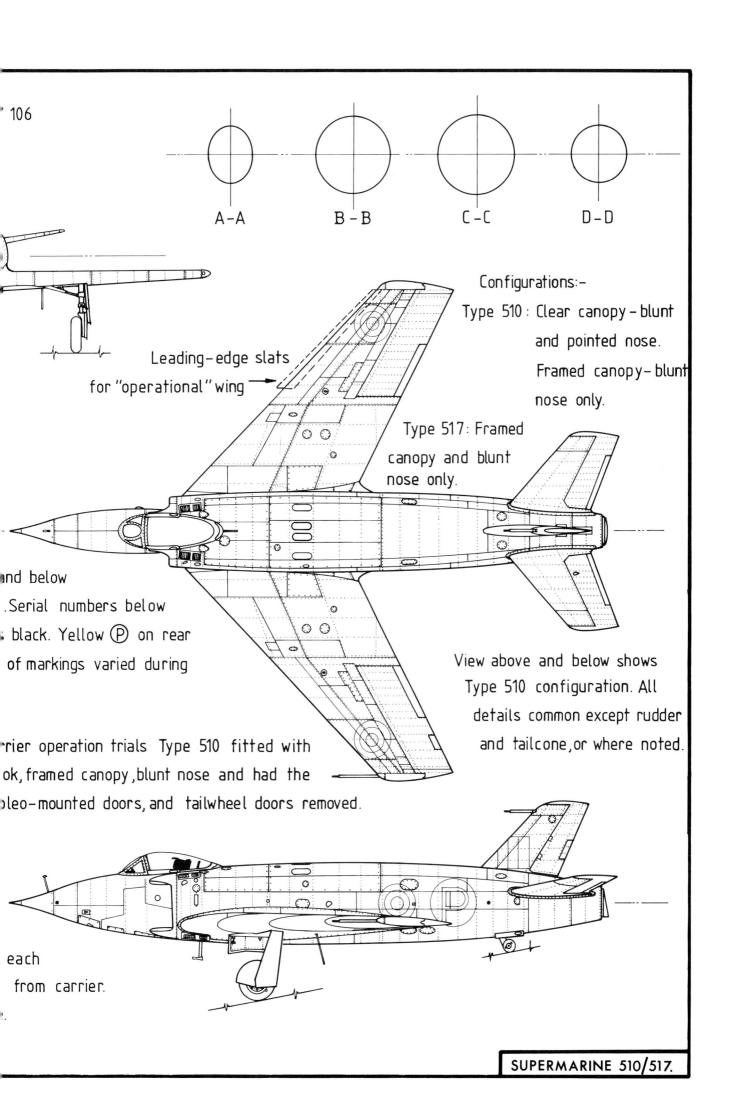

A-A    B-B    C-C    D-D

Configurations:-

Type 510: Clear canopy - blunt
and pointed nose.
Framed canopy - blunt
nose only.

Type 517: Framed
canopy and blunt
nose only.

Leading-edge slats
for "operational" wing →

View above and below shows
Type 510 configuration. All
details common except rudder
and tailcone, or where noted.

and below

.Serial numbers below

black. Yellow Ⓟ on rear

of markings varied during

rier operation trials Type 510 fitted with

ok, framed canopy, blunt nose and had the

leo-mounted doors, and tailwheel doors removed.

each

from carrier.

**SUPERMARINE 510/517.**

*The Meteor ancestry of its cockpit canopy and nosewheel oleo is very evident in this view. Note the extremely short nosecone forward of the wing root giving the pilot an exceptional forward view.*

# AVRO 707

| Manufacturer | A.V. Roe & Company Ltd |
|---|---|
| Specification | E.15/48 – 707,707B |
| | E.10/49 – 707A |
| Role | Aerodynamic Research Aircraft |
| First Flight Date | 707: VX 784 |
| | 4th September 1949 |
| | 707B VX 790 |
| | 6th September 1950 |
| | 707A: WD 280 |
| | 14th June 1951 |
| | WZ 736 |
| | 20th February 1953 |
| | 707C: WZ 744 |
| | 1st July 1953 |

On 1st January 1947, Specification B.35/46 was issued, calling for the most advanced bomber which the state of the art could produce, in the light of all recent advances in aerodynamic knowledge. Three firms tendered – Avro, Handley Page and Vickers. After extensive study, Avro decided that the best design to meet the requirement used a delta, or triangular, shaped wing. The true delta shape, an equilateral triangle with 60° sweep at the leading edge, had been thoroughly investigated by Lippisch in Germany, and was currently being flight tested on the XF–92A in America. However, the Avro wing differed in having less leading edge sweep, a much thicker section (to house the engines on the bomber), and with the point of maximum thickness closer to the leading edge the further inboard the section was to the wing root.

In the light of this, it was felt prudent to design a one-third scale single-seat research aircraft to investigate low speed stability and control, the area of the flight envelope causing most concern. The Specification E.15/48 was raised to cover the design of this research prototype which was designated the Avro 707. In the event, a whole family of aircraft evolved under this type number to fulfil various tasks associated with the bomber design, the Avro 698.

## DEVELOPMENT HISTORY

As part of the massive development programme for the Avro 698 (eventually to be named the Vulcan), and because of its unique aerodynamic shape, the 707 was to be only one of three research tools. As well as the very simple, low-speed 707, there was also planned a much larger, twin-engined Avro 710, to explore the stability and control at the upper end of the proposed bomber's performance envelope. It was also proposed that a full-scale prototype of the bomber, being solely an aerodynamic shell devoid of any military equipment, should be built; the idea was that this could probably be developed more quickly than a 'normal' prototype.

All except the 707 were cancelled by early 1948, and Specification E.15/48 was raised to cover two low-speed, and one high-speed, prototypes. Due to the use of very simple construction, plus the standard undercarriage and cockpit components, the aircraft was completed by August 1949. Brief taxi-ing trials were completed at the Avro airfield before dismantling and transporting by road to Boscombe Down, where a successful first flight was made on 4th September 1949. Two further flights were made to enable the aircraft to be displayed statically at the SBAC display.

However, on 30th September, the aircraft crashed during low-speed trials at Blackbushe, killing the pilot. The cause was never fully established, although it was thought that the fuselage-mounted airbrakes may have been a contributory factor, locking fully deployed due to a control malfunction. At high angles of attack during low-speed trials, considerable drag and very high rates of descent can be achieved. If these airbrakes had been deployed, with the already low thrust/drag ratio, it may have been impossible to recover before ground impact. Whatever may have been the cause, it is interesting to note that these aft-fuselage airbrakes were deleted on the subsequent aircraft and their place was taken by additional surfaces above the wing.

The second aircraft, the 707B, also covered by Specification E.15/48, was already under construction together with the 707A, which had been ordered under Specification E.10/49. The much longer nose of the latter was substituted for that originally intended for the 707B. It not only had aerodynamic benefits, but it also contributed to the centre of gravity, being much further forward than on the 707 (which might have been another factor in the accident). An added benefit, if only from the pilot's viewpoint, was that it could accommodate an ejection seat! As with the original 707, it was

transported to Boscombe Down, where a successful first flight was made on 6th September 1950, again just in time to take part statically in that year's SBAC display.

During the flight-test programme, the aircraft's characteristics were investigated through the whole envelope, from a minimum speed of some 80 kts., being taken beyond incidences of 25°, and up to approximately 350 kts. During these latter trials, it was found that airflow into the intake was being disrupted due to turbulence caused by the cockpit canopy and, to enable the high speed part of the envelope to be fully explored, the intake had to be radically redesigned.

Also, the nosewheel oleo was lengthened, to give a positive ground incidence, which allowed a lower unstick speed and thus a shorter take-off run. As with the later 707A, there were various stability and control problems, purely associated with the non-powered controls, which were solved when fully powered units were fitted on the 707A's. It did make some contribution to the 698 design, in that the latter's fin area was reduced and the jet exhausts angled to compensate for loss of longitudinal stability and trim changes with power change.

The 707B completed some 100 hours research at Avro's, before being sent to Boscombe Down in 1951 for further trials. It was involved in an accident on 21st September 1951, but was repairable and continued its programme of investigating the stability derivatives of delta wings. (There is also photographic evidence of the carriage of underwing stores at one stage, on a pylon just outboard of the

*A rear three-quarters view at the 1949 Farnborough Display, showing the control surface details well. Also note the fuselage airbrake resting on top of the fuselage skin rather than fairing flush when retracted.*

airbrakes, in front of the mainwheel bay. Only the right wing is visible, and the store looks very much like a finless bomb, but there are no further details available.) Eventually it was passed on to the Empire Test Pilots' School, Farnborough, for test pilot training, where once again it crashed during landing. There was extensive damage to the left wing, undercarriage, nosewheel, and fuselage, and it was deemed to be economically unrepairable. It was then taken to RAE Bedford where, on 8th November 1957, it was struck off charge to act as a source of spares for the 707A, and where it was eventually scrapped.

Meanwhile the 707A had joined the flight test programme, with a more representative wing and intake configuration. It had flown for the first time, again from Boscombe Down, on 14th July 1951. It, and its fellow 707A, which flew on 20th February 1953, had little influence on the bomber's design, with one exception. At high speed and high altitude, wing 'buzz' occurred. Large wing fences were tried to improve airflow over the tip, but the problem was eventually solved by a redesign of the outer wing leading edge, by reducing the sweep angle, and then increasing it again towards the tip, producing a 'kink'. This extension was also given a droop. The scaled-up version of this wing was applied to the bomber, but only after several production machines had flown. After the manufacturer's trials, both 707A's remained with the RAE for trials investigating position error and handling with powered controls, plus other general research, little of which was directly related to their aerodynamic shape. The first prototype was shipped to Australia on 8th May 1956 for further aerodynamic trials, and was fortuitously preserved on their completion. It was struck off charge on 10th February 1967 and is now privately owned and on display in Melbourne.

The second prototype 707A was used by the RAE for auto-throttle trials, to compensate automatically for the vast increase in drag due to high incidence on the approach (flying on the back of the drag curve) and during the landing phase. Although possibly not directly due to these trials, it is interesting to note that another delta still uses this technique throughout its landing phase – the Concorde. On completion of its working life, it went to Cosford Museum where

it was on display before being sent to RAF Finningley for refurbishment. It is now on display at the Transport Museum, Manchester.

The 707C was ordered in 1952, at the same time as the second 707A. Four prototypes were to be built, to act as dual-control trainers to convert pilots to fly the delta wing. This proved unnecessary, so the last three were cancelled and only the first was completed. It was taken by road to RAF Waddington where it flew for the first time on 1st July 1953. Subsequent manufacturer's trials were completed at Woodford. It flew later on research trials into 'fly-by-wire' systems at Farnborough before retiring in 1967. It is now preserved at Cosford Aerospace Museum.

The 707 family thus completed some valuable research, little of which was directly concerned with their original purpose, the resolving of aerodynamic problems of the delta wing planform. Virtually any 'ordinary-shaped' aircraft would have sufficed for most of them.

# CONSTRUCTION

### AVRO 707 (VX 784)
The fuselage was basically of circular cross-section, with the centre-section forward of the mainspar attachment frame and nose, and was built up from a relatively crude framework of welded steel tubing, the skin being from unstressed alloy panels, riveted to formers. To save time and money, a standard Meteor III cockpit canopy and nosewheel were used.

An instrument boom, 4'9" long, projected forward from the short, pointed nose, for the pitot head, above which was mounted a yaw vane. The cockpit was well forward to give a good field of view during the approach and landing, with the expected high angles of attack during these phases of flight. The pilot was not provided with an ejection seat and sat under an aft-sliding canopy. The fixed aft fairing of the canopy was not glazed, and under it was mounted the TR 1464 VHF radio, the whip-aerial for which was mounted above the fuselage centre-section. The nosewheel-well stretched from the aft cockpit bulkhead to the mainspar pickup frame, the nosewheel oleo being hinged to the rear face of

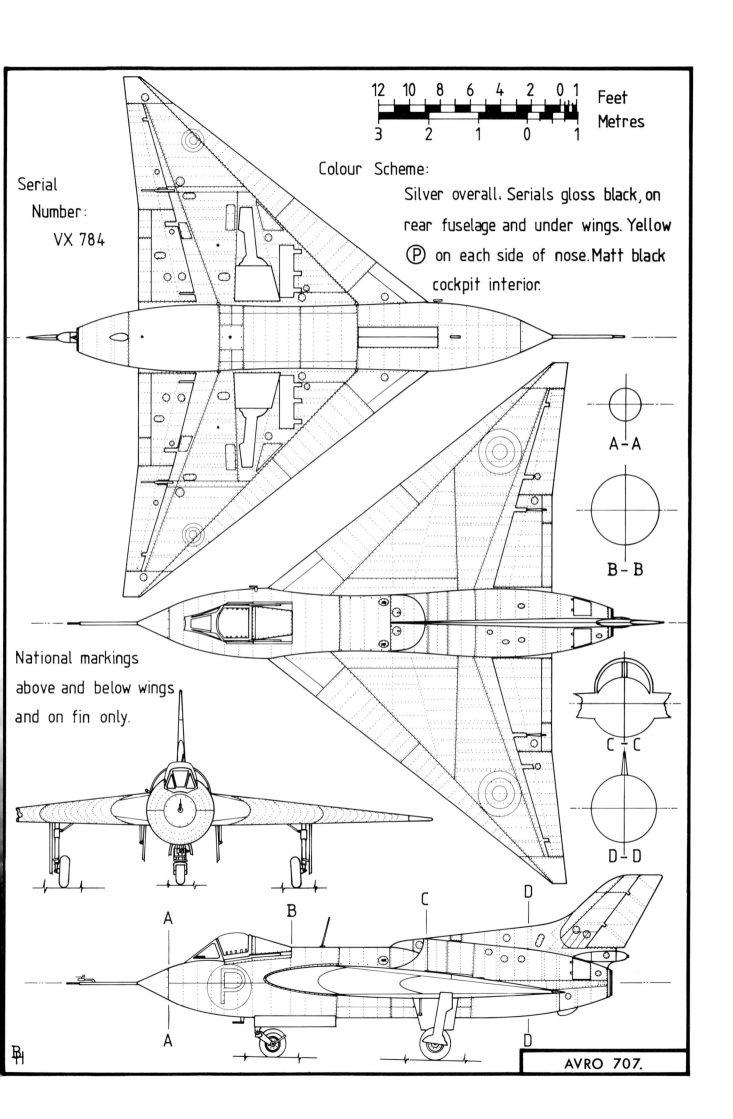

12 10 8 6 4 2 0 1   Feet
Metres
3 2 1 0 1

Serial
Number:
VX 784

Colour Scheme:
Silver overall. Serials gloss black, on
rear fuselage and under wings. Yellow
Ⓟ on each side of nose. Matt black
cockpit interior.

A – A

B – B

National markings
above and below wings
and on fin only.

C – C

D – D

A          B          C          D

A          D

AVRO 707.

the cockpit bulkhead and retracting aft into its bay, which was enclosed by two doors. The wheel was fitted with a 22" diameter standard 'Meteor' tyre. The aircraft had a pronounced nose-down attitude on the ground, which at that time was representative of the projected full-sized bomber design.

Within the nosewheel bay were mounted several auxiliary service panels, including those for the pneumatics, engine start and generator controls, as well as the aircraft accumulators. An air bottle was mounted vertically on the left side of the forward bulkhead, and a pneumatic bottle mounted transversely on the aft bulkhead. The ground starter socket was approximately midway along the bay, on the left side.

The fuselage centre-section was a 4'4" constant diameter tube and aft of the mainspar frame, and was of conventional frame and stringer construction, again with an alloy skin. In its upper side, forward of the intake and aft of the mainspar frame, was a rectangular panel for access to an equipment bay which contained the auto-observer panels. Aft of the rear wingspar attachment frame, on the lower side of the fuselage was a large panel both for engine access and removal.

A semi-circular, dorsal-bifurcated intake was positioned approximately midway along the fuselage to feed the engine via a sharply curved S-shaped duct, with the engine itself mounted on, and parallel to, the fuselage datum. The single fuel tank was mounted below the intake duct, venting through a panel to the left of the intake splitter plate, with the filler cap to the right, and had a capacity of 205 gallons. Between this and the rear spar bulkhead was a bay, accessible through a panel in the lower fuselage, containing the engine-driven Rotol gearbox. Just aft and above the wing trailing edge root, on each side of the fuselage, were fitted lateral airbrakes. These were not flush with the skin but, when retracted, laid flat on top of it. A substantial tail bumper was provided under the fuselage tail.

The fin was of two-spar construction attached to the fuselage at two reinforced frames, with a long dorsal fairing reaching to the intake lip, and having a leading edge sweep of 49°24'. The single surface rudder reached to the top, was hinged to the rear spar at two points and had no trim tab. (Manufacturer's drawings show one at the base of the rudder but photographs of the actual machine show its absence.) Rudder travel was ± 20°. Under the base of the rudder was a small streamlined fairing containing an anti-spin parachute, which could also act as a braking parachute for landing. Multiple panels were provided in the fin for access to the rudder push/pull rods and parachute cables.

The wing was mid-mounted on the fuselage, with an incidence of +2°30', being constructed around a forward mainspar, swept at 45°, and an aft auxiliary spar, to which were hinged the flying controls. The fuselage frames to which the spars were attached were unusual, in that they were set perpendicular to the wing and thus at an angle of 87°30' to the fuselage datum, as compared to all the other frames which were at 90° to it. Leading edge sweep was 52°43', chord at the centreline 21'8", and at the tip 12", section NACA.0010 to 80% chord, and dihedral zero. The trailing edge had zero sweep out to Wing Station 97.5 (measured in inches from the centreline), then had 6° sweep to the tip. This Wing Stn. also marked the break between the outer and inner control surfaces. The inner ones acted as elevators and had full length geared and trim tabs. The outer surfaces, acting as ailerons, stretched out to Wing Stn. 178 and each had a small trim tab at its inner end. All flying controls were manually operated.

The ribs between the spars were parallel to the aircraft centreline, as were those in the control surfaces; however, the leading edge ribs forward of the mainspar were perpendicular to it. The mainwheel bays were located at approximately mid root chord, between two bracing spars. The oleos were those of a standard Athena trainer, the wheels had 24" diameter tyres, and retracted inwards, each bay being faired by two doors, one attached to the oleo, and the other hinged on its inner edge next to the fuselage.

Just forward of each mainwheel bay, on the underside of the wing, was a rectangular airbrake panel, hinging down and forwards on the end of three arms.

*Extended landing gear on the first 707 was from the Athena Trainer*

*The 707B shown after receiving its lengthened nosewheel oleo and revised intake profile. Note unusual red fire extinguisher marking on nose. The white crosses in black circles are datum marks to aid tracking for cine camera recording. (Pilot Press Ltd.)*

## AVRO 707B (VX 790)

The fuselage aft of the mainspar attachment frame was originally identical to that of the 707, other than having the upper equipment bay access panel shortened by one frame, the intake splitter plate re-shaped, and the fuselage-mounted airbrakes deleted. The fuselage longitudinal datum zero was at the forward face of the mainspar. The equipment and instrumentation bay aft of this spar-frame contained an accelerometer, rate gyro and an inverter.

The forward fuselage was, however, of much improved fineness ratio, extended forward by some 2'6", with a frame and stringer monocoque construction. The cockpit canopy was also redesigned, having a fixed flat windscreen and curved quarter-lights, and the jettisonable hood being constructed primarily of light alloy, with a small rectangular window each side for limited lateral vision, and hinged on its right side for normal entry/exit. The pilot also now had a Martin-Baker Mk. 1 ejection seat. As on all of the 707 variants, the cockpit was unpressurised.

The cockpit was set much further back in relation to the longer and more streamlined nosecone. The nose horizontal datum, from the sloping rear cockpit bulkhead at Stn.–83.5" (ie. forward of the datum), was canted down by 2°30' to improve pilot visibility at high angles of attack. The vertical frame at Stn.–83.5" also marked the forward end of the nosewheel bay.

The detachable nosecone had a long three-pronged instrumentation boom fitted at its tip, with what appear to be three pitot heads, and with yaw vanes above and below the junction. Later, an alternative boom was fitted, similar to that to be used on the 707A, with a single pitot head and a yaw vane fitted underneath.

In the underside of the nose, immediately aft of the nosecone attachment frame, was a rectangular panel for access to the aircraft's battery, and also within the nose was an auto-observer. Above and below the fuselage, slightly forward of the mainspar frame, were mounted VHF whip-aerials.

The nosewheel oleo was a standard Hawker Sea Hawk unit, and was stowed, when retracted, in a bay which was enclosed by a single door hinged on its left edge. Trials showed that this gave too nose-down a ground attitude, and take-off performance would be enhanced by having a longer nose-oleo to give the fuselage a positive ground angle. The oleo was therefore lengthened by 9" and the bay was extended after to accommodate it.

During the flight test programme, the engine intake was also radically altered. It was enlarged in area, causing a marked 'hump' in the top fuselage line, with the lip now being vertical to the aircraft's datum, and moved forwards by 27". It also lost its central splitter plate and was no longer bifurcated. Long plate vortex walls were fitted extending forwards from the outer edges of the intake lip, and coming to a point just aft of the cockpit canopy aft fairing. In plan view, the geometry of the intake looked very similar to that of a NACA flush-type intake. This modification vastly improved flow to the engine, especially at high angles of attack. As in the original 707, a single tank was situated below the intake with a capacity of 205 gallons.

To compensate for the reduction in directional stability due to the longer nose, the fin tip was extended by 12", the rudder remaining the same, now being inset from the tip. A trim/geared tab was added to the rudder, with a movement range of ±12°, the rudder range staying at ±20°, and a pitot head boom fitted to the leading edge of the fin, in

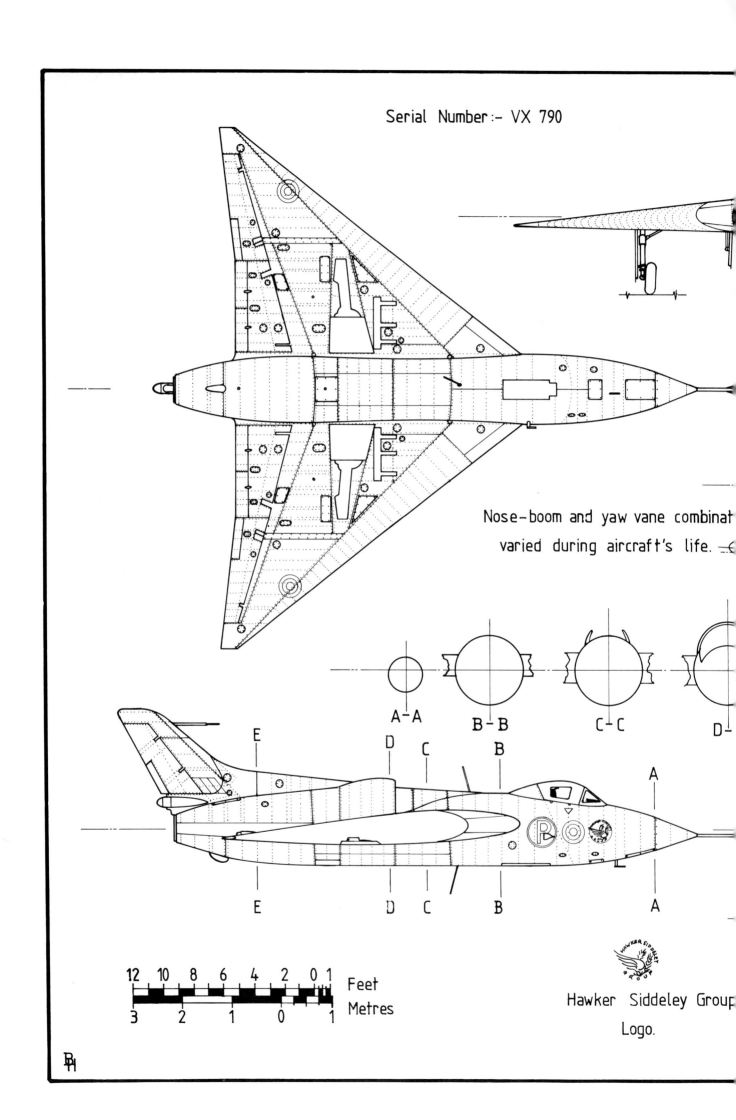

Serial Number :- VX 790

Nose-boom and yaw vane combinat
varied during aircraft's life.

A-A     B-B     C-C     D-

E     D  C     B     A

E     D  C     B     A

12  10  8  6  4  2  0 1    Feet
3    2    1    0    1    Metres

Hawker Siddeley Group

Logo.

BH

Colour Scheme:- Overall gloss blue, national markings above and below
wings, on nose and fin. Prototype "P" in circle, both yellow, on
nose. Hawker Siddeley emblem in white on a black circle either
side of nose, replaced on left side by a white cross in black circle.

Serial in black under wings
and on rear fuselage.

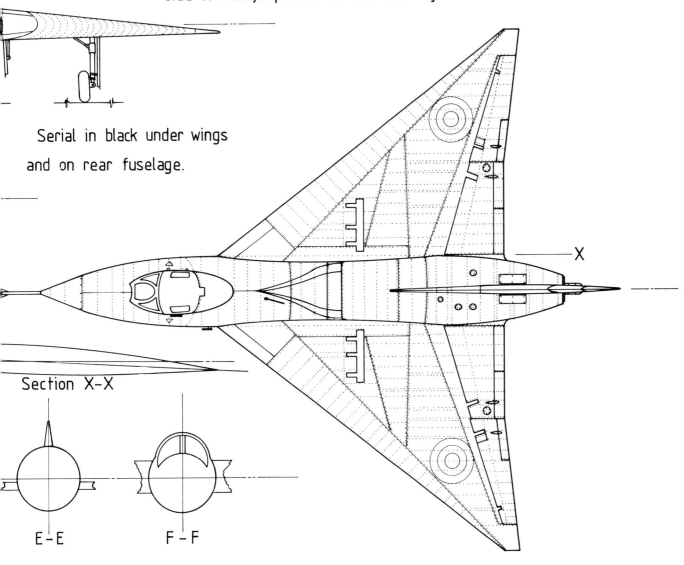

Section X-X

E-E          F-F

View below depicts aircraft in the original
configuration with a small "707" intake. All other views show
final configuration.

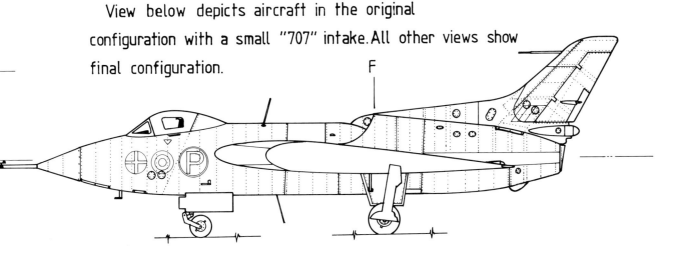

AVRO 707B.

line with the upper end of the rudder. Small changes were made to the shapes of the fairing below the parachute container and to the jetpipe nozzle to give a measure of downthrust to minimise trim drag.

The wing structure was basically identical to that on the 707, as were the main undercarriage units. However, the rectangular airbrakes on the underside were reduced in chord, but the distance from the hinge-line to their trailing edges remained the same. A similar pair of airbrakes to those on the underside were added immediately above them on

the wing topside. The panels were of the same area, but had slightly shorter pivot arms.

The control surfaces remained basically as before, and were manually operated. The inner pair acted as elevators, with a movement range of –24° and +6°, and the outer pair as ailerons, having a range of ±15.2°. However the whole system was re-engineered with the hinges now perpendicular to the rear spar, the servo/trim tabs on the elevators being re-proportioned (50:50 compared to 30:60 of the trailing edge), and geared tabs were fitted to both ailerons.

*(Above) The 707B banking away showing underside details well. (Right) This illustration shows the aircraft with its original markings and noseprobe but revised engine intake. Note the difference in the nose and fin markings from the photograph on page 73.*

*The 707A in its original salmon pink colour scheme. Well illustrated are the new wing root intakes and the much 'cleaner' looking rear fuselage compared to the earlier 707 and 707B. (Avro)*

## AVRO 707A (WD 280 and WZ 736)

Forward of the mainspar attachment frame, the fuselage was identical to that of the 707B at its later stage, ie. with the longer nosewheel oleo and bay. Aft of this, despite there being no dorsal intake, the structure was also virtually the same, except for some slightly repositioned frames, all being circular in cross-section, and with some in the centre-section having cut-outs to accommodate the ducting from the intakes which were now positioned in thickened wing roots. The cockpit was again unpressurised and had a large NACA flush intake on the right side of the fuselage for ventilation. A Martin-Baker Mk. 1 ejection seat was again fitted. Auxiliary suck-in doors, two on each side of the aft fuselage between Stn.117.04" and 125.09", provided additional airflow to the engine at low speeds and high power settings. The engine itself was mounted parallel to the aircraft datum, and the jetpipe nozzle geometry was returned to the original shape of that on the 707. Various access panels were altered on the fin and fuselage and the capacity of the fuel tank was slightly reduced to 196 gallons.

The fin and rudder were identical to those on the 707B, and the line of the dorsal fairing was continued forwards in a straight line to fair into the fuselage at the forward edge of the dorsal instrumentation compartment hatch. Rudder travel was, however, now limited to ±15°, and the fin-mounted pitot head deleted.

The wing was entirely changed and was more representative in planform of that on the full-sized bomber, but its section did not have the latter's forward-swept peak suction line. It also had the engine intakes in each root, generally of the same shape, but not bifurcated, as on the bomber. It was built around the same 45° swept mainspar as on the 707B, but with a repositioned rear spar and, despite being intended for higher speeds, had less leading edge sweep, this being 49°54. The aerofoil section at Rib 61.16 was NACA 0010. Chord at the centreline was 21'10", and at the tip 2'0". On the trailing edge, the unswept centre portion was reduced to extend out as far as Wing Stn.61.167", the outer trailing edge sweep angle being reduced to 4°. The wing's incidence remained at +2°30' and the dihedral zero.

The structure out to Wing Stn. 61.167" was also similar to the 707B, with all of the wing ribs being parallel to the centreline but, outboard of this point, between the spars, they were toed out at 10°, with the leading-edge ribs perpendicular to the mainspar. The ribs near to the leading edge root were cut out to accommodate the intake ducts. The main undercarriage bay structure and the undercarriage itself were identical to that fitted to the 707B. As with all the various versions, the wheel brakes were pneumatically operated.

The flight controls were also altered from the previous aircraft. The small inboard unswept trailing edge portion was now a separate control surface and acted as a dive recovery flap, being operated via a trim-wheel on the left cockpit wall. This flap was also deflected upwards at low speeds for the approach, to reduce the amount of up-elevator required for trimming purposes and to leave sufficient residual upwards movement of the elevator for control during the flare and landing.

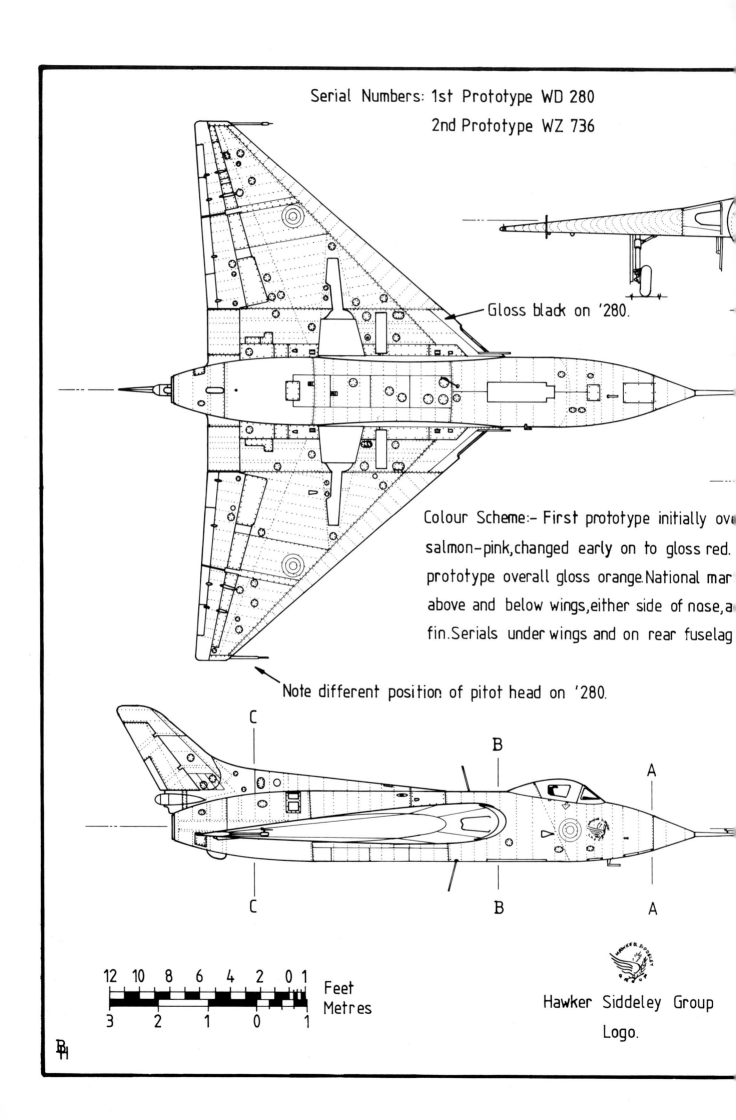

Serial Numbers: 1st Prototype WD 280
2nd Prototype WZ 736

Gloss black on '280.

Colour Scheme:- First prototype initially ove
salmon-pink, changed early on to gloss red.
prototype overall gloss orange. National mar
above and below wings, either side of nose, a
fin. Serials under wings and on rear fuselag

Note different position of pitot head on '280.

C        B           A

C        B           A

12  10  8  6  4  2  0 1     Feet
                            Metres
3    2    1    0    1

Hawker Siddeley Group
Logo.

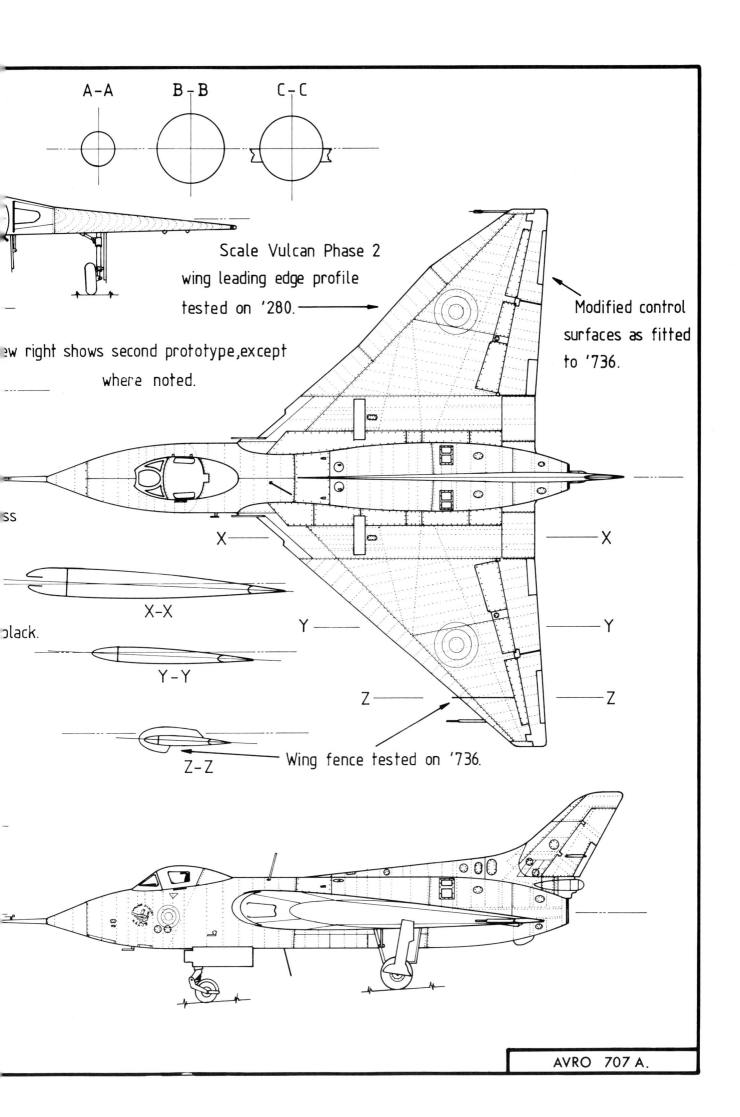

A-A    B-B    C-C

Scale Vulcan Phase 2
wing leading edge profile
tested on '280. ──────▶

ew right shows second prototype,except
where noted.

Modified control
surfaces as fitted
to '736.

ss

X-X

)lack.

Y-Y

Z-Z

X ──── ──── X

Y ──── ──── Y

Z ──── ──── Z

Wing fence tested on '736.

AVRO 707 A.

*Avro 707A banking away to show good underside details. Compared to the similar view of the 707B note the slightly revised wing planform with more blunt tips. (Avro)*

The aileron range of movement was +12°30' and −13°30'. The middle control surface acted as an elevator, with a movement of +8° and −20°. All the surfaces were pressure sealed, with hinges which were not inset, as they had been on the 707B.

The flying controls were originally manually operated, but flight trials revealed problems, especially longitudinally. Oscillations in pitch in one part of the flight envelope were divergent. The flight controls were therefore modified to be power operated, thus eliminating these characteristics. At the same time the geared and servo tabs on the surfaces were changed. Originally, the elevator had tabs across its entire trailing edge, in two pieces, and the inboard 75% of the aileron was also occupied by a two-section tab. These were altered to a small trim tab on the elevator at its inboard end, and a single one at mid-point on each aileron. The second prototype, WZ 736, had the powered flying controls and this new control layout from the beginning.

The dive brakes were also altered on the 707A. They were identical in size above and below the

wing but, instead of hinging out and forwards, they extended straight out from the wing surface on two 'rods' for each panel and, as they extended, the actual braking surface rotated to lie at approximately 80° relative to the airflow. Deployment of the airbrakes took 5 seconds.

Buffet boundary trials showed evidence of wing 'buzz', which increased severely with height and speed. A 'kinked' outboard leading edge was designed, with angles of sweep of 43°30'° and 57°30' and mild conical camber. This was fitted to WD 280 and was found to solve the problem, and a similar scaled-up version was eventually incorporated on the production bomber as the 'Phase 2' wing. This wing was not fitted to WZ 736, but this aircraft did at one stage have large wing fences fitted to the leading edge at approximately mid-aileron span. The other external difference between the two prototypes was that both the pitot head on the port tip, and the yaw vane probe on the starboard side were both at the very tip of the wing on the first aircraft, but the pitot head was moved inboard approximately 18" on the second.

*The larger two-seater cockpit canopy of the 707C is clearly shown. The remainder of the airframe was identical to that of the second prototype of the 707A. Note repositioned pitot head. (This also applied to the second 707A). (Avro)*

## AVRO 707C (WZ 744)

The sole 707C prototype was identical to the second 707A, except for the modified cockpit and canopy to accommodate the two pilots. The fuselage itself was not widened, and thus the room for the side-by-side seating arrangement was minimal and extremely cramped (which, together with the matt-black interior, made for a claustrophobic cockpit, as I can verify from my one flight in the aircraft).

To save space and weight, the ejection seat was removed and the pilots had normal bucket seats. The bulbous canopy was almost the same width as the fuselage and, like the 707A and B was mainly of light alloy, with limited lateral vision being provided by circular perspex windows on each side. It was still hinged on its right edge for access and entry.

The cockpit was not pressurised, but heating and ventilation were incorporated. During the trials at Farnborough, the flying controls were operated by two separate circuits: manual control by the left control column and rudder pedals, and hydraulic operation with electrical control from the right.

## POWER PLANT

707 and 707B: One Rolls-Royce Derwent 5 R.D.7 centrifugal flow turbojet developing a Sea Level Static Thrust of 3,500 lbs.
707A and 707C: One Rolls-Royce Derwent 8 R.D.7 centrifugal flow turbojet developing a Sea Level Static Thrust of 3,600 lbs.

## DATA

|  | 707 | 707B | 707A/C |
|---|---|---|---|
| Span | 33'0" | 33'0" | 34'2" |
| Length (including probe) | 40'2.25" | 41'3.5" | 42'4" |
| Length (excluding probe) | 35'5" | 37'9" | 37'9" |
| Height (ground static) | 11'3" | 12'3"(11'7")* | 11'7" |
| Track | 15'3" | 15'3" | 15'3" |
| Wheelbase | 11'0" | 12'0"(13'7.5") | 13'7.5" |

*With lengthened nose oleo

| Weight (gross) | | |
|---|---|---|
| 707 | | 8,600 lbs |
| 707B | | 9,500 lbs |
| 707A | | 9,800 lbs |
| 707C | | 10,000 lbs |

| AREAS | 707/707B | 707A/C |
|---|---|---|
| Wing (gross) | 366.5 sq ft | 408 sq ft |
| (net) | 278.3 sq ft | 319 sq ft |

### PERFORMANCE

| | |
|---|---|
| Minimum Speed | 100 kts IAS |
| Maximum Speed | 350 kts IAS |
| Maximum Mach No. | 0.88 Mach |
| Maximum Acceleration | 4.5g |
| Maximum Speed for Undercarriage Operation | 150 kts IAS |
| Maximum Speed with Undercarriage Down | 170 kts IAS |

### REFERENCES

| | |
|---|---|
| Avro 707A and 707C | —The aircraft |
| Avro 707A, 707B, 707C | —Pilots' Notes |
| Avro 707A, 707B and 707C | —Servicing Manuals |
| British Aerospace, Manchester | —Archives |
| Public Records Office | —Avia Files |
| RAE Farnborough | —Library |
| Aviation Bookshop | —Photographic Collection |

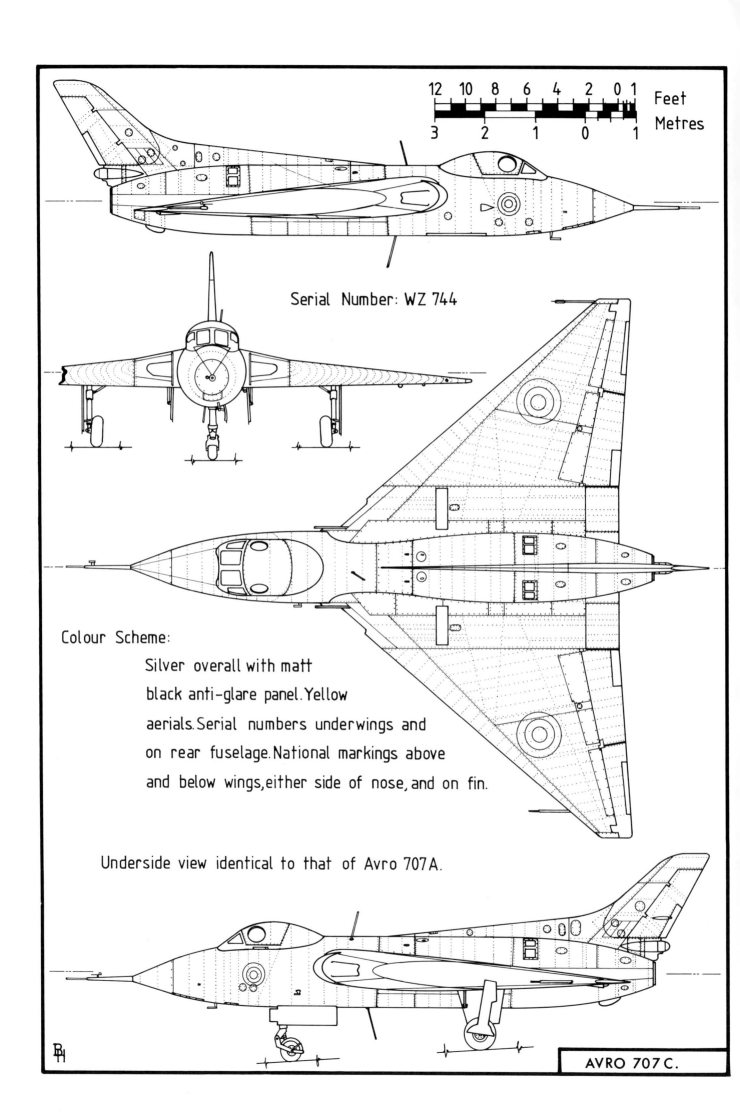

Feet
Metres

Serial Number: WZ 744

Colour Scheme:

    Silver overall with matt
    black anti-glare panel. Yellow
    aerials. Serial numbers underwings and
    on rear fuselage. National markings above
    and below wings, either side of nose, and on fin.

Underside view identical to that of Avro 707A.

AVRO 707 C.

*The afterburner jetpipe is just visible behind the fireman at the right. Compare this view with the almost identical one of the Type 510 on Page 61 illustrating the longer pointed nosecone fairing, shallower engine intake, revised form of boundary layer bleed, and slightly reduced static ground angle. (Vickers Armstrong)*

# SUPERMARINE TYPE 528/535

| Manufacturer | Vickers Armstrong (Aircraft) Ltd, Supermarine Division |
|---|---|
| Specification | E.41/46 |
| Role | Experimental Fighter Prototype |
| First Flight Date | Type 528 – VV 119 – 27th March 1950 |
| | Type 535 – VV 119 – 23rd August 1950 |

This variant was the next stage in the rather tortuous development leading eventually to an operational fighter originating in the Type 510 experimental prototype. The Type 528 was the second prototype Type 510, covered by the same Specification E.41/46, but was considerably modified compared to the original aircraft, including a provision in a modified rear fuselage for accommodating a 1500°K afterburner for the Nene engine, together with several other refinements. After brief trials, the aircraft was further modifed to emerge eventually as the Type 535 with a lengthened nose containing a new nosewheel undercarriage.

## DEVELOPMENT HISTORY
Within the company, the unofficial name 'Swift' was applied to the Types 510, 517, 528, 535 and 541, which causes considerable confusion when trying to trace the development history progression.

The earlier Type 510 was designed solely as an experimental prototype to test the theory of swept wing and tail surfaces. An operational version was proposed, with four wing-mounted 20mm cannon and outboard wing leading-edge slats, designated Type 520. An export version, retaining the same wing but with an extended pointed nose, designated the 'Swift' Type 510 'Australian' version was proposed, powered either by a Nene or Tay engine, with a large diameter jetpipe and rear fuselage. This was to have a nosewheel undercarriage, as was another variant, the 'Swift' Type 510 'RAF' version, which had an identical configuration to what was to become the Type 535. (Supermarine drawings identify both of these variants as the Type 535 (Sheets 1 and 4) as well as 'Australian' and 'RAF' Type 510, to add to the confusion!)

Despite the obvious limitations of a tailwheel undercarriage, there was no official requirement for a nosewheel undercarriage version of the aircraft. This, and the fitting of an afterburner to improve performance, were both private venture projects at the company's own expense, and thus no official contract was issued to cover the work.

After first emerging as the Type 528 and flying on 27th March 1950, VV 119 went back into the experimental shop barely more than one month later, on 6th May, for conversion to the Type 535. It flew in this guise on 23rd August 1950.

The main flap airbrake trials were conducted at Boscombe Down commencing 3rd December 1951. The aircraft crashed on landing on 19th January 1952, but the damage was slight and it was flying again by 14th March. Further general trials were conducted not specific to the type, including investigation into the carriage of up to four Fairey Fireflash guided weapons on swept wings. These commenced on 28th May 1953. The aircraft was then sent to the Central Fighter Establishment on 6th September 1954 for arrester barrier trials.

The aircraft was finally retired from its active life on 28th September 1955, when it was sent to RAF Halton as an instructional airframe, with the Instructional No.7285M. It was scrapped at the end of its useful life.

# CONSTRUCTION

## Type 528

The airframe of the Type 528 was essentially identical to that of Type 510. It retained the original pointed nosecone, together with the horizon datum bead, but was fitted with the strengthened cockpit canopy as fitted to the Type 517. The only visible external differences were in the rear fuselage, the tailcone of which was cut back allowing the jetpipe to protrude approximately 15" (although the afterburner was never actually fitted), and in having completely redesigned intakes.

The fuselage line was altered in planview forward of the attachment frame for the wing mainspar so that, instead of tapering slightly, it was now of constant width right forward to the intakes. These were moved forward 6" and made shallower to give a semi-circular cross-section, but had an overall increase of 20% in area compared to the earlier type. (The intake modifications were to allow for the increased mass flow of the engine when using the afterburner, and also to attempt to cure the intake problems described earlier in the chapter on the Type 510.) The raised boundary layer exhaust louvres found to be beneficial on the earlier Type were also retained. To cope with the increased fuel consumption with afterburner, the fuel capacity was increased.

Although retaining the same wing planform, the Type 528 had the 'operational' wing proposed for the Type 520 fitted (although minus the leading edge slats). This consisted of provision being made in the centre of each wing panel, outboard of Wing Stn. 72, for the carriage of two 20mm cannon, with their ammunition containers in the space between the main and auxiliary spars aft of the undercarriage bays. This also required that the ailerons be reduced in span, by moving their inboard ends a further 12" outboard, also reducing the size of the trim tabs by a similar amount. No armament was fitted, nor at this stage were any dummy cannon fairings.

The main undercarriage oleos were modified, being slightly shorter, and when extended were hinged to be vertical to the fuselage datum, giving the aircraft a reduced ground angle when static. Other minor external differences compared to the 510 were the removal of the small fairing doors to the tailwheel undercarriage bay, and the fitting of the second pitot head to the right wingtip, the one fitted to the fin tip having been deleted.

## TYPE 535

The aft end of the fuselage was lengthened to 'fair in' the protruding jetpipe of the Type 528. However, this did not affect the overall length of the aircraft, as the fuselage was lengthened to bring it in line with the trailing edge tips of the tailplane. The afterburner was fitted to the Nene engine for a brief period but was later removed to reduce weight. (The Type 535 was the only aircraft actually to fly with an operational afterburning Nene engine.)

The major fuselage modifications were to the nose section forward of the intakes. The entire fuselage forward of Frame 4 was modified and lengthened by 3'0" to allow a nosewheel undercarriage to be fitted. This retracted forwards to be enclosed by a single door hinged along its right edge. The nosewheel was fitted with a 23" diameter tyre. A large access panel on the left side of the nose gave access to an equipment bay which housed the G4F compass unit, and additional spring-loaded footsteps were added to the right side to afford access to the cockpit. The canopy framing and transparencies were also slightly altered in shape. A horizon datum bead was fitted to the nosecone,

*VV 119 in its guise as the Supermarine 535, showing the extended nosecone and nosewheel undercarriage layout. Note slightly extended engine intakes and suction relief doors at the aft end of the engine access panels indicating the moving aft of the engine to restore the centre of gravity position with the new, longer nose. (Crown Copyright)*

*A three-quarters front view. Note semi-circular intake shape with 20% increased area compared to those on the Type 510. Also illustrates well the nosewheel oleo and bay fairing door details.*
*(Crown Copyright)*

and a VHF whip-aerial under the fuselage aft of the wheel-well.

The boundary layer bleed inlet slots were initially within the intake as on the Type 510, but later in the aircraft's life were moved forwards to be in line with the cockpit windscreen arch fuselage mounting frame.

To compensate for the large change in the airframe's centre of gravity caused by the addition of the longer nose and new nosewheel undercarriage, the engine was mounted further aft in the fuselage to return it to its original position in relation to the wing. (*Note:* No existing documentary evidence mentions this, but study of the available photographs show that the intake relief doors in the engine bay access hatch were now right at the back end, compared to just forward of the mid-point. These would have to be in line with the engine's compressor intake to function satisfactorily, thus indicating the relocation of the engine.)

The Type 535 flew initially with the standard Type 510 fin and rudder, but with the former's pitot head removed. However, the longer fuselage nose caused a loss of directional stability, which was recovered by the fitting of a long tapered dorsal fairing which stretched forwards to the aft end of the engine access hatch. The standard tailplane and elevators were retained. A variable incidence tailplane had been proposed to be fitted at the same time as all the other modifications, but was rejected. (In this guise, the aircraft would have become the Type 531.) It was, however, fitted later in the trials programme, and had a movement range of –9° to +4°, although the Type number was not altered.

Initially, during take-off it was found that the nosewheel could not be raised until 120 kts., even

## DATA

### DIMENSIONS

|  | Type 528 | Type 535 |
|---|---|---|
| Span | 31′8.5″ | 31′8.5″ |
| Length | 38′1″ | 41′1″ |
| Height | 8′9.72″ | 12′7.5″ |
| Wheelbase | 16′8″ | 15′2″ |
| Track | 14′2.5″ | 14′2.5″ |
| Tailplane | | |
| Span | 12′7.2″ | 12′7.2″ |
| | Dihedral 10° | |

### AREAS

| | |
|---|---|
| Wing (gross) | 297.4 sq ft |
| Tailplane | 61.1 sq ft |
| Elevator | 15.6 sq ft |
| Fin and Rudder | 40.5 sq ft |
| Aspect Ratio | 3.41 |
| Fuel Capacity | 600 galls |

### WEIGHTS

| | |
|---|---|
| T/O weight | 14,390 lbs |
| Overload | 15,000 lbs |

### PERFORMANCE

| | | |
|---|---|---|
| Design $V_{max}$ | 607 kts IAS | achieved. 570 kts |
| Design $M_{max}$ | 0.975M | achieved: 0.94M at 30,000 ft |

Level Speed:

| | |
|---|---|
| 15,000 ft | 540 kts |
| 25,000 ft | 529 kts |
| 35,000 ft | 506 kts |

### REFERENCE

| | |
|---|---|
| Eric Morgan | —Supermarine Archives |
| Royal Air Force Museum | —Archives |
| Public Records Office | —Avia files |
| RAE Farnborough | —Library |
| Boscombe Down | —Science Library Archives |

Colour Scheme: Natural metal overall, matt black anti-glare panel (removed very early
in 535's career.) Serial numbers gloss black, on wing under surfaces
and rear fuselage below tailplane. National markings above and below
wings, on rear fuselage, and on fin.

Serial Number: VV 119.

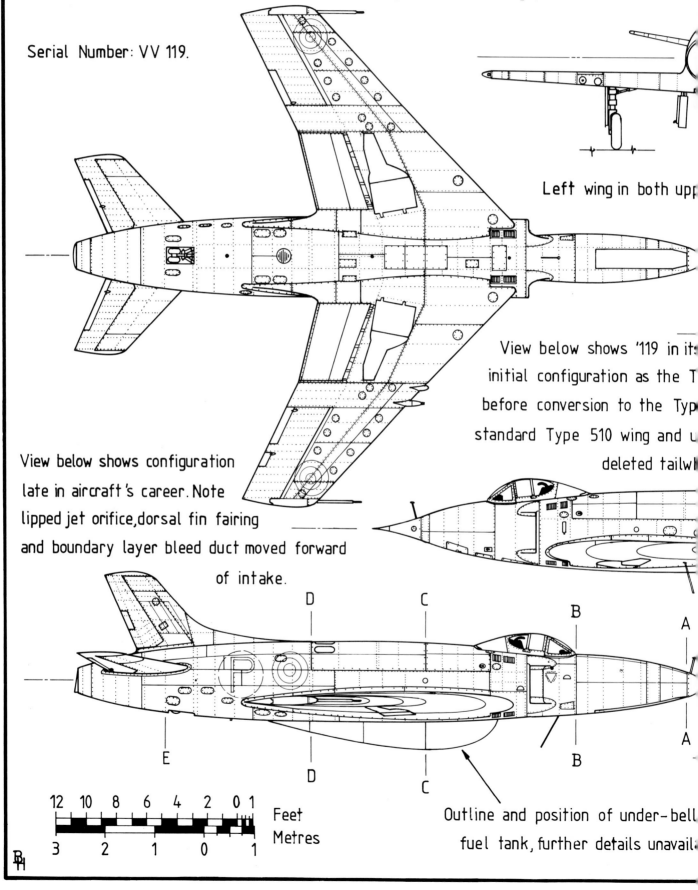

Left wing in both upp

View below shows '119 in its
initial configuration as the T
before conversion to the Typ
standard Type 510 wing and u
deleted tailw

View below shows configuration
late in aircraft's career. Note
lipped jet orifice, dorsal fin fairing
and boundary layer bleed duct moved forward
of intake.

D          C          B          A

E

D          C          B          A

12 10  8  6  4  2  0 1    Feet
3     2     1    0    1    Metres

Outline and position of under-bell
fuel tank, further details unavail

$B_H$

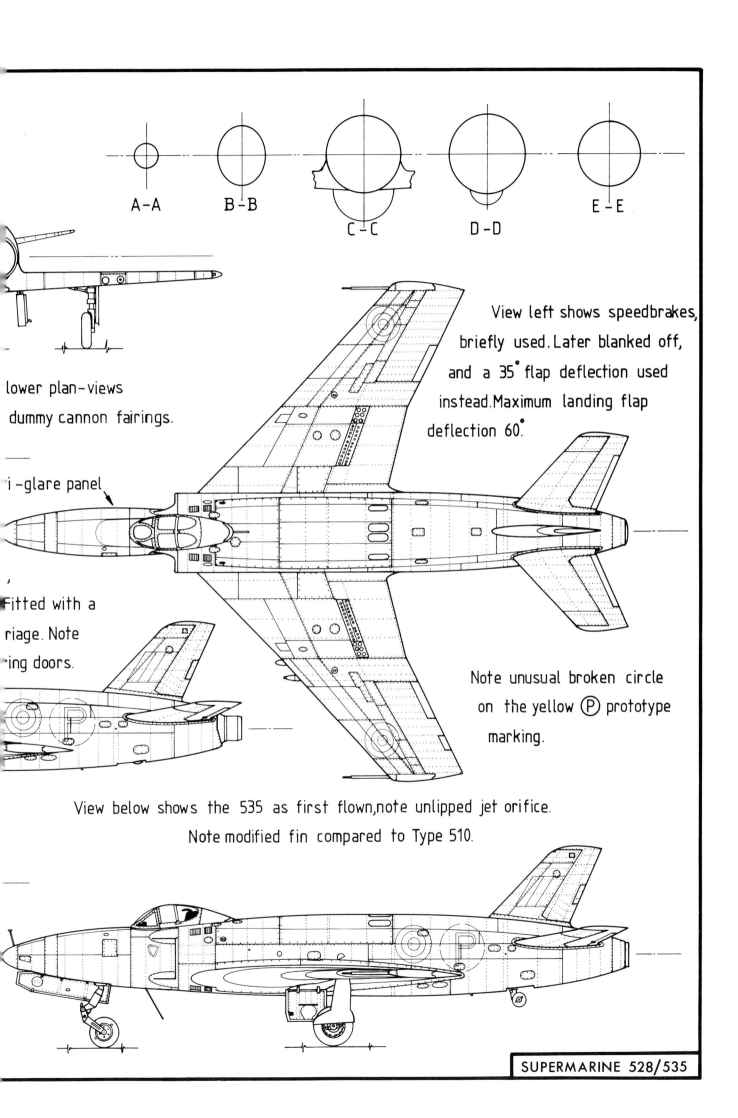

A-A   B-B   C-C   D-D   E-E

View left shows speedbrakes, briefly used. Later blanked off, and a 35° flap deflection used instead. Maximum landing flap deflection 60°.

lower plan-views
dummy cannon fairings.

i-glare panel

Fitted with a
riage. Note
ing doors.

Note unusual broken circle on the yellow Ⓟ prototype marking.

View below shows the 535 as first flown, note unlipped jet orifice.
Note modified fin compared to Type 510.

SUPERMARINE 528/535

with full elevator. A 'lipped' jetpipe was fitted which produced a down-load of approximately 200 lbs., enabling the nosewheel to be raised at just over 100 kts., reducing unstick distances by 300 – 350 yds. The landing distance could be shortened by keeping the tailwheel on the ground, using full up elevator and waiting for pitch-down at about 65 kts. Using this technique, there were no problems in stopping on a 1600 yds runway, although in a cross-wind it was desirable to lower the nosewheel early. A standard 'Attacker' type ventral auxiliary fuel tank could be carried. However, only one flight was attempted with it in place, but empty, due to the aircraft's take-off performance being seriously affected, as the aircraft was underpowered.

The wings were also considerably modified, although they retained the same basic construction as before. The wing root was extended slightly forwards and also backwards, increasing the inboard sweep angle very slightly on the leading edge and reducing it on the trailing edge inboard of Wing Stn. 72, increasing the gross wing area to 297.4 sq.ft., and also enabling a corresponding increase in flap area to a total of 28.12 sq.ft. Each flap surface had a span of 5'0" and mean chord of 2'9.75", with a sweep angle of 19.1° at the hinge line. These were multi-position flaps, stopping in any position when the cockpit control was released. Take-off position was 35°, with a maximum deflection of 60° for landing.

The main undercarriage bays were moved aft of the mainspar, retaining the same track as the Type 510/528. The oleos were the same as on the Type 528, retracting inwards, but the bay and fairing doors were modified in shape, a single door being attached to the oleo, and the inner one being much larger in size. The retractable tailwheel was retained, with the bay doors removed.

Although the proposed armament comprising 4 × 20mm cannon was never actually installed, four dummy fairings were fitted briefly to the wing leading edges for trials purposes.

Perforated upper surface mounted airbrakes were tested, hinged at the auxiliary spar, having a 12" chord, but were found to cause considerable buffet when deployed. The main flaps were then modified to act as airbrakes. The 35° take-off position was selectable by means of a switch on the end of the throttle lever. The deflection angle was 35° up to 400 kts., reducing to 16° at 570 kts. by blow-back action to prevent flap overstressing. They proved to be not very useful for a proposed fighter aircraft, causing a sharp nose-down change of attitude of approximately 3.5°, but with no change of trim. There was a corresponding nose-up change of attitude on retraction. These characteristics would have caused gun tracking problems during an attack.

Summary of the main differences from 510:
1. Redesigned intakes, shallower, but with 20% greater area.
2. Intakes moved forwards 6".
3. Rear fuselage extended by 12".
4. Nose extended by 3'0".
5. Pitot head on each wingtip.
6. Reduced span ailerons to accommodate wing-mounted cannon.
7. Main undercarriage moved aft of mainspar.
8. Modified inner wing leading and trailing edges.
9. Metal and perspex canopy of slightly different shape.
10. Engine moved aft in the fuselage.

### POWER PLANT
One Rolls-Royce R.B.41 Nene 3 R.N.2 centrifugal flow turbojet developing a Sea Level Static Thrust of 5,100 lbs. There is no record of the expected thrust rating with the 1,500°K afterburner fitted.

### ARMAMENT
Proposed armament of four 20 mm Mk.5 Hispano cannon, but never fitted.

*This three-quarters rear view showing tailplane, fin and rear fuselage details. Note large rearwards extension of the wing root fillet with the 'kinked' trailing edge shape. (Crown Copyright)*

*The Hawker P.1081 after the revised fin and rear fuselage were fitted and despite the more 'portly' shape of its rear fuselage, clearly showing its P.1052 ancestry. (British Aerospace)*

# HAWKER P.1081

| | |
|---|---|
| **Manufacturer** | **Hawker Aircraft Company Ltd** |
| **Specification** | **No specification – private venture design** |
| **Role** | **Interim Fighter prototype** |
| **First Flight Date** | **19th June 1950** |

The P.1081 was the final step in the long development of what was to be Hawker's first jet fighter to enter RAF service. It was a further progressive development of the earlier basic P.1040 design, via the P.1052, and in fact was a modification of the second P.1052 airframe.

## DEVELOPMENT HISTORY

Hawker submitted a proposal in January 1950 for a development of the P.1052, fitted with an afterburning Tay turbojet to improve performance, to satisfy an Australian interest in the P.1052. The fitting of an afterburner could not be done with the existing bifurcated exhausts, so the proposal needed a totally new rear fuselage with a straight-through single exhaust pipe.

The second prototype, P.1052, VX 279, was returned to Kingston in April of the same year, for conversion to this new configuration. Such was the change that a new designation, P.1081, was applied. Delays with the development of the Tay engine caused the standard Nene RN.2 to be retained, although this was planned to later have an afterburner fitted which, in the event, was never done.

The prototype was transported by road to Boscombe Down from where the first flight was made on 19th June 1950. Flight trials continued through the year to refine the aerodynamics with the modifications described.

The Australian interest in a production version waned, and the company was notified that work should cease on the project in November 1950. The aircraft was delivered to RAE Farnborough in January 1951 for further handling trials at high Mach

*Banking away and showing its swept wing planform and underside details. Despite having been painted gloss 'duck-egg' green, the join of the cleaner new rear fuselage and wing-root fillet can easily be seen. (British Aerospace)*

numbers. These were brief, as the aircraft crashed killing the pilot, on 3rd April 1951. The cause of the crash was never definitely determined.

# CONSTRUCTION

The fuselage of the P.1052 was removed aft of the rear engine-bay bulkhead, and thus the forward fuselage and wing panels were unchanged. A completely redesigned aft fuselage with a straight through jetpipe was added, the removal of the two bifurcated jet exhausts requiring redesigned wing-root fillets. The jetpipe bent upwards where it was attached to the engine giving a 3°30′ upthrust and, in place of the planned afterburner jetpipe, one from an Attacker was substituted. An aft fuselage fuel tank was wrapped around the forward end of

the jetpipe, giving a useful increase in capacity to 400 gallons.

A swept fin was fitted, constructed around multiple ribs and spars, sweep on the leading edge being 54° and on the trailing edge 20°, with the electrically-operated variable incidence tailplane mounted approximately one-third up from the fuselage. A relatively small rudder with trim tab was hinged to the rear spar, above the tailplane. A substantial, angled, and reinforced fuselage frame formed the main aft fin attachment point.

Initially the fuselage ended in a 'pen-nib' fairing above the jetpipe exhaust which extended aft of the fuselage structure at the bottom. Early flight trials showed a need to improve directional stability and the trailing edge of the fin below the rudder was modified to increase fin area. The fuselage was

90

also extended to enclose fully the jetpipe, and was faired to give the same 'sweep' as the trailing edge of the upper fin in side view. The tailcone aft of the fin attachment frame was detachable for jetpipe removal.

Early flight trials also highlighted the need to improve the airflow over the outer wing panels, so fences were fitted to the leading edge at approximately mid-aileron span. A slightly increased span tailplane was also tested.

The P.1081 was one of the first British prototypes to have wire recorders fitted.

## POWER PLANT
*Planned.* One Rolls-Royce Tay R.Ta.1 centrifugal flow turbojet developing a Sea Level Static Thrust of 6,250 lbs. The planned afterburner rating is not known.
*Prototype.* One Rolls-Royce Nene 4 R.N.2 centrifugal flow turbojet developing a Sea Level Static Thrust of 5,000 lbs. Afterburner planned but never fitted.

## DATA

**DIMENSIONS**

| | |
|---|---|
| Span | 31'6" |
| Length | 37'4" |
| Height | 13'3" |
| Wheelbase | 12'11" |
| Track | 8'8" |
| Tailplane Span | 9'6" |

**AREAS**

| | |
|---|---|
| Wing | 258 sq ft |

**WEIGHTS**

| | |
|---|---|
| Empty | 11,200 lbs |
| Loaded | 14,480 lbs |

**PERFORMANCE**

| | | |
|---|---|---|
| $V_{max}$ | at 36,000 ft | 0.89 Mach |
| $V_{max}$ | at Sea Level | 604 kts |
| Service Ceiling | | 45,600 ft |

**REFERENCES**

| | |
|---|---|
| British Aerospace (Kingston) | —Photographic Archives |
| British Aerospace (Kingston) | —Archives – Drawing E.169528 |
| RAE Farnborough | —Library |
| RAF Museum Cosford | —P.1052 – The Aircraft |

*A side view showing well the shape of the swept fin and rudder, with the extended fin root trailing edge and fillet, to increase area, and revised aft fuselage tailcone from that originally fitted. (British Aerospace)*

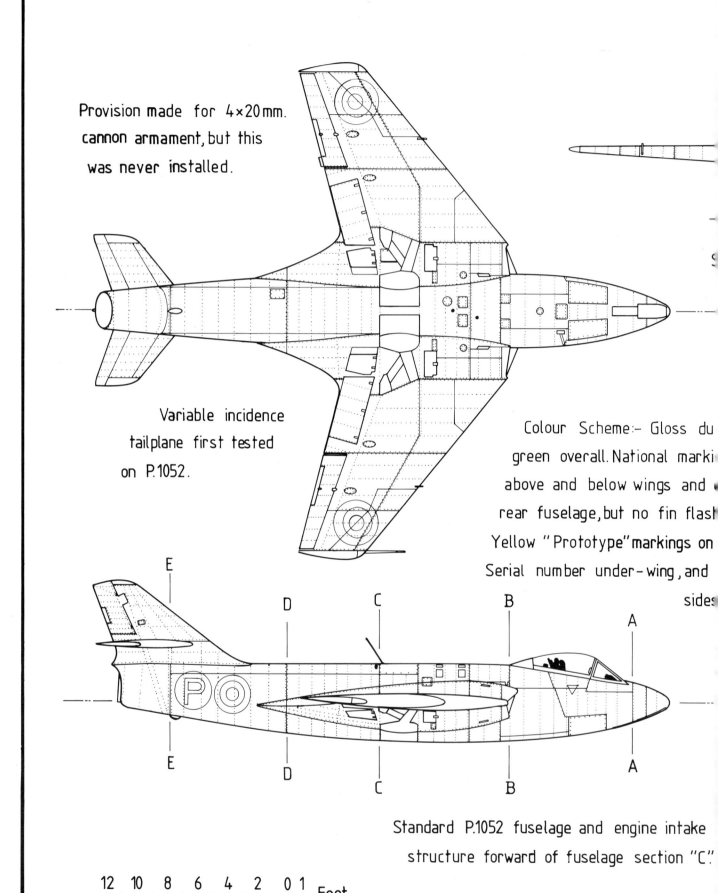

Provision made for 4×20mm. cannon armament, but this was never installed.

Variable incidence tailplane first tested on P.1052.

Colour Scheme:- Gloss du green overall. National marki above and below wings and rear fuselage, but no fin flash Yellow "Prototype" markings on Serial number under-wing, and sides

Standard P.1052 fuselage and engine intake structure forward of fuselage section "C".

| 12 | 10 | 8 | 6 | 4 | 2 | 0 | 1 | Feet |
| 3 | | 2 | | 1 | | 0 | 1 | Metres |

P O

E    D    C    B    A
E    D    C    B    A

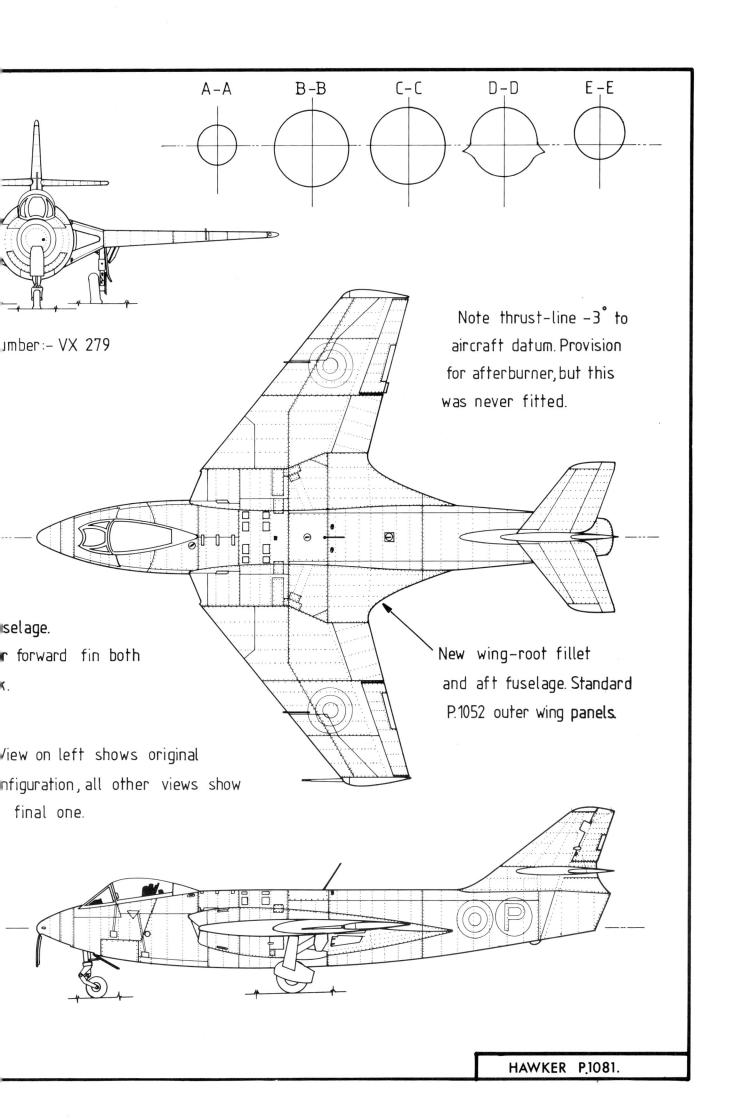

A-A  B-B  C-C  D-D  E-E

...umber :- VX 279

Note thrust-line -3° to aircraft datum. Provision for afterburner, but this was never fitted.

...selage.
...r forward fin both
...

...iew on left shows original
...nfiguration, all other views show
   final one.

New wing-root fillet and aft fuselage. Standard P.1052 outer wing panels.

HAWKER P.1081.

*Boulton Paul P.111 at first roll-out. Note the wing configuration is without either version of the extended tips fitted, span at 25' 8", which is how the aircraft is now preserved, but in its P.111a guise. (Crown Copyright)*

# BOULTON PAUL P.111/P.111a

| | |
|---|---|
| **Manufacturer** | **Boulton Paul Aircraft Ltd** |
| **Specification** | **E.27/46** |
| **Role** | **Research Prototype** |
| **First Flight Date** | **P.111 – VT 935 –** |
| | **10th October 1950** |
| | **P.111a – VT 935 –** |
| | **2nd July 1953** |

The Boulton Paul deltas were the first in Britain to be designed purely for academic research into the delta wing planform, to determine the basic aerodynamic stability and control derivatives, and for research at transonic speeds as part of an RAE programme, the earlier Avro 707 being a one-third scale model of the planned Avro 698 bomber design

## DEVELOPMENT HISTORY
In the light of German research data discovered after the War, interest was shown in the advantages inherent in the delta wing planform, which eliminated both the weight and drag of a conventional tailplane. As there were still many unknowns in the areas of stability and control, it was decided to fund a prototype for pure research, not aimed at any specific future project. A Specification E.27/46 was raised, the contract awarded to Boulton Paul Aircraft, and detailed design work and manufacture started in 1947. After construction was completed at their Wolverhampton factory, the aircraft was disassembled and transported by road to Boscombe Down where its first flight took place on 10th October 1950. (It is interesting to note that the Prototype Notes for the aircraft are titled 'E.27/46. Mk.1', although there is no information to hand as to further versions which were planned, other than the later P.120 to a new specification.)

The aircraft was found to be very sensitive longitudinally on take-off, causing pilot-induced oscillations which could be controlled with experience. During the first few flights, there was a lot of trouble experienced with the undercarriage retraction and sequencing, and several flights had to be completed with the undercarriage locked down before the problems were solved. On undercarriage retraction, it was found that there was a large nose-up trim change caused by the loss of drag from the relatively large nosewheel door.

As with many other aircraft, the first attempts at fully-powered controls and the associated artificial feel systems made the aircraft extremely sensitive in all axes. It was also found that the rudder was too slow to operate to give adequate control during cross-wind landings, so the hydraulic power was removed and the rudder operated purely manually.

In July 1951, after only 28 hours flying, a new, framed windscreen was fitted, together with a re-designed spring-feel system to try to reduce the aircraft's sensitivity.

The aircraft suffered damage on landing on 29th October 1951, but this was slight and the aircraft was able to resume flying after a short period. There were two further landing accidents on 5th January and 29th August 1952, the latter causing considerable damage as it was a completely wheels-up forced landing.

During the lengthy lay-up, the opportunity was taken to make further modifications to the airframe and systems. Such were the differences that the aircraft was re-designated the P.111a. Major external differences, apart from the eye-catching new paint scheme, were the long pitot head projecting from the intake splitter plate, redesigned nosewheel and main wheel fairing doors (which might have been modified in the light of earlier undercarriage problems), and the fitting of four 'petal' airbrakes,

sited unusually far forward around the mid-fuselage. Although these served the normal function of speed reduction, one of the prime reasons for their fitment was to increase drag during the approach to land. A minimum of 7,000 rpm was needed on the engine to keep the generators on line, the resulting high thrust requiring a very flat approach to land, together with difficulty in reducing airspeed for landing. The resulting drag against thrust with the airbrakes extended helped to alleviate the situation. The rear face of these surfaces also formed the intake duct wall; thus, when they were extended, there were four fairly large 'holes' around the duct, just forward of the engine compressor intake. These must have caused considerable turbulence in the duct, which resulted in a thrust loss from the engine.

After being transported by road to Boscombe Down, the first flight in this new guise was made on 2nd July 1953. The airbrakes were found to be very effective, but the landing speeds were still high and, to help reduce the ensuing landing roll, the anti-spin parachute was strengthened so that it could also be used as a braking parachute. Initially, it was streamed just after touchdown, but later it was usual to do this at about 10', just before touchdown.

Control sensitivity was still evident, with a tendency to overcontrol at high speed. A pilot-selectable, fully variable gearing system was introduced in both pitch and roll. Also, until now the automatic trimming system was functional, both when flying with the powered controls engaged

*Underside detail, with the aircraft having the intermediate sized wingtips fitted, increasing the span to 29' 9". (Royal Aeronautical Society.)*

and while in manual reversion. The tendency to overcontrol at high speed when in manual was eliminated by the automatic trimming being selected off. It was possible to control the aircraft adequately up to 400 kts. in manual but, above this speed, the controls became too heavy.

At the low speed end of the flight envelope, it was found that there was no stall in the accepted sense; the limit for speed reduction, and incidence increase was the onset of lateral rocking, but with no longitudinal pitching. The minimum speed achieved during flight testing was 108 kts.

After some forty flights by the manufacturer, the aircraft transferred to RAE Bedford on 24th February 1954 for continued reseach by the Aerodynamics Flight into delta wings, to establish the various basic parameters and stability derivatives. It was flown in the three wing configurations possible with the removable wingtips, causing some marked changes in the aircraft's lateral stability and control.

After the completion of its trials programme on 20th June 1958, it was transferred by road to the College of Aeronautics, Cranfield, on 28th April 1959, to act as an instructional airframe. At the end of its useful life there it made its final move on 13th July 1975 to the Midland Air Museum, Coventry, where it is still preserved.

# CONSTRUCTION

To extract the maximum performance from the relatively low-powered engines available at that time, the fuselage was as short as possible, with a wide oval plain pitot intake, a centre-body splitter plate bifurcating the intake around the cockpit and nosewheel bay, with the engine almost immediately behind the cockpit. It also had a short jetpipe to minimise intake duct and jetpipe thrust losses.

The cockpit sidewalls were formed by the intake inner walls and, to give the fuselage sufficient strength and stiffness, the outer intake walls and airframe skin were supported on very closely-spaced formers and stringers. The fully stressed monocoque structure was manufactured entirely from light alloy. The fuselage was made in three sections, the nose, from Stn.72" back to Stn.193", containing the intake, cockpit, nosewheel bay and instrumentation bay immediately behind the cockpit accessible through a removable panel in the spine which housed the flying control runs and electrical wiring. The centre-section, between Stn.193 and 290.88", comprised the engine bay, and the aft section aft of Stn.290.88 comprised the fuselage tailcone, and integral fin structure. The forward end of the tail section comprised a transport joint for removal of the complete rear fuselage and fin assembly for access and removal of the engine. (*Note:* The fuselage datum 0 was 72" forward of the intake lip, thus the fuselage structure 'started' 72" aft of the datum).

The cockpit initially had a one-piece curved windscreen, but this was soon replaced with one with an optically flat centre-panel, and curved quarter-lights. The new windscreen was heated for de-misting purposes. (It is not clear whether the change was made due to windscreen distortions through the curved panel, or whether it was changed for strength reasons.) Access was via the rearward hinging clamshell canopy, which had three small windows for sideways and upwards

*Boulton Paul P.111a with its bright new yellow and black colour scheme. External changes evident are the pitot probe fitted to the intake centre body, and just discernible, the new airbrake panels. (via Philip Jarrett)*

*Boulton Paul P.111a rear three-quarters view illustrating the four airbrake panels in the fully out position. (via Philip Jarrett)*

visibility. This could be jettisoned in an emergency, and the pilot was provided with a Martin-Baker ejection seat. Although the aircraft was well instrumented, the cockpit was small and spartan.

The rearwards retracting nosewheel was fitted with an 18″ diameter wheel and, when retracted, lay in its bay below the cockpit. As well as a long door attached to the oleo, two small doors faired the aft end of the bay. Electrical fuse panels, terminal blocks and voltage regulators were mounted on panels on either side of the bay, together with one 12 volt/25 amp. accumulator on each side.

A TR 1920 VHF radio was mounted in the spine immediately behind the cockpit, below which was the auto-observer panel recording some twenty control and engine parameters. There was little room left within the fuselage, so all the fuel was housed in the wings. In addition to the auto-observer, the aircraft carried continuous trace and voice recorders and had facilities for pressure plotting.

The entire centre-section was occupied by the Nene engine, mounted on and parallel to the aircraft's datum. Immediately in front of the compressor intake, the wing mainspar structure passed right across the fuselage which, together with the cockpit centre-body, formed a 'cross' effectively dividing the plenum chamber into four equal sections. Two strengthened frames at Stn.213.75″ and Stn.254.66″ formed the engine bay

firewalls, and acted as attachment frames for the wing's main and aft auxiliary spars. The bay formed between the latter frame and the transport joint at the aft end of the centre-section housed the powered flying control electro-hydraulic generators and various other items of electrical equipment arranged around and each side of the jetpipe. The flying control surfaces were actuated via normal push/pull rods.

Strengthened frames in the rear fuselage structure formed the attachment points for the fin spars. The triangular fin was constructed around three spars and multiple ribs. It had a leading edge and quarter chord sweep angles of 45° and 36°52′ respectively, the trailing edge being vertical. It had a symmetrical, Squires High Speed 'C' section, with a thickness/chord ratio of a constant 10%. Gross area of the fin and rudder was 48.3 sq. ft (to the fuselage datum line) with a net area of 34.55 sq. ft. The fibreglass fin-tip was designed to be removable for trials with a cropped fin but this was never done.

The power-operated rudder was hinged to the aft fin spar and had an area of 6.72 sq.ft aft of the hinge line and a movement range of ±15°. It also had a small trim tab of 1.04 sq.ft area and a movement range of ±6°.

A long bulged fairing was fitted on the left side of the fuselage at the base of the fin and it housed a 7′ diameter anti-spin parachute, its anchor point being a quick-release fitting on the fuselage

*A dramatic view of the aircraft in flight with the airbrakes partially extended. Study of the original photograph appears to confirm that the airbrakes were fully variable by pilot selection. (via Philip Jarrett)*

centreline at the base of the rudder. The jetpipe orifice protruded slightly from the rear of the fuselage tailcone, which had a substantial bumper beneath it to protect the structure and jetpipe in the event of a large touchdown incidence. The short-coupled fuselage and undercarriage layout allowed a tail-down incidence of 17° (static) reducing to 13°30′ with the main oleos fully compressed, making it extremely unlikely that there would be the possibility of a tail strike in normal operations. Wing incidence (ground static) was 6°. (This increased to 7° on the modified P.111a due to more compression on the main oleos.)

The wing was the main object for research and, to enable several different configurations to be investigated, had removable wingtips, allowing three different layouts. The basic wing spanned 25′8″, and tapered from a centreline chord of 17′2.5″ down to 4′8″ at the tip. It had a leading edge and quarter-chord sweep angle of 45° and 36°52′ respectively. It had 0° dihedral and was also set at 0° incidence to the aircraft datum, and possessed a symmetrical Squires High Speed 'C' section with a constant thickness/chord ratio of 10%.

It was constructed around multiple ribs, a forward mainspar and rear auxiliary spar, to which were hinged the two-piece flying control surfaces which comprised the entire wing trailing edge. These surfaces worked as elevons (eg. acting as both ailerons and elevators), and had a total area, aft of the hinge line, of 29.3 sq.ft. and their chord

was a constant 15% of the wing chord. Their movement range was ±15° as ailerons and –25° as elevators. The inner surfaces each had trim tabs whose total area was 5.67 sq.ft with a movement range of ±8°.

The main undercarriage bays were situated inboard between the two spars, the oleos retracting inwards giving the aircraft an unusually wide track compared to the wingspan and conferring exceptional stability during ground manoeuvring. The long-stroke oleos had a 26.5″ diameter wheel, with Maxaret anti-skid brakes fitted. Due to the lack of space in the fuselage, all of the fuel was carried in the wings. There were two tanks in each wing leading edge forward of the mainspar, extending out as far as the outer end of the undercarriage bays, and one tank in each wing aft of the undercarriage bay, total capacity being 230 gallons.

The left wing was instrumented for pressure plotting and a long yaw-vane boom was fitted to the right wing at about mid semi-span; a pitot head was fitted to the left wingtip.

Two different extended wingtips could be fitted, increasing the span to either 29′9″ or 33′6″. Both these additional configurations were tested during the aircraft's career.

Late in 1952/early 1953, the aircraft was extensively modified both internally and externally, and re-designated the P.111a. The exterior changes included the fitting of an instrumented pitot boom to the intake centre-body, modified undercarriage bay doors, the nosewheel twin doors being replaced by a single one hinged on its left edge, and the mainwheel bay doors having their relative lengths changed. (This small change might have been done to eliminate finally the undercarriage retraction problems which had been evident at the start of its programme.) The anti-spin parachute system was strengthened to allow it to be also used as a braking 'chute to reduce the aircraft's landing roll. The other major external change was the addition of four 'petal' airbrakes arranged equidistant around the fuselage at the forward end of the centre-section. Due to the fuselage having minimal structural depth between the outer skin and the intake duct wall, the inner surface of each airbrake formed part of the intake wall so that, when open, there were four fairly large 'holes' in the intake, just in front of the engine's compressor, which caused some airflow disturbance and thus loss of thrust. When fully extended, their opening angle was 80°–85°. Provision was also made for the fitting of a cine camera under a small fairing, approximately halfway up the fin, for view tufting on the left wing during airflow investigation.

The flying controls were fully power-operated by a duplicated hydraulic system, with spring feel and automatic trimming by means of electrically operated tabs. The latter was provided so that, in the event of reversion to manual, the controls would always be in trim. While trimming, there was no feedback to the pilot's control column, the controls having a datum-shift mechanism. Reversion to manual control was either automatic on the failure of both hydraulic systems or was selectable by the pilot. The initial flights showed the aircraft to be over-sensitive to pilot inputs causing pilot-induced oscillations and, early on in the programme, the spring-feel system was redesigned in an attempt to alleviate this.

When the aircraft was modified to the P.111a configuration, the flying control system was again changed to one that had variable gearing, fully pilot-selectable at any speed. This helped to solve the handling problems. While flying in manual, there was still a tendency to over-control at high speeds, but this was eliminated by disengaging the automatic trimming facility when in manual, allowing flight up to 400 kts, when the control forces became too heavy.

## POWER PLANT

One Rolls-Royce Nene 3 R.N.2. centrifugal flow turbojet developing a Sea Level Static Thrust of 5,100 lbs.

*The College of Aeronautics, Cranfield, is mentioned many times in this book as the keeper of experimental airframes. Here is the famous Hangar, with part of its exotic collection including VT935 in foreground with the Hawker P.1121 behind it. (Ron Moulton)*

## DATA

| Span | 33'6" | ; 29'9" ; 25'8" |
|---|---|---|
| Length | 26'1" | ; 31'6.1" (including nose probe) |
| Height | 12'6.5" | |
| Track | 14'5.3" | |
| Wheelbase | 11'0.5" | |

**AREAS**

| Wing (gross) | 269.25 sq ft (25'8" span) |
|---|---|
| | 284.16 sq ft (29'9" span) |
| | 290.13 sq ft (33'6" span) |

Wing Loading 35 lbs/sq ft (max)

**WEIGHTS**
(29'9" span)

| basic | 7,517 lbs | |
|---|---|---|
| pilot | 180 lbs | |
| fuel | 1860 lbs | |
| ballast | 570 lbs (fwd cg) | 230 lbs (aft cg) |
| auw | 10,127 lbs (fwd cg) | 9,787 lbs (aft cg) |

**PERFORMANCE**

| Minimum Speed Tested | 108 kts |
|---|---|
| Maximum Speed at Sea Level | 564 kts |
| 20,000 ft | 554 kts |
| 30,000 ft | 550 kts |
| 35,000 ft | 540 kts (0.93 Mach) |

Maximum Speed tested in a dive 0.96 Mach

Initial Climb Rate          9,400 ft/min

**REFERENCES**

| Midland Air Museum | —The aircraft |
|---|---|
| RAE Farnborough | —Historical Archives |
| Flying Review | —Vol. XIV. No. 11 |
| Prototype Notes | —General arrangement diagram |
| Boulton Paul Aircraft | —Anniversary brochure |
| RAF Museum | —Photographic Archives |

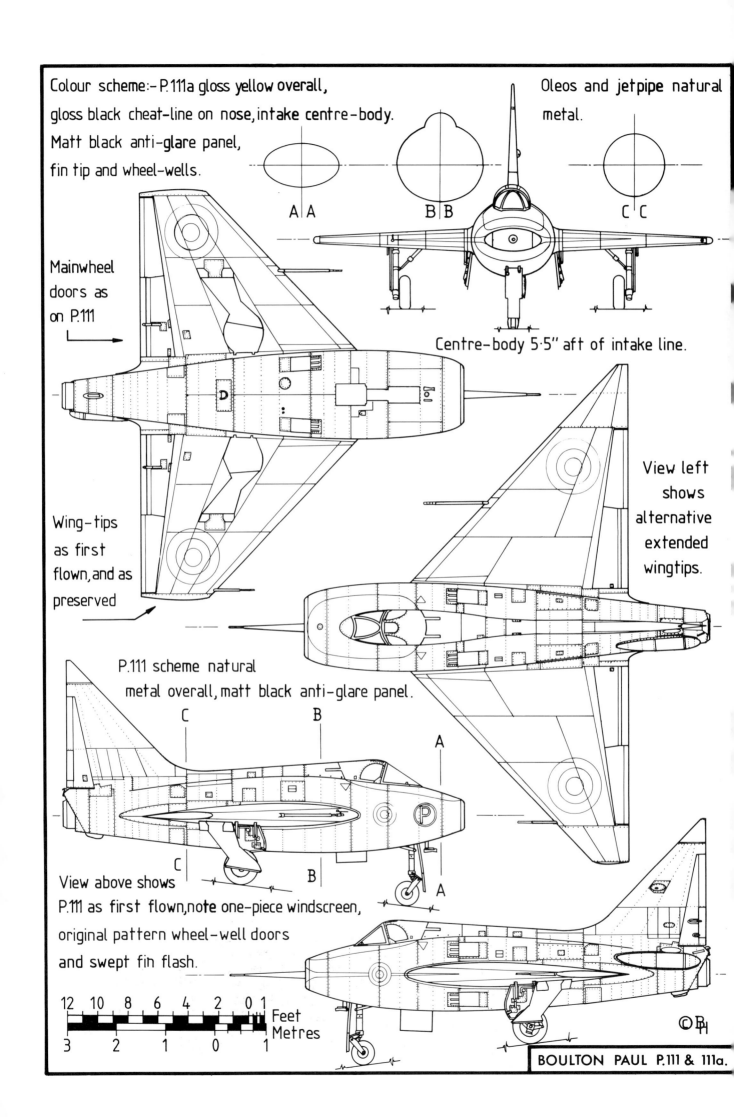

Colour scheme:- P.111a gloss yellow overall,
gloss black cheat-line on nose, intake centre-body.
Matt black anti-glare panel,
fin tip and wheel-wells.

Oleos and jetpipe natural metal.

A A    B B    C C

Centre-body 5·5" aft of intake line.

Mainwheel
doors as
on P.111

Wing-tips
as first
flown, and as
preserved

View left
shows
alternative
extended
wingtips.

P.111 scheme natural
metal overall, matt black anti-glare panel.

C    B    A

View above shows
P.111 as first flown, note one-piece windscreen,
original pattern wheel-well doors
and swept fin flash.

C    B    A

12 10 8 6 4 2 0 1   Feet
                    Metres
3    2   1   0   1

©B_H

BOULTON PAUL P.111 & 111a.

*Fairey F.D.1 after the removal of the two lateral fairings at the wing root. The lower fairing has been modified to house the braking parachute. The fixed leading-edge slats are well shown as is the horizontal tail surface, which is also fixed.*

# FAIREY DELTA 1

| | |
|---|---|
| **Manufacturer** | **Fairey Aviation Company Ltd** |
| **Specification** | **E.10/47** |
| **Role** | **Single-Seat Research Prototype** |
| **First Flight Date** | **VX 350 – 10th March 1951** |
| | **VX 357; VX 364 – Not flown** |

When all of the captured German data was evaluated after the War, one of the aircraft that seemed really to impress the Air Ministry was the Bachem Natter vertical take-off interceptor. This was a lethal machine, designed to be rocket-powered, take-off from an almost vertical ramp, fire its unguided missile battery in one pass at its target, then glide down to a 'safe' altitude. At this point in the very brief sortie, the pilot jettisoned the complete nose-section, fell out to descend by his parachute, and the aft fuselage containing the more 'valuable' rocket motor also descended by parachute to be re-used for the next sortie. The only known manned launch attempted broke the pilot's neck. Hardly a fighter-pilot's dream aircraft!

However, a proposal for a vertical-take-off interceptor was made, and the contract awarded to Fairey's for prototype construction. The first, and only, prototype to fly was modified to allow normal take-off and landing from a runway for trials purposes.

## DEVELOPMENT HISTORY

In July 1946 the Air Ministry proposed a series of tests with rocket-powered scale models, culminating in full-scale trials of the ultimate VTO fighter. Control at low speeds, before there was sufficient airflow over the normal control surfaces, was to be by gyroscopic servo units driving four swivelling jetpipe nozzles, as well as by the normal aerodynamic controls.

Specification E.10/47 was raised to cover the project and Fairey was awarded the development contract and construction of three prototypes serialed VX 350, VX 357 and VX 364. The first was modified to have a nosewheel undercarriage to allow normal flight trials.

The first prototype, VX 350, flew its initial trials with the four fairings around its normal jet orifice, originally intended for the swivelling nozzles, still fitted. However, early in the trials the fairings for the two vertical control nozzles (those at the wing trailing edge roots) were removed, the one in the lower fuselage was modified to house a braking parachute. The full system of control nozzles was to be fitted to the second and third prototypes, their fuselages being strengthened, and wings stressed for the mounting of the four booster rockets at their roots, to enable them to be capable of ramp launching. (No records could be found as to whether a lighter, modified undercarriage was to be fitted for landing.) The booster rockets were to be mounted in pairs under each wing root, and were externally almost carbon copies of a German design, the Schmidding 109–553 solid-fuel unit fitted to the Enzian missile. Four different layouts were designed, with downthrust angles between 6° and 12°54', and thrust lines angled out between 5° and 26° relative to the fuselage datum.

Model tests had indicated the launch acceleration would be 'acceptable'. With the ramp elevated to 45°, longitudinal acceleration was calculated to be 2.6g but it was planned to increase ramp angle to up to 80° during the trials. A special mobile crane was designed to lift the fully-loaded aircraft onto the ramp when it was horizontal. The trials were to be made from Boscombe Down, and a suitable site for the launching ramp was chosen to the right of the main runway 24 threshold, launch trajectory to be parallel to the runway.

However, events overtook the project, and it was decided that there was no longer a requirement for a VTO ramp-launched fighter; therefore the second and third prototypes were cancelled. The second prototype, VX 357, was in an advanced stage of construction, having had its Derwent 8 engine installed at Stockport on 8th January 1951. The first was to be completed solely for research into the aerodynamic characteristics of a delta wing.

Construction of VX 350 was completed at Fairey's Heaton Chapel, Stockport factory, and taxi-ing trials commenced on 12th May 1950 at Ringway Airport (now Manchester International). It was then dismantled and transported by road to Boscombe Down, where it eventually made its first flight on 12th March 1951, some ten months later. At the time of its first flight it was the smallest delta-winged aircraft to have flown, and the first with a horizontal tail surface fitted. All subsequent flights were to be made from either Boscombe Down or Farnborough.

The initial trials investigated the longitudinal and lateral control and stability characteristics. Despite its tiny size, with the small control moment-arms, the aircraft was found to be particularly steady, with longitudinal stability large and positive. Longitudinal control was satisfactory although sensitive at high speed. Lateral stability and control were also good, with high roll-rates being possible due to the relatively large elevons compared to the small span. Braking parachute trials were also made. The aircraft was damaged during a landing accident in September 1951. During repairs, other modifications were carried out. The two swivelling-nozzle fairings at the wing roots were removed and the wing fillet altered. Down-time was almost two years and the aircraft did not fly again until May 1953. (Having said

*Fairey F.D.1. Almost circular intake with its prominent centre-body fairing and with the split airbrakes extended. (Flight International)*

the foregoing the aircraft was grounded at Boscombe Down early in 1953, quote, "as a dangerous aircraft"!)

During the subsequent trials, the fixed leading-edge slats were also removed, as were the wingtip mounted anti-spin parachutes. The tip fairings then acquiring long 'spike' aerials protruding from their rear ends.

Another landing accident occurred on 6th February 1956, causing the aircraft to veer off the runway and the undercarriage to be torn off. Repair was deemed to be uneconomical and the aircraft was allocated to the Mechanical Engineering Department, Farnborough. On 9th October 1956 it was transported to Shoeburyness Range for use as a gunnery target for airframe battle damage assessment. Presumably, at the end of these tests, what remained of the airframe was scrapped.

## CONSTRUCTION

The airframe was of standard frame and stringer construction with a stressed light alloy skin. To keep weight and thrust losses to a minimum, the airframe was the smallest practicable to be able to be designed around the engine, leaving little space for the pilot and fuel.

The portly fuselage had an oval intake in the nose, which was bifurcated by a wide, curved, centre-body to accommodate the nosewheel bay and cockpit. The nosewheel oleo retracted aft into its bay, being enclosed by two doors, one attached to the oleo and the other sequenced closed after nosewheel extension. There was a large hatch in the upper side of the nose above the undercarriage bay for access to an instrumentation compartment. A small 'horizon-datum' mast was fitted on this hatch for reference purposes for the pilot through the curved, frameless windscreen. (The mast was to be removed later in the test programme.) The cockpit was quite cramped, with its side-walls forming the intake inner walls, passing each side of it. However, there was just sufficient room for an ejection seat to be provided. The canopy slid aft for normal entry and exit and could be jettisoned in an emergency by operation of a push-button. It was made mainly from light alloy, three small oval windows allowing limited lateral and vertical vision for the pilot. A VHF whip-aerial was mounted on the canopy's metal aft fairing.

A large rectangular panel in the upper fuselage, between the cockpit and the fin leading edge, provided access to the engine and for its removal. Four square spring-loaded suction-relief panels were situated above the engine's plenum chamber, in the engine-access panel, to provide additional air to the engine at low speeds. They were hinged along their upper edges, and were springloaded closed until sucked open at high thrust settings.

There was a corresponding rectangular panel in the bottom of the fuselage for access to the engine's auxiliary equipment. The engine was started electrically and the 24-volt external power socket was situated in the right main undercarriage bay.

In either side of the fuselage, at approximately mid wing-root chord, were the two main undercarriage bays. The main oleos retracted aft to lie almost horizontal in the fuselage, and were stressed to accept a 12 ft./sec. rate of descent at touchdown. They were enclosed by three doors each, the large horizontally-hinged doors sequenced closed after undercarriage extension. The smaller forward doors were hinged at their top and bottom respectively, the lower ones having an additional novel function. They were sequenced open only after the main undercarriage was fully extended then, when these doors opened, brackets attached to their inner surfaces were placed fore and aft of the oleo, thus effectively locking it in position. On retraction, these lower doors closed first, removing the down-lock and allowing the gear to retract. (It may be interesting to speculate that this sequence may have failed on one side, causing the down-lock not to be engaged during the second landing accident, making the aircraft veer off the runway.)

The fuselage terminated at the jet orifice, the engine having a minimal length jetpipe to reduce thrust losses. Above, below, and on each side were the fairings for the intended swivelling jet nozzles. Initially, each of these had a conical fairing at its rear end. The two fairings on each side were eventually to be removed completely and the wing-root fillet extended. The upper fairing retained its conical 'bullet' throughout the life of the aircraft, but that on the lower one was removed and a braking-parachute container added. A substantial bumper was fitted below the lower fairing to protect the lower fuselage during landing, as there was minimal clearance at the landing attitude.

The stubby delta wings were mid-mounted, with a relatively thick root-section. The broad tips had streamlined fairings attached, which initially contained anti-spin parachutes, but these were later removed and the fairings may have contained instrumentation, as each sprouted a 'spike' aerial at its aft end. A pitot head was fitted to the nose of the fairing on the right wingtip and a yaw-vane boom on the left. The fuel tanks were located in the wing leading edges, forward of the mainspar, as there was little available space within the small fuselage. Fully power-operated elevons occupied most of the trailing edges for pitch and roll control, each fitted with a trim tab at its inboard end. Below the wing root/fuselage junction on each side forward of the mainspar was a streamlined fairing covering the flying control hydraulic actuators. Between the elevon and the fuselage on each wing was a split

*Fairey F.D.1 in flight showing good topside detail. Note the leading-edge slats have been removed. (Flight International)*

airbrake, each surface opening equally above and below the wing to eliminate any trim change.

Initially, fixed leading-edge slats were fitted from approximately mid semi-span out to the wingtip fairings. However, these were removed early in the test programme.

Due to the short moment arm, a relatively large fin and rudder were fitted to give adequate directional stability, with a small fairing between its leading edge root and the cockpit. The fin overhung the jet orifice, to put the rudder hinge as far aft as possible, and a horizontal tail surface was fitted at the fin tip. It was not a tailplane in the true sense, being a fixed slab surface at approximately –5° to the aircraft datum. Later in the programme, for high speed trials, it was intended to remove this tail surface, the fin tip then being faired into the top of the rudder. However, this was never done throughout the aircraft's life. A second VHF whip aerial was fitted to the upper tailplane surface. (The FD.1 was the first delta to fly with a horizontal tail surface.)

## POWER PLANT
Original proposal to be fitted with a special Rolls-Royce turbojet engine intended for the vertically launched fighter, the specified type being unknown. The actual aircraft was fitted with one Rolls-Royce Derwent 5 R.D.7 centrifugal flow turbojet developing a Sea Level Static Thrust of 3,500 lbs. The second prototype had a Derwent 8 R.D.7 fitted, of 3,600 lbs. Static Thrust. The four rocket booster motors were each to have a thrust of 5,000 lbs., with a burn time of 6 seconds.

## DATA
**DIMENSIONS**

| | |
|---|---|
| Span | 19'6.5" |
| Length | 26'3" |
| Height | 11'5" |
| Track | 6'0" |
| Wheelbase | 11'10.5" |
| Tailplane Span | 7'4.5" |

**AREAS**

| | |
|---|---|
| Wing (gross) | 155.7 sq ft |
| Tailplane | 15.0 sq ft |
| Fin and Rudder | 37.0 sq ft |
| Rudder (aft of hinge) | 6.63 sq ft |

**WEIGHTS**

| | |
|---|---|
| All-Up Weight (with boosters) | 8,000 lbs |
| All-Up Weight (without boosters) | 6,600 lbs |

**LOADING**

| | |
|---|---|
| Wing Loading (with boosters) | 51.4 lbs/sq ft |
| Wing Loading (without boosters) | 42.5 lbs/sq ft |
| Stressed for Maximum +8g | |

**PERFORMANCE**

| | |
|---|---|
| Critical Mach Number | 0.85 |
| Maximum Speed | 345 kts |
| Stalling Speed | 115 kts |

**REFERENCES**

| | |
|---|---|
| Public Records Office | —Avia Files |
| Royal Air Force Museum | —Archives |
| Flight International | —Photographic Archives |

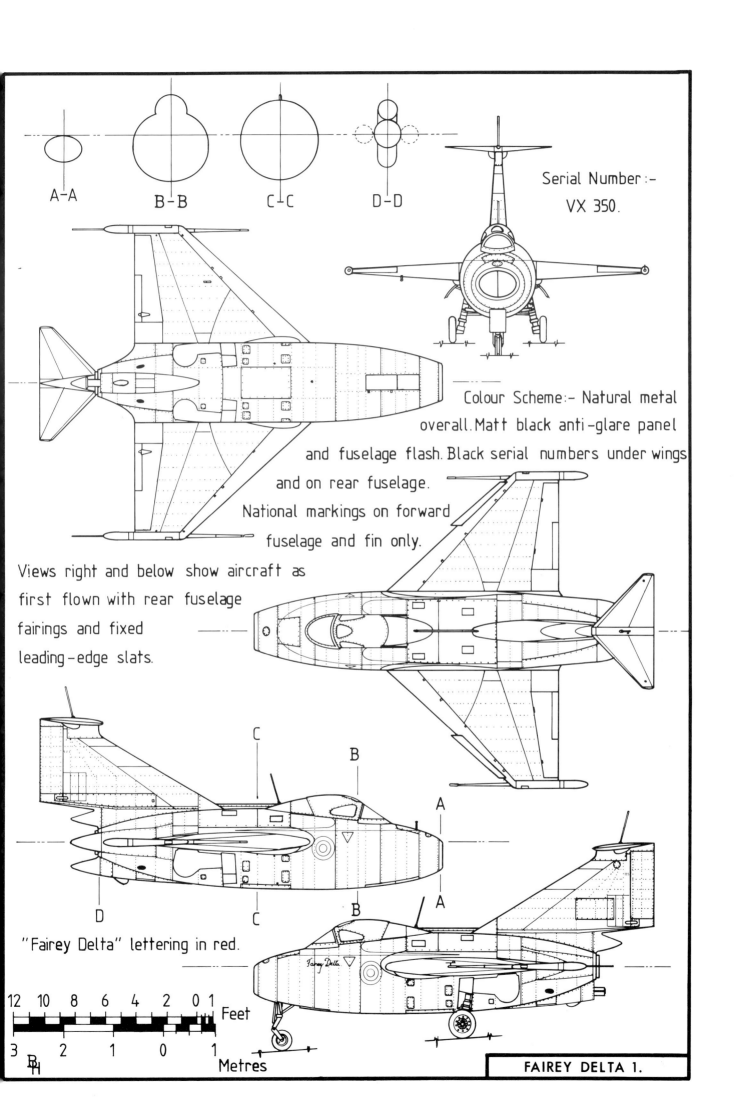

A-A  B-B  C-C  D-D

Serial Number :-
VX 350.

Colour Scheme:- Natural metal
overall. Matt black anti-glare panel
and fuselage flash. Black serial numbers under wings
and on rear fuselage.
National markings on forward
fuselage and fin only.

Views right and below show aircraft as
first flown with rear fuselage
fairings and fixed
leading-edge slats.

C
B
A

D
C
B
A

"Fairey Delta" lettering in red.

*Fairey Delta*

12 10 8 6 4 2 0 1   Feet

3        2        1        0        1
                                    Metres

B.H.

FAIREY DELTA 1.

*Handley Page HP.88 at first roll-out. Its Supermarine ancestry is apparent. Note the aileron mass-balance arms and the fin mounted instrument boom, yet to have the yaw vane fitted at its tip. The ejection seat has yet to be installed. (British Aerospace (Brough))*

# HANDLEY PAGE HP.88

| | |
|---|---|
| **Manufacturer** | **Blackburn & General Aircraft Ltd** |
| **Specification** | **E.6/48** |
| **Role** | **Single-Seat Research Prototype** |
| **First Flight Date** | **VX 330 – 21st June 1951** |

When Handley Page was awarded the contract to develop the HP.80, the HP.88 was built to test the crescent-wing planform of the proposed bomber, as its aerodynamic properties were an unknown quantity. The wing was intended to be a 0.36 scale representation of that to be used on the bomber, but design changes overtook the project. The wing, which was actually manufactured, was not representative either in planform or in control layout to that finally used on the larger aircraft, and therefore its usefulness in providing data for the HP.80 would have been strictly limited.

## DEVELOPMENT HISTORY

At the end of the War, some of Handley Page's design staff were among the teams of intelligence experts sent to Germany to evaluate the advances in aeronautics. Among other firms, the work of Arado on swept, and 'crescent' wing planforms to delay the onset of compressibility effects at high Mach numbers, made a marked impression, the latter shape being intended for trials on the Arado 234 twin-jet bomber.

When the firm successfully tendered for the development of a four-jet bomber to meet Specification B.35/46, designated HP.80, they proposed

to use this radically new shape of wing, and it was felt prudent to flight test a reduced scale version of the wing to prove its aerodynamics, as was also done with Avro's competing design, producing the Avro 707 family of aircraft. A Specification E.6/48 was raised on 12th March 1948 to cover the contract for the development of the proposed proof-of-concept prototype. In June of that year, construction of one prototype was authorised, designated HP.88 and serial-numbered VX 330. (An earlier design study, designated HP.87, for a towed one-third scale glider version was abandoned.)

To save time and costs, it was decided to use a Supermarine Attacker fuselage, marrying it with a new wing and tail unit. Thus, right from the start, the layout of this machine was not representative of the full-sized bomber as it had a low-set wing, compared to the high, shoulder-mounted wing of the HP.80. Also, the airflow disturbances around the tail unit on deployment of the large airbrakes would have made a nonsense of any read-across to the larger machine.

The wing planform chosen was representative of that of the HP.80 as it was in 1949, with a sweep in two stages on the trailing edge, and a section with a critical Mach no. of 0.83. In 1950, after the wing for the HP.88 had been manufactured, the HP.80 wing-root section was modified to raise the critical Mach no. to 0.86 and its outer kink moved inboard, making the scale wing even less representative of the full-sized version.

The Handley Page HP.88 must have had more designations in its very brief career than virtually any other type! Having decided to use a Supermarine fuselage, this was changed from the Attacker's to one similar to that on the Supermarine 510, as this had already been redesigned to mount a 45° swept wing. The fuselage for the HP.88 was quite extensively modified and was therefore allocated a new Supermarine Type No. 521.

Due to the heavy commitments of Handley Page in the development of the HP.80, detail design of the 0.36 scale wing and the prototype was subcontracted to General Aircraft Ltd., receiving their design number GAL.63. General Aircraft Ltd. was taken over by Blackburn Aircraft Ltd. and the whole project was transferred to Brough, receiving yet another designation, Blackburn Y.B.2., and it was this firm who actually got the contract for the building of the prototype. They finished the modifications to the fuselage and completed construction of the aircraft in June 1951. (Although photographs showing what appears to be a complete aircraft prior to being painted are dated 15th December 1950.)

After brief taxi-ing trials at Brough, the aircraft was taken by road to Carnaby airfield which, having been an emergency landing field during the war, had a much longer runway. Arriving there on 14th June, only seven days later it made a successful short five-minute maiden flight, consisting of one circuit and landing using its tail parachute for braking. Grounded for adjustments, it did not fly again until 7th July, when it was airborne twice.

However, control problems were already showing themselves as the aircraft was over-sensitive in pitch. Any small disturbance caused the aircraft to pitch and any corrective action caused divergent pilot-induced oscillations. The resulting low amplitude porpoising could only be damped by holding the control column fixed. This phenomenon occurred at speeds as low as 230 kts., and the aircraft became extremely difficult to control above 255 kts.

To try to remedy the situation, a strip of light alloy angle bracket was riveted to the upper surface of the tailplane trailing edge, and control became acceptable up to about 270 kts. Lengthening of the strip, and adding another to the under surface, eventually produced satisfactory characteristics up to 450 kts./Mach 0.82. After a disturbance, the aircraft pitched for two cycles before being damped out by steady back-pressure on the control column.

Having confirmed these results, the Handley Page Deputy Chief Test Pilot accepted the aircraft and on 23rd August ferried it to Stansted for airspeed calibration flights, in progressive stages up to 550 kts./Mach 0.85. On 26th August, the aircraft took off on what was to be its final flight.

Until approximately 14 minutes into the flight nothing untoward had been reported and, seconds before the accident, the last contact was quite normal. On completion of the flight test schedule, a straight, fast run at approximately 300 feet altitude was made over the field. Witnesses observed a pitching oscillation, immediately followed by structural failure, the aircraft disintegrating before the pilot was able to eject. The rear fuselage detached at Frame 14, just aft of the wing trailing edge, and the nose section then broke off upwards prior to wing failure.

Subsequent examination of the flight recorder and wreckage indicated that an attempt had been made to reduce speed by selecting the emergency control lever for the airbrakes. Recorder traces showed a divergent oscillation at 475 kts., with peak accelerations of +7g and –5g. A second trace, at 525 kts, showed peaks of at least +12g and –5g. (The true values could actually have been much higher for these were the instrument stops!) The aircraft was at a greater speed at low level than on any previous flight, although this speed had been successfully achieved at higher altitudes.

The loss of the aircraft had little effect on the HP.80 development, the design of which had bypassed the HP.88, as construction of the bomber prototypes was well advanced.

The total life of the aircraft from the first flight on the 21st June 1951 to the date of its crash was only 36 days! Not including the final flight, it had flown a total of approximately 14 hours in 28 sorties.

# CONSTRUCTION

The fuselage was basically similar to that of the Supermarine Type 510, except for the necessary modifications to suit the mounting of the new wing and tail unit, plus the addition of hydraulically-operated airbrakes on each side, and it was constructed of light alloy.

The main changes to compensate for the modified weight distribution and tail unit position were as follows:

Frames 25 and 27 were reinforced to carry the attachment points for the repositioned fin. Fore and aft intercostal diaphragms between Frames 23 and 27 were riveted to the top skin, and to the fin attachment brackets at Frames 25 and 27. The skinning aft of Frame 23 was stiffened by an external doubling plate, and the rear slinging joint at Frame 23 was reinforced. Two additional Frames – 19a and 21a – were added to carry the airbrake hinge loads and operating jack attachment points.

A stressed panel was inserted into the top of the fuselage skin for access to the electro-hydraulic control unit for the rudder and tailplane, and an additional fuel tank was mounted aft of Frame 17. The engine and forward main fuel tank access panel attachment points were also strengthened. The outer ends of the mainspar attachments were modified and a new wing leading edge attachment point provided. The rear wing spar attachment point was redesigned and the frames adjacent to the engine mount were reinforced by external doubling plates.

The cockpit was pressurised and had a sliding hood for entry/exit, which could be jettisoned in an emergency. A Martin-Baker Mk. 1A ejection seat

*One of the very few photographs taken of the Handley Page HP.88 airborne. The lighting highlights the prominent flap actuator fairings, the aileron mass-balances, the airbrake fairings and the heavily waisted fin/tailplane bullet fairing. (British Aerospace (Brough))*

was provided for the pilot.

Immediately aft of the cockpit was the fuel tank bay, the rear bulkhead of which formed the division between the tank and engine bays, and to which the mainspar was attached. The engine had a three-point mounting and was fed via intakes either side of the cockpit, each having full depth boundary layer bleed ducts, which exhausted through louvres above and below the intake lips. Engine starting was electrical.

Fuel was carried in four fuselage mounted tanks, with the addition of an optional ventral tank. The main tank aft of the cockpit had a capacity of 74.5 gallons, the side tanks a total of 111 gallons, and the aft tank 51 gals. The ventral tank (which in the event, was never fitted) contained 60 gallons, bringing total capacity to 296.5 gallons. Two electric booster pumps were fitted in the main tank, one for normal, and the other for inverted flight.

Several stressed panels were provided in the bottom of the fuselage to give access to the control runs and other equipment. The skinning was double-plated for reinforcement allowing for the many cut-outs for controls, electrics and instrumentation. The undercarriage was of standard Supermarine 510 type, except for minor changes to the tailwheel unit, and the design of new crosshead and folding strut assemblies for the main gear to suit the new layout.

Construction of the wing was around a forward mainspar and aft auxiliary spar, with multiple ribs, and was attached to the fuselage at Frames 12 and 14 respectively, a pick-up point for the leading edge being provided at Frame 9. Chord at the aircraft's centreline was 13'0". Root incidence was +3°, but marked washout gave a tip chord incidence of –2°. Geometric plane inclination was –2° and dihedral +0°54'. Aspect ratio was 5.58, and the thickness/chord ratio varied from 14% at the root, 10% at first

'kink', 6% at the second and 5% at the tip. Gross wing area was 285.726 sq.ft. Leading edge sweep varied in three stages, the inboard being 50°, with the inboard 'kink' at Wing Station 54.75 (measured in inches from Station 0 which was 24" from the centreline). The middle sweep angle was 40° and the outer 30°. The outboard kink was at Wing Stn.128.28. The trailing edge had only two stages of sweep, changing from 25° to 12° at the outboard kink line.

The mainspar was continuous to the wingtip, bending at the outboard kink, but the rear spar reached only out to Wing Stn.86.4. A 'new' rear spar further aft, to which was hinged the aileron, overlapped the inner rear spar. Each aileron was hinged at three points and mass-balanced externally at the tip. Also inboard, in line with the outer wing kink, were two long mass-balance arms in the form of upper and lower surface 'struts' angled forwards at 40°. There were no trim tabs, lateral trim adjustment being a ground operation by adjustment of the control surface rigging.

Powered control layout for the ailerons was unusual. Instead of the operating jack being mounted adjacent to each surface in the normal fashion and operating it directly from the ram, a single electro-hydraulic unit was mounted in the inboard port wing panel, behind the mainspar, accessible through a large stressed panel in the undersurface. Operation of the control surfaces then was via a system of linkages and push/pull rods. The control unit had duplicated systems so that, in the event of the failure of one, the other would take over automatically. Spring feel was provided as there was no feedback of control loads. In an identical position to the electro-hydraulic units, but in the starboard wing, was mounted the TR.1920 VHF radio, with its aerial outboard under the middle wing panel.

The wing control surfaces acted both as ailerons and for pitch trim. Lowering of the trailing edge flaps caused an exceptionally large nose-down trim-change, which could not be countered by the tailplane alone. Therefore the ailerons were inter-linked with the flaps so that, as the flap angle increased, so the ailerons were biased upwards, thus achieving an overall zero trim change. This system was completely automatic, the pilot having no overriding control. If the flaps and ailerons failed to keep in correct relationship, this was sensed, and all flap movement and aileron bias stopped. The aircraft was safe to fly and land with the flaps in any position, provided that the ailerons were biased to the correct degree. With zero bias, aileron movement range was from –18° to +16°30' but, with 15° upwards bias, this changed to –20° to +17°30' (all angles measured relative to the ailerons 'neutral' position).

Leading edge flaps in two sections were fitted on the centre and outer panels of each wing and were driven through torsion shafts by a single hydraulic actuator in the fuselage underside. An emergency air accumulator allowed one emergency extension. The inboard surfaces could be locked closed, only as a ground operation, to allow the aircraft to fly with only the outboard surfaces functioning. Large trailing edge 'Fowler' flaps were fitted to the inboard wing surfaces and had a total area of 27.44 sq ft. These extended aft so that their leading edge was level with the wing trailing edge before deflecting, in selectable stages, to a maximum angle of 50° for landing, an intermediate setting of 15° being used for take-off. Their screw-jacks were housed in prominent fairings on the upper surface of each wing, extending aft of the trailing edge.

A long pitot tube was fitted to the left wing just outboard of Rib 73.8. Within the pitot static system, a pressure switch activated a stall warning system as it sensed a decreasing airspeed of approximately 144 kts., illuminating a light adjacent to the airspeed indicator, together with one in the undercarriage position indicator if the undercarriage had not been lowered. The lights went out as speed increased past 160 kts.

The main undercarriage was housed in the inboard wing panel, retracting inwards, and was hinged just forward of the mainspar. It was fitted with a 26" diameter tyre with a pressure of 180 psi. The tailwheel assembly was fully castoring, self-centring and could be locked. It was fitted with twin wheels, whose tyre pressures were 140 psi., and retracted aft, with its bay faired by two doors when retracted. Compressed air allowed one emergency lowering of the undercarriage.

The tail unit was mounted further aft than on the Supermarine 510. The fin was built around two spars, attached to the fuselage at Frames 25 and 27.

To the rear spar was hinged the rudder, which had no trim tabs, trimming being by spring bias. The fin had a leading edge sweep of 46°, and a quarter-chord sweep of 35°. Maximum thickness was 35% chord and the section had a thickness/chord ratio of 12%. Gross fin area, including the fairing, was 49,1 sq.ft. The rudder area was 6.5 sq.ft, and it had a range of movement, in a plane normal to the hinge line, of ±36°. It could also be trimmed through a range of ±13°.

Hinge point for the slab tailplane was midway between the two spars, near the top of the fin. The fin/tailplane junction was faired by a massive 9'0" long bullet, heavily waisted in the middle and extending fore and aft of the fin leading and trailing edge, from the front of which protruded a long tube on which as mounted a yaw vane. The aft end of the bullet was detachable and housed an anti-spin parachute, which could also be used for extra braking action after touchdown. The tailplane was of symmetrical section and constructed around three mainspars at 20%, 45% and 68% chord; the

## DATA

**DIMENSIONS**

| | |
|---|---|
| Span | 40'0" |
| Length | 39'10" |
| Height (tail up) | 12'8" |
| Tailplane Span | 8'4.5" |
| Track | 12'1" |
| Wheelbase | 14'8" |

**AREAS**

| | |
|---|---|
| Wing (gross) | 285.726 sq ft |
| Wing (net) | 237.6 sq ft |
| Tailplane Gross | 28.27 sq ft |
| Tailplane Movable | 18.79 sq ft |
| Fin and Rudder | 49.07 sq ft |
| Rudder | 6.5 sq ft |
| Aileron | 15.53 sq ft |
| Flap | 27.44 sq ft |
| Rudder | 7.3 sq ft |
| Airbrake (approx) | 12.5 sq ft |

**LOADING**

| | |
|---|---|
| Wing Loading at 13,197 a u w | 46 lbs/sq ft |

**WEIGHTS**

| | |
|---|---|
| Zero Fuel Weight | 10,841 lbs |
| Fuel | 2,148 lbs |
| Pilot and Equipment | 208 lbs |
| All-Up Weight | 13,197 lbs |

**REFERENCES**

| | |
|---|---|
| Blackburn YB2 | —Type Record |
| Handley Page Association | —Archives |
| Handley Page Association | —Prototype and Servicing Notes |
| British Aerospace, Brough | —Archives |
| British Aerospace, Brough | —Photographic Archives |
| RAE Structures Dept. | —Report No. ACC.245 |

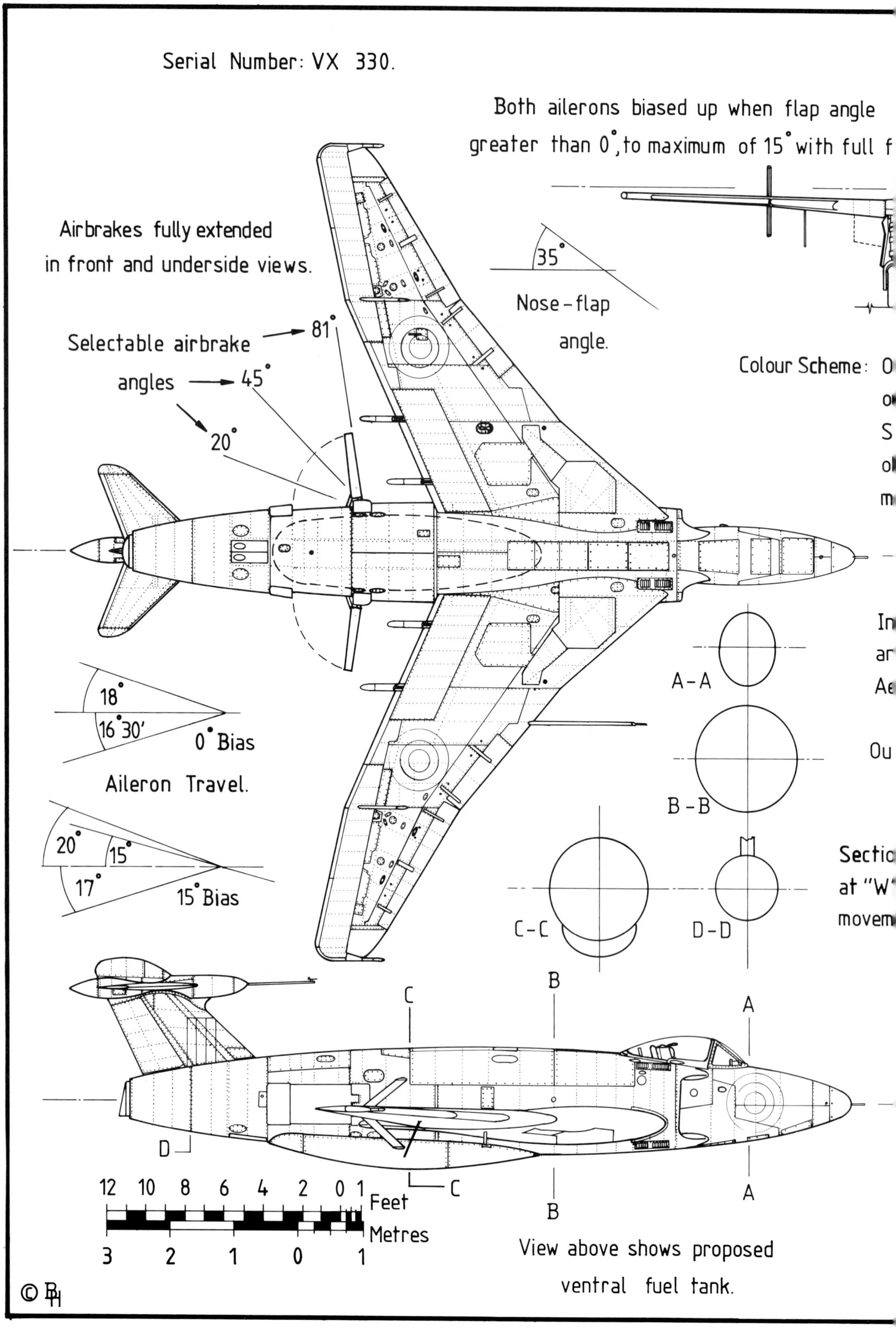

Serial Number: VX 330.

Both ailerons biased up when flap angle
greater than 0°, to maximum of 15° with full f

Airbrakes fully extended
in front and underside views.

35°

Nose-flap
angle.

Selectable airbrake
angles → 81°

angles → 45°

20°

Colour Scheme: O
o
S
o
m

18°
16°30'      0° Bias

Aileron Travel.

A-A

In
ar
Ae

20°  15°
17°      15° Bias

B-B

Ou

C-C          D-D

Sectio
at "W
movem

B

C

A

D          C

A

B

A

View above shows proposed
ventral fuel tank.

© BH

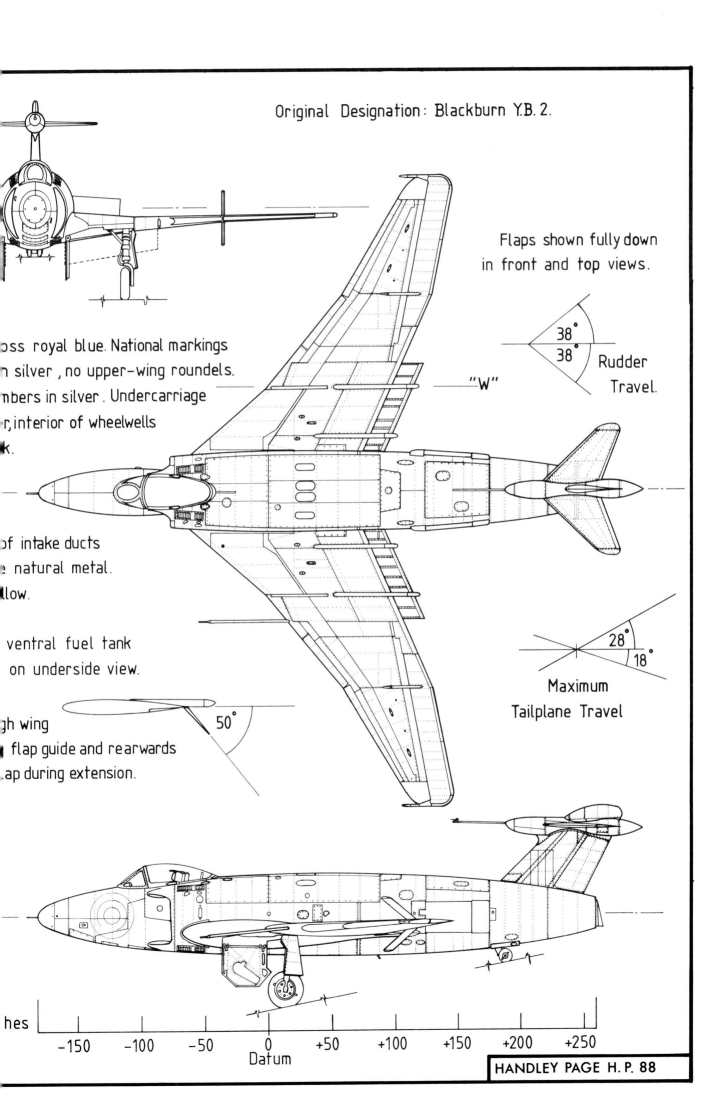

Original Designation: Blackburn Y.B. 2.

Flaps shown fully down
in front and top views.

38°
38°    Rudder
       Travel.

"W"

oss royal blue. National markings
n silver, no upper-wing roundels.
nbers in silver. Undercarriage
r, interior of wheelwells
k.

of intake ducts
natural metal.
low.

28°
18°

Maximum
Tailplane Travel

ventral fuel tank
on underside view.

gh wing
flap guide and rearwards
ap during extension.

50°

hes

-150    -100    -50    0    +50    +100    +150    +200    +250
                    Datum

HANDLEY PAGE H. P. 88

*Starboard side of the aircraft with the airbrakes fully deployed, flaps in the landing position and full aileron upwards bias. Note the leading edge flaps are locked up and the ejection seat is now in place. (via Philip Jarrett)*

thickness/chord ratio was 9% and root chord 4'2.25". Normal setting to the fin datum was +2°1.44'. It could be trimmed through a range of –16° to +8° and had a maximum range of movement of –28° to +18° relative to the aircraft datum. Artificial feel was effected by spring feel and a g-restrictor bob-weight in the control circuit. As with the ailerons, the powered flying controls units for the rudder and tailplane were remotely fitted, being located in the upper fuselage just forward of the fin leading edge root. From there, surface movement was via push/pull rods.

All control surfaces were power-operated by Boulton & Paul electro-hydraulic units, with no feedback in the circuits, and the flaps, nose-flaps, airbrakes and wheel-brakes were also hydraulically operated from the 2,500 psi. system. After initial flights, the power operation of the rudder was disconnected and direct rudder bar control substituted, as it was found that the powered response was insufficient to maintain adequate directional control during take-off and landing.

The surfaces of the wing, aileron, trailing and leading edge flaps on the starboard side, together with both sides of the tailplane, were extensively drilled for pressure plotting purposes.

The airbrakes were mounted on the outside of the existing skin, with fore and aft fairing bulges. Each panel was hinged at two points and they had a single operating jack. They were opened by means of compressed air, acting on one side of the jack piston, hydraulic pressure applied to the other side of the piston closing the airbrakes, and re-compressing the air. Four buttons in the cockpit controlled the angle of the brakes, allowing zero (closed), 20°, 45° and 81° (fully open) and, in emergency, could be fully opened and closed once controlled by a lever in the cockpit.

## POWER PLANT
Previous publications state that a Rolls-Royce Nene 3 turbojet was fitted, developing 5,100 Static Thrust at Sea Level. However, the official Type Record reports the fitting of one Rolls-Royce 2 R.N.2 Nene (No.259) centrifugual flow turbojet developing a Sea Level Static Thrust of 5,000 lbs.

## OUTLINE SPECIFICATION
i) Strength requirements for all cases based on maximum take-off weight with full fuel and equipment.
ii) Dive speed of Mach 0.95, but not to exceed 600 kts. E.A.S.
iii) Maximum normal acceleration 7.3g.

*Supermarine 541 showing the cockpit canopy changes and the repositioned boundary layer bleed slot ahead of the engine intake. (Crown Copyright)*

# SUPERMARINE TYPE 541

| | |
|---|---|
| **Manufacturer** | **Vickers Armstrong (Aircraft) Ltd Supermarine Division** |
| **Specification** | **Ministry of Supply Specification – F.105** |
| **Role** | **Fighter Prototype** |
| **First Flight Date** | **WJ 960 – 1st August 1951** |

As a contingency against the failure of the rival fighter design, the Hawker P.1067 Hunter, it was decided to develop a fully-equipped fighter version of the Type 535. As this latter aircraft was so very underpowered, the new aircraft was to be fitted with an Avon turbojet which would confer an increase of approximately 50% more thrust. To speed development, an interim prototype was constructed which was virtually identical to the Type 535 but re-engined with the Avon for trials purposes.

## DEVELOPMENT HISTORY

The benefits of the much increased power available from the Avon were immediately apparent, especially in take-off and climb performance. However, the high-speed end of the flight envelope could not be extended further for aerodynamic reasons, and the aircraft remained subsonic. The longer span ailerons, together with their spring tabs, were prone to flutter at high Mach numbers, thus limiting performance. In the event, geared tabs were not fitted until the production prototype Type 541, WJ 965 when, at last, the Swift went supersonic in a dive.

The early Avon engines were prone to their own problems. The aircraft suffered an engine failure on 3rd August 1951 only three days after its first flight, and also, following another engine failure, the aircraft crashed on 8th September 1951 during an approach to land. Luckily, the pilot escaped, with repairable damage being caused to the aircraft's tail section, which enabled it to re-commence trials some three months later. The aircraft suffered more engine damage on 8th April 1952.

The aircraft was returned to the manufacturers on 14th August 1953 for the installation of a variable incidence tailplane and geared aileron tabs. There is no record that the tabs were fitted, but the tailplane was, having a travel of –9° to +4°, and the first flight with it installed was in February 1954. Early in 1955, a brake unit was fitted to the nosewheel, and trials were carried out during April 1955. During 1956 the aircraft moved to RAE Bedford for Arrester Barrier trials.

After suffering a final accident, WJ960 was finally struck off charge on 15th September 1959 and sold for scrap. During its relatively short flying career, the aircraft was fitted with no less than seven different Avon engines.

*Supermarine 541 three-quarters rear view shows the changes to the aft fuselage compared to the Type 535. (Crown Copyright)*

# CONSTRUCTION

The basic construction and external appearance of the Type 541 was virtually identical to the Type 535, except for minor modifications to the wing and fuselage. These changes were as follows:-

1.   The nosecone now carried a pitot boom, at various times either a standard boom or a stream-lined fairing. The horizon-datum bead above the nose was deleted.

2.   The canopy main transparencies were slightly altered in shape, by moving the narrow frame just aft of mid-point about 6" further aft. A Martin-Baker Mk.2G ejection seat was fitted.

3.   The large engine-bay access doors along the top of the mid-fuselage were completely re-designed, and lengthened by 4'0" to allow the removal/installation of the longer axial-flow engine. The four auxiliary intake doors were removed and two smaller intake louvres were substituted. Four large rectangular louvres were fitted under the fuselage in line with the wing-root fairing.

4.   The tailcone was lengthened slightly and faired to enclose fully the tailpipe.

5.   The tailwheels regained their fairing doors although, later in the programme, the tailwheel assembly, together with these doors, was deleted completely.

6.   The fin regained its pitot head and retained the dorsal fairing developed on the 535.

7.   The wingtips were modified to give a more streamwise flow, increasing the wingspan by approximately 8"; however, the overall wing area was little changed. The sweepback at quarter-chord was 40° on all flying surfaces. There were no pitot heads fitted to the wings. Although externally identical, the flaps were modified to make their operation as airbrakes simpler.

8.   The ailerons were extended inboard slightly, as

## DATA

**DIMENSIONS**

| | |
|---|---|
| Span | 32'4" |
| Length | 41'6.5" |
| Height | 12'7.5" |
| Wheelbase | 15'2" |
| Track | 14'2.5" |
| Wing | |
|    Incidence | 2.5° |
|    Dihedral | 2° |
| Tailplane | |
|    Span | 12'7.2" |
|    Dihedral | 10° |

**AREAS**

| | |
|---|---|
| Wing (gross) | 297.4 sq ft |
| Tailplane | 61.1 sq ft |
| Aileron | 34.5 sq ft |
| Flap | 35.4 sq ft |
| Elevator | 15.6 sq ft |
| Fin and Rudder | 40.5 sq ft |

**WEIGHTS**
Unknown

**REFERENCES**

| | |
|---|---|
| Boscombe Down | —Science Library |
| | —Archives |
| Public Records Office | —Avia files |
| RAE Farnborough | —Library |

*The new streamwise wing tips compared to the more square-cut versions on the Type 535 are clearly illustrated. Just discernible is the slight leading edge kink where the wing root chord has been increased by extending the leading edge forwards. Note also the later version of the noseprobe compared to the earlier photographs.*

the provision for wing-mounted guns was not required, the proposed armament bay having been moved to the fuselage under the intakes. Spring/trim tabs extended virtually the whole length of the aileron trailing edges.

The primary internal modifications were confined to those required to accommodate the new engine. Being much less bulky than the earlier centrifugal flow Nene, there was sufficient space available to alter the fuel system, which was modified to ensure supply after combat damage, and the capacity was also increased by 25% over the Type 535 to a total of 750 galls. The hydraulic services were fed from a 3,000 psi. system.

## POWER PLANT
One Rolls-Royce Avon R.A.7. axial-flow turbojet developing a Sea Level Static Thrust of 7,500 lbs. No afterburner was fitted.

*This head-on view emphasizes the thick wing section of this aircraft, especially at the root. It would also appear that the boundary layer outlet louvres on the right intake are raised, while those on the left are still flush. (Crown Copyright)*

Colour Scheme : Natural metal overall. Serial numbers gloss black,
under wings and on rear fuselage below tailplane.
National markings above and below wings, on rear
fuselage, and on fin.

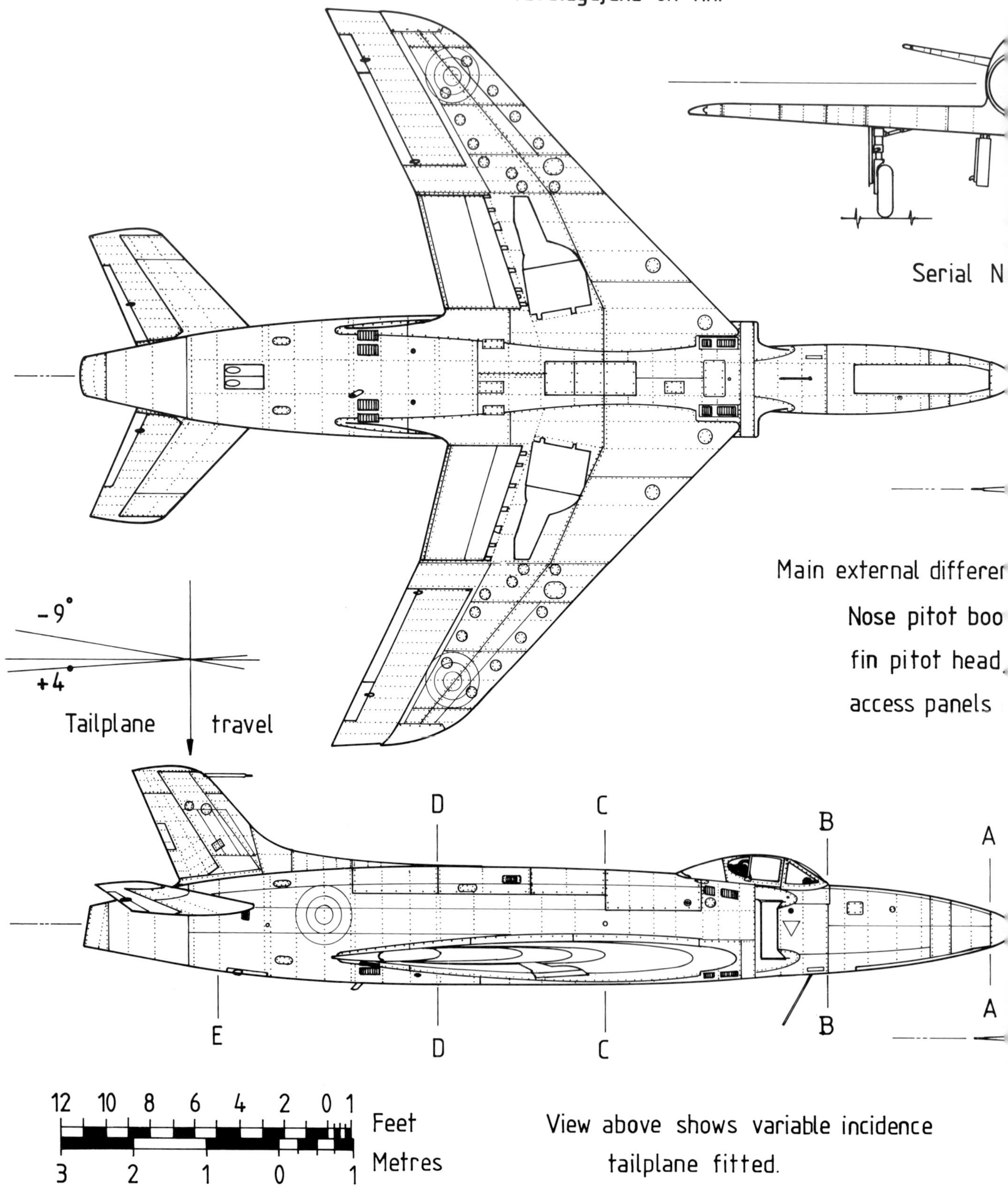

Serial N

Main external differer

Nose pitot boo

fin pitot head,

access panels

−9°

+4°

Tailplane    travel

D          C          B          A

E

D          C          B          A

12  10  8  6  4  2  0 1    Feet

3    2    1    0    1    Metres

View above shows variable incidence
tailplane fitted.

BH

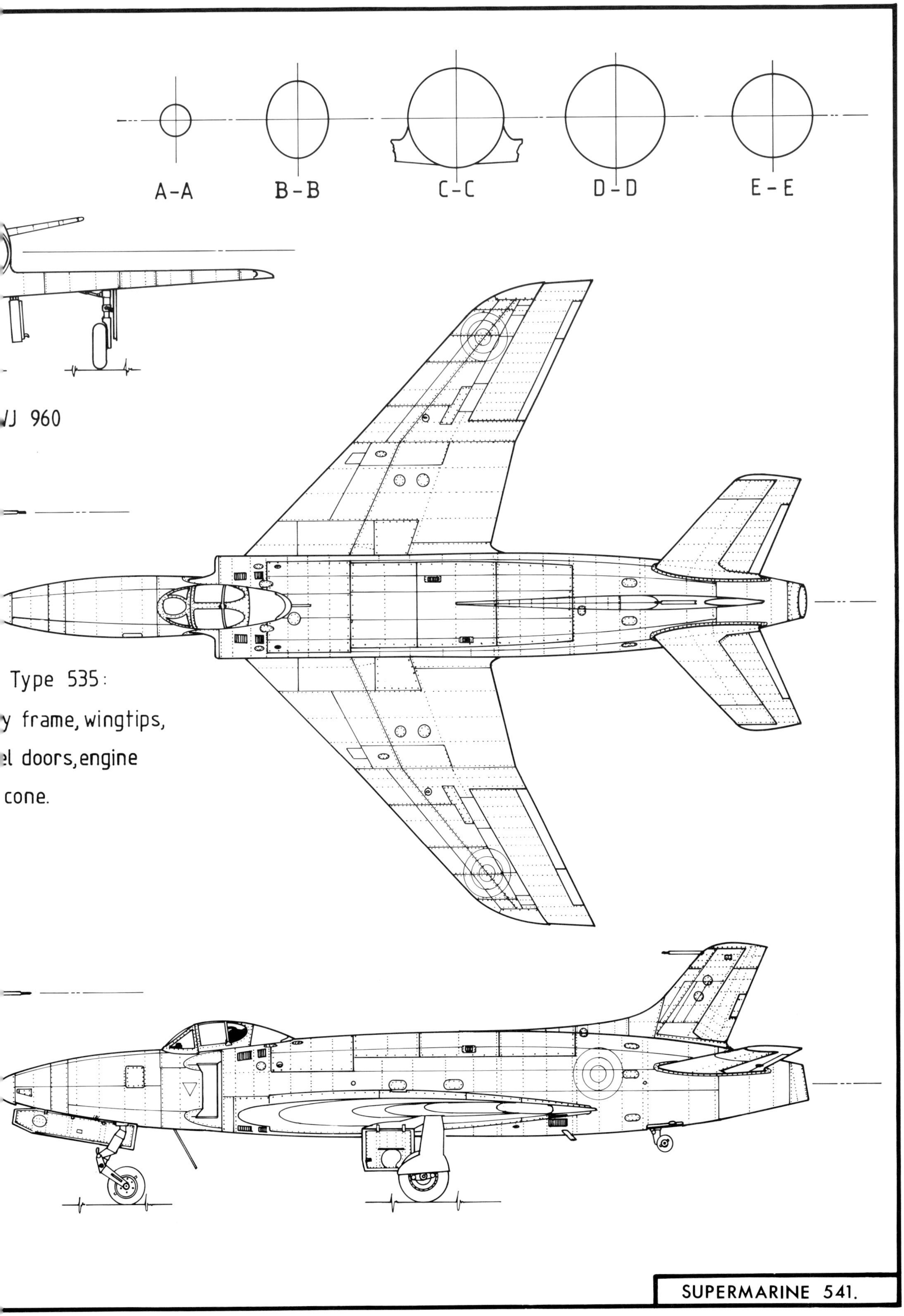

A-A    B-B    C-C    D-D    E-E

J 960

Type 535:

y frame, wingtips,

l doors, engine

cone.

SUPERMARINE 541.

*Short S.A.4 Sperrin showing the topside details and the inboard fillets at the leading edge/engine nacelle junction. Interestingly it appears that the pitot head has been removed from the right wingtip, the boom on the left being a yaw vane mount. (Shorts)*

# SHORT S.A.4. 'SPERRIN'

| | |
|---|---|
| Manufacturer | Short Brothers and Harland |
| Specification | B.14/46 |
| Role | Interim Bomber Prototype |
| First Flight Date | VX 158 – 10th August 1951 |
| | VX 161 – 12th August 1952 |

The Royal Air Force required a jet-powered replacement for its latest heavy, piston-engined bomber, the Lincoln, and tenders were requested from various firms, including the three main 'bomber' firms Avro, Vickers and Handley Page. Types were ordered from all three, which eventually materialised as the 'V-bombers', the Vulcan, Valiant and Victor. However, as these were to be a quantum leap in capability and the state of the art, it was felt prudent to order another type as a low risk 'insurance' in case the planned higher performance 'definitive' designs failed to come up to expectation. Thus, a Specification was raised in 1946 and the contract awarded to Shorts for manufacture of the aircraft. The ensuing aircraft more than fulfilled the official requirement.

## DEVELOPMENT HISTORY

Although formulated in 1946, and given the number B.14/46, the Specification was not actually issued until 6th October 1948. However, preliminary design work had started in 1947 and was allocated the firm's designation S.A.4. At this time, the firm was based at Rochester, Kent but, for political reasons, they were forced to move to Belfast, Northern Ireland. First went the production staff, followed later in the year by the technical and design offices, thus considerably delaying completion of the prototypes. Three were being constructed – two for flight trials and the third for structural testing. Although a conventional 'low-risk' design, it was to be the first four-jet British bomber to fly, with many aerodynamic unknowns. The aircraft was larger, and had almost twice the performance of anything that they had built before. There was inevitably a cautious approach to the many problems and, to assist in its development, items were tested on other aircraft, including the basic fin shape which was flight tested on a Sunderland flying-boat.

Even before the aircraft's first flight, the decision had already been taken that the type would not be put into production, but was nevertheless urgently required for experimental work concerned with new weapons and for trials of radar bombing equipment intended for the V-bombers.

Construction of the first prototype was completed in early 1951, but then the airframe had to be dismantled and transported by road to RAF Aldergrove, as the runway at Sydenham was at that time too short. Later in the aircraft's life, after work on extending the runway, trials were conducted from Short's 'home-base'. After re-erection, systems test and taxi trials, the first flight of VX 158 was successfully made on 10th August 1951.

The aircraft required few changes after this flight, the main one being that the elevator tab gearing needed altering to reduce sensitivity. During later flight trials, various other problems were solved including the elimination of undercarriage door vibration, the dive recovery flaps being locked shut as they caused severe buffet when deployed above 0.75 Mach. Local buffeting around the engine nacelles was cured by adding drooped triangular leading edge fillets and small boat-tail fairings between the jetpipe exit shrouds. There were also problems with the flying-control screw-jacks freezing at altitude and low ambient temperatures, plus airflow to the fuel tank pressurisation system had to be increased to prevent collapsing during rapid descents.

Heavy buffet with bomb bay doors open was experienced above 200 kts. and was cured by the addition of a row of retractable 'gills' about 1'0" ahead of bomb bay, opening to 60°. After these modifications, the maximum speed achieved with bomb doors open was 375 kts. IAS., with a recommended maximum of 340 kts.

The engines' extensive wetted area caused a loss in performance, but this was more than compensated for by the weight saved using an uncomplicated wing structure, engine servicing was easy, and propulsive efficiency high.

Results from tests on the static test airframe proved the basic design, with the wing failing at 104% of the ultimate load and the fuselage at 108%. The pressure cabin was tested to nearly three times the proposed differential before distortion of the escape hatch aperture.

Originally, it had been planned to have the forward end of the fuselage jettisoned in an emergency as an escape capsule for the crew, with large parachutes being deployed from the aft end, but wind tunnel trials had shown this was extremely unstable in descent. It could be made more stable by moving the capsule's centre of gravity further forward, but this entailed a marked aircraft and system redesign which incurred a weight penalty of over 1,000 lbs., and thus militated against its adoption. The crew of five included two pilots, a bomb-aimer, navigator and signaller seated in what was to become the 'standard' V-bomber layout,

with the last three sitting in a row facing aft in the cockpit. Maximum speed for crew safe escape was 330 kts. EAS.

The second prototype, VX 161, was completed and flew for the first time just over one year after the first, on 12th August 1952. It was virtually identical to the first, apart from the use of uprated Avon engines and a redesigned rudder leading edge seal.

The two prototypes followed very different careers. The first prototype completed its manufacturer's trials by May 1953 and went to RAE Farnborough for radar navigation and bombing trials. It had an operational radar system, but an inactive bomb bay, marker flares being dropped through a small door in one of the main bomb doors. It was then kept in storage at Belfast from 23rd December 1953. During 1954, the S.A.4 received the name 'Sperrin', the name deriving from a range of hills in Northern Ireland.

The unusual engine layout made the basic airframe ideally suited for the task of being a test bed for different engines. It embarked on this new career when fitted with one of the new de Havilland supersonic engines, the Gyron, in its lower left nacelle. Little redesign was necessary to accommodate the engine, other than a larger, re-contoured, lower nacelle and slight strengthening of the wing structure. The first flight in this configuration was made on 7th July 1955, and the aircraft was subsequently flown to Hatfield on 29th July for continuation of the trials. On successful completion of this phase a second Gyron was fitted in a similarly redesigned lower nacelle on the right wing and the first flight with two Gyrons was on 26th June 1956. During this flight, the left outer undercarriage door was lost. It was not felt to be economical to manufacture a replacement, so the second prototype was flown to Belfast and cannibalised for the spare, and it never flew again. Such was the increase in thrust available compared to that from the earlier engines that, with only one Gyron operating at its 20,000 lbs. rating, there was almost as much thrust available as with all four of the original Avons at full power!

On completing the basic Gyron trials and, as that engine was not adopted for any airframe application (it was intended to be used to power the Hawker P.1121 private venture multi-role aircraft, but that had itself also been cancelled), further research was carried out starting on 20th November 1957, into measuring the infra-red radiation from the Gyron engine. The aircraft was sold to the de Havilland engine company on 21st September 1959 and subsequently scrapped.

After completion of its manufacturer's trials, VX 161 went to Woodbridge on 11th April 1953 for weapons trials concerned mainly with the loading, release and aiming concrete dummy aerodynamic shapes of 'new weapons'. The bomb bay was designed to accommodate the first British nuclear weapons, but these were actually slightly smaller than the original 30′. After a period of storage at Farnborough, flight trials recommenced on 28th September 1955, when the cockpit roof escape hatch came off in flight, but this was recovered successfully. As described previously, it was later flown to Belfast to be cannibalised to replace the undercarriage fairing door on VX 158 and never flew again. It was finally struck off charge and sold for scrap on 2nd June 1958.

# CONSTRUCTION

The structure was of conventional, light alloy, stressed skin throughout, with few innovations except for the use of a new alloy, the use of hot dimpling for cutting holes in the skin and a company-developed method of milling rivet-heads to ensure the smoothest exterior finish. The complete fuselage was built as one unit, with transport joints between the nose, centre and tail sections.

The slab-sided centre-section was of constant cross-section throughout virtually its whole 50′9″ length, with fuselage frames at 20″ intervals, and had four massive transverse beams, at the ends of which were the wing attachment points. The upper structure, in line with the wing leading and trailing edges, was occupied by the fuselage fuel tanks. The lower structure was occupied by the 30′3″ long bomb bay, enclosed by two full-length doors, hydraulically operated via jacks at each end. The space between the forward end of the doors and the forward bulkhead was occupied by the crew entry and escape hatch, hinged at its forward end to act as a wind-break for escape at high speeds. Aft of the bomb doors was the camera bay, again faired by two small doors, which were inter-linked to open and close with the bomb doors. The rearmost access panel allowed access to the aft of the centre section, and via a ladder to the walkway between the rear group of fuselage fuel tanks.

The main equipment bay was at the forward end of the centre-section and contained the oxygen bottles, dinghy and electrical inverters, the electrical accumulators being stowed aft of the bomb bay. The dinghy external release was on top of the fuselage, causing it to deploy through a hatch just forward and above the left wing root leading edge.

The aft fuselage was of similar construction to the centre-section, with two reinforced frames for attachment of the fin spars. The air from the bomb bay was free-flowing through the aft fuselage, and exhausted through four louvres just below the right tailplane trailing edge. The tailcone formed the stowage for a braking parachute assembly, consisting of an auxiliary, a retarder and two main parachutes. The parachutes were streamed electrically, the end of the tailcone hinging downwards to allow their deployment. When the aircraft had slowed sufficiently, the parachutes were jettisoned.

The tailplane and fin were both constructed around two spars and multiple ribs, and the spars of both surfaces shared reinforced fuselage frames for attachment points. The elevators and rudder were hinged to the aft spar of their respective surfaces, and were mass, and Irving, balanced.

The fixed tailplane, set high on the fuselage, was of RAE 103 symmetrical section, having a thickness/chord ratio of 10.6%, aspect ratio of 4.28:1, and possessed a dihedral angle of 13°. The chord tapered from 12′8.5″ at the centreline to 5′0″ at the rounded tips.

The S.A.4 was the first aircraft to fly with no direct connection between the flying control surfaces and the pilot. Movement of his cockpit controls, via cable-driven screw jacks, moved the full-span aerodynamic servo-tabs which, in turn, caused the main surfaces to deflect. Artificial feel was provided on all three axes, by springs for the rudder and ailerons, and additionally a 'g-restrictor' in the elevator circuit, designed to cut in between +1.7 and 1.8g. An autopilot was designed but never fitted.

Elevator movement range was between −22°15′ and +9°25′ for the left elevator and −23°45′ and +8°35′ for the right, there being no direct connection between the two and, that for the servo tabs movement range was between −3°30′ and +8°30′.

The fin also had a symmetrical RAE 103 section with the same 10.6% thickness/chord ratio. The rudder servo tab movement was ±16°, producing a rudder movement range of −14°30′ and +14°.

The forward 24′4″ of the fuselage comprised the crew compartment and radar installation. Thought was given early on to having the whole nose-section jettisonable as a capsule for emergency escape of the whole crew. Due to instability during trials, and the weight penalty incurred, as well as the complication, this was abandoned. Only the First Pilot had an ejection seat, a Martin-Baker Mk.1D, adjustable for height only, and mounted to enable it to be hinged slightly inwards and backwards, by means of an hydraulic jack and spring-loaded cable, before allowing ejection through a 50″×32″ escape hatch in the left side of the cabin roof. The remaining crew members, the co-pilot who sat to his right, and the three aft-facing navigator/radar operators, all had to exit via the entrance door in the bottom of the fuselage. This had a power operated hatch to act as a windshield and was used for normal crew entry and exit. Access to the cockpit was via a sloping tunnel and through a pressure-door below the aft crew members' console and table, the centre seat hinging to allow access. When armed, the centre seat was also connected to jettison the pressure door and open the entry hatch for more rapid evacuation.

The main windscreen had ten window panels, with one on the left side being openable for use as a direct vision panel. The rear crew had only a small circular porthole on each side for limited lateral vision.

When first flown, neither prototype had a visual

bomb-aiming position, both having a plain hemispherical metal nosecone. Later in its life, VX 158 had a more streamlined cone fitted, which added some 15" to the aircraft's overall length, incorporating three windows in its lower side for the bomb-aimer, the centre one being optically flat. To get to his position, he had a sloping cylindrical tunnel extending into the extreme nose from under the centre of the pilots' main instrument panel. Access was made easier by a powered ramp running on rollers.

The entire cabin was pressurised by two Godfrey superchargers, fitted one on each accessory gearbox in the leading edge of the wing. This allowed a differential pressure of 8.5 psi., (8,000 ft. cabin altitude at 40,000 ft. true) for normal use, and 3.5 psi. for combat. The pressure was regulated through a discharge valve in the rear cockpit bulkhead, and

passed through the bomb bay for heating and ventilation, and eventually overboard at the aircraft's tail.

The steerable nosewheel oleo retracted aft to lie in its bay below the cabin and immediately in front of the crew entry hatch. The oleo was free to castor until a clutch was engaged to allow steering via the normal aileron handwheel on the pilot's column. (Originally the steering was via rudder pedal operation but this was abandoned in favour of the later system.) The twin wheels were fitted with 30" diameter tyres at 98 psi. pressure.

The rest of the nose section underside forward of the nosewheel bay was taken up with the large unpressurised radome, although this was actually fitted to only one of the aircraft, the other being faired over by a light alloy skin. The radar was a development of the earlier wartime H2S. A

## DATA

### DIMENSIONS

| | |
|---|---|
| Span | 109'1.25" |
| Length | 102'2.6" (103'6" with modified nosecone) |
| Height | 28'6.2" (static) |
| Tailplane span | 42'0" |
| Distance between nacelles | 40'6" |
| Track | 32'2" |
| Wheelbase | 30'3.7" |

### AREAS (VX 161)

| | |
|---|---|
| Wing (gross) | 1,896.77 sq ft |
| Wing (net) | 1,675.72 sq ft |
| Tailplane (gross) | 364.02 sq ft |
| Tailplane (net) | 304.37 sq ft |
| Fin and Rudder (net) | 159.0 sq ft (excluding dorsal fairing) |
| Flaps (inboard) | 146.0 sq ft |
| Flaps (outboard) | 85.0 sq ft |

### WEIGHTS

| | |
|---|---|
| Empty | 72,000 lbs |
| Loaded | 115,000 lbs |
| Landing | 81,310 lbs |

### PERFORMANCE

Climb Speed (between 100,000 and 115,000 lbs, weight): 260 kts/0.65 Mach

| | |
|---|---|
| Ceiling | 42,000 ft |
| Maximum Speed | 564 mph |
| Range | 3,860 miles |
| $V_{dive}$ | 390 kts |
| Design Mach: | 0.85M |

(This was limited to 0.78M (indicated) due to aileron flutter. This was eventually raised to 0.81M on VX 161, defined by sudden and severe airframe buffet. A 6'0" strip on the rudder trailing edge also eliminated a divergent directional oscillation at 0.75M.)

### VX 158 (Avon R.A.2)

**Take-off**

| Weight | Distance |
|---|---|
| 85,000 lbs | 2,190 ft |
| 95,000 lbs | 2,700 ft |
| 100,000 lbs | 2,790 ft |
| 105,000 lbs | 2,970 ft |
| 115,000 lbs | 3,120 ft |

**Level Speed (at 95,000 lbs)**

| Height | True Airspeed |
|---|---|
| Sea Level | 494 kts |
| 10,000 ft | 496 kts |
| 20,000 ft | 486 kts |
| 30,000 ft | 468 kts |
| 40,000 ft | 443 kts |

### VX 161 (Avon R.A.3)

**Rate of Climb**

| Height | 115,000 lbs auw | 100,000 lbs auw |
|---|---|---|
| Sea Level | 3,100 ft/min | 3,500 ft/min |
| 10,000 ft | 2,600 ft/min | 3,150 ft/min |
| 20,000 ft | 1,700 ft/min | 2,100 ft/min |
| 30,000 ft | 750 ft/min | 1,150 ft/min |
| 40,000 ft | — | 250 ft/min |

**TIME TO ALTITUDE**

| Height | 115,000 lbs auw | 100,000 lbs auw |
|---|---|---|
| 10,000 ft | 3 mins | 2 mins |
| 20,000 ft | 8 mins | 6 mins |
| 30,000 ft | 17 mins | 13 mins |
| 35,000 ft | 27 mins | 18 mins |
| 40,000 ft | — | 32 mins 30 secs |

### REFERENCES

| | |
|---|---|
| Public Records Office | —Avia Files |
| RAE Farnborough | —Library |
| Short Brothers | —Archives |
| 'Flight' | —17th December 1954 |
| | —21st January 1955 |
| 'Aeroplane' | —18th February 1955 |

requirement for a further radar scanner to be mounted under the rear fuselage was cancelled early on in the design state.

The wing was shoulder-mounted, with no fillets fairing it at 90° to the fuselage. It had a symmetrical RAE 103 section, with a thickness/chord ratio of 12% and aspect ratio of 6.18:1. It was set at an incidence of 4°30' to the fuselage datum and had a dihedral of 1°. The wing tapered from a root chord of 26'0" to tip chord of 7'6", giving a leading edge sweep of 18°15', and was built around a torsion-box mainspar and aft auxiliary spar. It was attached to the four heavy transverse booms in the fuselage centre-section. To increase the critical Mach number of the wing, large fillets were attached to the leading edge either side of the engine nacelles at a negative incidence of 5° to the wing chord-line.

The section inboard of the engine nacelles, which were set 40'6" apart, was of massive structure and housed the main undercarriage bays. The mainwheel oleos were originally to have one extremely large wheel each, but were in the event fitted with four-wheel trucks which retracted inwards to lie within the wing. The wheels were fitted with 35" diameter tyres inflated to a pressure of 105 psi. The wheels were originally fitted with ordinary brakes but, later, Maxaret units were fitted to reduce tyre wear. A hydraulic accumulator allowed six full applications of brake in the event of main system failure. Fuel tanks whose capacity totalled 557 gallons were fitted in front and behind the forward mainspar in each wing inboard of the engines. Dive recovery flaps were fitted forward of the mainwheel bays but were never used. A pair of large landing lights were fitted underwing on the left side aft of the mainwheel bays, plus a further single taxi-ing light almost at the wingtip on each side, all retractable when not in use.

The engine pods were mounted parallel to the wing chord and were originally designed around the R.A.3 Avon, but were redesigned to accommodate the R.A.2 version as the earlier engines were not available at the time. The engines were mounted one above and one below the wing structure which was continuous from root to tip. They were mounted in a tubular structure attached at four points to fittings at the front mainspar. For fire-protection the nacelle was divided by horizontal and vertical firewalls. The lower engine's jetpipe was parallel to the fuselage datum, but that of the upper one had a substantial downthrust. Although producing more drag than a buried installation, this was more than compensated for by easier access for servicing and simpler design. In the event, this proved to be a bonus when the aircraft took on its new role as an engine test-bed, modification required to take the much larger Gyron being minimal.

Each outer wing panel accommodated fuel tanks totalling 1053 gallons between the two spars and had pitot heads fitted at each tip. The static ports were mounted on the fuselage.

The entire trailing edge aft of the rear spar and inboard of the engine nacelles was taken up by a single rectangular plain flap. Another flap panel was mounted on each side just outboard of the nacelle, incorporating an airbrake over most of its trailing edge. This was originally to be a single surface hinged centrally so that the area above the wing, when deployed, balanced that below. This was changed to two separate 'split' surfaces hinged at their leading edge to open above and below the wing. The flaps could be selected to four positions – 0°, 7°, 25° and 40°. The 7° position was an altitude manoeuvring position and could be attained by the use of a switch on the control column wheel, the 25° and 40° by use of a spring-loaded lever on a side console in the cockpit. The airbrakes could only be extended with flaps up or in the 7° position, producing a slight nose-up trim change.

The remainder of the wing trailing edges outboard of the flaps was occupied by the ailerons, with their full span servo tabs which had a movement range of ±11°. This produced a movement of –15° and +15°50' on the left aileron and –15°30' and +15°10' on the right.

## FUEL SYSTEM

A total of 6,170 gallons was carried in fourteen tanks in the wings and eight in the fuselage above the bomb bay in line with the root leading and trailing edges of the wing. An automatic system for the control of the fuel system was provided to keep the aircraft's centre of gravity within limits, with an emergency manual back-up. The fuel in the fuselage tanks had to be used first to relieve wing bending loads, and wing fuel could not be used with more than 100 gallons in each fuselage tank. The tanks were pressurised by ram air through scoops mounted on the fuselage and engine nacelle sides, fitted over the vent lines. Pressure refuelling points were provided on each side of the lower fuselage just aft of the bomb doors. In an emergency, the tanks could be gravity filled from panels in the upper fuselage.

## ELECTRICAL SYSTEM

This was basically 24 volt DC, driven from four 6kw generators, one on each engine, with a maximum rating 200 amps. Alternating current from the inverters fed instrumentation and the radar.

## HYDRAULIC SYSTEM

The hydraulic system had a working pressure of 4,000 psi driven from two pumps on each of the accessory gearboxes, and served the undercarriage, wheel brakes, nosewheel steering, flaps, airbrakes, bomb and camera doors. An emergency electrical back-up system allowed the lowering of the undercarriage, the flaps, and opening and closing of the bomb bay doors. There were accumulators for emergency operation of wheel-brakes and airbrakes.

## ARMAMENT

No defensive armament was fitted, reliance being made on the aircraft's speed and altitude performance.

A maximum load of 20,000 lbs. could be carried in the internal bomb bay comprising either conventional or nuclear weapons. The size of the bay, 30'×10'×10', was determined by the size of the nuclear weapons then in existence. Loading of the weapons was originally intended to be via built-in winches attached to the roof of the bomb bay, but this was subsequently changed to the use of a crane with access through panels in the upper fuselage top skin. Vinten K and F.52 strike cameras were carried in a bay aft of the bomb bay whose doors were hydraulically linked to open with the bomb doors. Their bay was heated by air tapped from the bomb bay, which itself was heated by air tapped from the engine 7th stage compressor.

## POWER PLANT

*First Prototype VX 158*
Four Rolls-Royce Avon R.A.2 axial flow turbojets developing a Sea Level Static Thrust of 6,000 lbs.

Later fitted with three Avon R.A.2. turbojets, plus one de Havilland D.Gy.1 Gyron axial flow turbojet developing a Sea Level Static Thrust of 15,000 lbs. in lower left nacelle. Final configuration was two Avons in the upper nacelles and two Gyrons in the lower. The Gyron, in its D.Gy.2 version, had an increased Static Thrust rating of 20,000 lbs.
*Second Prototype, VX 161*
Four Rolls-Royce Avon R.A.3. axial flow turbojets developing a Sea Level Static Thrust of 6,500 lbs.

## OUTLINE SPECIFICATION

1  Range 3,350 miles with a 10,000 lbs. bomb load.
2  Ceiling over target to be 45,000 ft.
3  Maximum bomb load 20,000 lbs., to be accommodated internally, either nuclear or conventional bombs.
4  Crew of 5.
5  No defensive armament, navigation and bomb-aiming to be by an advanced version of H2S radar, with a visual station in the nose.
6  To be capable of rapid quantity production, easy maintenance and avoid unproven techniques and materials.

*Short S.A.4 Sperrin showing underside detail to advantage. Note hot air exhausts in the tailcone with the prominent ventilation scoops above the bomb bay. (Shorts)*

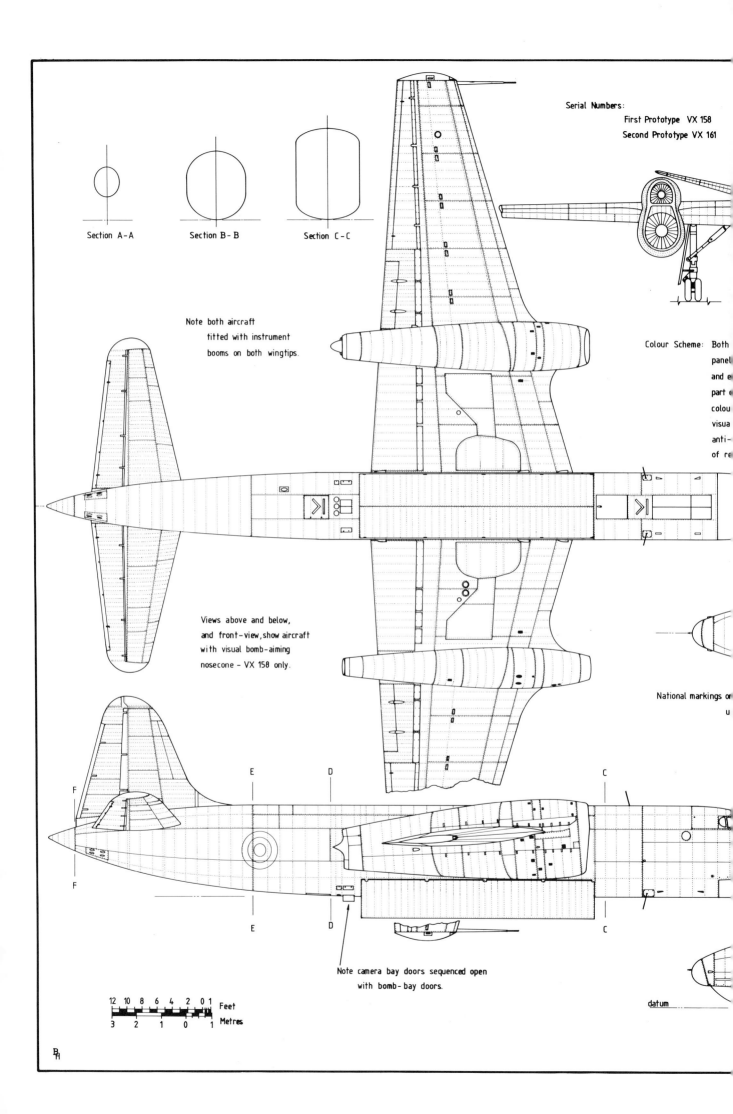

Section A–A  Section B–B  Section C–C

Serial Numbers:

First Prototype  VX 158
Second Prototype VX 161

Note both aircraft
fitted with instrument
booms on both wingtips.

Colour Scheme: Both
panel
and e
part
colou
visua
anti-
of re

Views above and below,
and front–view, show aircraft
with visual bomb–aiming
nosecone – VX 158 only.

National markings or
u

F

E       D                                      C

F

E       D                                      C

Note camera bay doors sequenced open
with bomb–bay doors.

datum

12 10 8 6 4 2 0 1  Feet
3    2    1    0    1  Metres

B
H

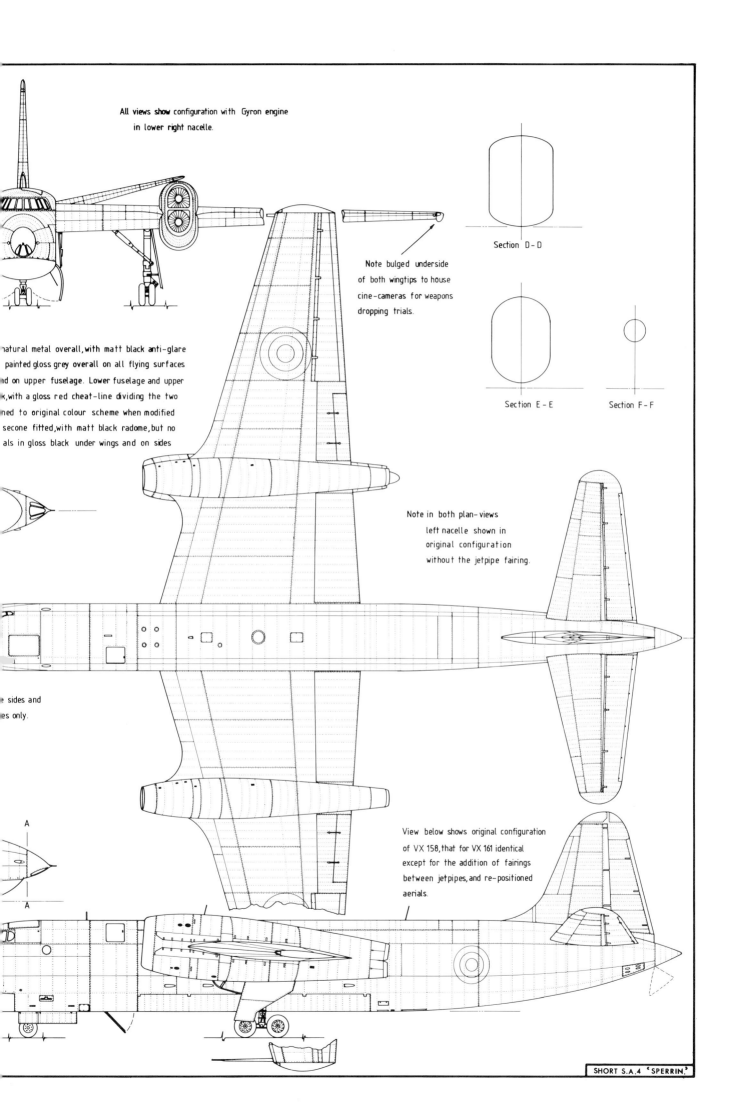

All views show configuration with Gyron engine
in lower right nacelle.

Section D–D

Note bulged underside
of both wingtips to house
cine-cameras for weapons
dropping trials.

Section E–E

Section F–F

natural metal overall,with matt black anti-glare
painted gloss grey overall on all flying surfaces
nd on upper fuselage. Lower fuselage and upper
k,with a gloss red cheat-line dividing the two
ned to original colour scheme when modified
secone fitted,with matt black radome, but no
als in gloss black under wings and on sides

Note in both plan-views
left nacelle shown in
original configuration
without the jetpipe fairing.

sides and
es only.

View below shows original configuration
of VX 158,that for VX 161 identical
except for the addition of fairings
between jetpipes, and re-positioned
aerials.

A

A

SHORT S.A.4 'SPERRIN.'

# SUPERMARINE TYPE 508/529

*Supermarine 508 banking low over Chilbolton showing topside detail to advantage with the multitude of engine bay cooling vent panels. Note also the positive position of the tail cone trimmer for high speed flight.*

| Manufacturer | Vickers Armstrong (Aircraft) Ltd., Supermarine Division |
|---|---|
| Specification | N.9/47 |
| Role | Experimental Fighter Prototype |
| First Flight Date | VX 133 – 31st August 1951 |
| | VX 136 – 29th August 1952 |

Initially designed to use the new technique of landing on its belly on a flexible deck, the Type 508 family developed before flight into a relatively conventional airframe. It was then the most powerful and heaviest aircraft ever designed for the Royal Navy. However, its straight-wing design limited its performance, especially at high subsonic speed, and further development and production were not continued.

## DEVELOPMENT HISTORY

After the end of the War, one avenue of research followed briefly by the Navy was the use of a flexible deck for an aircraft carrier, which would eliminate the need for an aircraft to have an undercarriage except for a very lightweight type solely for ground manoeuvring. This would have saved considerable weight and system complexity. Brief trials were made at Farnborough using a Sea

Vampire but these only served to show the basic impracticability of the whole scheme. However, a requirement was raised for a twin-jet interceptor to use this method of operation and the Supermarine Type 508 was initially designed to have no undercarriage at all and, to keep it well clear of the deck, the tail was of unusual 'butterfly' design. Early in the design stage, the new Specification to N.9/47 was raised, and the aircraft's wing was increased in thickness to enable it to accommodate a long-stroke main undercarriage capable of absorbing a deck landing.

Three prototypes were ordered under the contract awarded to Supermarine, the 1st and 3rd aircraft to be fully instrumented and the 2nd to be fitted to operational standard with radar-ranging for armament trials with the new 30 mm Aden cannon. Other operational equipment also specified included the fitting of two vertical and one oblique cameras in the nosecone for reconnaissance. A normal gun-sight recording camera was fitted in a streamline fairing under the nose. One of the two wingtip-mounted pitot heads was to be replaced by a sideslip/incidence vane for handling trials, but both pitots were to be used during performance trials. Other instrumentation included an automatic observer fitted aft of Frame 32.

It was decided to fit the third prototype with

swept wing and tail surfaces, and this was re-designated the Type 525. A de-navalised version was offered to meet Specification F.43/46 for the RAF, with a reduced span and length, two cannon, and wingtip-mounted fuel tanks, but this tender was not accepted.

On completion of construction of the first prototype, serialed VX 133, and transportation by road to Boscombe Down, the first flight was made on 31st August 1951. It was followed into the air almost a year later, on 29th August 1952, by the second prototype, serialed VX 136 but such were the changes in this aircraft that it had received the new designation of Type 529.

The Type 508, despite having four open gun ports, carried ballast in place of the cannon. The Type 529 had the cannon fitted, and a white fibreglass nose cap for the radar-ranging. It also had a small 6" extension to the very end of the tailcone, covered by another small fibreglass fairing to house tail-warning radar. However, as it transpired, neither of the latter were fitted as there were considerable supply problems at the time of both radio and radar-ranging equipment. Therefore, the requirement for its fitting, together with its associated Mk. 5 gyro gun-sight, was withdrawn on 18th February 1953.

Flight trials revealed that both aircraft were prone to wing flutter which severely limited their use in their intended role, although their take-off and climb performance were very good for their era. The proposed armament trials were never carried out on the Type 529, but both aircraft were deployed for carrier trials at sea to investigate the problems of operating large, powerful jet aircraft in preparation for those types still on the drawing board. (During research, detailed records could only be found covering the Type 529, VX 136.)

The Type 529 was involved in tail-down landing trials conducted at RAE Bedford, starting on 15th April 1953 and curtailed by a forced landing on 5th May. Damage was slight and, after repair, it was then involved in catapult acceleration trials, commencing 16th June. Its research programme was completed towards the end of the year and it went back to Supermarine at Chilbolton for further development trials on 19th November 1953. It was again involved in an emergency landing on 19th December.

Repair was uneconomic in view of the later Type 525 development, and the airframe was put into storage on 13th January 1954 and finally struck off charge on 27th October of the same year. After languishing for some considerable time, its fuselage and wings were sent to the P&EE on 29th June 1956.

The Type 508 airframe minus its outer wing panels, was used for several years by the School of Flight Deck Handling at RNAS Culdrose. On retirement, it was

*An underside view of the Supermarine 529 with flaps extended, but undercarriage up. Note arrester hook stowage and tail mounted radar bullet increasing overall length, the under-nose gun camera fairing and blanked-off cannon ports under the intakes.*

destroyed by being used for fire-practice, its importance for preservation being realised too late to save it.

# CONSTRUCTION

For a ship-board fighter, the airframe was massive by any standards, with its extremely bulky centre section housing the side-by-side Avon turbojets. Construction was conventional and entirely of light alloy with a stressed skin, and its fuselage followed closely the 'traditional' Supermarine layout of a nosecone containing the cockpit, projecting forwards from lateral 'elephant-ear' intakes. However, it was the first twin-jet aircraft designed by the company.

Each engine was fed from its own intake, which featured prominent boundary layer bleed slots. They were mounted in the centre-section, accessible through large, stressed, twin doors in the upper skin, and exhausted through twin orifices just aft of the wing root trailing edges, with prominent fuselage protection fairings projecting aft. The engine datum and thrust line were at +6° to the aircraft datum, and the exhausts imparted a thrust-line toe-out of 6°40'. Provision was made for three cartridge starts per engine before reloading.

The cockpit had a large, heavily framed canopy which slid back for normal entry and exit, and could be jettisoned in an emergency before the pilot ejected. Initially provision was made for a Martin-Baker Mk.1 seat, but this was later replaced by a Mk.3 version. Entry without a ladder was provided for, on the right side, by a retractable footstep inset in to the single nosewheel bay door. The whole bay was offset to the right by 4" so that the 25" diameter nosewheel avoided the deck-mounted catapult guide.

As with several other early jet designs (to compensate for the lack of the usual lateral reference provided by the wing on a piston-engined aircraft), an 'horizon' reference bead was mounted on a rod just aft of the nosecone cap. Roughly in line, and below, the fuselage was a streamlined fairing for the gun-camera.

The armament of four 30mm Aden cannon was mounted in the lower fuselage, two on each side of the fuselage central keel members, forward of the main undercarriage bays, and the outer pair were mounted forward of the inner ones. Access was through two large doors, which contained link and shell-case ejection chutes, and the gun-ports were just aft of each intake.

Catapult-hook attachment points were fitted just forward of the wing root leading edges, outboard of the gun bay doors, and the hold-back attachment was under the tailcone to allow a tail-down launch, giving a wing incidence of 11°30'.

The mainwheels, fitted with 34" diameter, low-pressure tyres retracted into bays which occupied the full width of the fuselage at approximately mid wing chord. Each oleo had a rather complicated set of three doors attached to it, with a further small one hinged at the fuselage centreline, to fair the undercarriage bay when the gear was retracted. Five fuel tanks were situated in the fuselage, the first between the intake ducts just aft of the cockpit and the remainder in the aft end of the centre-section

*Supermarine 529 during deck trials showing the method of wing folding to advantage. Note the dorsal strakes extending forward of the fins on the fixed part of the tailcone, and also that the tail-mounted warning radar bullet is not fitted in this view.*

above and between the jetpipes. A large equipment bay was situated approximately level with the jet orifices, which contained the auto-observer, among other items. The structure continued aft to Frame 41, at which point the tailcone was attached.

One of the most distinctive features of the aircraft was its so-called 'butterfly' tailplane, comprising two large surfaces mounted at a 35° dihedral angle which acted as both fin and tailplane surfaces. Construction was about a mainspar at mid-chord, and an aft auxiliary spar, with multiple ribs. Quarter-chord sweep was zero. The 'ruddervators' were hinged to the rear spar, acting differentially when operated by the pilot's rudder pedals for directional control, and in unison for their elevator function (ie, when used for rudder control one moved up and the other down and, for elevator control, both moved up or down as required.) A very small trim tab was provided in both surfaces at about quarter span, for directional trim only. Longitudinal trim was provided by the whole tailcone moving up and down, the tail surfaces being fixed to it, hinged at the attachment point on Frame 41. Movement range was 9° tailcone up, to 3° down. A retractable tail-skid and an 'A-frame' arrester hook were attached below the tailcone, the hook hanging down at 60° when deployed.

The external differences on the Type 529 included the relocation of the radio aerial about 10' further back behind the aft equipment bay, with provision in the extreme end of the tailcone, which was extended by 6", for the installation of warning radar, and fixed strakes, about 7'9" long, extending forwards from the tail surface root leading edges. These were attached to the fixed structure of the fuselage forward of Frame 41 and did not move with the tailcone. Also, although the actual arrester hook was of the same design, that on the Type 508 when retracted was faired completely by a rather complicated set of retractable doors and, on the Type 529, this was simplified to rest in two open, unfaired, channels each side of the tail-skid.

The wings were mounted just below the central fuselage datum, with an incidence of +2° and a dihedral of 3°. Chord at the centreline was 11'8", and thickness/chord ratio 9%. The leading edge was swept 8°, and the trailing edge swept forward 11°, giving an overall zero sweep angle at quarter-chord, wing fold 90° to wing datum giving a 3° toe-in.

Construction was around a forward mainspar and aft auxiliary spar. Full-span leading edge flaps were hinged to the forward spar, and the plain trailing edge flaps and ailerons to the aft one. Rectangular dive recovery flaps were fitted to the wing-underside at about one-third chord under the inner wing panels. Both ailerons were fitted with full-span servo tabs. All flying control surfaces were manually operated.

Wing folding was provided, reducing the overall span to 20'0" to enable the aircraft to fit the carrier lifts then in use. This split both the leading edge and trailing edge flaps. When folded, the outer panels were perpendicular to the wing datum, which imparted each with a 3° toe-in angle. Provision was made for the carriage of two underwing fuel drop-tanks on the wing fixed inboard panels, but these were never carried. Vent pipes for fuel dumping were fitted at the outer ends of the trailing edge flaps.

Pitot heads (or, as noted above, one pitot head and one yaw/incidence vane) were fitted to the extreme tips of the wings, together with standard navigation lights.

## POWER PLANT

Both Types 508 and 529 fitted with two Rolls Royce R.A.3 Avon axial flow turbojets developing a Sea Level Static Thrust of 6,500 lbs.

# DATA

## DIMENSIONS

| | |
|---|---|
| Span (wings extended) | 41'0" |
| (wings folded) | 20'0" |
| Length (Type 508) | 50'0" |
| (Type 529) | 50'6" |
| Height (static) | 12'4" |
| (wings folded) | 16'7" |
| Track | 13'0.25" |
| Wheelbase | 15'11" |
| Tailplane Span | 17'2.5" |

## AREAS

| | |
|---|---|
| Wing (gross) | 340 sq ft |

## WEIGHTS

| | |
|---|---|
| Normal loaded (Type 508) | 18,850 lbs |
| Overload with drop tanks (Type 529) | 25,630 lbs |

## PERFORMANCE

$V_{max}$ (level flight)

| | |
|---|---|
| at 30,000 ft | 524 kts/0.89 Mach |
| at 40,000 ft | 510 kts/0.887 Mach |
| at 45,000 ft | 500 kts/0.873 Mach |

Climb Time to Height

| | |
|---|---|
| to 30,000 ft | 2.5 mins |
| 40,000 ft | 3.9 mins |
| 45,000 ft | 5.1 mins |

(Note: all times calculated from attaining climb speed)

| | |
|---|---|
| Ceiling (1,000 ft/min) | 50,000 ft |

## REFERENCES

| | |
|---|---|
| Public Records Office | —Avia Files |
| Aviation Bookshop | —Photographic Archives |
| Fleet Air Arm Museum, Yeovilton | —Library |

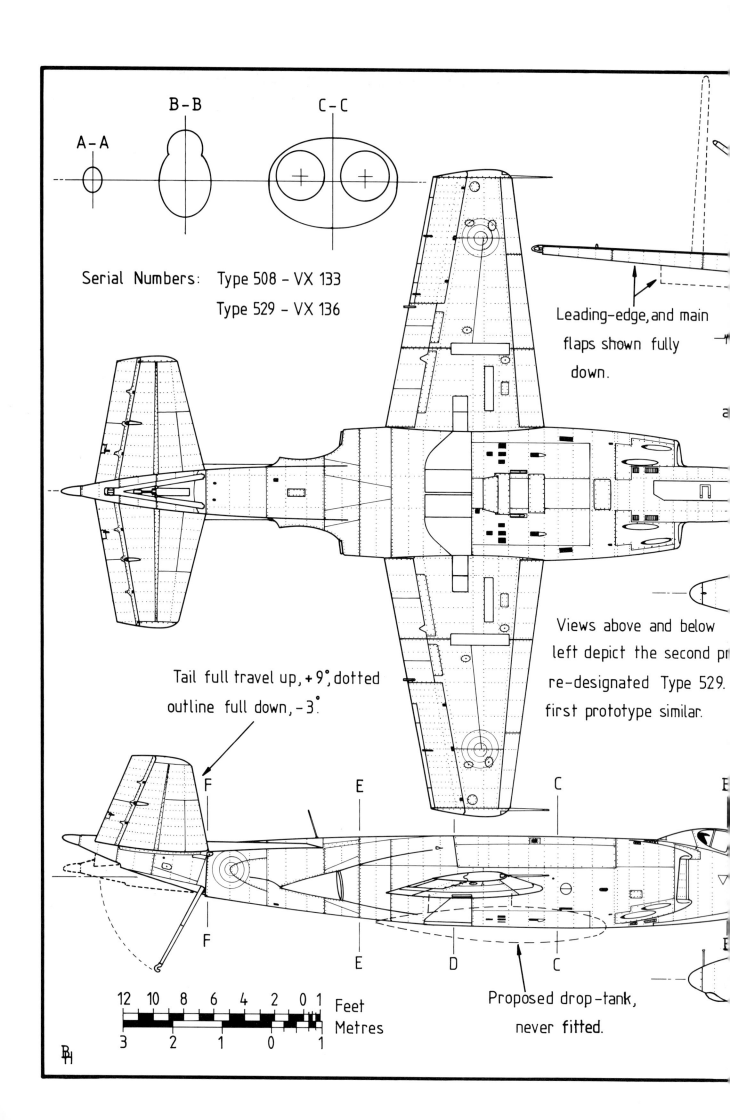

A-A    B-B    C-C

Serial Numbers:   Type 508 - VX 133

Type 529 - VX 136

Leading-edge, and main
flaps shown fully
down.

Views above and below
left depict the second pr
re-designated Type 529.
first prototype similar.

Tail full travel up, + 9°, dotted
outline full down, -3°.

F

F

E

E

C

C

D

Proposed drop-tank,
never fitted.

12   10   8   6   4   2   0 1   Feet
                         Metres
3    2    1    0    1

BH

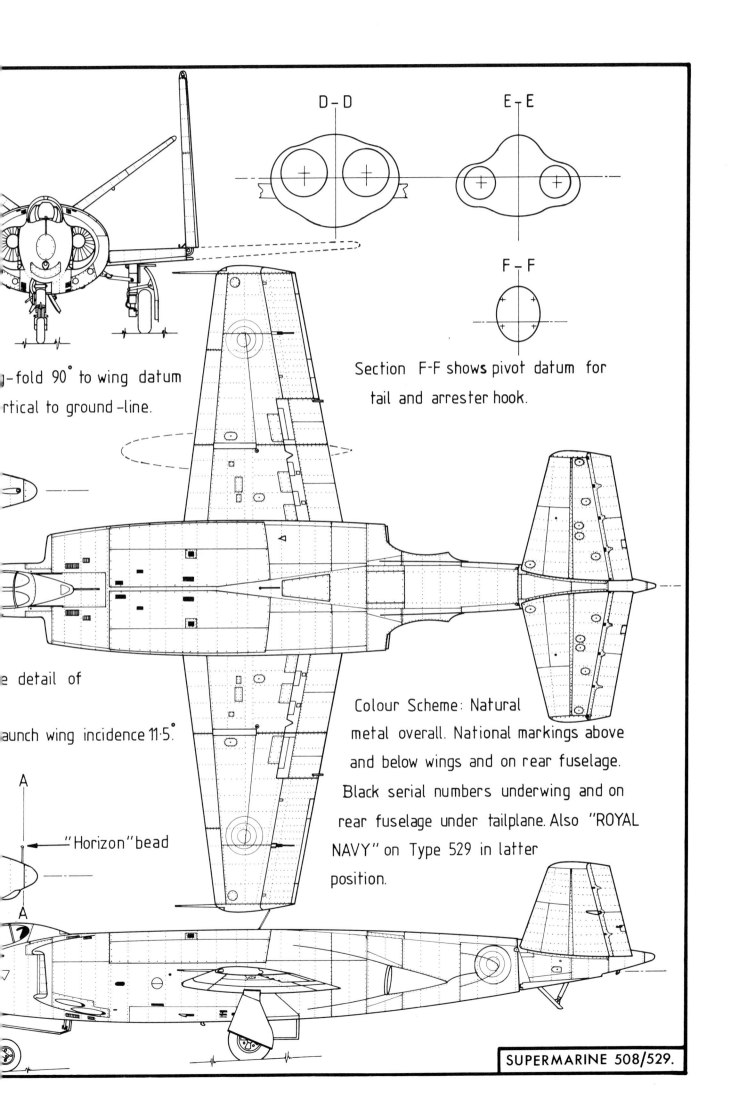

D–D

E–E

F–F

Section F-F shows pivot datum for
tail and arrester hook.

-fold 90° to wing datum
rtical to ground–line.

e detail of

aunch wing incidence 11·5°

A

← "Horizon" bead

A

Colour Scheme: Natural
metal overall. National markings above
and below wings and on rear fuselage.
Black serial numbers underwing and on
rear fuselage under tailplane. Also "ROYAL
NAVY" on Type 529 in latter
position.

SUPERMARINE 508/529.

Boulton Paul P.120 illustrating the modified tail surfaces, repositioned parachute container fairing and modified jetpipe cowling to advantage. Also note the two longitudinal fairings on the main undercarriage doors. The unpainted state allows much panel detail to be seen. (Dowty Boulton Paul Ltd.)

# BOULTON PAUL P.120

| Manufacturer | Boulton Paul Aircraft Ltd |
|---|---|
| Specification | E.27/49 |
| Role | Research Prototype |
| First Flight Date | VT 951 – 6th August 1952 |

The P.120 was a development of the earlier P.111 and 111a and was intended to further the programme of basic research into the characteristics of the delta wing planform. Although it looked like a straightforward modification of the earlier airframe, with the provision of a swept fin and rudder and a horizontal tail surface to improve longitudinal and directional stability, it also had provision for movable wingtips, which was a major departure from the original design. These radical differences might be thought to have contributed to the aircraft's short life but, as is shown later, had no bearing on the accident.

## DEVELOPMENT HISTORY

The aircraft had one of the briefest of careers, lasting only 23 days from first flight to its destruction in a crash on 29th August 1952. The first flight had not been without incident and immediately showed the very powerful effect of the horizontal tailplane trimmer. On its first take-off, the pilot had been unable to raise the nosewheel for take-off until almost the entire length the main runway at Boscombe Down had been used up, and a much higher speed attained than required for take-off on the earlier P.111. This was subsequently found to be

due to the wrong tailplane angle being calculated for take-off, thus requiring a higher speed to be achieved before lift-off could be made. Tests were continued to open up the flight envelope and to investigate the effects of the aircraft's novel control layout. There are no records as to whether the wingtip surfaces were ever activated during the brief test programme, as all photographs show them to be only in the neutral position.

On the final flight, tests were being carried out at a relatively low altitude of approximately 4,000 ft. At 450 kts. (the highest speed attained during the flight test programme), a very intense buzz was noted and the pilot saw the tab position indicator flicker. Almost immediately, there was a loud bang and the aircraft rolled to the left. After two complete revolutions, a modicum of control was successfully achieved, with wing level being maintained with full right aileron and full right rudder applied. It was later found by the pilot, looking over his shoulder after the canopy had been jettisoned and before ejection, that the entire left elevon and tab assembly had broken off.

A slow climb was made to 12,000 ft. with full power on the engine, the control column fully forward and 45° to the right, with full right rudder applied. During this time there was no indication of airspeed, as the pitot tube had bent fully back with the wing vibration before the elevon had separated. It was found that, if there was any reduction of power or the control column or rudder were moved, the left wing immediately dropped. After much difficulty, a gentle descent was made to approximately 6,000 ft. and the cockpit canopy jettisoned which, for some reason, seemed to stabilise the aircraft. However, after further descent to approximately 3,000 ft., turbulent air was encountered which contributed to the onset of violent lateral oscillations. These proved uncontrollable and the pilot ejected with the bank angle at 60° and rapidly increasing, the aircraft being totally destroyed in the ensuing crash. Total flying was only eleven hours.

Investigation after the crash showed that the entire left elevon and tab assembly had broken off due to flutter, the onset of which was caused by lack of stiffness in the tab control mechanism. Before breaking off, the tab had been forced downwards to some 45° and the elevon upwards to over 60°. Subsequent tests on the tab linkage showed that a load of less than half of the design load was needed to produce movement consistent with the evidence found. On test specimens at Boulton Paul, no movement was noted in the linkage until 1.36 times the design load was applied.

The cause of the crash was therefore in no way directly connected with the aircraft's aerodynamic qualities, or control layout. This tail layout was still intended to be a part of the on-going RAE research programme and, at one time, plans were in hand to modify the P.111a, although this never happened.

Nothing, of course, remains of the actual aircraft, but portions of the structural test airframe still exist. The complete tailplane is used for instructional purposes at Hatfield Polytechnic and, at nearby St. Albans, certainly until a short time ago, the rear fuselage and fin were used for apprentice instruction into airframe construction and repair.

# CONSTRUCTION

Fuselage construction was identical to that of the P.111a back to Frame 290.88. (The datum point was 72" forward of the intake lip.) The four airbrakes were retained, but the pitot tube mounted on the intake splitter was not. The only other external difference on the forward fuselage was the mounting of a VHF whip-aerial on the spine just aft of the canopy. The large panel upon which it was mounted could be removed for access to the auto-observer mounted below the TR.1920 radio. As with its predecessor, it was extensively instrumented for pressure plotting and, in addition to the auto-observer, had continuous tape and voice recorders.

The fuselage was extensively modified aft of Frame 290.88, and a swept fin and horizontal tail surface added. The jetpipe was very slightly lengthened, and the large bulge on the left of the fuselage fairing housing the 7' diameter braking and anti-spin parachute was removed. Instead, a circular-section fairing containing the parachute was added to the top of the fuselage immediately below the rudder, projecting aft of the jetpipe orifice. The fuselage section was blended smoothly around the fairing. The underlying fuselage structure was strengthened with the addition of extra

formers to cope with the added stresses at the attachment points of the swept fin. This was constructed around a mainspar at approximately mid-chord, with forward and aft auxiliary spars, the rudder being hinged to the aft spar. Fin leading and trailing edge sweep angles were 55°50' and 39°45' respectively, and the thickness/chord ratio 10%. Chord at the centreline was 10'4.5" and at the extended tip 6'3.3" giving a gross area of 58.98 sq. ft. (including fuselage to the centreline) and a net area of 49.56 sq. ft. Provision was made at its tip to mount

## DATA

### DIMENSIONS

| | |
|---|---|
| Span | 33'5.5" |
| Length | 29'7.5" |
| Height (static) | 9'6.5" |
| Track | 14'5.3" |
| Wheelbase | 11'0.5" |
| Tailplane Span | 9'4" |

| | |
|---|---|
| Wing incidence (ground static) | 7° |
| Tail down incidence (static) | 17° |
| Tail down incidence (fully compressed) | 13°30' |

### WING DATA

| | |
|---|---|
| Aspect ratio | 3.0 |
| Sweep (l/e) | 45° |
| Sweep (quarter-chord) | 36°52' |
| Dihedral | 0° |
| Chord at centreline | 17'2½" |
| Chord at root | 14'5" |
| Section | Squires High Speed section 'C' |
| Thickness/Chord ratio | 10% (constant) |
| Incidence to a/c datum | 0° |
| Loading | 43.46 lbs/sq ft |
| Elevons | chord 15% of wing chord |
| | range of movement |
| | ±15° as ailerons |
| | −25° as elevators |
| | tab range of movement ±8° |

### AREAS

| | |
|---|---|
| Wing (gross) | 290.13 sq ft |
| Tailplane (gross) | 30.74 sq ft |
| Fin and Rudder (gross) | 58.98 sq ft (including fuselage) |
| Fin and Rudder (net) | 49.56 sq ft |
| Elevons | 29.3 sq ft (aft of hinge line) |
| Elevon tab | 5.67 sq ft |
| Rudder | 6.27 sq ft |
| Rudder tab | 1.04 sq ft |

### WEIGHTS

| | |
|---|---|
| Empty | 10,656 lbs |
| Pilot | 180 lbs |
| Fuel | 1,860 lbs |
| Loaded | 12,580 |

### REFERENCES

| | |
|---|---|
| Midland Museum | —Boulton Paul P.111a (the aircraft) |
| RAE Farnborough | —Structures Report ACC.248 |
| Boulton Paul | —P.120 Electrical Installation Drawing |
| Hatfield Polytechnic | —Structural Test Tailplane |

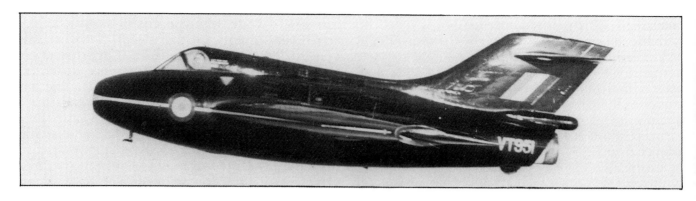

*Boulton Paul P.120 in its gloss black and yellow colour scheme towards the end of the brief 23 day flight test period.*

a cine camera for viewing the left wing during planned tufting for airflow investigation. The rudder was power operated and had an area of 6.27 sq.ft. and range of movement of ±15°, its tab's movement range being ±6°. (Early in the test programme, the rudder was modified to be solely manually operated.)

The horizontal tail surface was mounted approximately two-thirds up the fin, having a 45° sweep leading edge and a thickness/chord ratio of 10%. Root chord was 5'9" tapering to 10" at the tip, giving a gross area of 30.74 sq.ft. It was a slab surface, but was not a tailplane in the accepted sense, in that it was only a trimming surface, lateral and pitch control being identical to that of the P.111 by the wing-mounted elevons. There is no record of its movement range, but it was electrically activated by a switch mounted on a panel on the left cockpit wall, its actuator being mounted on the aft of the fin mainspar accessible through panels on the right side. This cockpit panel also had mounted, at its forward end, the parachute stream and jettison switches.

Wing planform, and basic construction were the same as for the P.111 in its pointed tip configuration. The only obvious differences externally were the two fairing bulges added to each outboard main undercarriage door. However, there was one major change to the earlier aircraft and that was the provision of movable wingtips. (However, as stated earlier, it is not known whether the system was ever activated during the aircraft's short life.) Outboard of Wing Station 151 (measured from the centreline) which was also the outboard end of the elevons, the tips comprised movable slab surfaces and, like the tailplane, they were for trimming purposes only. No movement range is available, but they were electrically activated from switches on the same cockpit side-panel as that mounting the tailplane control switch. Three switches controlled the system – a master ON/OFF switch, and two others, one moving the tips in unison for pitch trim, and the other differentially for lateral trim. The two actuators were mounted in the fuselage in a bay between Frames 254.66 and 290.88, which also housed the electro-hydraulic flying control actuators. An elliptically-shaped fence was fitted at the leading edge of the wing/wingtip junction to control spanwise flow. The pitot head mounted on the left wing was also moved very slightly inboard.

## POWER PLANT
One Rolls-Royce Nene 3 R.N.2. centrifugal flow turbojet developing a Sea Level Static Thrust of 5,100 lbs.

*Boulton Paul P.120 square sectioned nosewheel tyre and wing fence at the junction of the fixed wing structure and the moveable tips, here shown in their neutral position. (These may have been locked in this position during the aircraft's very brief life.) (Dowty Boulton Paul Ltd.)*

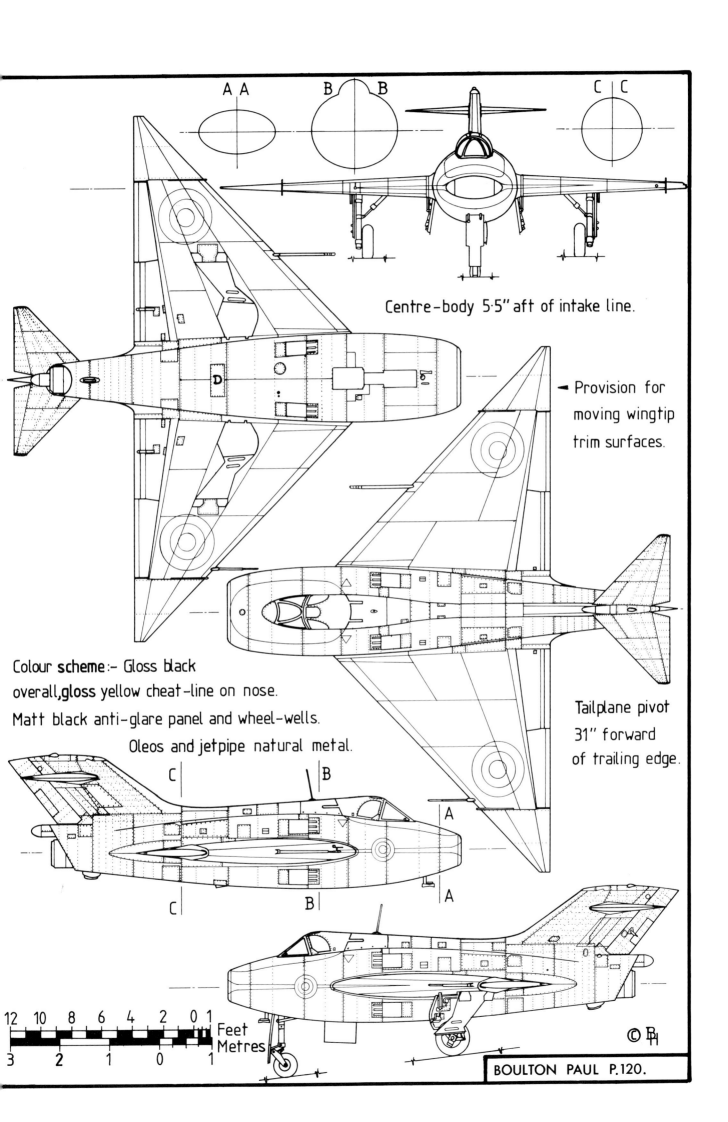

A A     B   B            C   C

Centre-body 5·5" aft of intake line.

◄ Provision for
moving wingtip
trim surfaces.

Colour scheme :- Gloss black
overall, gloss yellow cheat-line on nose.
Matt black anti-glare panel and wheel-wells.
Oleos and jetpipe natural metal.

Tailplane pivot
31" forward
of trailing edge.

C      B

A

C      B      A

12 10 8 6 4 2 0 1
3    2    1    0    1
Feet
Metres

© BP H

BOULTON PAUL P.120.

*Short S.B.5 as it appeared with full-span leading edge droop and high-set tailplane. Note what appears to be a stub pitot boom on the intake right edge with its end angled down to allow for the airflow direction at slow speed.*

# SHORT S.B.5

| Manufacturer | Short Brothers and Harland |
|---|---|
| Specification | ER.100 |
| Role | Research Prototype |
| First Flight Date | WG 768 – 2nd December 1952 |

Originally designed to a requirement to test the low speed characteristics of the unique aerodynamic configuration for the forthcoming English Electric P.1a, and to solve the argument of the merits of a high or low set tailplane for this aircraft, the S.B.5 was to become, together with the Handley Page HP.115, one of the most versatile and cost-effective research tools into the characteristics of highly-swept wing surfaces. Not only were basic derivatives established, but it was also possible to verify wind tunnel results with a full-scale aircraft.

## DEVELOPMENT HISTORY

So radical was the design of the English Electric P.1a at the time that it was conceived, and the fact that it had a more highly-swept wing than anything until then tested in Britain, there were many unknowns regarding its likely flight characteristics, some of which wind tunnel tests had suggested were likely to be dangerous. It was therefore felt prudent to build a near full-sized, cheap and simple aerodynamic test-bed to investigate the likely low speed characteristics of the aircraft. There was also much controversy at the time over the positioning of the tailplane, RAE Farnborough theory indicating that its proposed low-set position on the fuselage

might prove dangerous due to wing-wake under certain flight conditions. They therefore favoured one in a high-set position mounted on top of the fin.

Due to these factors, the requirement E.R.100 was raised in 1949 for a simple aircraft with fixed undercarriage, with a wing which could be set at three progressively more swept angles, a leading edge which could be easily modified to test various configurations, and the tailplane mounted either on the fin tip or low on the rear fuselage. Shorts was awarded the contract and bowed to RAE pressure, with the aircraft being built first with the tailplane on top of the fin. As there was then no experience in Britain with sweep angles as high as 60°, the aircraft was designed to allow a gradual approach to this configuration, with the wing initially set with a leading edge sweep angle of 50° and a full-span leading edge droop of 20°6' (measured in the line of flight).

Following completion of construction, the aircraft was moved by sea and road from the works in Belfast to Boscombe Down, where it made its first flight on 2nd December 1952. Right from the start of flight testing, it was painfully obvious that the aircraft was extremely under-powered with its Derwent engine, flight being virtually at the stall the whole time, especially in the very slow, shallow climb.

Once the basic handling characteristics had been checked, the aircraft was returned to Belfast for the fitting of the wing at the 60° position to enable work to commence which directly related to the P.1

research programme. Initially, the high-set tailplane was retained, as was the drooped leading edge, and the aircraft first flew in this configuration on 29th July 1953. As nothing untoward was revealed, the aircraft was once again withdrawn from flying to have the tailplane moved to the low-set position in October 1953, and the inboard leading edge of the wing modified to have pronounced droop to simulate the, then, proposed inboard leading edge flap on the P.1. However, the droop outboard of the flap was still retained on the leading edge to keep the aerodynamic changes to a minimum before testing commenced.

The first flight in this configuration was made in January 1954 at Boscombe Down and the aircraft was then ferried to RAE Bedford. Flying was kept to a minimum for essential flight clearance, in order that the definitive P.1a configuration could be tested before that aircraft was due to fly. The change to this was made in February 1954 when the outboard droop was finally removed, the aircraft having returned to Boscombe Down for the initial flying. The S.B.5 then resembled a 7/8 model of P.1a with leading edge flap down. The majority of the aircraft's flight tests were to be made with the wing at this angle. The aircraft moved from Boscombe Down to Farnborough in June 1954, and finally to Bedford in August 1956. It was determined that the minimum speed achievable was in the order of 80 kts., identified by a sudden yaw to the right together with a sharp wing drop to about 60°, the nose dropping to 45°–50°, despite control column fully back and full left rudder applied. It was found that there was no tendency to spin after the stall. The limiting factor was rudder power and, with extreme caution using only outside visual reference, a speed as low as 75 kts. was achieved before the start of the yaw.

Other tests included asymmetric load tests carrying underwing canisters which could be loaded with up to 420 lbs. each, although tests were confined to weights varying from 60 lbs. through 100, 200 and 300 lbs. on either wing, the limit being determined by lateral control availability for making a safe landing. The speed range investigated was from a minimum of 90 kts. up to 200 kts.

Testing in the 60° configuration was completed in April 1958. Total flying at 60° sweep, excluding miscellaneous flying, was 185 hours, and most tests were carried out at or below an altitude of 5,000 ft.

As previously stated, the aircraft was extremely under-powered, and the possibility of adding a small auxiliary turbojet was considered. During 1957, the decision was taken to completely re-engine the aircraft with a more powerful Bristol Siddeley Orpheus axial flow turbojet. The aircraft was therefore shipped back to the manufacturer's works at Belfast for a complete rebuild in 1958. Not only was a new engine fitted, but also the wing was swept even further to 69°, its instrumentation

*Configuration with drooped wing root nose flaps and outer wing leading edge. The tailplane is now low set. Note heavy dome riveting on the fuselage nose. (Shorts)*

updated, and the pilot provided with a Martin-Baker zero-zero ejection seat. The aircraft was also repainted an overall bright blue. It returned by sea and overland to RAE Bedford during September 1960 and made its first flight on 18th October of that year.

At this extreme sweep angle, its programme included trials with and without full-span leading edge droop, to confirm wind tunnel predictions and establish derivatives in the general research programme, together with the HP.115, into the control and stability of highly-swept aerofoils. The left wing was at times heavily tufted to investigate airflow patterns and these were recorded by a cine camera mounted in a small fairing on the left side of the fin. To improve picture clarity, a small 'search-light' was fitted on the fuselage spine, shining on the left wing upper-surface.

Aircraft handling was overshadowed by the lack of power, and for take-off only up to 15° trailing edge flap could be used, although with little improvement in runway performance, any greater angle causing excessive drag which prolonged the take-off roll and caused buffet. Minimum unstick speed was approximately 130 kts. after about 5,400 ft. ground roll.

The same applied in flight. Flap deflection caused a very strong nose-down trim change, and buffet became progressively worse with increasing flap angle. With full flap, the aircraft would not maintain level flight at any speed!

Approaches were flown at approximately 145 kts., usually with no flap deflected, although up to 20° could be used producing a slightly lower approach speed. Touchdown was achieved at between 125 and 130 kts.; any lower speed and there was risk of tail strike. The technique after touchdown was to lower full flap, thus reducing the required landing roll.

At the end of its long and productive test programme, it was offered for use by the Australian Aeronautical Research Laboratory but the offer was declined. It was therefore delivered to the Empire Test Pilots' School at Farnborough, and was used during 1967 for the familiarisation of pilots in the low-speed handling characteristics of slender aircraft.

This soon came to an end when the airframe was due for a major inspection and it was no longer cost effective to keep it flying. It was struck off charge and is now preserved at the Royal Air Force Museum, Cosford.

# DATA

## DIMENSIONS

### Span

| Sweep angle | 50° | 35'2" | |
| | 60° | 30'6" | |
| | 69° | 26'0" | |
| Length | | 47'9" | (high tail, excluding probes) |
| | | 45'9" | (low tail, excluding probes) |

(overall length increased by 7'0" when including probes)

| Height | | 17'4" | (static, high tail) |
| | | 16'3" | (static, low tail) |
| Tailplane span | | 9'7" | (high set) |
| | | 11'7.4" | (low set) |

### Track

| Sweep angle | 50° | 13'1.5" |
| | 60° | 11'6" |
| | 69° | 10'8" |
| Nosewheels | | 10" |

### Wheelbase

| Sweep angle | 50° | 17'9" |
| | 60° | 18'3" |
| | 69° | 18'3" |

## AREAS

| Sweep angle | 50° | 273.1 sq ft (net) |
| | 60° | 276.9 sq ft (net) |
| | | 351.0 sq ft (gross) |
| | 69° | 281.7 sq ft (net) |
| Leading edge flap | | 6.77 sq ft (each) |
| Trailing edge flap | | 18.44 sq ft (each) |
| Ailerons | | 8.65 sq ft (each aft of hinge line) |
| tailplane | | 74.5 sq ft (gross) |
| | | 43.85 sq ft (net) |
| elevator | | 7.81 sq ft (each aft of hinge line) |
| fin | | 51.98 sq ft (net) |
| rudder | | 13.69 sq ft (aft of hinge line) |

## WEIGHTS

| Empty | 9,196 lbs |
| Loaded | 11,500 lbs–12,700 lbs (varies dependent on centre of gravity position and wing canister loads) Max loaded 13,000 lbs (maximum permissible at take-off) |
| Tip canisters max load | 420 lbs |

## PERFORMANCE

| $V_{max}$ | 350 kts |
| duration | 45 mins |
| ceiling | 10,000 ft |
| max load | 4.5g |

## REFERENCES

RAF Museum Cosford – The Aircraft
RAE Farnborough – Library

# CONSTRUCTION

Primary construction of the fuselage, fin and tailplane was light alloy, and was conventional throughout, and bore an overall general similarity to that of the English Electric P.1a. The skin was riveted to the fuselage formers using dome-headed rivets, and no attempt was made to obtain a smooth exterior surface as high-speed flight was not required (however, in view of the limited power of the engine, any reduction in drag would have been appreciated!) The fuselage split just aft of the wing root trailing edge to allow access to the engine. The skinning contained multiple access and servicing panels. The cockpit was set above the circular engine intake duct and, aft of this, the fuselage was of constant cross-section right back almost to the leading edge of the fin-root. The jetpipe occupied the lower half of the rear fuselage and the upper

*Short S.B.5 at lift-off showing the fixed wing root nose flaps and drooped outer wing leading edge. The wing is at its 60° swept position. (Shorts)*

part above the orifice housed the parachute container. This contained two 20' diameter braking

parachutes and one 20' diameter anti-spin parachute. A spine along the top of the fuselage between the cockpit and fin contained electrical and control runs.

(*Note:* Some reports state that there were two separate aft fuselage sections manufactured, one with the tailplane set on top of the fin and the other with it in its low-set fuselage mounted position. It would appear more likely that only one aft fuselage was completed, the necessary modifications being made to it and the fin to accommodate the two different configurations.)

The cockpit canopy hinged aft for normal access and entry. It was initially multi-framed and had to be jettisoned before the pilot could eject but, when the aircraft was fitted with its wing at 69° sweep, a zero-zero ejection seat was fitted, and thus insufficient time would have been available to do this. The framing at the top of the canopy was therefore drastically reduced, allowing the seat to eject through the canopy in the event of an emergency.

Two large instrument booms were fittted on either side of the circular intake lip. That on the right was a pitot head, the tip of which was deflected down 15° relative to the aircraft datum to reduce position error at high angles of incidence. The left boom carried pitch and yaw vanes. During position error measurements, an electrically-

*Short S.B.5 showing the wing at its maximum sweep angle. Note also the redesigned cockpit canopy framing. The aircraft is now in its bright blue colour scheme. (Royal Aeronautical Society)*

*Short S.B.5 rear view, again with the wing at maximum sweep angle. This is one of the few views showing the rear fuselage/tailpipe detail detail. (Royal Aeronautical Society)*

powered winch was fitted forward of the fuselage fuel tank, and was connected across an airspeed indicator to a venturi pitot on the right side of the fuselage. A large hatch was fitted in the extreme nose of the aircraft above the intake duct, giving access to an equipment bay which contained ballast, which was removed or added to vary the aircraft's centre of gravity.

The fixed nosewheel oleo was mounted below the fuselage in line with the cockpit windscreen. It was fully castoring and had twin wheels, whose tyre diameter was 16" fixed to a live axle.

The single 300-gallon capacity fuel tank was mounted in the upper fuselage half, and was sited so that centre of gravity movement with fuel usage

was kept to a minimum. An auto-observer was fitted just forward of the fuel tank together with its camera.

All controls surfaces were manually operated, all having set back hinges and, with the exception of the right elevator, geared balance tabs. The tab on the right elevator was a pilot-operated trim tab.

The fin was constructed around a mainspar at approximately mid-chord, and a forward auxiliary spar. It had an aspect ratio of 6:1 and a thickness/chord ratio of 8%. Root and tip chords were 11'0" and 5'0" respectively. Leading edge sweep was 60°, and that on the trailing edge 37°. The rudder was hinged to the mainspar and had a hinge line sweep of 44°30'. Its range of movement was ±25° and it

*Short S.B.5 as now preserved at Cosford. It has been re-painted to the colour scheme when it first flew, but this is incorrect as it never carried this scheme with the wing in its present fully swept position. (Ron Moulton)*

was fitted with a geared balance tab whose movement was through ±20°.

The tailplane was initially fitted on a small 'mast' right at the fin tip, adjustable electrically in flight through ±10°. It was in the form of a cropped delta whose centreline chord was 9'10", with a tip chord of 1'4.5", a leading edge sweep of 60°, and it had a thickness/chord ratio of 6%

When moved to its fuselage-mounted position, the overall span increased by just over 2'0", giving a centreline chord of 11'5.25" and root chord of 8'2.9", and reducing its aspect ratio to 1.81:1.

The elevator was one continuous surface when the tailplane was fin-mounted, but split into two when in the other position. The movement range was through ±20°. As mentioned previously, the tab on the left was of the geared balance type with a movement range of ±20° and that on the right was a trim tab with a range of ±17°30'. The elevator hinges featured prominent control horns, and the rudder and its tab also had large external operating rods on the left side.

The wing was the primary novelty of the design. It was constructed around a rigid light alloy box-spar, with multiple spanwise stringers attached above and below to sheets so as to form sandwich skin panels for both upper and lower surfaces. They had a symmetrical section, profile of which was completed by plywood-covered leading and trailing edges to allow easy modification or change. Its root attachment points were designed so that it could be set at three different leading edge sweep angles on the ground. The change to the angles, which were 50°, 60° and 69°, was a lengthy procedure requiring major modification especially to the leading edges.

The main undercarriage was also non-retractable and had oleos of novel design which could be 'twisted' to retain the wheels' direction parallel to the aircraft centreline at the three sweep angles, and whose rake was also adjustable to compensate for the centre of gravity changes incurred with sweep change. The undercarriage track and wheelbase therefore varied slightly with configuration. The wheels were fitted with Maxaret brakes operated by toe pedals, and had tyres of 28" diameter.

The wing data varied with the sweep angle and those quoted are with it at 60°, at which angle the major proportion of test work was done. The aspect ratio was 2.64:1, thickness/chord ratio 5.26% at the root and 7.735% at the tip, with a symmetrical section. It was set at an incidence of 2° to the aircraft datum, with no washout, and an anhedral angle of 3°. Centreline chord was 17'0.36", while that at the root and tip were 16'2.6" and 1'2" respectively.

The trailing edge flaps were also of novel design, and bore no relationship whatsoever to those intended for the P.1a. They were of a 'split-cum-Zap' variety which meant that, as the flaps deflected downwards to their maximum angle of 54° (measured in the line of flight), their hinge lines rotated, decreasing sweepback from 51°30' to 27° about a fixed pivot at their outboard ends.

When the wing was swept at 60°, the ailerons were perpendicular to the line of flight. Their range of movement was ±12° and that of their geared balance tabs ±20°.

As well as the change in sweep angle, the wing went through eight distinct configuration changes, as follows:

1  Sweep 50° with full span drooped leading edge at 20°6' (measured in line of flight).
2  Sweep 60° with the same full span leading edge droop.
3  Sweep 60° with leading edge inboard flap deflected at 4° or 24° 24' (measured in line of flight, 26°30' perpendicular to hinge line).
4  Sweep 60° with inboard flap deflected and outboard droop removed.
5  Sweep 60° with full span leading edge droop of 10°42' (measured in line of flight, 20° perpendicular to hinge line).
6  Sweep 60° no droop or leading edge flap.
7  Sweep 69° with full span leading edge droop.
8  Sweep 69° with no droop.

(*Note.* One further minor variation at the two higher sweep angles was the fitting of a notch in the leading edge at 70% semi-span. The wing's characteristics were tested with this both sealed and cut. The notch was fitted to eliminate a wing drop which had not been present with the full span droop. Before fitting the notch, leading edge spoilers were tried in four sections totalling 101" from the wing tip. The wing drop was still present until the last inboard section was fitted. The much simpler notch eliminated the problem entirely and was therefore adopted.) The nose flaps were ground adjustable only. The aircraft is preserved in the last configuration.

(*Note* As a direct result of the testing on the S.B.5, and brief confirmation on the actual aircraft, the leading edge flaps were deleted on the P.1a.)

## POWER PLANT

Originally fitted with one Rolls-Royce Derwent 8 R.D.7 centrifugal flow turbojet developing a Sea Level Static Thrust of 3,500 lbs.

Later fitted with one Bristol Siddeley B.E.26 Orpheus axial flow turbojet developing a Sea Level Static Thrust of 4,850 lbs.

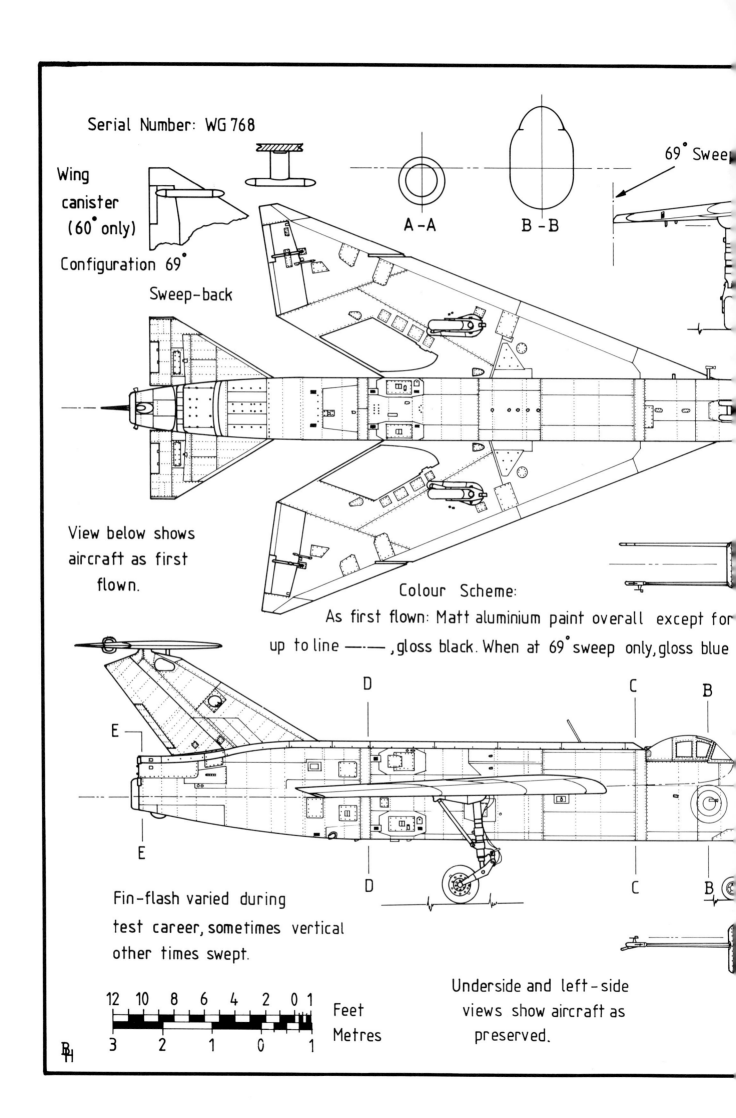

Serial Number: WG 768

Wing
canister
(60° only)

Configuration 69°

Sweep-back

A - A    B - B

69° Swee

View below shows
aircraft as first
flown.

Colour Scheme:

As first flown: Matt aluminium paint overall  except for
up to line —·—, gloss black. When at 69° sweep only, gloss blue

D          C       B

E

E

D          C       B

Fin-flash varied during
test career, sometimes vertical
other times swept.

12  10   8   6   4   2   0 1
3        2        1        0        1    Feet
Metres

Underside and left-side
views show aircraft as
preserved.

B H

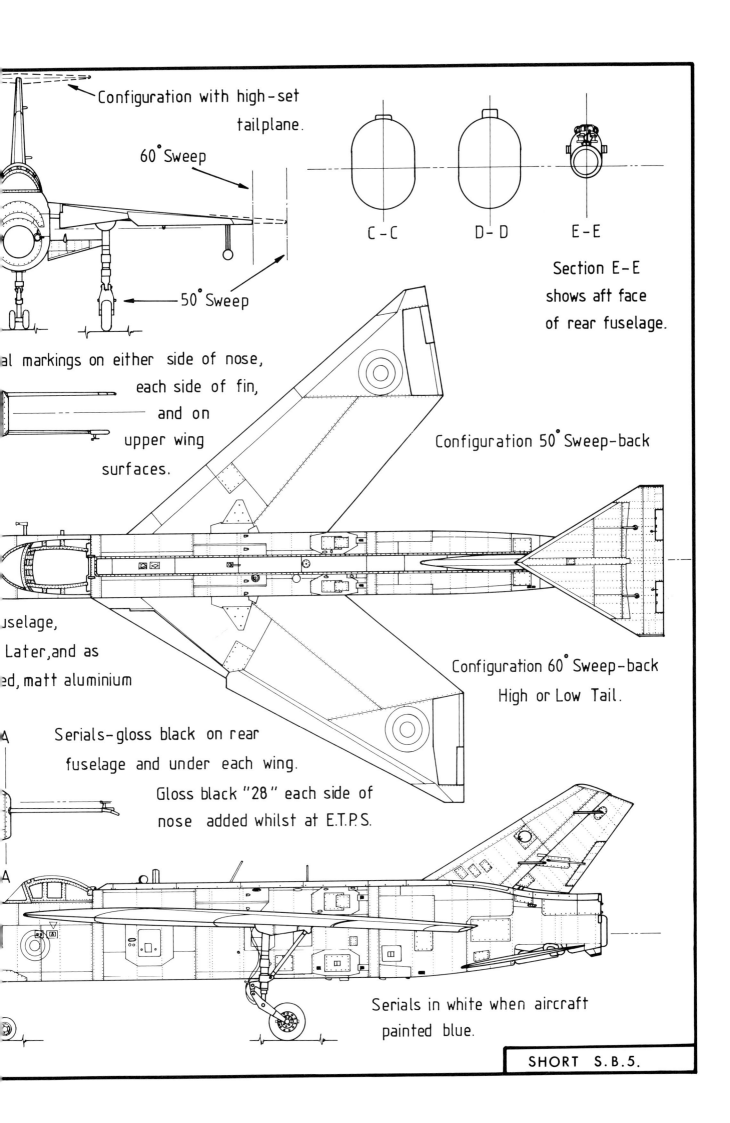

Configuration with high-set tailplane.

60° Sweep

50° Sweep

C-C    D-D    E-E

Section E-E shows aft face of rear fuselage.

al markings on either side of nose, each side of fin, and on upper wing surfaces.

Configuration 50° Sweep-back

uselage,

Later, and as ed, matt aluminium

Configuration 60° Sweep-back High or Low Tail.

Serials—gloss black on rear fuselage and under each wing.

Gloss black "28" each side of nose added whilst at E.T.P.S.

Serials in white when aircraft painted blue.

SHORT S.B.5.

# HAWKER P.1083

| | |
|---|---|
| Manufacturer | Hawker Aircraft Company Ltd |
| Specification | F.119D |
| Role | Fighter Prototype |
| First Flight Date | WN 470–Not Flown |

Designed as a successor for the Hunter and, in parallel with the proposed Swift replacement the Supermarine 545, to a similar specification, the Hawker aircraft differed from the latter in that it was a minimal change to the original airframe rather than an entirely new design.

## DEVELOPMENT HISTORY

The Hunter was barely capable of exceeding Mach1, even in a fairly steep dive although, having said that, its 'manners were impeccable' in doing so, which sadly was more than could be said for the Swift at that time. Although there were much higher performance fighters already in the project stage in Britain, there was a requirement for an interim transonic aircraft of a similar performance capability to the North American F-100, pending their availability and entry into service.

Preliminary design work on the Hunter's successor had been started as early as November 1951, with Instructions to Proceed in the following February. The Hawker submission was allocated the Specification F.119D to meet this requirement, which was issued to the company on 18th April 1952.

It was felt that the basic Hunter airframe could be adapted successfully to meet the requirements, the major redesign being limited to the wing and to the aft fuselage to accommodate the afterburner. As was the case with the earlier Hunter, the aircraft was to be powered by either a Rolls-Royce Avon or an Armstrong Siddeley Sapphire engine, both with afterburners.

To speed construction, the fuselage of the fourth prototype P.1067, WN 470, was used with the Rolls-Royce Avon selected as its power plant. Progress was such that the starboard wing had been completed by October 1952, together with a mock-up rear fuselage to accommodate an Avon RA.14R engine. At this stage, it was decided to substitute an Avon RA.19R. However, there was a problem, in that a diameter of at least 36" was required to accommodate the afterburner jetpipe, but the standard Hunter fuselage structure allowed a diameter of only 31". To overcome this, the design was modified so that the afterburner jetpipe outer skin formed the actual skin of the rear fuselage itself, not only providing a large enough diameter, but also a substantial weight saving.

No authentic pictorial data could be found showing this final development, and there is some evidence to suggest that WN 470 would have been completed purely to prove the aerodynamic characteristics of the new wing, the rear fuselage being of the same design as was proposed and later flown for the Hunter F.3, with its same engine, the Avon RA.7R. The drawings depict the aircraft in this configuration.

It had been hoped to have the aircraft flying in time for the 1953 Farnborough Air Display, but this was not to be. Following the end of the Korean War, the inevitable cutbacks were made and more interest was shown by the Royal Air Force in Hunter developments with a larger, non-afterburning engine, to give more thrust with a better specific fuel consumption. The enthusiasm for afterburner-equipped engines had waned. The blow finally fell on 13th July 1953 when the requirement was officially cancelled. The company decided not to continue construction of the prototype as a private venture, and work ceased.

Although most of the airframe components were scrapped, the story does not quite end there, as part of the P.1083 actually did fly. Its forward fuselage was used for the first prototype F.6, the P.1099, serialed XF 833, which had its first flight on 23rd January 1954.

Several theories have been put forward for the final cancellation. Doubts have been expressed that the aircraft would have been able to achieve its design performance (an accusation also levelled at its rival, the Supermarine 545). Another was that the basic wing design did not allow the easy carriage of external stores for any future developments. Another was that the predicted performance of the Supermarine 545 was much better and, therefore, the P.1083 was cancelled in its favour.

The most likely reason was purely financial. There have always been massive cutbacks of expenditure whenever a crisis is over, and in this case the urgency for new aircraft faded with the cessation of the Korean War. It was felt that an interim, just-supersonic fighter, was not needed but, to save money, a 'two-generation' leap would be made to the promising new Mach 2 design emerging from the English Electric factory, the P.1.

## CONSTRUCTION

The forward fuselage was identical to that of the basic Hunter back to the main fuselage transport joint between the centre and rear sections, the construction of which has been described in many other sources.

As the design progressed, it was gradually refined in detail. At first a new, taller, and slimmer fin was proposed, with a low-set all flying tailplane at the junction of the fin and fuselage structure. However, dated drawings show that this was gradually changed until the final design had a standard Hunter fin and rudder, with the tailplane mid-set in the normal position. (It is not clear whether these later drawings referred to the prototype solely as built, or whether the proposed production versions would also have the standard fin/tailplane configuration.)

With the low-set tailplane the aft fuselage ended in a 'pen-nib' fairing above the afterburner nozzle but, with the change to the standard fin/tailplane combination, this became the same as that eventually fitted to the Hunter F.3, with an angled cut-off to the fuselage and the afterburner nozzle protruding slightly. The tailcone below the fin was attached by four quick-release fasteners to allow access for removal of the jetpipe. (As noted earlier, there is strong evidence that the prototype was designed purely to prove the aerodynamic characteristics of the wing, being fitted with a RA7.R with two-position eyelid afterburner nozzles.) A further change to the rear fuselage shows a large, ventral, NACA-type flush intake, to provide cooling to the rear fuselage structure.

The wing-root intakes and fairings were again identical to the standard Hunter, at least on the prototype. The production version would probably have redesigned intakes to allow for the great mass flow of the more powerful engines proposed.

Outboard of the intakes, the wing structure was completely new. The actual internal structural layout followed closely that of the original Hunter wing, but had a greater span and fineness ratio. It was constructed around a forward mainspar and rear auxiliary spar, to which were hinged the flaps inboard, and the fully powered ailerons outboard, and multiple ribs. Sweepback on the leading edge was increased to 52°, giving a quarter-chord sweep of 48°36′ with a thickness/chord ratio of 7.5%. The left aileron had a small trim tab fitted approximately midway along its trailing edge. Dive brakes were fitted on the upper surfaces, forward of the flaps and just inboard of the ailerons. Standard Hunter mainwheel oleos were fitted, with the upper hinge modified to allow them to retract into the more swept area between the inner ends of the spars, and the bays stretched further outboard to increase the

## DATA

### DIMENSIONS

| | |
|---|---|
| Span | 34′4″ |
| Length | 45′10.5″ |
| Height | 13′2″ |
| Track | 15′7″ |
| Wheelbase | 17′8″ |
| Quarter chord sweep | 48°36′ |
| Leading edge sweep | 52° |
| t/c ratio | 7.5% |

### AREAS

| | |
|---|---|
| Wing | 358 sq ft |

### WEIGHTS

| | |
|---|---|
| Zero Fuel Weight | 15,400 lbs |
| Normal All-Up Weight | 20,000 lbs |
| Half Fuel Weight | 17,700 lbs |

### PERFORMANCE

| | |
|---|---|
| $V_{max}$  SL | 712 kts/1.08 Mach |
| | 36,000 ft 686 kts/1.2 Mach |
| Sea Level Rate of Climb | 50,000 ft./min |
| Service Ceiling | 59,500 ft |
| Take Off Distance to 50′ | 1,040 yds |

### REFERENCES

| | |
|---|---|
| Public Records Office | —Avia files |
| British Aerospace (Kingston) | —Archives |
| British Aerospace (Kingston) | —Photographic Archives |

Note   While I was carrying out research at British Aerospace, Kingston, their photographic records were found to be incomplete, and a large section covering the period of the P.1083 had been misplaced. It is therefore not possible to provide a photograph, even of the mockup.

track to 15′7. A pitot head was fitted to the left wingtip.

The fuel tanks, of 600 gallons total capacity, were housed in the wing leading edge. Integral tanks were being developed at the time, but drawings suggest that the prototype's tanks were of the bag-type, in two sections in each wing panel.

## POWER PLANT

Prototype: One Rolls-Royce Avon RA.7R axial flow turbojet developing a Sea Level Static Thrust of 7,130 lbs. dry, and 9,600 lbs. thrust with two-position afterburner nozzle.

Production Version: One Rolls-Royce RA.19R Avon axial flow turbojet developing a Sea Level Static Thrust of 12,250 lbs. dry, and 17,750 lbs., thrust with a fully variable nozzled, 1,800°K afterburner.

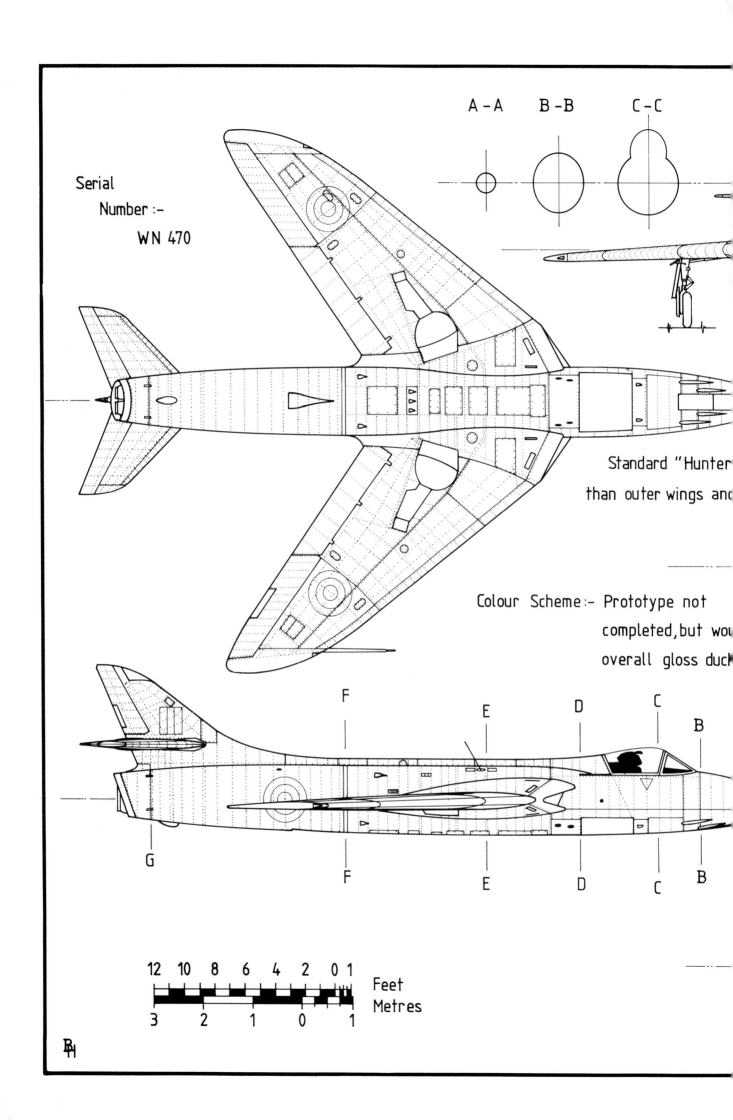

Serial
Number :-
WN 470

A - A    B -B    C-C

Standard "Hunter
than outer wings and

Colour Scheme:- Prototype not
completed, but wou
overall gloss duc

F        E        D        C        B

G

F        E        D        C        B

12  10  8  6  4  2  0 1    Feet
                          Metres
3       2     1     0     1

BH

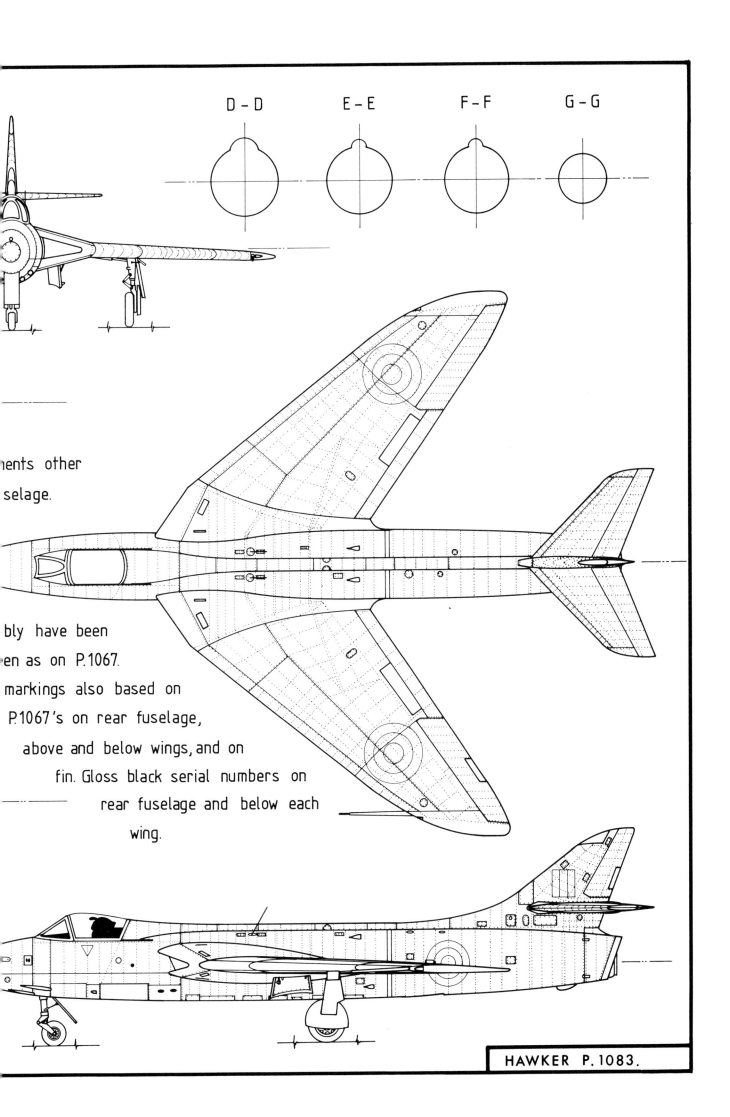

D - D    E - E    F - F    G - G

ments other

selage.

bly have been

en as on P.1067.

markings also based on

P.1067's on rear fuselage,

above and below wings, and on

fin. Gloss black serial numbers on

rear fuselage and below each

wing.

HAWKER P.1083.

Short S.B.4 Sherpa. Topside view showing to advantage the clean wing profile and engine intake. The aircraft is depicted before its first flight and has yet to have its serial numbers applied. (Royal Aeronautical Society.)

# SHORT S.B.4 'SHERPA'

| Manufacturer | Short Brothers and Harland Ltd |
|---|---|
| Specification | Private Venture – No Specification Allocated |
| Role | Research Prototype |
| First Flight Date | G–14–1–4th October 1953 |
| | G–36–1 – (later serial number) |

Having designed the Short S.A.4 four-jet bomber, the company proposed a further development based on this aircraft, but with a swept fin, no horizontal tail surfaces, and a swept wing of entirely new concept. At high subsonic speeds, the normal swept wing suffered in various degrees from lateral and longitudinal stability problems. To overcome these, the entire wingtip formed the control surface for both roll and pitch control, and the whole structure of the wing flexed under load, allowing the incidence of the wing to remain constant. The new principle was called 'aero-isoclinic'. The S.B.4 was built as a proof-of-concept prototype.

## DEVELOPMENT HISTORY

The company's interest in the revolutionary new wing concept started in 1945. It was designed to keep its angle of attack unchanged and thus free from buffet, whatever the deflection under load. This was achieved by placing the torsion box much further aft than normal. This resulted in the torsional and flexural axes being coincidental so that, when the wing flexed upwards, it did not twist and, conversely, when it did twist, the incidence remained constant. The lower skin of the leading edge was separated from the bottom edge of the box-spar to allow this flexure and also avoid local buckling. It was claimed that the use of wingtip control surfaces overcame the potential problems of both aileron and elevator reversal at high subsonic speeds. Also, tip stalling could be avoided and adverse yaw with aileron could be eliminated.

The company designed a large bomber around this new wing, using the basically identical fuselage from the S.A.4 and, to prove the basic aerodynamic theory, a cheap, small, proof-of-concept prototype was developed. This had the company designation S.B.1 and was unpowered. It was launched by towing behind a Short Sturgeon and first flew on 14th July 1951, but crashed on its second flight which did not occur until 14th October 1951.

The wings were found to be repairable, but it was decided that the glider and towed launch were too hazardous, and that a powered version would make a more valuable contribution to the overall research programme by allowing longer sorties and a much expanded flight envelope. Therefore, it was decided to design a new light alloy fuselage and to add propulsion in the form of two small turbojets. The design received the company designation of S.B.4 and the name 'Sherpa'.

The common NACA-type engine intake in the top of the fuselage proved to be efficient at all speeds and angles of attack. To cancel out any possible wing-flexure due to centre of gravity change from fuel usage, the two 25–gallon tanks were set very close to the fuselage centreline, and equally balanced about the centre of gravity. Despite the overall simplicity of the design, an auto-observer was fitted in the rear fuselage, its power supplied by the propeller-driven windmill generator in the nose.

After construction was completed at the Belfast factory, the aircraft was transported by road to Aldergrove airfield from where the first flight was made on 4th October 1953, just under two years from the crash of the glider.

Trials continued at Aldergrove and Belfast, with visits to Farnborough and, although the basic design concept was proven, no further development was undertaken. The originally planned bomber was still-born but other designs were proposed, including one to meet Specification M.148T, which was raised to cover the Naval requirement N.A.39 which eventually resulted in the Blackburn Buccaneer.

In the light of the lack of official interest (more 'normal' solutions having been found to the problems of high subsonic flight problems), following the completion of these trials the aircraft was transferred to the College of Aeronautics, Institute of Technology at Cranfield in April 1957, and re-serialed G–36–1. It was involved in a research programme which included investigation into the roll response of the wingtip controllers. These continued until the engines were time-expired during 1964, when the machine was transferred to Bristol College of Advanced Technology for use in laboratory work, continuing in this role until May 1966.

It was transferred by road to the Skyfame Museum, Staverton but, when this establishment closed and its exhibits dispersed, it went on its final journey (to date) to be preserved in the Imperial War Museum collection at Duxford, where it is currently held in storage.

This was effectively the first variable camber wing

to have successfully flown. It proved the idea of an aero-isoclinic wing to be feasible, and in itself was a successful research programme. Only in the late 1980s were further trials being made into the variable camber wing, but now with computers to control it and composite materials for construction. The 'Sherpa' was well ahead of its time.

# CONSTRUCTION

The fuselage structure was manufactured in three sections, each from different materials. The nose, back to Station 31.5, was made of fibreglass and was split horizontally to give access to the equipment accommodated inside, which included the radio transmitter and receiver, fuse-panel, pneumatic accumulators and a generator to charge storage batteries, which was driven by a small propeller attached to the tip of the nose. This was the sole source of electrical power for the radio, voice and auto-observer, the last two being housed in the rear fuselage. A charging point for the pneumatic system was provided in the upper left skin of the nosecone, and the radio aerial was mounted on the top centreline (this probably also doubled as a reference for the pilot). The fixed, fully castoring, nosewheel was fitted below the fuselage, the oleo having a fibreglass streamlined fairing, and had centring springs acting on a cam at the top of the unit.

The centre-section was of light alloy monocoque construction with a stressed skin, frames and stringers. A substantial longeron ran the full length of the centre-section along each side, above which there was no structure aft of Station 112, allowing the mounting of the engines and wing. Bulkheads were fitted only at the nosecone/centre-section junction, to absorb the nosewheel loads, and at the attachment points for the wing front and rear spars, and main undercarriage.

The cockpit was set well forward in the centre section for good visibility. The pilot had no ejection seat, and sat under a sliding canopy which could be jettisoned in an emergency. A venturi-type pressure head was fitted on the right side of the fuselage in line with the front of the one-piece windscreen, with its associated static ports on the left side below the wing root leading edge.

Immediately aft of the canopy, set flush into the fuselage topline, was a wide common NACA-type intake feeding both engines, which were mounted approximately level with the wing trailing edge and with their thrust lines at 10° to the centreline, each exhausting through jetpipes on each side of the fuselage aft of the wing trailing edge. Fireproof bulkheads, together with a sheet-steel compartment floor, isolated the engines from the rest of the fuselage structure. The two 25-gallon fuel tanks were mounted immediately below the engines. Mounted between the engines were two recuperators, for air-starting, a 1-gallon tank for ground-starts, and an oil tank. Three large air scoops were fitted on the engine access bay hatch to provide ventilation.

The fixed, oleo-pneumatic main undercarriage was attached immediately below the engines, with the shock-absorbers attached to a central anchor point, with radius rods and drag links. Wheel braking was pneumatic.

The aft fuselage was constructed from spruce frames, with a plywood skin and bulkheads. It was attached to the centre-section by a metal butt strap. A substantial tail bumper was fitted below the tailcone, as there was little physical ground clearance.

The fin and rudder were also of wooden construction, built around a single spar to which the rudder was hinged. This had two large external mass-balance horns, attached at approximately mid-height, and had a movement range of ±24°30'. An instrumentation boom, mounting a yaw vane, was fitted at the very top of the fin.

The wing was also primarily constructed from spruce for the main and the auxiliary spars at 35% and 60% chord. The main ribs forward of the mainspar were of light alloy, and of plywood and spruce aft of this. The skinning was of plywood for the lower surface, except where the flaps were fitted, and outboard of Rib 5 where it was fabric-covered. Plywood covered the top surface back to 60% chord, and aft of this it was also fabric-covered. The ribs aft of this spar were of spruce, as was the trailing edge member. Fittings were of light alloy at certain strategic high-stress points. It was built as a continuous structure out to the elevons, and was bolted to the fuselage at three points. Ribs 6 and 8 were all alloy to carry the elevon attachments.

The leading edge ribs were all of light alloy, with their upper part fixed to the 30% spar and their lower ends free to move, the entire leading edge being plywood covered. This construction effectively provided a 'slot' along the entire wing leading edge which prevented the lower surface form buckling during wing flexure. If necessary, for trials with different wing characteristics, the leading edge which prevented the lower surface from of this the wing was permanently aero-isoclinic. Leading edge sweep was 42°22', but the trailing edge was 'kinked', the angle being zero out to Station 58.5 and then 30° outboard of this to Stn. 148". Although the elevons' leading edge sweep was the same, the trailing edges were at 18°30'. It was of symmetrical Piercy 425 section, with an aspect ratio

## DATA

### DIMENSIONS

| | |
|---|---|
| Span | 38'0" |
| Length | 31'10.5" |
| Height | 9'1.12" |
| Track | 4'0" |
| Wheelbase | 13'1.45" |

### AREAS

| | |
|---|---|
| Wing (gross) | 261.5 sq ft |
| (net) | 230.0 sq ft |
| Elevon | 23.5 sq ft (each) |
| Balance tab | 3.42 sq ft (each) |
| Flap | 17.75 sq ft (each) |
| Fin and Rudder | 19.72 sq ft |
| Rudder | 9.75 sq ft |

### WEIGHTS

| | |
|---|---|
| Empty | 3,000 lbs |
| Loaded | 3,125 lbs (initially, but later 3,300 lbs) |

### PERFORMANCE

| | |
|---|---|
| Design Limiting Speed | 250 mph |
| Maximum Speed | 170 mph |
| Ceiling | 5,000 ft |
| Duration | 50 mins |

### REFERENCES

| | |
|---|---|
| 'The Aeroplane' | —18th December 1953 |
| 'Aeroplane Monthly' | —October 1977 |
| RAE Farnborough | —Library |

of 5.6:1 and an unloaded anhedral of 1°. Root chord was 11'9", decreasing to 5'8" at the elevon joint and 1'10" at the tips. The wing had considerable twist, with an incidence of +1°49' at the root, –0.53' at the elevon joint, and –6°4' at the tip.

The elevons were hinged at 23% of tip chord, and were made from spruce and plywood with an octagonal metal spar. The skinning was of plywood to about mid-chord, and fabric aft of this. Each surface had an anti-balance tab inboard. Connection to the main wing was via machined fittings, with the connecting control runs through the wing leading edge. When acting in unison for pitch control movement range was +5° to –17°30', and differentially for roll control ±9°. However, the maximum movement available was +9° and –26°30' combining both pitch and roll inputs. The anti-balance tabs were operated by torque rods, but an electric motor allowed the tabs' hinge point to be varied, giving an extra ±8° movement if required.

## POWER PLANT

Two Blackburn-Turbomeca Palas axial flow turbojets developing a Sea Level Static Thrust of 353 lbs.

*The all-moving Short S.B.4 Sherpa wingtip controls shown with aircraft taxi-ing out for take-off. (Royal Aeronautical Society.)*

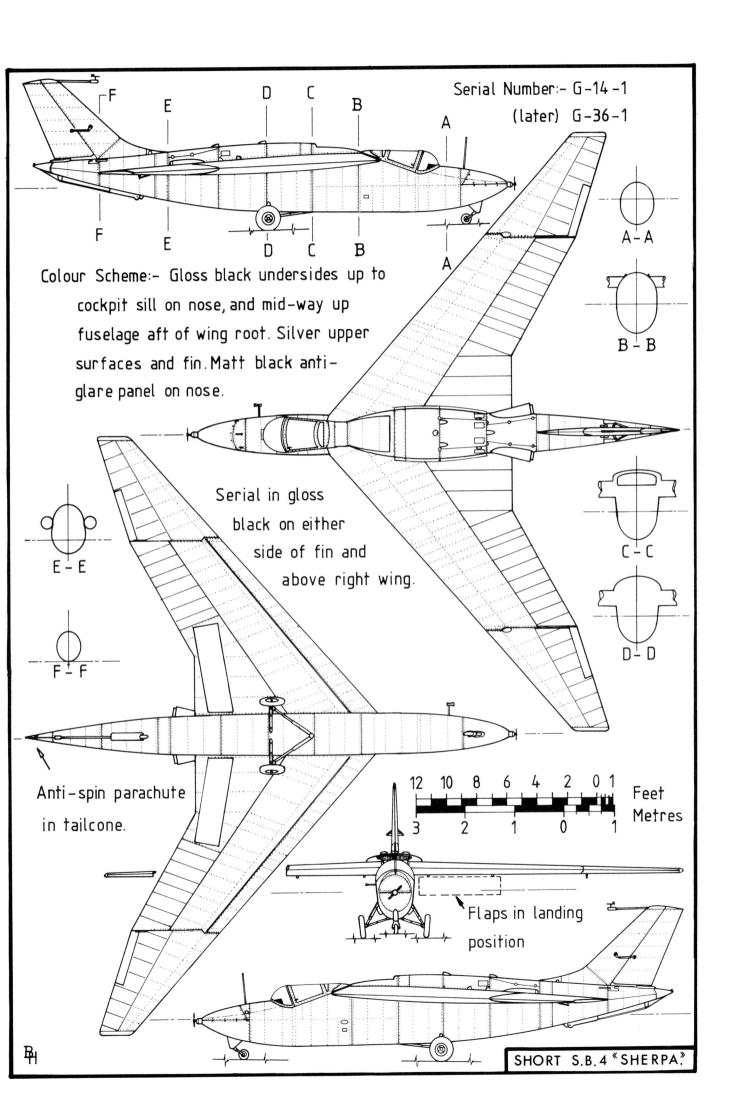

Serial Number:- G-14-1
(later) G-36-1

A-A

B-B

C-C

D-D

E-E

F-F

F E D C B A

Colour Scheme:- Gloss black undersides up to
cockpit sill on nose, and mid-way up
fuselage aft of wing root. Silver upper
surfaces and fin. Matt black anti-
glare panel on nose.

Serial in gloss
black on either
side of fin and
above right wing.

Anti-spin parachute
in tailcone.

12 10 8 6 4 2 0 1    Feet
3    2    1    0    1    Metres

Flaps in landing
position

SHORT S.B.4 "SHERPA."

*Supermarine 525 at first roll-out. Note 'string-type' arrester hook and clean topline to fuselage compared to later in its career. Note also early shape to fin tip.*

# SUPERMARINE TYPE 525

| | |
|---|---|
| **Manufacturer** | **Vickers Armstrong (Aircraft) Ltd., Supermarine Division** |
| **Specification** | **N.9/47** |
| **Role** | **Interim Fighter Prototype** |
| **First Flight Date** | **VX 138 – 27th April 1954** |

Although eventually to be put into production in a much modified form as the Scimitar, this aircraft is included as it was actually the third prototype of the earlier Type 508, suitably modified to have a swept wing, and entirely new tailplane and fin of conventional design. It bore a resemblance to the production aircraft in overall shape only, the latter having been completely redesigned.

## DEVELOPMENT HISTORY

The contract to develop an aircraft to Navy Specification N.9/47 was awarded to Supermarine for the construction of three prototypes and the project was given the company designation of Type 508. Only the first two were completed in this form, the third, early on being developed to incorporate swept wing and tail surfaces, and therefore allocated a new Type number, 525. It was still, however, covered by the original specification as no new one was written around it.

Following completion at the Supermarine Works, the airframe was disassembled and transported by road to Boscombe Down, where the first flight was made successfully on 27th April 1954. Subsequent trials showed under certain phases of flight that directional stability needed improvement, resulting in a redesigned fin leading edge, increasing the area. Company drawings show the intention of adding outboard leading edge extensions to form a small 'dog-tooth' discontinuity at approximately mid semi-span; these were not fitted to the Type 525 but did feature on the later Type 544, the forerunner of the Scimitar. Ventilation of the engine bay was also improved by adding scoops to some of the existing ventilation holes. In fact the aircraft had more changes to its paint scheme than it had modifications!

A modified, and de-navalised, version, designated the Type 526, was offered to meet Specification F.3/48 but was not proceeded with. A trainer version, with the pilots sitting in tandem, was also designed, still at that time with the swept 'butterfly' tailplane and allocated the designation Type 539, but was not proceeded with.

Despite having more powerful engines and

swept surfaces, the speed increase over the earlier Types 508/529 was only in the order of 30–40 kts. In fact, the time to height climb performance was, if anything, slightly worse. Also, despite being the swept-wing aircraft with about the most powerful installed thrust in the world, it still remained subsonic in level flight. It could just go supersonic in a dive.

Suggested modifications to improve performance included marked area-ruling of the fuselage and other changes to the wing and tail. This resulted in a complete redesign to eventually become the Type 544, to the definitive Specification N.113D and production under Specification N.113P.

The aircraft's career was destined to be relatively short, however, as on 5th July 1955 it spun into the ground and was totally destroyed.

# CONSTRUCTION

The fuselage was identical in construction to the Type 508/529 as far back as Frame 41 in the rear fuselage to which the tailcone was hinged. Aft of this was added a fixed cone, shortened by 3'6" compared to the earlier one. The overall length, however, increased due to the swept tail surfaces. The retractable tail skid was moved slightly aft and redesigned, as was the arrester hook. This now faired fully into the tailcone and extended aft before pivoting down to 60° when in use, together with its fuselage fairing panel.

Although originally designed with a swept 'butterfly' tailplane, this was changed early on to a design of more conventional form. The fin structure was built integrally with the new fuselage tailcone and was of two-spar construction with multiple ribs. It had a leading and trailing edge sweep of 50° and 28°30' respectively. The rudder was in two sections, one above and the other below the tailplane, neither having any trim tab. The trailing edge of the fin between the two surfaces was inset slightly compared to the rudder trailing edges. A long dorsal fairing projected forwards from the root leading edge to just short of the aft end of the engine access panels. During trials, it was found that directional stability was insufficient, and the fin leading edge shape was altered near the tip to slightly increase area.

An all-flying tailplane was fitted at approximately $\frac{1}{3}$ up the fin. The whole surface pivoted through a range of –10° to +5° for trimming purposes and as a follow-up control for the normal elevators. It had no dihedral and had a chord at the centreline of 7'5", and a leading and trailing edge sweep of 50° and 30° respectively. A long pointed bullet fairing projected aft from the junction of the fin and tailplane to improve airflow, and was used to house the braking parachute to shorten the landing run. This was unusual in consisting of three very small diameter parachutes on a common cable which, when deployed, were almost 60'0" behind the tail. It

is not clear whether they could also be used for anti-spin purposes.

No operational equipment was carried, the four cannon installation of the Type 529 having been removed and the ports faired over. There were also minor changes to the boundary layer exhaust louvres above and below the intake. Initially, the vents in the engine bay access doors on top of the fuselage were the same as before but, during tests, they were modified to incorporate scoops to improve efficiency.

Despite having the wing mounted further forward to keep the centre of pressure/centre of gravity relationship the same, it was possible to use the same main undercarriage bays in the fuselage centre-section, the design of the fairing doors was considerably changed, with a much smaller one attached to the oleo itself. The nosewheel oleo was unchanged but the single fairing door of the Type 508 was changed to two smaller ones that attached to the oleo hinged at its forward edge.

Fore and aft of these bays were the main changes from the earlier aircraft, with the inclusion of additional flap sections and two airbrake surfaces. The two new rectangular sections of flap were hinged across the fuselage at the frame to which the rear spar attached, to which were hinged the main wing flaps. Thus, when extended, the flaps were in line and acted in effect almost as if they were a continuous surface. The airbrakes were two curved

---

## DATA

**DIMENSIONS**

| | |
|---|---|
| Span | 37'2" |
| Length | 53'0.4" |
| Height | 14'11" |
| Wheelbase | 16'9" |
| Track | 13'6" |
| Tailplane span | 14'3" |

**AREAS**

| | |
|---|---|
| Wing (gross) | 450 sq ft |

**WEIGHTS**

| | |
|---|---|
| Normal loaded | 19,910 lbs |
| Maximum Overload | 28,169 lbs |

**PERFORMANCE**

| $V_{max}$ (level flight) at 30,000 ft | —562 kts/0.954 Mach |
|---|---|
| 40,000 ft | —545 kts/0.95 Mach |
| 45,000 ft | —535 kts/0.936 Mach |

The aircraft was capable of achieving supersonic speed in a dive.

**TIME TO HEIGHT**

to 30,000 ft—2.5 mins
40,000 ft—4.0 mins
45,000 ft—5.25 mins

(Note: Time calculated from attainment of climb speed).

**REFERENCES**

| Public Records Office | —Avia Files |
|---|---|
| Aviation Book Shop | —Photographic Archives |
| Vickers Armstrong | —Photographic Archives |
| RAF Museum | —Supermarine Archives |

Originally third prototype Type 508.

A-A        B-B        C-C

Serial Number: VX 138

Tailplane range of
movement.

10°
5°

Note enlarged fin area
in view below.

Structure designed for
wing-fold, but not operable

F
F

E        D        C

E        D        C

National markings above and below each
outer wing panel and on rear fuselage.
No fin flash. Serial number, gloss black,
on outer underwing panels and
above roundel on rear fuselage. Also,
"ROYAL NAVY" on rear fuselage above roundel.

12  10  8  6  4  2  0 1
                              Feet
                              Metres
3      2      1      0      1

BH

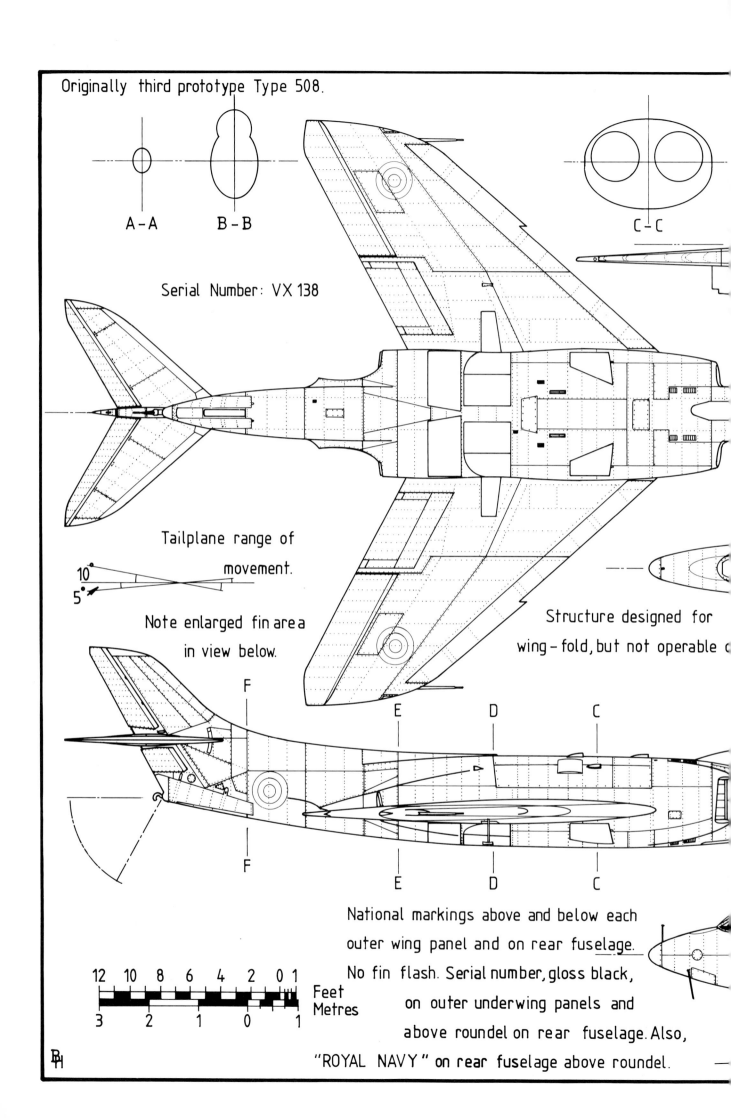

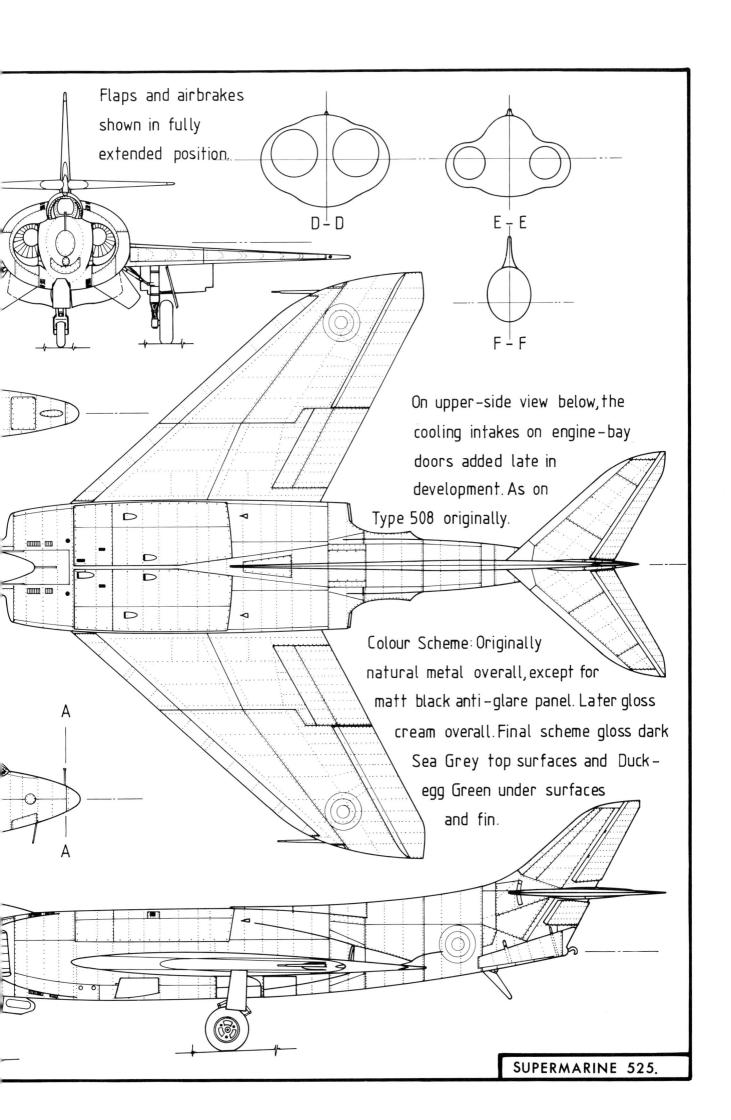

Flaps and airbrakes shown in fully extended position.

D - D

E - E

F - F

On upper-side view below, the cooling intakes on engine-bay doors added late in development. As on Type 508 originally.

Colour Scheme: Originally natural metal overall, except for matt black anti-glare panel. Later gloss cream overall. Final scheme gloss dark Sea Grey top surfaces and Duck-egg Green under surfaces and fin.

A
A

A
A

SUPERMARINE 525.

*In flight with a stormy background, again showing the multiple ventilation scoops on the top of the fuselage. The aircraft is shown in its gloss cream colour scheme. Below: Supermarine 525 painted in Naval colour scheme of dark sea grey/duck-egg green. Note the multiple scoop intakes sprouted on the engine bay doors and the revised leading edge to the fin tip.*

surfaces set unusually far forward situated just aft of the wing root leading edge on the fuselage underside.

The entirely new wing was set much further forward on the fuselage, and thus required some modification to the structure to cater for the new locations of the wing spar attachment points. It was constructed around a forward mainspar and aft auxiliary spar together with multiple ribs. It was of symmetrical section, with a thickness/chord ratio of 8% and chord at the centreline being 18'9". It had a quarter-chord sweep of 45° and anhedral angle of 1°. Leading and trailing edge sweep were 50° and 28°30' respectively.

The main wing fuel was accommodated between the two spars around the small main undercarriage bays. The structure was designed on the assumption that wing folding for carrier stowage would be needed in any developed version, but the Type 525 wing had no facility for this. The inboard end of the ailerons and the outboard end of the flaps coincided with the point where the wing would have folded to give the required 20'0" span. Plain trailing edge flaps and unusually large ailerons were hinged to the aft auxiliary spar. The ailerons had no trim tabs, as lateral trim was achieved by datum bias. The flaps had a flap-blowing system fed by bleed air from the engines, to help reduce approach speeds. Acting in conjunction with the main flaps, the entire wing leading edge was occupied by slats. All control surfaces were fully power operated from the hydraulic system.

The main undercarriage bays intruded very little into the wing structure and required only small cut-outs, despite the increase in wheel track. Changes to the pivot design of the oleos allowed an increase in wheelbase, while still enabling the same stowage in the fuselage for the wheels when retracted. The actual oleos were slightly lengthened compared to those on the Type 508, and were stressed for carrier-type landings.

## POWER PLANT
Two Rolls Royce R.A.7 axial flow turbojets developing a Sea Level Static Thrust of 7,500 lbs. Proposed R.A.7R version with afterburner never fitted.

English Electric P.1a first prototype WG 760 in flight. Note wing leading edge notches and inboard leading edge flaps. (English Electric)

# ENGLISH ELECTRIC P.1a

| Manufacturer | English Electric Company Ltd |
|---|---|
| Specification | ER.103; F.23/49 |
| Role | Interceptor Fighter |
| First Flight Date | WG 760 – 4th August 1954 |
| | WG 763 – 18th July 1955 |
| | WG 765 – Not Flown |

The English Electric P.1a was to gain fame as the first British fighter prototype capable of exceeding the speed of sound. Despite being described by a contemporary journal as having "all the shapeliness of a suitcase", the aircraft was certainly a very efficient aerodynamic machine and, at the time of writing, was eventually to be developed into the RAF's last single-seat interceptor. (Note The P.1a has been included in the book as it is unique in being the first successful British supersonic aircraft, and due to the fact that in its production form it was virtually an entirely different aircraft, after major re-design).

## DEVELOPMENT HISTORY

Early in 1948 at RAE Farnborough, a committee was set up whose terms of reference were to make recommendations for the future development of advanced fighters. Their findings were that, instead of the normal, customary, slow conservative approach, a short cut should be taken and work should proceed immediately on the development of a fully operational supersonic fighter.

Specification ER.103 was raised, calling for an aircraft capable of attaining at least 1.4 Mach and, after receiving tenders from the various firms, the contract was awarded to both Fairey Aviation and English Electric, each for two flying prototypes (and in the case of the latter a static test airframe as well) which, although experimental, had to be capable of development into an operational fighter. The choice of both companies was a departure from the accepted norm as neither were 'fighter companies' and neither had any previous experience of producing aircraft with anywhere near the

157

performance required. Fairey, at least, had a background of designing and building aircraft, but English Electric was very new to the game, having started solely as a production facility for other types such as the Vampire, and had designed only one aircraft of their own, although it was the most successful first jet-powered bomber for the RAF – the Canberra.

The shape of the aircraft was radically different from any previous design, the wing having a 60° leading edge sweep, and was virtually untapered. In effect, it was a delta wing with a notch cut-out in its trailing edge. However, there was more controversy over the positioning of the tailplane. After many model tests, the company had come out with a low-set position, much in the same position as that on the contemporary North American F-100. However, for some reason RAE Farnborough was convinced that this would be extremely dangerous, and felt that it should be repositioned on the top of the fin. So unconvinced were they by the firm's findings that eventually the Ministry issued a requirement for the construction of a near full-scale low-powered experimental aircraft to test the theories, resulting in the Short SB.5. This had the facility of the tailplane fitted in either the fin tip, or low-fuselage positions and also, as there was some worry over the "exceptionally large sweep angle", the wing could be ground adjusted from 50° to 69°. By the time it had flown, and finally been tested in the 60° sweep position with both high and low-set tail, the P.1 was so advanced in construction that it made little difference to the design, other than proving that the original concept had been correct from the start!

Even before the aircraft had been completed, it was obvious that a viable fighter could be developed from it, although it required some major redesign work especially to the forward fuselage and cockpit areas. Specification F.23/49 was raised, and the aircraft eventually developed, via the P.1b prototypes, into the Lightning fighter, the story of which is outside the scope of this book.

Construction of the first prototype, WG 760, was completed at the firm's Warton factory and, after dismantling, the aircraft was taken by road to Boscombe Down for its initial test flights. Taxi-ing trials commenced on 24th July and were completed in eight sessions by 2nd August, the aircraft having completed one very brief 'hop'. These trials were used also to prove the tail braking parachute operation, brake performance and runway performance up to nose lift-off. The first flight was made on 4th August 1954 and, by its third flight, had undramatically become the first British aircraft to exceed the speed of sound in level flight. (In fact, unknown to the pilot, it had gone supersonic earlier in a slight climb, all a little different to some of the earlier experiences on such as the DH.108!) All of this was done without the benefit of afterburners. On completion of the initial trials, the aircraft operated for the rest of the time mainly from its base at Warton.

From the outset, it proved to be a remarkably easy aircraft to fly, and required little in the way of aerodynamic modifications, although the extremely limited amount of fuel able to be carried proved an embarrassment. After the first flight, adjustment had to be made to the tailplane movement range as insufficient nose-down trim could be applied. Initially, the triangular leading edge flaps were used for landing but these were eventually locked closed as they were found to be superfluous. (These had also been fitted at the insistence of the RAE in the light of their wind tunnel tests, the results of which were to prove as erroneous as those for the tailplane position.) One other problem which was never solved was that of the airbrakes. These were of unusual design as they were hinged about their aft edges and, when opened, caused severe nose-up trim change and buffeting. Eventually it was decided that they could be used only in an emergency, as a new design was not thought worthwhile on the P.1a, but they were redesigned and repositioned on the P.1b.

For a British fighter-type, the cockpit was exceptionally roomy, with a sill width of 37" which at that time was unprecedented (soon to be rectified back to the normal 'squeeze' on the P.1b. One had the impression that aircraft were completely designed and then some small space found for the pilot almost as an afterthought!) However, its locking mechanism was of poor design, in that the lever could indicate that the canopy was locked closed when in fact it was not. Consequently, canopies were lost during high speed flight on 5th March and 13th August 1956 although luckily the pilot was able to decelerate and recover to base successfully. (To lose a canopy once is bad enough but to lose it twice for the same reason is not really on!)

Meanwhile, the second prototype WG 763 had joined the test programme and made its maiden flight on 18th July 1955. The only external differences readily apparent were two cannon ports high on the nose, an under-fuselage fuel tank, and slight changes to the equipment hatch immediately aft of the cockpit canopy. The additional fuel in the belly tank was probably very welcome! (Contrary to other reports, the aircraft retained the same split flaps as the earlier machine, the change being made to plain flaps on the second P.1b prototype.) Later in 1955 it became the first British aircraft to fire its guns at supersonic speeds.

Initially, neither aircraft had flown with afterburners but, during late 1955, WG 760's engines were fitted with very rudimentary ones with the nozzles fixed in a position for optimum thrust with the afterburners operating. This drastically reduced the maximum 'dry' thrust to approximately 4,200 lbs. for each engine, badly handicapping performance. The aircraft first flew with these engines on 31st January 1956 and the climb performance, with afterburners, dramatically improved, giving a time

*English Electric P.1a first prototype showing the planform of the development wing with increased tip chord to reduce subsonic drag. (Royal Aeronautical Society)*

to 40,000 ft. of only 3.5 minutes; however, in the event of an engine failure in the landing configuration, the aircraft was not able to maintain altitude, so much was the dry thrust reduced.

By this time, both aircraft had been evaluated by Service pilots who were all favourably impressed, the performance capability being well out of any class previously experienced. However, adverse comment was made about the endurance caused by the severe lack of fuel, and the ejection seat was found to be very uncomfortable and, with the low canopy line, caused taller pilots to have to hunch over, thus causing the windscreen arch to encroach further on the forward view.

The brakes on WG 763 were also criticised. On the first aircraft, these were operated by a lever on the control column, standard practice in British fighters until that time, with differential braking being achieved by deflecting the rudder and applying brakes. WG 763 had toe-brakes which initially had only half an inch of movement of the pedals from full off to full on, and the pilots found it impossible to keep a straight line during taxi-ing as they were far too sensitive. The ratio of pedal movement to braking amount was altered to

improve matters. (Toe-brakes were an art to get used to in those days when one had only had the hand-operated variety before, as I found when I first flew the Javelin and Viscount. Luckily it did not take long to adapt!)

A modified wing with extended tip chord, had by now appeared on WG 760 giving a kinked leading edge profile. This reduced subsonic drag by as much as 20% but caused a small increase at supersonic speeds, which it was thought could be easily accommodated by a small increase in available thrust.

Both aircraft left their Warton base during 1957, WG 760 going to Boscombe Down on 6th May and Finningley on 20th May for wet runway braking trials, and then back to Boscombe Down on 25th November for preview handling by the Service pilots. WG 763 meanwhile had gone to Bedford on 19th June for longitudinal stability and tail-load measurement in flight trials. It was joined slightly later, on 23rd January 1958, by WG 760 for Safeland barrier arrester trials. It was still involved in these when, on 12th November of the same year, it suffered damage when engaging the barrier and subsequently in the hangar, mainly restricted to the tailplanes.

*The second prototype English Electric P.1a just after take-off. Note ventral fuel tank and only one pitot boom fitted on the nose. (Royal Aeronautical Society)*

The second machine was involved in ground resonance trials in December 1960 and, during the early part of 1962, in parachute streaming trials. The third aircraft, serialed WG 765, remained throughout at Warton as a structural test airframe and was scrapped at the end of the trials programme.

WG 760 was finally retired from active flight trials on 2nd July 1962 and transported to Weeton for ground instructional purposes, with the Maintenance Serial of 7755M. It was transferred to St. Athan for storage in September 1965, and then to Henlow, being joined by WG 763 (now serialed 7816M) on 21st January 1964. WG 763 had been allocated to Aero Flight at RAE Bedford on 21st June 1957 before being retired to Henlow. Between them, they had completed over 500 flights and had made a valuable contribution to the initial development of the Lightning fighter. For some years they were displayed side by side alongside the parade ground. Due to deterioration in the open air, and because of their historical significance, they were removed from there, the first going for refurbishment and preservation to the only remaining operational Lightning base at Binbrook, and the second, after similar treatment, was exhibited at the Manchester Air and Space Museum, where it is to this day. WG 760 made one final move from Binbrook to the RAF Museum, Cosford, where it is now on display.

(*Note* Much has been written recently regarding the flight trials of the P.1a aircraft, providing much interesting, first-hand detail. Therefore, this will not be more fully dealt with and the reader is referred to the several publications which cover this aspect.)

## CONSTRUCTION

The structure was made from light alloy with a stressed skin, except for certain areas around the engines and jetpipes which were manufactured from titanium. The fuselage was a flat-sided, constant cross-section tube over virtually its whole length, totally unlike earlier 'more elegant' shapes, eliciting the previously mentioned analogy to a suitcase. The majority of space was taken up with the intake and exhaust ducts for the two engines. These had a common, sharp-lipped, pear-shaped intake right in the nose. Two long pitot booms were mounted to the lip, one above and one below. The bottom one was always carried but the top was deleted on occasion. The duct narrowed slightly immediately aft of the lower lip, the slight bulge being caused by the need to house the nosewheel oleo in its bay after it had retracted forward, turning 90° whilst so doing, to lie horizontally in the bay. The wheel was fitted with a very narrow profile, 22.6" diameter tyre which had, for that period, an extremely high pressure of 200 psi. (later increased to 250 psi.).

Further aft, a slightly narrower 'throat' was created by the duct reducing in area from the top, this bulge being created by the cockpit floor. Just aft of this, the duct bifurcated horizontally, the mainplane structure passing right through the fuselage. The engines were mounted one above the other, the depth of the fuselage being kept to a minimum by the engines being staggered, the bottom one being in front of the top, and aligned so that the compressor of the latter was just behind the turbine of the former. Even so the fuselage depth was quite large at 6'6" (width being only 4'4" in comparison). The jetpipes continued straight aft to exhaust eventually at the very rear of the fuselage.

The cockpit canopy was virtually flush with the top line of the fuselage and was unusually broad. The main canopy hinged at its rear edge for normal entry and exit and was actuated and held open by two small hydraulic rams on each side. The pilot was provided with a Martin-Baker Mk.3 ejection seat, which automatically jettisoned the canopy when the ejection sequence was initiated. Instrument layout was surprisingly simple for such an advanced aircraft, with the main forward panel divided into three and the side sections angled to give the pilot a 'no-parallax' view of the instruments. The sharply raked windscreen had a flat rectangular centre panel, and unusually large curved side quarter-lights, the left one of which had embedded heating elements for demisting and poor weather visibility. A wide, but shallow, equipment bay was provided between the intake lip and the windscreen base, and a further one was situated immediately aft of the cockpit canopy, covered by two doors hinged at their top edges.

Multiple access panels were provided around the nose and forward fuselage skin for access to the various pieces of equipment and instrumentation. There were also two pairs of small rectangular doors on each side of the fuselage, one pair low on the side just aft of the nosewheel bay and the other pair on the sides of the upper fuselage above the wing. These were suction relief doors to provide added airflow to the engines at high power settings and low speeds. For servicing and removal, each engine had an 11'0" long access panel in the lower and upper fuselage skins, the upper ones having large rectangular ventilation louvres set in them.

The fin and rudder were mounted with the fin root leading edge at the aft end of the upper engine access panel. The fin height above the fuselage was 7'0.5", with its thickness/chord ratio varying from 4% at its root to 6% at the tip. It was built around multiple vertical spars and ribs, the aft spar being swept and to which the constant chord rudder was hinged. The leading and trailing edge sweep angles were 57°30' and 10° respectively. The anchorage point for the braking parachute cable was attached to the top of the fuselage immediately aft of the fin trailing edge root, the actual stowage for the parachute being below the fuselage under the tailplane. When stowed, the cable was clipped around the left edge of the two jetpipes and was pulled loose when the parachute was streamed. Two rectangular airbrakes were mounted either side of the jetpipes, hinged at their aft edges. These caused a lot of problems and were only used in an emergency.

The low-set tail was mounted on a bulged fairing either side of the fuselage with an interconnection between the two surfaces. It was a slab surface with no separate elevators and the whole surface moved as one for pitch control and trim. Like the wing, it was virtually untapered, with its thickness/chord ratio varying from 6.5% at the root to 5% at the tip. Its leading edge sweep was 60° and that at the trailing edge, 56°30'. It was built around a mid-chord mainspar and two auxiliary spars. The movement range of the tail was initially +3° to –18°, but in the light of the flight testing this was altered to +1° to –20° relative to the aircraft datum.

The wing was mid-mounted at an incidence of +2° and with an overall anhedral of 3°. It was built around a main forward spar which curved towards the root to be attached perpendicular at the fuselage side, and there were three further primary auxiliary spars aft, with additional spanwise stiffeners. There were multiple ribs perpendicular to the leading edge. The wing hardly tapered at all towards its tip, the chord at the centreline being 19'5.6", aspect ratio 2.65:1, and the leading and

## DATA
### DIMENSIONS
| | |
|---|---|
| Span | 34'10" |
| Length | 50'11" |
| Fuselage length | 48'6.8" |
| Tailplane span | 14'6" |
| Height | 17'3" (on ground) |
| Track | 12'9.25" |
| Wheelbase | 17'11" |

### AREAS
| | |
|---|---|
| Wing (gross) | 458 sq ft |
| (net) | 380 sq ft |
| Ailerons | 30.42 sq ft |
| Tailplane (gross) | 75.24 sq ft |
| (net) | 52.91 sq ft |
| Fin and Rudder (gross) | 118.7 sq ft (including fuselage) |
| (net) | 45.86 sq ft |

### WEIGHTS
| | |
|---|---|
| loaded | 27,100 lbs |
| max landing | 21,100 lbs |

### PERFORMANCE
**Climb**

| | |
|---|---|
| Wheels roll to 1,000 ft (400 kts) | —1 min |
| to 10,000 ft (410 kts) | —1 min 50 secs |
| to 20,000 ft (0.9 Mach) | —2 min 40 secs |
| to 30,000 ft | —3 min 32 secs |
| to 40,000 ft | —4 min 43 secs |

(all the above times to height without afterburner!)

$V_{max}$ 1.51 Mach (limited by directional stability due to fin area)

### REFERENCES
| | |
|---|---|
| Manchester Museum | —The aircraft |
| RAF Museum, Cosford | —The aircraft |
| A & AEE, Boscombe Down | —Library Archives— Report No. 909. |

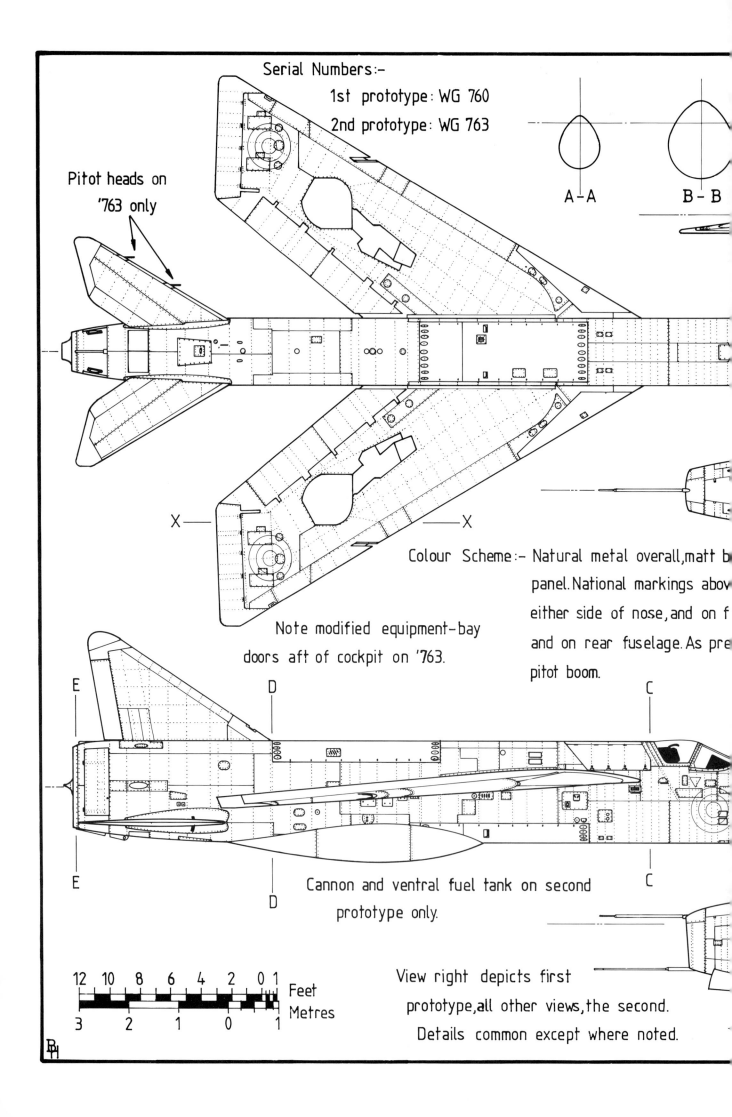

Serial Numbers:-
1st prototype: WG 760
2nd prototype: WG 763

Pitot heads on
'763 only

A-A          B-B

X ———— X

Colour Scheme:- Natural metal overall, matt b
panel. National markings abov
either side of nose, and on f
and on rear fuselage. As pre
pitot boom.

Note modified equipment-bay
doors aft of cockpit on '763.

E          D          C

E          C

D

Cannon and ventral fuel tank on second
prototype only.

12  10  8  6  4  2  0 1   Feet
3       2      1     0   1   Metres

View right depicts first
prototype, all other views, the second.
Details common except where noted.

BH

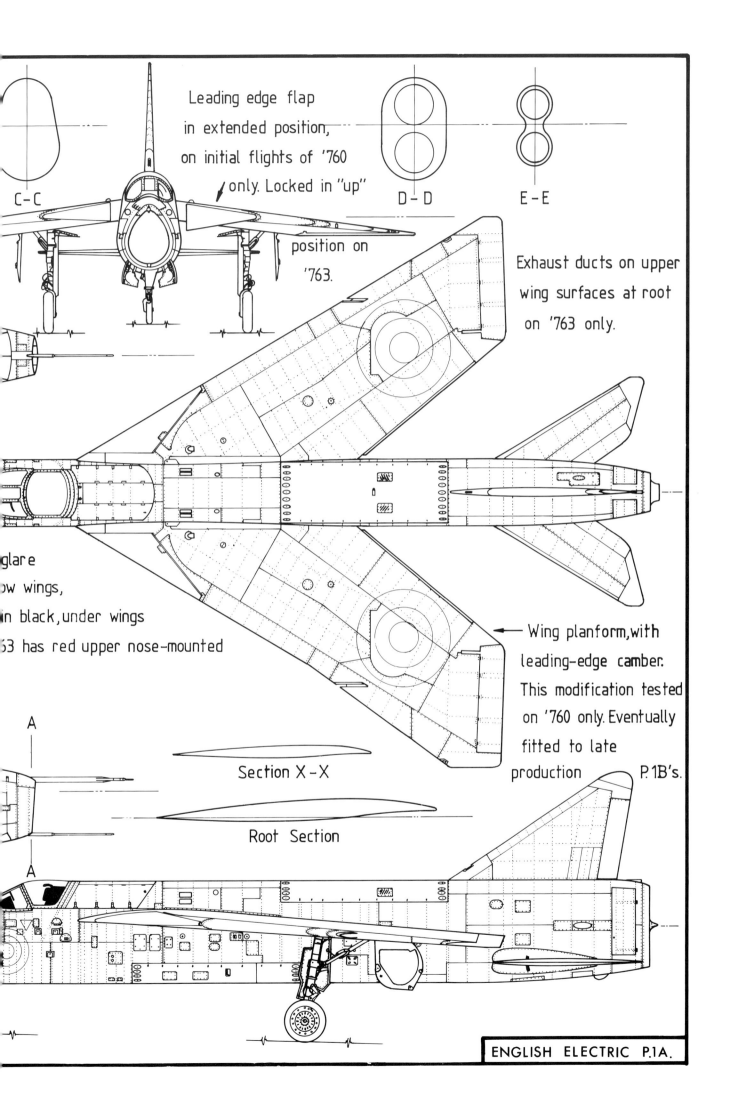

C-C

Leading edge flap
in extended position,
on initial flights of '760
only. Locked in "up"
position on
'763.

D-D

E-E

Exhaust ducts on upper
wing surfaces at root
on '763 only.

glare
ow wings,
in black, under wings
63 has red upper nose-mounted

A

Section X-X

Root Section

A

Wing planform, with
leading-edge camber.
This modification tested
on '760 only. Eventually
fitted to late
production        P.1B's.

ENGLISH ELECTRIC P.1A.

trailing edge sweeps being 60° and 51°30' respectively. Thickness/chord ratio increased from 5.25% at the root to 6.19% at the tip. The constant chord ailerons were hinged across the tips, which were not quite at 90° to the fuselage but had a forward sweep of 2°. The ailerons had a horn balance at the tip, except when WG 760 was fitted with the wing with extended tip chord, when they were inset. The 'kinked' wing had its leading edge sweep reduced to 55° from Wing Stn. 130" measured from the centreline, the new tip profile also having slight conical camber. Fuel was carried in integral tanks between the main and aft auxiliary spars. All control surfaces were fully powered, with irreversible jacks.

The main undercarriage retracted outwards into its bay, with the outer fairing door hinged at its inner edge, in what was to become the distinctive and unique 'Lightning' fashion. Each wheel was fitted with a narrow, 33.4" diameter tyre inflated to the high pressure of 250 psi.

The main Fowler-type split flaps occupied virtually the entire trailing edge and had a maximum deflection angle of 50°. As they deflected downwards, they also moved aft, effectively increasing the wing area. For initial trials, there were also triangular leading edge flaps at the root of the wing, which were deflected down for take-off and landing by 26°30'. They proved to be superfluous, the low-speed handling being perfectly satisfactory without them, and so they were soon locked in the up position (in fact, the second prototype had them deleted completely).

## WG 763

The basic airframe was identical to the earlier aircraft. The only external difference was in the fitting of a 250 gallon capacity ventral fuel tank, which could be jettisoned in an emergency, to add to the ludicrously small internal fuel capacity.

Apart from the tiny difference in the shape of the equipment bay doors aft of the cockpit, the only other major difference was the fitting of two 30 mm Aden cannon either side of the cockpit, with their troughs either side of the upper nose. Spent cartridges and links were retained on board. They caused no difference in the aircraft's handling but the open ports produced a deep resonant sound that could be heard from the cockpit at all times. Firing trials, even at supersonic speeds, caused no engine surge problems, as the ports were well aft of the intake; however their closeness to the pilot's line of sight must have caused problems with muzzle flash, especially at night. When the cannon were fitted, the upper pitot boom was not, so that the radar ranging antenna could be fitted, with its very slim di-electric cover forming the upper tip of the intake lip. Other 'operational' equipment was carried, although no record can be found specifying just what this comprised. As has been noted previously, toe-operated wheel brakes were fitted rather than those actuated by a hand-lever.

## POWER PLANT
Two Armstrong Siddeley Sapphire A.S.Sa.5 axial flow turbojet engines with a Sea Level Static Thrust of 7,200 lbs.. Later WG 760 fitted with two Armstrong Siddeley A.S.Sa.5R axial flow turbojet engines with a Sea Level Static Thrust of 4,200 lbs., dry, and 9,200 lbs., with afterburner.

*English Electric P.1a first prototype as preserved at Cosford. Note sharp intake lips, and just discernible within the intake, the throat caused by the bulge of the nosewheel bay.*
*(Ron Moulton)*

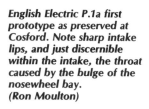

*Fairey Delta 2 in flight during its early trials and still in its polished natural metal finish. (Royal Aeronautical Society)*

# FAIREY DELTA 2

| | |
|---|---|
| **Manufacturer** | **Fairey Aviation Company Ltd** |
| **Specification** | **ER.103** |
| **Role** | **Research Prototype** |
| **First Flight Date** | **WG 774 – 6th August 1954** |
| | **WG 777 – 15th February 1956** |

The FD.2 was one of those fortunate designs that was correct from the start and no major aerodynamic changes were required in the light of flight tests. It far exceeded its original specification regarding performance, and proved to be one of Britain's most valuable research tools, with programmes stretching over many years. However, apart from gaining the speed record, it was rarely in the public eye.

## DEVELOPMENT HISTORY

In September 1947, the Ministry of Supply discussed how Britain might catch up in supersonic aircraft development, a sphere in which it had fallen badly behind. One of the companies consulted was Fairey Aviation, which was unusual in that its previous work had mainly been a succession of designs for the Navy. Specification ER.103 was raised for the design and development of a supersonic aircraft.

The preliminary design work produced an aircraft with highly-swept wings, a conventional tailplane, all-moving wingtips and twin engines fed by a nose intake, very similar to the English Electric layout. However, early in 1949 the firm reconsidered the whole project in the light of their acquired experience in the new techniques of drag and performance estimation, and completely redesigned their submission. By December of that year, it materialised very much in the form in which it eventually flew.

The design was of delta planform, with a minimum diameter fuselage to house an afterburning Avon RA.5 axial flow turbojet and wingroot intakes. The contract was not placed until October 1950 and was awarded to both English Electric and Fairey, covering the construction of two flight prototypes and one airframe for structural testing. By this time, the design had received the company designation of FD.2

*In flight with the nosewheel bay doors removed. Note the correct angle of the nosewheel oleo compared to the aircraft's fuselage datum, plus the yaw vane boom on the fin tip.*

Work was seriously delayed, as the company almost immediately became involved in a 'super-priority' programme producing the Gannet, and a fully effective start on detailed design and construction could not properly begin until Summer 1952. Little priority was given to the design and little wind tunnel work had been done before the aircraft made its maiden flight. In fact, some of the supersonic wind tunnel tests had not even been analysed until the aircraft itself had flown supersonically!

The aircraft's final form differed little from the original configuration. A company drawing, No. A.79411, dated 3rd July 1950, shows that the original plans were for a small horizontal tailplane fitted at the tip of the fin, as per the specification. However, a letter from the company to the Ministry in May the following year described the disadvantages of this layout. In their opinion the tailplane should be removed on three counts: there was a decrease in stability at high coefficients of lift; the fin structure weight could be made much lighter without the necessity of it being fitted; and the tailplane increased overall drag. The decision was taken on 18th May to delete the requirement "in the light of experience gained in America with a 60° delta design."

The fuselage was redesigned so that the engine could be withdrawn out the rear after unbolting the complete rear fuselage, instead of the original idea of upwards through large dorsal doors. A further major change did not take place until after the aircraft had actually flown. Main wing flaps were originally fitted at approximately mid-chord, and the decision to have them deleted was taken before the aircraft flew. However, for the first flights on WG 774, they were still in place but locked in the up position. They were deleted entirely on WG 777.

An original idea was that the aircraft should first fly with a raised 'slow' cockpit canopy with a flat windscreen, later to be substituted for a more streamlined, near flush 'high-speed' canopy. The latter was adopted, and the earlier one deleted. However, then the problem arose of the forward and downward visibility during the approach and landing phase, at the characteristic high angles of attack of a delta planform. The novel idea of a 'droop-snoot' nose was put forward at a meeting on 19th December 1951, in which the whole nose section was pivoted at the cockpit's aft bulkhead down through 10° to improve the pilot's vision. This was adopted, and proved most successful. Westland Aircraft inherited this Fairey patent when it took the company over and it was subsequently purchased by BAC. Today it is still seen on another delta – Concorde.

The first prototype – serial WG 774 – was completed in mid–1954 at the company's Hayes factory, and transported by road to Boscombe Down where its successful maiden flight was made on 6th October 1954.

No major modifications or adjustments were necessary as the pilot considered that it showed "every promise of being a very pleasant aircraft to fly". However, the contractor's flight trials were not to be without incident. On its fourteenth flight, on 11th November (which in itself demonstrates the soundness of the design in achieving so many flights on a new prototype in just over a month), a fuel problem caused the engine to stop. Luckily, the aircraft was close enough to Boscombe Down for the pilot skilfully to execute a 'dead-stick' wheels-up landing. Damage was limited to the wing, which was entirely replaced by that from the structural test specimen and, after an eight month lay-up, the aircraft resumed its programme, showing no different handling characteristics with the substitute wing.

Despite the aircraft not having yet used its afterburner, the first supersonic flight was achieved, without any fuss, on 28th October 1955.

It was by now becoming very obvious to the

company that the design had far greater speed potential than at first envisaged. With the after-burner working, they were looking at thrust v drag curves which did not cross until very high speeds had been attained. They realised that, in the FD.2, they had an aircraft which could successfully regain the speed record from the Americans. The only problem seemed to be in convincing the Ministry who, to say the least, did not appear enthusiastic, or even to believe that the aircraft was capable of such performance! In the end, reluctant permission was given for the attempt, provided it was mostly at the company's expense!

After practices starting on 8th March, the record attempts were made on 10th March 1956. The aircraft made two runs, one in each direction and, even though these had to be made within 30 minutes of each other, the pilot was able to land and refuel, and climb back to height between them, as there was insufficient fuel to do both. The runs were made at 38,000 ft: on the first run the aircraft achieved 1,117.6 mph. (971.17 kts.) and, on the second, 1,146.9 mph. (996.62 kts.) Therefore, the average of the two, 1,132.136 mph. (983.8 kts.) was sufficient to beat the previous record by a handsome 300 mph., held at the time by a North American F-100C. This large margin caused not a little consternation in the USA! What was not released at the time was that the aircraft was still accelerating throughout each run, and the only apparent limit to its top speed was fuel available. The speed achieved was equivalent to approximately 1.73 Mach.

Just before the record attempt, the second prototype WG 777 had joined the test programme, having completed its first flight on 15th February 1956. It differed little, other than having the underwing flap system completely removed and slight differences in equipment and instrumentation. After its brief manufacturer's trials, it went to RAE Bedford and was operated by Aero Flight, completing many research programmes into high-speed flight stability and control.

Due to restrictions in low-level supersonic trials over Britain, agreement was reached with the French authorities to conduct them in the South of France. Therefore, WG 774 was based at Cauzaux between 11th October and 15th November 1956. In this relatively short time, no less than 52 sorties were flown, and supersonic flight was achieved as low as 3,500 ft. altitude. At the time, Dassault had several people at Cazaux, and it would appear that the FD.2 impressed them and had not a little bearing on the design of their next creation – the Mirage III!

WG 774 returned to Britain, and was handed over to Aero Flight by RAE Bedford, for operation with its companion on various research programmes, until 5th September 1960 when WG 774 departed

for BAC. Filton for conversion into the BAC Type 221.

WG 777 soldiered on alone until 1st July 1966, when it was put up for disposal as UHF radio could not be fitted. This was a requirement for all aircraft being operated from that time. By now, total airframe hours were only 198 hrs. 15 mins., with total engine hours (Engine No. 7482/A651729) standing at 169 hrs. 4 mins. (These low hours were an indication of the short duration of some of the flight test sorties, considering the number that had been made.)

The decision was taken that the airframe should be preserved but, although the shell was kept intact, equipment and systems parts were cannibalised from it to keep the BAC.221 flying, this latter aircraft by now being back at Bedford.

When it was no longer required, WG 777 was transferred to the RAF Museum, Cosford, where it is on display still. Strangely, though, during one of its refurbishments, someone put the nosewheel oleo on the wrong way round! The aircraft now has a totally unnatural 'sit' on the ground, with the nosewheel oleo angled much too far forward. (If photographs of the FD.2 are checked, it will be seen that the attachment pivot for the retraction drag brace should be on the front of the main-leg; at present it is on the back!)

The company was, of course, keen to develop a fighter from the obviously successful configuration of the FD.2. It proposed, first, an interim ER.103B design, retaining the original wing but having an enlarged fuselage housing either a de Havilland Gyron, or a Rolls-Royce RB.122. The ultimate design was to be the ER.103C, again with the same choice of engine but with a weapons system based on a monopulse radar and tip-mounted Firestreak missiles. The company did, in fact, win the competition for a contract arising from the F.155T specification calling for a mixed power plant interceptor, but this was cancelled before any real progress was made on it.

Looking back, the FD.2 was an exceptional experimental aircraft. Other than the one forced landing due to engine failure, there were few problems, and it looked identical externally from the first to the last flight, as no major modifications were required. It far exceeded its specification and it contributed much to Britain's knowledge of supersonic flight characteristics.

## CONSTRUCTION

The whole airframe design was geared towards one having the minimal frontal areas to reduce drag. Unfortunately, this meant that there was very little room in the whole airframe for equipment, engine, fuel and pilot. The fuselage was a long, slim,

*Fairey Delta 2 painted in its attractive mauve and white colour scheme after its successful attempt at the World Speed Record. (Royal Aeronautical Society)*

cylinder of sufficient diameter just to accommodate the engine, with only the minimum of clearance around it for the fuselage structure. From the aft cockpit pressure bulkhead, it was of constant section to just aft of the fin leading edge root, when it gently tapered down to the afterburner nozzle. The nose tapered into an oval section in a long fine point to the interchangeable nose-mounted pitot instrumentation boom (dependent on which boom was fitted, the actual fuselage length varied resulting in some different quoted dimensions). In the very nose of the fuselage structure proper was the compass detector unit, and just in front of the cockpit was an equipment bay containing the oxygen bottle, radio, brake control valve and undercarriage selector valve. Whip-aerials for the radio were fitted below the nosecone and above and behind the cockpit canopy. A 'squared U-shape' di-electric fairing was also fitted under the nosecone. The cockpit canopy hardly broke the line of the fuselage, the curved windscreen consisting of a cast magnesium-alloy frame containing a pair of single curvature glass panels, with a slim centre pillar and raked at 62°. The mainly metal canopy was hinged on its right-hand edge and had only three tiny square windows, and two even smaller tear-drop shaped windows, to give the pilot barely adequate forward, sideways and upwards vision. There was no rearward vision possible at all. The cockpit was very small and cramped, and many of the normal instruments were miniaturised to fit them all in. The pilot was provided with a modified Martin-Baker Mk.3FDV ejection seat and the whole canopy could be blown off in an emergency. There was also an external canopy jettison button on the left side, just forward of the windscreen, for rescue in the event of a crash landing.

The extremely limited visibility for the pilot, especially during the approach and landing phase, was overcome to some extent by the whole nose of the aircraft being hinged down by 10°, pivoted at the base of the rear cockpit bulkhead. It was controlled by the pilot and was operated by a centrally-mounted single hydraulic jack. In order that the underside of the nose structure did not foul the forward ends of the nosewheel bay doors these were sequenced open whenever the 'droop' was selected down, so that on many occasions the aircraft could be seen flying with all undercarriage up, nose droop down, and the nosewheel doors open. (This must be one of the few systems on a modern aircraft where the doors were not connected to, and sequenced automatically by, the undercarriage.) Various services were accessible within the nosewheel bay including the 24 volt accumulator, electrical ground socket, hydraulic system charging points and the electrical connection for engine starting. The nosewheel oleo was fitted with twin wheels mounted on a live axle, each wheel having an 18″ tyre inflated to a pressure of 80 psi. The oleo retracted backwards into the bay which was faired over by two large doors.

The central fuselage section was designed as slim as possible around the Avon engine; in fact, there was barely five inches between the engine and the outside skin of the aircraft. Due to this lack of physical depth, the main load-bearing fuselage frames had to be machined from solid forgings, and were made from special high-strength light alloy. The datum for the fuselage was measured from the trailing edge of the wings, and the centre-section stretched forward from Frame 27.5 to the sloping front frame behind the cockpit rear bulkhead at Frame 292.5. Most of the frames around the engine bay were not continuous hoops but were manufactured in three sections and pin-jointed together. Six prominent intake scoops were provided along the fuselage for engine bay ventilation.

The engine was fed by two relatively small simple oval intakes on each side of the fuselage, with prominent boundary layer bleed ducts. Each duct curved sharply inwards to form the common, circular inlet for the engine. The sharp lips of the intakes were swept, and the lower one raked behind the upper to enable it to stay within the shock-cone formed by the upper one, up to maximum design speed. The flying control and hydraulic services were all led along the top of the fuselage under a series of easily removable panels for servicing access. The fuel system was gravity-filled through a filler cap in the upper fuselage just aft of the intakes.

The fuel was contained in four integral tanks in the wings, and a collector tank between the intake ducts in the fuselage. A recuperator was provided in the collector tank for negative-g manoeuvres. (Problems with this caused the engine failure and forced landing.) Provision was made for the carriage of a ventral fuel tank to supplement the meagre internal capacity, but this was never fitted. The electrical circuit was 28 volt, energised by a single engine-driven generator charging the battery mounted in the fuselage bay aft of the nosewheel well, with an inverter for generating alternating current for the instrumentation. Hydraulic power for the control surfaces, airbrakes, nose droop, undercarriage and wheel brakes was from two duplicated systems operating at 3,000 psi. Emergency operation of the flying controls and the under-carriage was provided from a drop-out ram air turbine housed in the lower fuselage, approximately in line with the elevator root leading edges.

The whole rear fuselage could be removed after undoing thirty-five bolts at Frame 27.5, and the associated control runs to the rudder. The structure was made from a series of continuous hoop frames, three being strengthened to act as fin attachment points. Immediately below the base of the fin and rudder was a long cylindrical fairing, integrally built with the rear fuselage structure, and containing three small braking parachutes attached to one common cable. The fixed fuselage structure ended at Frame 27 aft of the datum. The structure aft of this frame consisted of four large airbrake 'petals', equally spaced around the jetpipe, each surface actuated open by being pulled forwards by its own electrically-signalled hydraulic jack. When in the open position, the last three feet of the jetpipe was

completely exposed. The jetpipe orifice had a two-position afterburner eyelid shutters, unusally split horizontally (unlike other applications on which it was split more conventionally, vertically). Only two positions were available – either fully open or fully closed – dependent on whether the afterburner was in use or not.

The fin was built around three spars and only five ribs. It had leading and trailing edge sweep angles of 60° and 30° respectively and a square 3'6" tip. Thickness/chord ratio was 4%. The fully power operated rudder was hinged to the aft spar and had no trim tabs.

At the time of design, the 4% wing thickness/chord ratio chosen was the lowest attempted to date. The structure was entirely of light alloy with a stressed skin, and consisted of a series of rectangular cells formed by members parallel to the longitudinal and lateral axis of the aircraft. The wing torsion box was built around three main spars and two auxiliary ones, all at 90° to the fuselage and attached via the strengthened, milled, fuselage frames. The wing skins were exceptionally thick, being 0.25". This structure changed at Wing Stn. 105, outboard of which the spars were swept to conform to the delta planform. The main torsion box extended forward to Stn. 108 measured from the trailing edge, and forward of this was a triangular structure of relatively light construction, with the skin being of much thinner gauge to help accommodate the undercarriage. Only the fore and aft spars stretched from root to tip. Fences were fitted to the upper wing surface at Stn. 60 set back slightly from the

## DATA

**DIMENSIONS**

| | |
|---|---|
| Span | 26'10" |
| Length | 51'7.5" (including nose probe) |
| Height | 11'0" |
| Track | 7'7.6" |
| Wheelbase | 12'8" |
| Ground angle | 5° (to datum) |

**AREAS**

| | |
|---|---|
| Wing (gross) | 360.0 sq ft |
| Elevators (each) | 20.22 sq ft |
| Ailerons (each) | 16.0 sq ft (approximately) |
| Fin and Rudder | 40.0 sq ft (approximately) |

**WEIGHTS**

| | |
|---|---|
| Normal loaded | 13,400 lbs |
| Heaviest auw tested | 14,532 lbs |

**PERFORMANCE**

| | |
|---|---|
| $V_{max}$ | 1.73 Mach |
| Limiting 'g' | +4 |

**REFERENCES**

| | |
|---|---|
| RAF Museum, Cosford | —The Aircraft |
| Public Records Office | —Avia Files |
| RAE Farnborough | —Library Archives |
| 'Flight' | —25th April 1958 |

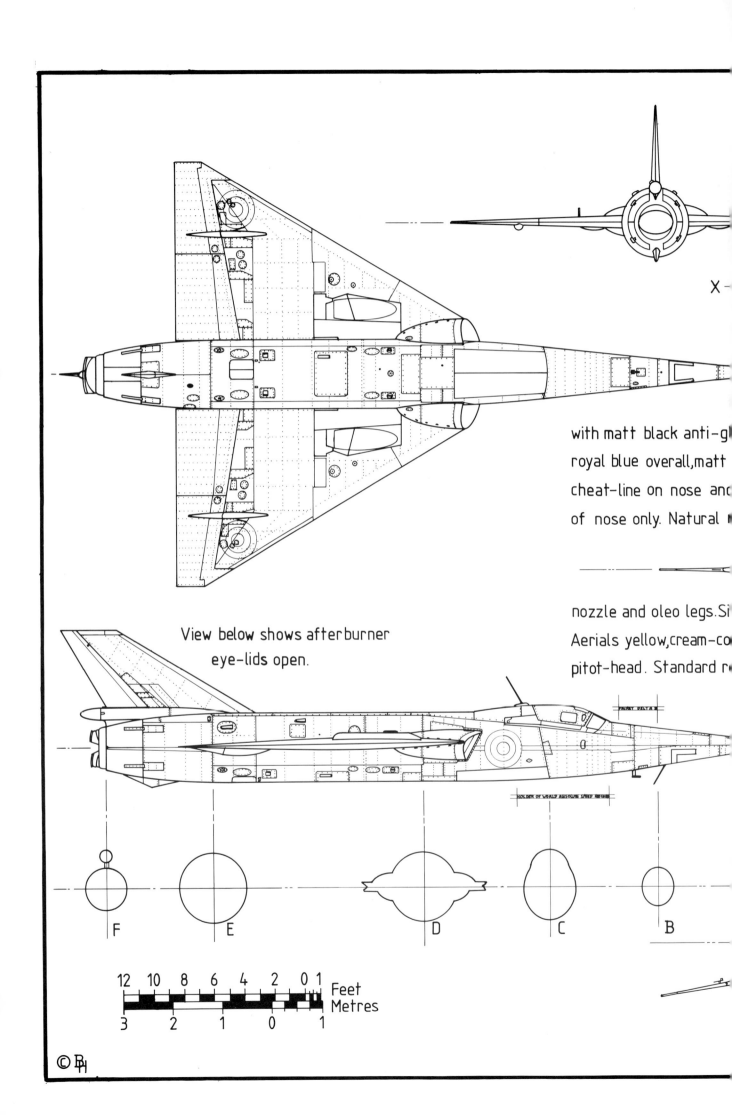

s:- First prototype WG 774, second
prototype WG 777.

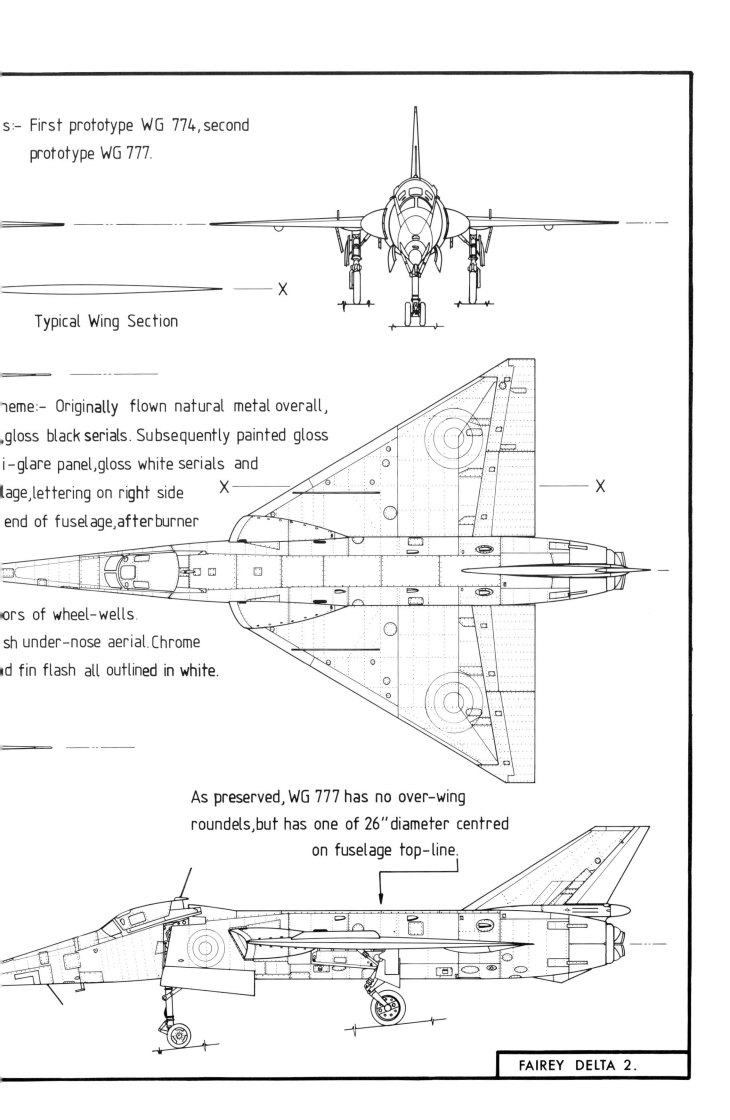

Typical Wing Section

heme:- Originally flown natural metal overall,
gloss black serials. Subsequently painted gloss
i-glare panel, gloss white serials and
lage, lettering on right side
end of fuselage, afterburner

ors of wheel-wells.
sh under-nose aerial. Chrome
d fin flash all outlined in white.

As preserved, WG 777 has no over-wing
roundels, but has one of 26" diameter centred
on fuselage top-line.

X

X

FAIREY DELTA 2.

round-section leading edge. The wing was mounted at an incidence of +1°30' to the fuselage datum, had an aspect ratio of 2:1, with leading edge and quarter-chord sweep angles of 60° and 52°30' respectively.

The main undercarriage, like the nosewheel oleo, was designed by Fairey themselves, and each oleo was a levered-suspension unit with an extremely thin wheel and 27″ tyre. Tyre pressures were very high for the time, at 225 psi. The wheels had hydraulically-operated Maxaret anti-skid brake units fitted. Each mainwheel oleo and strut was pivoted in such a fashion that, while they retracted, they hinged about two axes so that the unit moved forwards and upwards, rotating through 90° so that the wheels lay flat within the very thin wing, requiring only very slightly bulged fairing doors to accommodate them when retracted. Unusually, the main undercarriage units were made primarily from steel.

The flying control surfaces were hinged to the rear spar and occupied the entire wing trailing edges. There were two surfaces on each wing: the inner acting as an elevator for pitch control, and the outer ones as ailerons for roll control. Neither had trim tabs fitted and both were fully powered. The operating jacks for the elevators were within the fuselage at the surface root, but those for the ailerons were housed in long streamlined fairings on the wing undersurfaces. The ailerons each had a horn balance at the tips.

Spring feel was provided on all surfaces including the rudder, the feel units also being used to trim the aircraft by re-datuming the neutral position of the control circuits. The aileron and elevator circuits also incorporated an electrically-operated variable-ratio gearing, selectable from the cockpit.

## OUTLINE SPECIFICATION ER.103

1   To investigate transonic and supersonic flight up to 1.5 Mach.

2   The design as a research machine should not be compromised by any possible requirement for its use operationally.
3   Aircraft to be fitted with an Avon RA.5 with a 1,500°K afterburner with an alternative of a Sapphire engine to be considered.
4   A trimming tailplane to be fitted.
5   Cabin pressure of 3.5 psi., differential.
6   Martin-Baker Mk.1 ejection seat to be fitted.
7   Originally two interchangeable jetpipe nozzles to be fitted changeable on ground, one for afterburner, and other without.
8   Anti-spin parachute to be fitted, also to be suitable for use when braking.
9   Airbrakes to be fitted giving 0.5g deceleration at 350 kts., EAS. with negligible trim change.
10  Provision to be made for pressure plotting the wings.
11  Leading edge sweep to be 60°.
12  De-icing and anti-icing not required.
13  To be capable of exceeding 1.3 Mach at 36,000 ft. in afterburner.
14  Sufficient fuel for: start-up and take-off without afterburner; climb to 45,000 ft.; 15 mins. cruise without afterburner; 10 mins. at full power with afterburner; 80 gallons reserve for descent and landing.
15  Take-off distance to 50' not to exceed 1,500 yds. at maximum all up-weight. Landing distance from 50' not to exceed 1,500 yds.
16  Stressed to 8g.
17  $V_{dive}$ = 650 kts., EAS. or 1.7 Mach whichever is less.
18  Undercarriage stressed for a 14 ft./sec. touch-down rate.

## POWER PLANT
One Rolls-Royce R.A.14R Avon axial flow turbojet with 1,500°K afterburner. Dry Sea Level Static Thrust 9,500 lbs., and 14,500 lbs., with afterburner.

*The second prototype preserved at Costford. Note angle of nosewheel oleo as compared to previous photographs (page 166), the attachment pivot for the retraction link now being on the rear face instead of where it should be on the front, thus giving the aircraft a totally false static ground angle.*

*Supermarine 545 when at Cranfield. This photograph has been previously published, but reversed! That this shows the left side correctly is confirmed by the Lincoln and Me163 in the background (having its canopy hinged on the right-hand side this time).*

# SUPERMARINE TYPE 545

| | |
|---|---|
| **Manufacturer** | **Vickers Armstrong (Aircraft) Ltd., Supermarine Division** |
| **Specification** | **F.105.D.2** |
| **Role** | **Single-Seat Fighter/Interceptor** |
| **First Flight Date** | **Planned for Spring 1954** |

Although it was an entirely new design, the Type 545 had an easily recognisable 'Swift' ancestry in its general layout, with its low-mounted wing, tailplane and fin layout, but with the cheek intakes extended forward almost to the tip of the nose. The Swift had a wing with compound sweep on the leading edge, but this was developed into a true crescent shape to give a sharp sweep angle on the inboard leading edge, allowing for a thick centre-section providing generous stowage space for the undercarriage, ammunition and fuel tanks. This was allied with progressively less sweep outboard, together with thinner-sectioned outer panels for good high altitude performance and manoeuvrability.

## DEVELOPMENT HISTORY
From the various submissions to meet Specification F.105D2, Hawker Aircraft and Supermarine were chosen to build prototypes of their designs, the P.1083 and Type 545 respectively, the contract for their construction being placed in February 1952. The 545 was a much more radical design than the P.1083 and, on paper at least, promised a markedly better performance. This contributed to the eventual

cancellation of the P.1083 in July 1953.

Detailed design and construction of the two prototypes proceeded apace, with a planned first flight date in Spring 1954 for the first aircraft and early 1955 for the second. Marked delays to the programme occurred and, during 1954, a development of the basic 545 was offered which, in its final form, powered by the projected R.B.106 engine with fully variable afterburner, theoretically promised a maximum speed of Mach 1.68. Meanwhile, calculations of drag versus available thrust indicated that the first prototype would only attain its design speed of Mach 1.3 in a dive. Also, about the end of 1954/early 1955, the failure of its predecessor, the Swift, was becoming apparent. In addition, the prototype of the much higher performance English Electric P.1 had already flown in August 1954. These circumstances caused a major review of the whole project. As a first step the contract covering the second prototype was cancelled on 9th November 1954, and it was scrapped.

While construction of the sole remaining prototype continued, the specification around which it had originally been designed was superseded. The Royal Air Force indicated that it no longer had a requirement for the aircraft, thus losing its second intermediate design between the subsonic fighters then in service and the still far-distant Mach 2 replacement. Attempts were made to salvage the project, to allow the aircraft to be completed and flown solely for research purposes. A new specification was written around it, E.7/54., and the aircraft was intended to be used by the Royal Aircraft Establishment for experimental purposes after the initial manufacturer's trials. (*Note*: This information is contained in an official document held in the PRO, yet this system of numbering for specifications supposedly ceased in 1949/50!.) Overall configuration was to be unaltered, except for a long instrumentation boom to be attached to the nose and the armament and all associated equipment to be removed. Replacement with a R.A.28R Avon was also planned, with a revised first flight date of July 1955.

All efforts were in vain, and the whole programme was finally cancelled in early 1955, the ultimate single-seat interceptor, and the two-seater trainer versions remaining drawing-board projects. The airframe was transferred to the College of Aeronautics, Cranfield, for instructional purposes, where it remained, still virtually unknown to the general public, until it was scrapped in the early 1960's. (This seemed a very odd decision, in retrospect. It was virtually a complete airframe, designed to meet an official specification for the RAF, and was scrapped; yet its stable-mate at Cranfield, the Hawker P.1121, a private venture design and nowhere near completion, was saved and now forms part of the reserve collection of the Royal Air Force Museum, at Cardington!)

However, the story does not quite end there. It was discovered that, hidden away in a shed belonging to the Midland Aircraft Museum, Coventry, the cockpit canopy still survived and it is now the only known piece of the aircraft remaining in existence.

# CONSTRUCTION

## FIRST PROTOTYPE: XA 181

The area-ruled fuselage was of all-metal, conventional frame and stringer construction, with the engine fed through a bifurcated intake duct, which passed either side of the cockpit, converging just aft of Frame 15. The intake lip, and the engine, were provided with hot air anti-icing but there was no system for de-icing the actual airframe. The steerable nosewheel oleo retracted forwards into its bay within the intake centre-body, and was enclosed by a single door hinged on its left edge. Within the bay were located valves for replenishing the pilot's oxygen system, and recharging the hydraulic and brake accumulators, and the pilot's anti-g system with compressed air. The cockpit had an exceptionally large, single-skin, blown canopy, which slid aft for normal entry and exit and, in an emergency, could be jettisoned explosively. The canopy could be opened and closed externally, controlled by two buttons on the left side of the fuselage just below the cockpit sill.

There was also an external control, comprising a ring and lanyard housed behind a frangible panel, for hood jettison, low down on the left side of the

fuselage. Normal access to the cockpit was via a ladder which could be hooked into slots, again on the left. A tank containing fluid for windscreen anti-icing was located just forward of the windscreen to the left of the centreline. In the lower framing of the windscreen quarter-lights were large boundary layer bleed louvres. The fore and aft pressure bulkheads for the cockpit were made from solid steel, and also formed the armour plating protection for the pilot. (It had ben specified that the protection provided for the pilot should be to the same standard as that in the Swift F.2. Efforts had been made by the company to persuade the Ministry to allow them to reduce the thickness of the armour plating, thus allowing them to save valuable weight, and argued that the intake ducts along each side of the cockpit afforded added protection and thus the thickness of armour needed was less. This request, was however, refused.)

No details of the cockpit layout survive. However, it was intended to be of standard fighter-type but, unlike its forebear, was to have had fully faired side consoles, with the interior finished in black, which was standard for the period. A Martin-Baker Mk. 3G ejection seat was provided for the pilot.

Below the cockpit floor, flanking the aft end of the nosewheel bay, were the tubes for the cannon barrels, with the armament bay itself in the lower fuselage between Frames 10 and 14. Almost the entire dorsal spine area was taken up by large rectangular panels for access to the flying control rods. Both fuselage sides were dominated by three large access panels to electrical, ancillary and air conditioning equipment. In the latter panels were located hot air exhaust outlets: on the right for the heat exchanger and, on the left, for generator cooling. On the left were also panels allowing replenishment of the hydraulic header tanks and engine gearbox oil tank. In the underside, aft of the main undercarriage bay, were panels for access to the wing surface flying control rods and to the engine bay fire extinguisher system.

The mainwheels were fitted with 31" diameter, high-pressure tyres (162 psi.), with the oleos stressed to accept a 13 ft./sec. vertical velocity at touchdown on the prototype, but this was to be increased on the production aircraft. A Maxaret anti-skid braking system was fitted to the mainwheels only. These retracted inwards to lie within a bay in the bottom of the fuselage centre-section. A novel system of doors enclosed the wheel-bay in the belly. Instead of the normal fore/aft hinge line, three doors were provided, hinged laterally. The two smaller aft doors opened rearwards, and the single forward door hinged forwards, all being sequenced to close after undercarriage extension. The forward door doubled as a fully variable airbrake and its centrally mounted single actuating jack nestled between the mainwheels when they were retracted. It could be extended, if required, after the undercarriage extension sequence had completed, to give extra drag on the approach. A compressed air system was installed to allow emergency lowering of the undercarriage.

The fuselage transport joint was at Frame 22, allowing detachment of the entire rear fuselage for engine access and removal. This was achieved by means of nine bolted joints around the circumference of the fuselage, accessible through small panels in the aft fuselage skin. Multiple locating spigots around the mating surface on the fuselage frame ensured correct alignment on reassembly. While this operation was in progress, the aircraft had to be jacked up level. The main jacking points were at Frame 8 and at Wing Station 50 (measured in inches from the aircraft's centreline), just aft of the wheel bays in the wing. Additional trestle strong points were provided along the fuselage and at Rib 8 on the wings. In the bottom of the fuselage, in line with the tailplane, was a large compartment for ballast weights. The tailcone had provision for the stowage of an anti-spin parachute in a compartment on the right side, and could be removed completely by undoing six hinged quick-release fasteners.

The swept fin was constructed around two spars which were attached to the fuselage at Frames 28 and 29. It had a long dorsal fairing ending in a split intake providing air for cooling of the aft fuselage around the jetpipe and for the tailplane's 'q' feel system. Construction was all-metal, except for the fin tip which was made from di-electric material, housing a suppressed VHF radio aerial. The rudder was hinged to the rear spar at four points, was mass-balanced and had a small trim tab.

The tailplane was of the 'slab' type with no separate elevators or trim tabs, and was set at a 10° dihedral angle with a symmetrical RAE 103 aerofoil section. It was constructed around three ribs and channel members, and had its pivot point at fuselage Frame 30, access to the spigots being through panels in the lower and upper tailplane skins. Two independent operating jacks were fitted one on each side of the jetpipe, giving the tailplane a range of movement between +9° and –16°.

The engine was housed in the centre fuselage, and had a liquid isopropyl nitrate (Avpin) starter system with sufficient for four starts. Frame 21 formed a solid firewall between engine bay zones 1 and 2. The jetpipe was inclined at an angle of –1°34' relative to the fuselage datum to give a measure of upthrust. The afterburner nozzle was of the open/close eyelid type hinged in the vertical plane, as on the earlier Swift.

The wing was built around four spars, and was bolted to the fuselage at Frames 14, 16 and 19, with the leading edge attached at Frame 11. The quarter-chord sweep angles of the crescent planform were 50°, 40° and 30°, with the 'kinks' at Wing Stations

## DATA

### DIMENSIONS

|  | XA 181 | XA 186 | F.1 | Trainer |
|---|---|---|---|---|
| Span | 39'0" | 39'0" | 39'0" | 39'0" |
| Length | 47'0" | 48'6" | 46'3" | 45'10.5" |
| Height | 14'4.75" | 14'4.75" | 14'4.75" | 14'4.75" |
| Tailplane Span | 12'5" | 12'5" | 12'5" | 12'5" |
| Wheelbase | 17'0" | 17'0" | 17'0" | 17'0" |
| Track | 9'6.25" | 9'6.25" | 9'6.25" | 9'6.25" |

### AREAS

| | |
|---|---|
| Wing (gross) | 380.9 sq ft |
| Flap | 37.58 sq ft |
| Airbrake | 9.0 sq ft |

### WEIGHTS XA 181

| | |
|---|---|
| Empty | 13,862 lbs |
| Basic Equipped | 16,548 lbs |
| Operating | 17,260 lbs |
| Combat | 19,000 lbs |
| Landing | 19,149 lbs |
| Take-Off | 20,147 lbs (with 515 gallons of fuel) |
| Gross | 22,777 lbs |
| Overload | 24,000 lbs |

### WEIGHTS XA 186
No specific weights available, but the carriage of the external armament of four Firestreak missiles added 640 lbs, of internal equipment, plus 1,240 lbs, for the pylons and missiles.

### PERFORMANCE ESTIMATES

| | | |
|---|---|---|
| Design Limit Speed | 1.3 Mach | (1.68 Mach for F.1) |
| Diving Speed | 693 knots | |
| Load Factor | 11g at Combat Weight | |

### MAXIMUM SPEEDS

|  | XA 181 R.A.14R | XA 186 R.A.24R | XA 186 with 2 cannon + 2 Firestreak |
|---|---|---|---|
| Sea Level | 655 kts | 661 kts | — |
| 20,000 ft | 629 kts | — | — |
| 45,000 ft | 580 kts | 597 kts | 576 kts |
| 55,000 ft | 530 kts | — | — |

### TIME TO

|  |  |  |  |
|---|---|---|---|
| 45,000 ft | 5.5 mins | 3.9 mins | 4.7 mins |
| 1,000 ft/min Ceiling | 53,600 ft | 52,800 ft | 51,000 ft |

### XA 181 only

Initial Climb Rate 34,600 ft/min at Sea Level
Initial Climb Rate 28,200 ft/min at 10,000 ft
Initial Climb Rate 21,500 ft/min at 20,000 ft

Endurance on internal fuel alone was estimated to be 75 minutes, and with two 125 gallon drop tanks increasing to 105 minutes.

### REFERENCES

| | |
|---|---|
| Prototype Notes Type 545 (XA 181) | —Technical Manual |
| Public Records Office | —Avia 54 |
| RAF Museum | —Supermarine Archives |
| Eric Morgan | —Supermarine Archives |
| Dowty Archives | —Drawings E.59427/E.5961Y |
| Rolls-Royce Archives | —Drawings BTS 8050/8082 |

102 and 162. The wing had an overall dihedral angle of 1.5° and was mounted at an incidence of +1.75° at the root, whose chord at the centreline was 17′9″, with an RAE 100 symmetrical section having a thickness/chord ratio of 8.3%. It possessed a complex twist moving further outboard. The inner kink had an incidence of +0.35°, a chord of 9′3.5″, an RAE 101 section and t/c ratio also of 8.3%. The outer kink's incidence was +1.05°, chord 6′8.25″, had an RAE 102 section and a t/c ratio of 7.4%. The extended tip chord was 5′8″, section RAE 104, with similar incidence and t/c ratio. Wing construction was all-metal, with the heavy gauge skin being screwed and riveted to the spars and ribs. The inboard leading edge, forward of the front spar, housed the ammunition bays.

Aft, and outboard, of these were the integral wing fuel tanks extending out to Rib 8. The fully powered ailerons, with spring feel, were hinged to the rearmost spar, as were the split flaps inboard, which had a maximum deflection of 60° for landing. The ailerons had no tabs, trim being achieved by biassing the centring spring on the control column, with large panels in the top wing-skin providing access to their operating jacks. The wingtips were removable each having a navigation light and the left also housing a compass detector unit. Large pitot heads were mounted on each outboard leading edge, that on the left for test purposes only, the right being retained for the production aircraft.

### FUEL SYSTEM
The total internal capacity of 627 gallons was contained in two fuselage and two integral wing tanks. The flexible forward fuselage tank was situated between the intake ducts aft of the cockpit and held 128 gallons. The aft, metal, tank with a capacity of 129 gallons, was wrapped around the jetpipe. The wing tanks each held 180 gallons. A small 10 gallon recuperate tank was fitted aft of the fuselage forward tank to cater for negative 'g' manoeuvres. A single pressure-refuelling point was provided on the lower right fuselage side. There was no provision on the first prototype for carriage of underwing tanks, but the second prototype was planned to carry two 125 gallon tanks on the outboard pylons.

### ARMAMENT
The first prototype had provision for four 30mm Aden cannon, each with 150 rounds. The guns were mounted in the underbelly below the intake ducts, with the spent link and cartridge ejection chutes in line with the wing root leading edge. (From this arrangement, it would seem highly likely that damage to the airbrake skin would have been caused if the guns were fired while it was extended) Access to the gun bays was via two large doors hinged on their outer edges and to the ammunition bays in the wing root via large panels in the upper wing skins.

# SECOND PROTOTYPE: XA 186
Contrary to previously published information, the second prototype was virtually identical externally to the first, except for the fuselage nose being extended forward by 18″. The intake lip was also re-designed, having a more semi-circular cross-section, and a wider centre-body, to allow the installation of a radar scanner for the additional external armament of four Blue Jay (Firestreak) missiles to be carried on underwing pylons, the same internal armament being retained. The original requirement called for the weapons system to be fully operational although this was later cancelled, but dummy rounds were to be carried for aerodynamic research purposes. The outer pylons were also plumbed to allow carriage of drop tanks. The aircraft was also to have a secondary ground-attack role but no details of the proposed weapons load survive.

There were some changes to the centre fuselage structure, as the mainwheel bays were moved aft by one Frame. As the mainwheel oleo pivot points remained in the same position, this necessitated some additional minor alteration to the wing root structure.

### PRODUCTION VERSION
The ultimate proposed production interceptor used the same wing, fin and tailplane, with a slightly fatter rear fuselage to cater for the larger diameter afterburner jetpipe, but the forward fuselage was radically altered. The nose was shorter by 9″ than the first prototype and a conical, pointed and more circular cross-sectioned nosecone was added to house an 18″ diameter radar scanner. The nosecone was faired into the intake upper lip, which was also moved aft, the resulting profile being very similar in appearance to that of the F–86D Sabre. The 'chin' intake thus formed was bifurcated internally forming the nosewheel bay and passing either side of the cockpit as before. The fuselage nose topline was raised so that, although the cockpit canopy topline itself was virtually unaltered, the sill did not slope down at such a sharp angle; this also made the fixed windscreen and quarter-lights shallower. The nosewheel oleo now retracted aft, its bay being directly under the cockpit floor. However, the resulting wheelbase remained the same as before.

Aft of Frame 8, the forward fuselage was un-altered back to the transport joint. As mentioned above, the aft fuselage was slightly fatter to accommodate the larger diameter afterburner section. It also terminated at Frame 30 as there was no tailcone attached.

When fitted with the RB 106 engine, there was to be an additional fuel tank fitted around the jetpipe. From the rear of the fuselage structure jutted the long convergent/divergent, fully variable afterburner nozzle. Its throat diameter was 34.4″, in the dry thrust (closed) position, nozzle diameter was 25.7" and, when fully open, 43.0".

The same external armament of four Firestreak missiles was to be carried underwing, as on the second prototype, but the internal weapon layout was drastically revised. The inner pair of cannon were identically placed to the earlier prototypes, but the outer pair were moved up the fuselage sides either side of the intake ducts, to a position level with the bottom line of the radome. The ammunition boxes were still housed in the forward wing roots.

## TRAINER VERSION

One further version of the basic design was proposed, a two-seater advanced trainer to meet the requirements of O.R.318, and designated Type 554. This had basically the same external layout as the single-seat production interceptor, but with a more rounded nosecone, the main external difference being the side-by-side two-seater cockpit and canopy. Existing drawings of the aircraft do not make it clear whether the canopy slid aft for entry and exit, or whether it was of the 'clamshell' variety, as on the Hunter T.7. Each pilot sat on a Folland/Saab lightweight ejection seat.

An operational capability was retained, together with the radome housing the same 18" diameter radar scanner which, although no records remain to confirm this, presumably meant that the missile armament could be carried. The nosewheel oleo retracted aft to lie under the cockpit floor between the internally bifurcated intake, the ducts of which lay entirely under the wider cockpit. All internal armament was deleted except for a single Aden

cannon mounted on the left side of the fuselage nose, with 200 rounds (giving 10 seconds fire) being housed in the left wing root leading edge. Wing fuel capacity was slightly reduced, each holding only 150 gallons; the aft fuselage tank was also reduced to 110 gallons capacity but the forward tank was increased to hold 175 gallons. The power plant was to be a Rolls-Royce R.A.19R Avon with a 2,000°K afterburner with fully variable nozzle.

## POWER PLANT

Actually fitted

*1st prototype.* One Rolls-Royce R.A.14R Avon axial flow turbojet with 1,500°K afterburner. Dry Sea Level Static Thrust 9,500 lbs., and 14,500 lbs. with afterburner.

*2nd prototype.* One Rolls-Royce R.A.24R Avon axial flow turbojet with 2,000°K afterburner. Dry Sea Level Static Thrust 11,250 lbs., and 14,350 lbs. with afterburner.

Proposed:

*1st prototype.* One Rolls-Royce R.A.28R Avon axial flow turbojet with 2,000°K afterburner. Dry Sea Level Static Thrust 10,150 lbs., and 14,000 lbs. with afterburner.

*Production Version.* One Rolls-Royce R.A.35R Avon axial flow turbojet with 2,000°K afterburner. Dry Sea Level Static Thrust 11,000 lbs., and 16,300 lbs. with afterburner. Or one Rolls-Royce R.B.106 axial flow turbojet with 2,000°K afterburner. Dry Sea Level Static Thrust 15,000 lbs., and (??) lbs., with afterburner. In the event this latter engine also remained a drawing board project.

*Trainer Version.* As for 2nd prototype.

*Supermarine 545 intake shape with relatively blunt lips and exceptionally high canopy for good all-round visibility. Of interest also is the small model on the table which gives a good idea of the forward fuselage structure.*

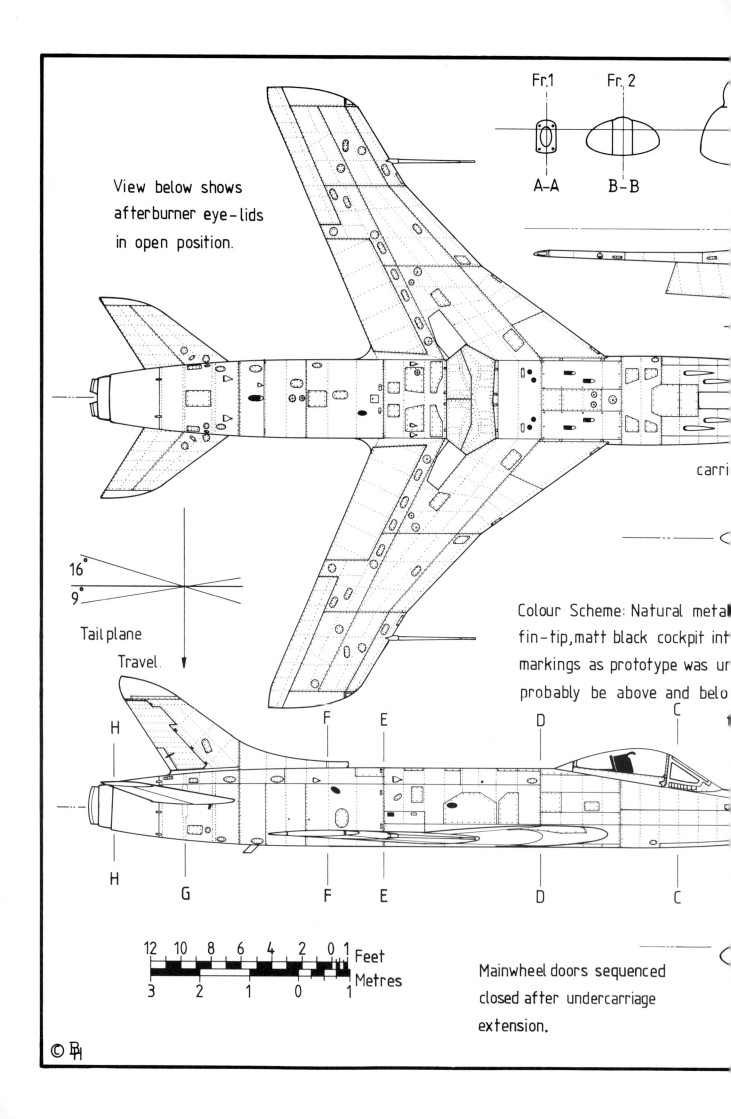

View below shows
afterburner eye-lids
in open position.

Fr.1        Fr.2
A-A        B-B

16°
9°

Tailplane
Travel.

H        F        E        D        C

H        G        F        E        D        C

carri

Colour Scheme: Natural meta
fin-tip, matt black cockpit int
markings as prototype was un
probably be above and belo

12  10  8   6   4   2   0  1   Feet
3       2       1      0      1   Metres

Mainwheel doors sequenced
closed after undercarriage
extension.

© BH

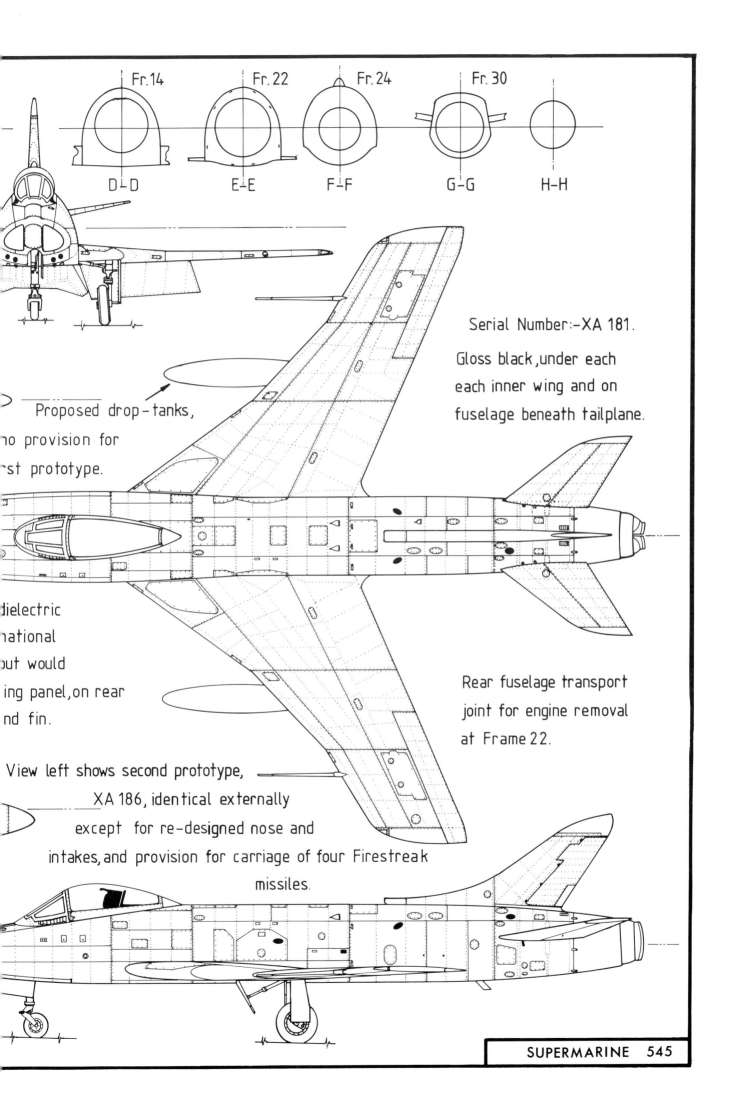

Fr.14    Fr.22    Fr.24    Fr.30

D–D    E–E    F–F    G–G    H–H

Proposed drop-tanks,
no provision for
rst prototype.

Serial Number:–XA 181.

Gloss black, under each
each inner wing and on
fuselage beneath tailplane.

dielectric
national
ut would
ing panel, on rear
nd fin.

Rear fuselage transport
joint for engine removal
at Frame 22.

View left shows second prototype,
XA 186, identical externally
except for re-designed nose and
intakes, and provision for carriage of four Firestreak
missiles.

*The mock-up with wheels down, (note only one mainwheel, there was no starboard wing fitted!)*
*This photograph has previously been erroneously identified as that of the actual prototype. (Avro)*

# AVRO 720

| | |
|---|---|
| **Manufacturer** | **A.V. Roe Ltd** |
| **Specification** | **F.137D** |
| **Role** | **Single-seat Interceptor** |
| **First Flight Date** | **Planned 1956** |

During the early 1950's, the RAF assessed that the enemy attack threat would be from bombers operating at speeds between 1.5 and 2.0 Mach, and at heights anywhere between 60,000 and 80,000 ft. Therefore, they raised an Operational Requirement for an interceptor capable of dealing with this perceived threat. The aircraft envisaged was very much a 'one-shot' point defence interceptor which, after shooting down its target, had to glide back to base and land on a very rudimentary, light undercarriage. In response to OR.301, several firms tendered and two – Saunders-Roe and Avro – actually constructed prototypes. In the event, only the Saunders-Roe was to get into the air, and both designs were far more viable than originally envisaged; however, each was very different in their approach to answer the requirement.

## DEVELOPMENT HISTORY

Following the study in 1951, the Ministry issued a draft Specification F.124T covering a rocket fighter capable of meeting the requirements of OR.301. Five firms tendered designs – Blackburn, Bristol, Fairey, A.V. Roe and Westland. One firm to whom the Specification was not even sent was Saunders-Roe. After some very intensive lobbying by the firm, they were allowed to tender and, in the event, won the competition. All except Blackburn and Saunders-Roe submitted two designs and, in the assessment after Saunders-Roe had been awarded the contract for further development, Bristol were

judged runner-up and were also awarded a contract to build a research aircraft, Type 178B, as a back-up. Avro's design came a close third. However, due to some intense political lobbying, Avro were also issued a contract to develop their design, the Avro 720. (Interestingly, having studied the various layouts submitted, the one from Avro is the only one which really bears any similarity between the original design and what was actually built, that from Saunders-Roe having only a nebulous conection!)

Specification F.138D was written to cover the Saunders-Roe design, and the contract called for the construction of three prototypes. This aircraft, in addition to its Viper turbojet engine, was powered by a Spectre rocket motor fuelled with HTP/kerosene. As an alternative, the Ministry also wished to investigate an alternative type of fuel combination and, therefore, when they awarded a contract to Avro under Specification F.137D, it was for an aircraft whose rocket fuel was to be liquid oxygen/kerosene, the motor being a Screamer rocket. The contract covered the construction of two flight prototypes and a structural test specimen.

Avro's original submissions were for identical aircraft externally, the only difference between the two being their power plant, one being a de Havilland Spectre and the other an Armstrong Siddeley Screamer. As mentioned above, the general arrangement drawing shows an aircraft virtually identical in overall layout to that which was built. The only noticeable differences externally were that there was no turbojet installed, a braking parachute fairing was sited on the rear fuselage aft of the rudder, airbrakes were at the aft end of the tailcone, hinged at their trailing edges and, as the original specification called for an armament of 50 unguided rockets to be carried, these were in a fixed fairing around the lower section of the centre fuselage from wing root to wing root. Span was 28'3.6" and length (not including nose probe) 44'0".

The specification was changed in the light of further deliberation, requiring the aircraft to have an additional turbojet engine to allow more recovery flexibility, and the unguided missiles were deleted in favour of the carriage of two Blue Jay infra-red homing missiles (Firestreak). Avro adapted their design very easily. Instead of altering the whole structure and layout of the fuselage, they simply added the turbojet housing, including intake and exhaust in an under-fuselage fairing, with the missiles carried one under each wing. To add to the complexities of design and manufacture, for some reason Avro had decided to manufacture the aircraft from stainless-steel honeycomb. The performance envelope of the aircraft in its original form did not warrant the use of such an 'exotic' material; light alloy was well able to cope, only requiring replacement when speeds were in excess of 2.3 to 2.5 Mach. Stainless steel was a notoriously difficult material to machine and work with, which makes its selection peculiar.

While still in the design stage, the company proposed an aircraft with a more powerful turbojet engine, an 8,000 lbs. thrust de Havilland P.S.37 engine, but otherwise little changed externally except for the application of area rule. This was followed by a completely revised, much larger design, with a better balance between the turbojet power output and that of the rocket. The aircraft was much larger, powered by a de Havilland Gyron Junior turbojet with an afterburner, and a de Havilland Spectre rocket motor. However, the real improvement was in the carriage of an interception radar. A Naval version was also proposed as the Avro 728. Neither was developed.

Some sources report that the first prototype, XD 696, was virtually complete by 1956, and could have flown almost a year before its Saunders-Roe competitor, but this appears unlikely. No specific records could be found, so reliance had to be placed on recollection which, as time passes, is difficult. In view of the radical nature of the structure, it would appear that the structural test specimen was completed first, before the first prototype's construction started. Under test, the structural specimen's fin failed at 110% load, causing the whole leading edge to buckle. The only two photographs known to have been published so far, although carrying the serial of the first machine, are in fact of the light alloy mock-up. Close study of the photographs show the aircraft to be on trestles, with only one mainwheel extended. In fact, when the complete series of photographs came to hand, a three-quarters front view shows that the fuselage is hard up against a hangar wall without any right wing at all! They do not show the aircraft in the configuration in which it was actually built, as the cockpit canopy and windscreen had been compltely changed. These were now similar to those which finally appeared on the Convair F–102, with a knife-edged windscreen with flat side panels, and a canopy faired into it with a single oval transparency on each side, in place of the two on the mock-up (as shown in the drawing).

Before the project could be taken any further, the contract for the Avro 720 was cancelled for two primary reasons: one, the cost of undertaking two expensive programmes and, two, the worries about operating with the liquid oxygen/kerosene combination of fuels. The company offered to change the design to accommodate the Spectre engine using HTP and kerosene, but this was turned down on the grounds that the SR.53 was to fly with this type of engine (quite what this had to do with which was the better aerodynamic design is hard to see). Consequently the programme was terminated and the airframes were scrapped.

# CONSTRUCTION

The structure was made from light alloy frames and spars, with a stainless-steel honeycomb skinning. The fuselage was circular in cross-section through-

*Avro 720 final mock-up confirming the aircraft's clean lines. Note shape of early cockpit canopy. This was changed on the actual first prototype to one with a 'vee-shaped' windscreen and a single larger side window.*

out its whole length, and was built in four major sections. The forward section comprised the long tapered nosecone which carried the long pitot boom at its tip. The next section was the forward fuselage and cockpit section. The datum of the whole nose area in front of the cockpit rear bulkhead was canted down 2°30' in relation to the aircraft's datum for better downwards visibility over the nose during the high angle of attack approaches to land. As schemed originally, the cockpit windscreen was to have been a central optically flat panel with two flat quarter-lights. The canopy itself was to be hinged on two arms attached to its sill edge, and have two windows on each side and one in the top for upwards vision. This layout is shown on the mock-up. However, the actual aircraft had a knife-edged windscreen with two flat panels either side of a slim central pillar. The canopy was again to be of the clamshell type, but with only one window on each side, as on the drawing. The structural specimen had this type of canopy, as did a separate fuselage section pressure tested in a water tank. The pilot was to be provided with a Martin-Baker Mk.4 ejection seat and the instrument panel was to be of the standard OR.946 layout.

The centre-section of the fuselage was basically a 19'0" long cylinder, of which the first 11'3" was of constant 4'4" diameter. Virtually the whole of the section was occupied by flexible fuel tanks, with the liquid oxygen tank at the forward end, a small kerosene tank containing fuel for the turbojet sandwiched in the middle, and a larger rear tank for the rocket motor's kerosene fuel at the rear. The latter occupied only the upper two-thirds of the fuselage, with a tank containing water below it. Solid bulkheads sealed each end of the section and also separated the fuel tanks. The aft end of the centre-section tapered slightly to the transport joint with the aft fuselage and tailcone, which were integral with the fin. The complete section of the fuselage below the wing main torsion box was removable for access, as was the jetpipe shroud attached to it.

The rocket motor was mounted on a strengthened frame, which also acted as the rear fin spar attachment point. The motor's combustion chamber was set so that it had an upthrust angle of 1°. The fuselage had tapered to a diameter of only 13.5", just sufficient for the rocket chamber, and the aft most section of the tailcone could be removed completely for access to the rocket motor. Rectangular airbrakes were mounted on each side of the fuselage. The ones in the original submission were hinged at their rear edges, but it is not known whether they still functioned in this way or whether they had been altered to the more conventionally hinged variety. There were also two equipment bay access doors low down on each side of the tailcone.

The fin was built around two main and two auxiliary spars, with a leading edge spar to the tip. The main spars were attached to the fuselage structure at two strengthened frames. It had a chord at the fuselage centreline of 14'5", with a leading edge sweep of 60° and the trailing edge of the rudder swept forward 5°. A semi-circular dorsal fairing joined the rear of the cockpit canopy to the fin root leading edge, accommodating electrical wiring and the control runs to the rudder. The power control unit for the rudder was in the leading edge of the fin structure forward of the front mainspar, moving the surface via push/pull rods attached to the right side of the rudder. This was hinged to the rear spar at three points and had no trim tabs.

The turbojet engine was mounted in a long semi-circular fairing under the fuselage which, aft of the nosewheel bay, could be completely removed for engine access and removal. Although the engine itself was mounted parallel to the aircraft's datum, its jetpipe and final nozzle were angled to give a downthrust of no less than 11°. The simple fixed intake was at the front of the ventral fairing in line with the base of the cockpit windscreen. Its lip was angled forwards slightly, and was of almost square cross-section, and its top edge was set about 3" away from the fuselage skin with a prominent, horizontal splitter plate to separate the boundary layer before entry to the duct. The intake duct was bifurcated internally some distance back from the intake lip to pass either side of the nosewheel bay, before returning to a single duct to enter the engine's compressor. The nosewheel oleo was hinged to the aft face of the cockpit rear pressure bulkhead, retracting aft into its bay, faired by a single door hinged on its left edge. The single wheel was fitted with a 17.5" diameter, high pressure tyre. Above the wheel well, aft of the cockpit and

| DATA | |
|---|---|
| **DIMENSIONS** | |
| Span | 27'3.6" |
| Length | 48'6" (including nose probe) |
| | 43'2.75" (excluding nose probe) |
| Height | 12'7.5" |
| Track | 11'4.25" |
| Wheelbase | 15'11.5" |
| | |
| **AREAS** | |
| Wing (gross) | 360.0 sq ft |
| Fin and Rudder (gross) | 57.22 sq ft |
| | |
| **WEIGHTS** | |
| Empty | 7,812 lbs |
| Loaded | 17,575 lbs |
| Max. overload | 18,750 lbs |
| | |
| **PERFORMANCE** | |
| $V_{max}$ | 2.0 Mach |
| Initial Rate of Climb | 25,300 ft/min |
| Maximum Rate of Climb | 41,200 ft/min |
| Ceiling | 60,000 ft |
| Full Power Endurance | 5 mins |
| Sortie Endurance | 35 mins (including return to base) |
| | |
| **REFERENCES** | |
| Public Records Office | —Avia Files |
| BAe., Manchester Division | —Archives |
| BAe., Manchester Division | —Photographic Archives |

forward of the liquid oxygen tank, was a substantial equipment bay.

The delta wing was mid-mounted on the fuselage, at an incidence of 1°, with the main torsion box structure continuous from tip to tip, passing through a cut-out in the fuselage structure. The two principle spars formed the forward and aft end of the torsion box whose structure was a series of cells made up from no less than seven additional spanwise formers perpendicular to the longitudinal axis of the aircraft, and ten formers parallel to it, covered by three heavy-gauge skin panels which were continuous from tip to tip. The outer boundary of the main box was formed by the leading edge spar which was continuous from root to tip and swept at 60°, as was the leading edge of the wing itself. The wing had an RAE 101 symmetrical section with an aspect ratio of 2.07:1. Its chord at the centreline and tip was 25'7.25" and 9.23" respectively, giving a taper ratio of 0.03. As with the fin and rudder, the trailing edge was swept forwards at an angle of 5°. A relatively light structure forwards of the mainspar completed the triangular planform, within which the main undercarriage was housed when retracted. The oleos were hinged to the front face of the mainspar and rotated through 90° whilst retracting so that the wheel, with its 25" high pressure tyre, lay horizontally within the wing structure in the apex of the wing. The bays were faired by two doors each, one attached to the oleo. The wing was able to accommodate the under-carriage without the need for any fairing bulges.

The entire wing trailing edges were occupied by two-section elevons, each hinged at four points to the aft mainspar. Their control runs passed along the forward face of the leading edge spar from the cockpit to a single power control unit in each outer wing. They moved in unison for pitch control and differentially for lateral control, none of the surfaces having any trim tabs. Small underwing fairings, two per section, faired the control operating rods.

Armament was planned to be two Blue Jay (Firestreak) missiles carried on underwing pylons. These were attached to hard points in the wing at Stn. 68.12" from the centreline. Initially, drawings show these pylons to be swept aft, but these were redesigned to sweep forwards (also as shown on the mock-up), so that the missile nosecones were just in front of the wing leading edges. As with the Sr.53, there would have only been space enough in the fuselage nosecone for a small radar-ranging type antenna, as used for a cannon armament.

## POWER PLANT

One Armstrong Siddeley A.S.V.8 Viper 101 axial flow turbojet developing a Sea Level Static Thrust of 1,640 lbs., plus one Armstrong Siddeley Screamer rocket engine with a Sea Level Static Thrust of 8,000 lbs., utilising liquid oxygen and kerosene as fuels.

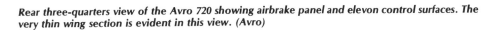

*Rear three-quarters view of the Avro 720 showing airbrake panel and elevon control surfaces. The very thin wing section is evident in this view. (Avro)*

A-A    B-B    C-C    D-

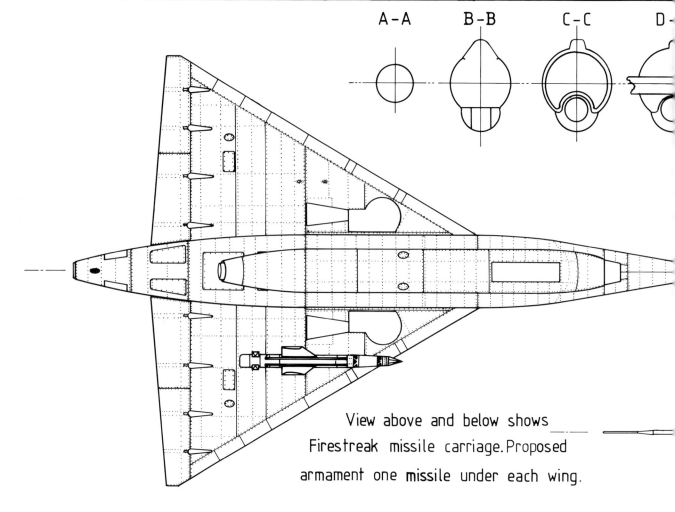

View above and below shows
Firestreak missile carriage. Proposed
armament one missile under each wing.

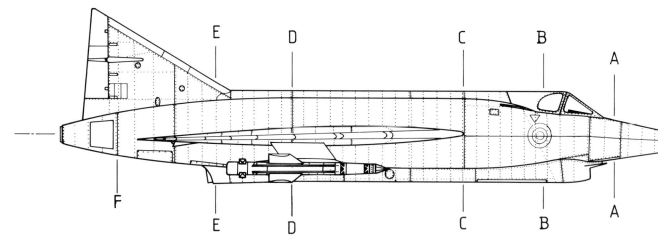

E    D    C    B    A

F

E    D    C    B    A

Colour Scheme :- Polished stainless steel overall. Mock-up shows
National markings in the form of roundels each side of nose,
and fin-flash only. Serial number in black on rear fuselage,
and under wings.

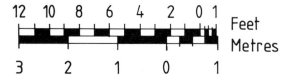

12  10   8   6   4   2   0 1
                              Feet
                              Metres
 3       2       1       0   1

B̶H̶

E-E    F-F

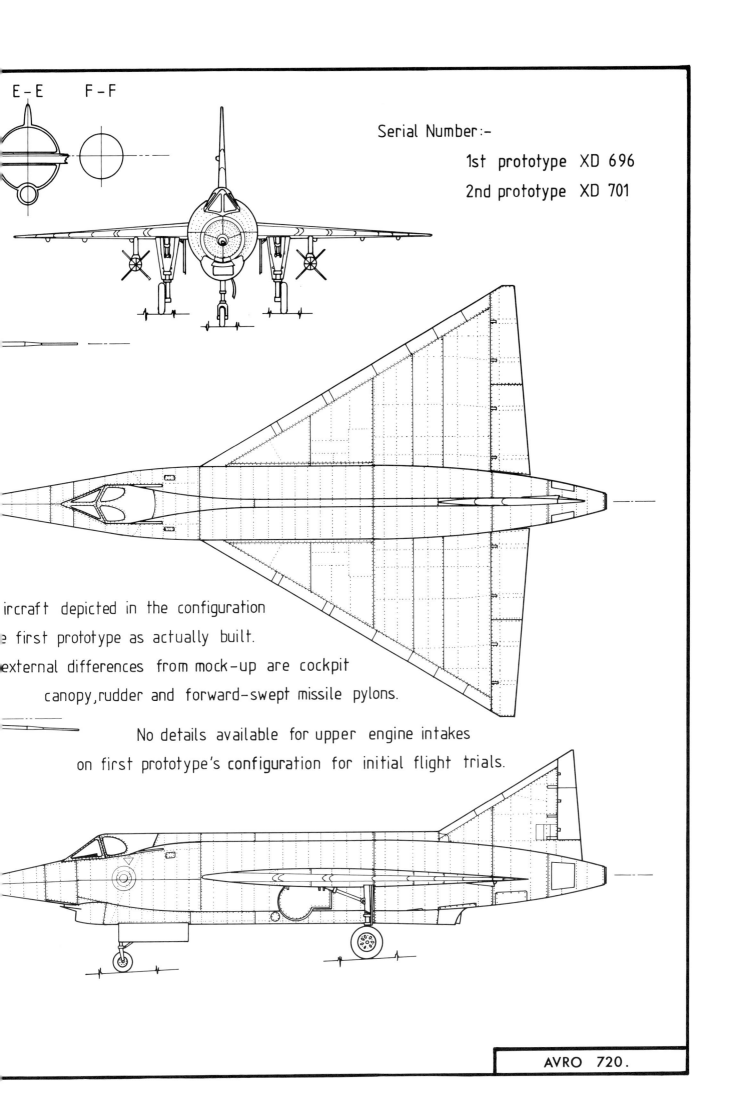

Serial Number:-

1st prototype  XD 696
2nd prototype  XD 701

ircraft depicted in the configuration
e first prototype as actually built.
external differences from mock-up are cockpit
      canopy,rudder and forward-swept missile pylons.

No details available for upper engine intakes
on first prototype's configuration for initial flight trials.

AVRO 720.

Short S.C.1. The aircraft landing conventionally after an early flight. Note forward raked main undercarriage legs and long stroke nosewheel oleo, none of which have fairings attached at this stage. (Shorts)

# SHORT S.C1

| Manufacturer | Short Brothers and Harland |
|---|---|
| Specification | ER.143 |
| Role | Vertical Take-Off Research Prototype |
| First Flight Date | XG 900 – 2nd April 1957 |
| | XG 905 – 23rd May 1958 |

During 1953, a very strange-looking contraption, powered by two horizontally-mounted Nene engines, began the first tentative trials into the use of jet engines for vertical take-off and landing. Although officially known as the Rolls-Royce Thrust Measuring Rig, it became quickly known as the 'Flying Bedstead'. Lateral and longitudinal control was from 'puffer-jets' mounted on the end of long poles. Following these successful trials which proved the principle feasible, Rolls-Royce developed special engines capable of being mounted vertically in an airframe for lift purposes. Specification ER.143 was raised to cover the development of a research aircraft to accommodate these engines and further explore the principle. The Short SC.1. was born.

## DEVELOPMENT HISTORY

Having been awarded the contract for the construction of two prototypes, Shorts started design work in 1954, the aircraft being evolved from their P.D.11 design. There was no precedent for the design, so virtually every problem was being encountered for the first time. It was fairly easy to design the airframe for conventional flight in the same manner as other aircraft, but the jet-borne flight was an entirely new problem. The airframe obviously had to be small and as light as possible to give sufficient thrust margin over weight, and therefore the airframe was the smallest possible in which to mount the lift engines, accommodate the pilot and equipment and contain just sufficient fuel for a worthwhile sortie length. As, until that time, helicopters were the only vehicles capable of vertical flight, the design of the cockpit area was based very much on their principles of operation, the cockpit canopy also bearing a passing relationship to that of a helicopter, with maximum visibility for the pilot in all directions.

At RAE insistence, a method of quick change-over from automatic to manual control, and vice-versa, was installed, using a fail-safe design for the servo-controllers. This incorporated three separate channels in parallel, so that a runaway in one could be contained by the other two, until it could be cut out by the pilot. It was also stipulated that no single fault in the system could be catastrophic. As far as possible, the pilot was to have conventional controls in the cockpit depending on the nature of the operation.

Construction of the first prototype, XG 900, was completed by the end of 1956, and the aircraft was ready for the engine runs and taxi-ing trials on 7th December of that year. No lift engines were installed and their bay, both top and bottom, was faired over with light alloy sheets. The aircraft was then taken by sea and road to Boscombe Down where it made it first conventional flight on 2nd April 1957. Its flight characteristics were found not to be too pleasant, due to its size and small control arms, nor was it found to be a very efficient airframe (bearing in mind that even on its wings there were many dome-headed rivets, which did not exactly help airflow patterns and drag!) However, this was considered satisfactory as the aircraft's prime task was not in conventional flight anyway. The lack of directional stability, however, was such that a dorsal fairing was added to the fin root leading edge.

One design peculiarity not found on conventional aircraft was the two-position main landing-gear oleos. These could be set either in a forward-raked position, for conventional, or with a slight aft-rake for vertical, take-offs and landings. It was felt that, if a vertical landing was made with the legs in their forward position, there was a risk of the aircraft tipping onto its tail. They were adjustable on the ground only and were fixed in either position. After the full transition flight had been achieved, they were left in the aft position.

The construction of the second machine, XG 905, had meanwhile been completed and this had its lift engines installed from the start. They were mounted about the aircraft's centre of gravity in pairs, and were tiltable fore and aft through 35° to assist the transition to horizontal flight and for rapid deceleration to vertical flight. They were protected from foreign object ingestion by wire mesh grills. The first tethered flight was made at Belfast on 23rd May 1958. Inevitably, adjustments were required to systems for control response, etc., and the pilot had to become accustomed to the new method of flight but, eventually, free flights started on 25th October of the same year.

XG 900 returned to Belfast to have its lift engines installed, plus oleo leg fairings, improved 'puffer' valves and automatic inlet louvres for the lift engines, before returning to RAE Bedford. Then the two aircraft gradually narrowed the gap between conventional wing-borne and jet-borne flight until, on 6th April 1960, the first full transition to horizontal flight from a vertical take-off, and back again to a vertical landing, was made at RAE Bedford. It was found that, other than the aircraft becoming a little more responsive to control inputs, the transition from one to the other was hardly noticeable. Minimum speed for wing-borne flight without the lift engines was found to be 134 kts.

After completion of the manufacturer's trials, XG 900 was handed over to Aero Flight, Bedford, in April 1961, for continuing with the research programme. It was later joined by XG 905 which had returned briefly to Belfast for installation of better autostabilisation.

Luckily, the trials had until then been without any real incident. However, on 2nd October 1963, XG 905 crashed, killing the pilot. Despite all of the built-in safeguards, the autostabilisation gyros failed. All three did not cage, despite the pilot reverting to manual control and this caused a false vertical reference for the autostabilisers. The aircraft flew into the ground from a height of 30 feet and the pilot had no chance to escape. The wreckage was returned to Belfast where it was rebuilt by May 1966. Its gyros, and those on its sister aircraft, had been modified so that the fault could not happen again. Just to be sure, the first flights were again tethered ones, starting on 17th June 1966 (the other aircraft had meanwhile been grounded until these were successfully completed). While being repaired, a head-up display and ground data link were installed, the aircraft finally returning to Bedford in June 1967, where its trials programme continued with the Blind Landing and Experimental Unit. These trials were aimed at the development of techniques for the operation of VTOL aircraft at night and in bad weather conditions.

The trials programmes were entirely successful and contributed much to the art of operating aircraft with similar capabilities, such as the Harrier. One problem with an aircraft with dedicated lift engines was that they were so much 'dead-weight' when not being used, and so the Harrier's principle of a combined engine was obviously much more desirable. It was found also that, to prevent re-

## DATA

### DIMENSIONS

| | |
|---|---|
| Span | 23′6″ |
| Length | 29′10″ (overall, including nose probe) |
| | 24′5″ (structure, excluding nose probe) |
| | 25′6″ (structure, including nozzle fairing) |
| Height | 9′10″ (ground static, mainwheels forward) |
| | 10′8″ (ground static, mainwheels aft) |
| Track | 11′6″ |
| Wheelbase | 8′4″ (mainwheels forward) |
| | 9′1″ (mainwheels aft) |

### AREAS

| | |
|---|---|
| Wing (gross) | 211.5 sq ft |
| Wing (net) | 141.9 sq ft |
| Elevators (each) | 7.38 sq ft |
| Ailerons (each) | 4.27 sq ft |
| Fin and Rudder (gross) | 28.64 sq ft |
| Fin (net) | 7.19 sq ft |
| Rudder (net) | 4.44 sq ft |

### WEIGHTS

| | |
|---|---|
| Empty | 6,000 lbs |
| Max. Loaded (VTO) | 7,700 lbs |
| Max. Loaded (STO) | 8,050 lbs |

### PERFORMANCE

| | |
|---|---|
| $V_{max}$ | 215 kts |
| Range | 150 miles |

### REFERENCES

| | |
|---|---|
| Science Museum | —The aircraft |
| RAE Farnborough | —Library Archives |
| 'Flight' | —10th June 1960 |

circulation of hot air from the lift engines' efflux the SC.1 had to be operated from a special forty feet square metal platform, approximately twelve inches from the ground, with a central octagonal hole.

In the light of their experience, Shorts put forward several variations on the theme of vertical take-off aircraft, culminating in a 'lifting-platform' capable of carrying English Electric's TSR.2 candidate, which had no less than *sixty* lift engines and *ten* propulsion engines! Hardly surprisingly, this monstrosity was not pursued past the design stage.

When their active careers were over, both aircraft were preserved. XG 905 was returned to Ireland for exhibition in the Belfast Museum. The first prototype, XG 900, was allocated to the Science Museum with the original intention of exhibiting it next to its ancestor the 'Flying Bedstead', but this was not to be. It was stored for some time at the museum's facility at Hayes before being transported to its present location at the Science Museum 'satellite' at Wroughton.

# CONSTRUCTION

The 'dumpy' fuselage was dominated at its front end by the extensively glazed, helicopter-like cockpit and canopy, giving the pilot exceptional all-round view except directly backwards, the lower edge of the glazing being well below elbow level. Originally the canopy was faired into the fuselage top-line and its roof panel was hinged at its rear edge for emergency exit, and it had a small separate forward-hinged entry and exit hatch. This was changed to a bulged roof hatch, which completely hinged aft for normal entry and exit, had no framework cross-members and was easily broken, enabling the pilot to eject through it. Initially, a Folland lightweight ejection seat was fitted but this was replaced by a Martin-Baker Mk.V4 zero-zero seat. The cockpit was not heated or pressurised. Instrumentation looked surprisingly conventional, the main instruments being mounted in a wide, central binnacle, with autostabiliser controls on the right, and engine and other test controls on the left. The only unusual lever noticeable for a jet aircraft was the helicopter-style 'collective lever' to the left of the seat. Some instruments and switches were attached around the main windscreen hoop. (For some reason the aircraft had two standby E4B compasses mounted here.) The two prototypes differed in the shape of their windscreens. That on the XG 900 had a smaller forward auxiliary hoop below the pilot's line of sight, while on XG 905 this was missing, and instead there was a narrow horizontal frame low down, with a metal fairing around the nose behind the main instrument panel. A long instrumentation boom projected forwards from the base of the windscreen, braced by three wires attached to the fuselage, mounting yaw and pitch vanes and a pitot head.

The forward fuselage structure was around closely spaced frames, together with stringers attached to the skin, all manufactured from light alloy. The long-stroke nosewheel undercarriage was attached to the aft face of the cockpit's sloping rear bulkhead. As with the maingear it was fixed and originally flew with no fairing 'trouser' around the shock absorber. The small twin wheels were mounted on a live axle, and were free to castor through ±180° during a vertical landing. The entire undercarriage was stressed to accept an 18 ft./sec., descent rate.

Between the cockpit aft bulkhead and that of the engine bay was a box structure, in the upper part of which was an equipment bay accessible through a hatch on each side. This contained an air turbine unit, a hydraulic pump and the 24v generator. The ground supply socket for the electrical system was on the right side of the fuselage nose below the cockpit sill.

The structure of the centre-section between the wing roots changed to four reinforced longerons, with close frames and ribs but no stringers. The top and bottom of the bay were open. Construction was again of light alloy, with an interior skin of titanium to act as a heat-shield. The fore and aft bulkheads of the engine bay sloped outwards both above and below the wing to allow for the lift engines to tilt fore and aft through 35°.

The fuselage had a maximum width of only 4'6" and had a flat bottom at the centre-section, below which the lift engine orifices protruded. The four engines were mounted in pairs on two common transverse axles, which were connected together so that all engines moved in unison. Their intakes were guarded from foreign object ingestion by a wire-mesh screen, and the top of the engine bay could be sealed by longitudinal spring-loaded louvres pivoted at their ends. They opened automatically by suction when the lift engines were started. They were started on the ground by bleeding air from the propulsion engine and, while in the air, by ram effect through manually controlled 'gills' around the forward end of the engine bay. The louvres and gills were closed during normal wing-borne flight when the lift engines were to be shut down.

Control of the lift engines from the cockpit was via a helicopter-style 'collective lever'. Called a 'Lift Control', the thrust from the engines was increased or decreased by raising and lowering the lever. For conventional flight, the propulsion engine was controlled from a normal console-mounted throttle lever, but, during jet-borne flight, its control was through a twist grip on the end of the Lift Control, giving the pilot control over all five engines without moving his hand. The tilting of the lift engines was controlled through a control column mounted spring-loaded electrical switch. (On conventional aircraft, this would be the electrical trim switch.)

The aft fuselage was again of conventional construction with an integral fin, whose forward mainspar was a continuation of a strong sloping fuselage frame at the aft end of the rear equipment bay, which contained the fuel pumps, engine oil

*Short S.C.1 hovering over its special platform at R.A.E. Bedford. Note main undercarriage legs now in their raked aft position and with 'trousers'. Engine intake gills are prominent. Pilot emphasizes small size of this aircraft. (Pilot Press Ltd.)*

tanks, and flying control linkages. The top of the rear fuselage was occupied by the propulsion engine, which was fed from an oval dorsal intake, all of which, together with the fins dorsal fairing, forming a large detachable panel for engine access and removal. The engine itself was mounted at an angle of 30° to the aircraft datum to ensure the proper functioning of its lubrication system, the engine having been designed for vertical mounting. With the exhaust orifice being in the lower rear face of the fuselage, this meant that the duct was in the form of a large 'S', which must have incurred some thrust losses. The braking parachute container was mounted in the rear fuselage immediately below the fin and above the jetpipe orifice.

The fin structure was around the forward mainspar and a rear auxiliary spar and multiple ribs. The rudder was hinged to the aft spar and was manually operated by the pilot's rudder pedals and had no trim tab. The height of the fin tip was only 8'2.5" above the fuselage datum (which was the base of the fuselage).

The wing was unusual, in that its design was not dictated by any performance requirements. It was of delta planform with a leading and trailing edge

sweep angle of 54° and 3° respectively, and had a root thickness/chord ratio of 10%. It was of three spar construction with the two forward spars attached to the fuselage at the frames at the forward and aft ends of the engine bay. Its rear auxiliary spar had the flying controls hinged to it. The rounded leading edge of the wing was a sealed unit containing fuel and was detachable from the forward spar by quick release fasteners. More fuel was carried in bag tanks between the mainspars. The main undercarriage was attached at approximately mid-chord and, like the nosewheel, consisted of a single shock absorber on each oleo, which had twin wheels on a live axle, free to castor through ±180°, (Like the nosewheel the oleos were 'bare' for initial flights but were later fitted with streamlined 'trousers'.) Each of the mainwheels was fitted with pneumatically operated brakes. As has been mentioned previously, the oleos could be fixed either in a forward or aft raked position depending on whether conventional or jet-borne trials were being conducted.

The flying controls occupied the whole of the wing trailing edge, with elevator inboard and ailerons outboard. Each aileron had a small balance tab; the right elevator had an electrically-operated trim tab, whilst that on the left was an automatic balance tab. The ailerons were manual, but the elevators were powered with manual reversion, the operating jacks being housed in large underwing fairings.

While the flying control surfaces could be used for conventional flight, they were of little use during low speed and hovering flight. Control was effected by the use of engine bleed air being fed to four air nozzles. The mounting trunnions of the lift engines were hollow, bleed air from the engines' compressors being fed into a 'ring-main' circuit for distribution to the nozzles. One was mounted in a fairing which bulged out from the base of the fuselage nose (this fairing stretching back to the nosewheel oleo on the second prototype) acting with another nozzle mounted in a fairing under the rear of the fuselage for pitch control. As it was connected to the pilot's rudder bar, this aft nozzle could also be rotated for yaw control. Distance between the two nozzles was 22'7.8". The roll control nozzles were mounted near the wingtips, pointing downwards. They were 14'6.92" aft of the wing's apex, and were sited 8'9.14" out from the centreline. The nozzles were all normally half closed, pitch and roll control being effected by differential opening of each pair, and were controlled by the autostabiliser, the pilot controlling attitude by moving the datum of the gyro-platform.

The autostabiliser system had three pilot-selectable modes, via so-called 'transition units'. The modes were: fully manual, with direct control of both surfaces and nozzles; manual surfaces and autostabiliser controlled nozzles; and fully stabilised with the autostabiliser controlling both surfaces and nozzles. (However, in the last two cases the rudder and rotating nozzle for yaw remain manually controlled.) When operating in the autostabilised modes, control column inputs were electrical rather than via the push/pull rods.

To eliminate thrust losses from the engines, no shaft-driven systems were taken from them but were driven by a compressor bleed air turbine mounted behind the cockpit. The hydraulic system operated at 2,500 psi. and drove the autostabiliser, transition mechanism, control nozzle servos, elevator power control unit, and lift engine tilt. It had a 1,200 psi emergency accumulator supply for 50 secs., to enable the pilot to select manual control. The electrical system was fed from a 28 volt generator with two inverters for a.c. power for the instrumentation, with a third acting as standby. The pneumatic system for the wheel brakes was supplied from three accumulators which were also used as an emergency supply for operation of the transition mechanism.

## POWER PLANT
Five Rolls-Royce R.B.108 axial flow turbojets developing a Sea Level Static Thrust of 2,130 lbs. Four grouped and mounted vertically acting as lift engines, and one for horizontal thrust.

*Short S.C.1 in the hover with a good view of the flat fuselage underside and paired lift jet engines angled slightly aft. The large canopy offers excellent forwards and downwards range of vision for the pilot.*
*(Pilot Press Ltd)*

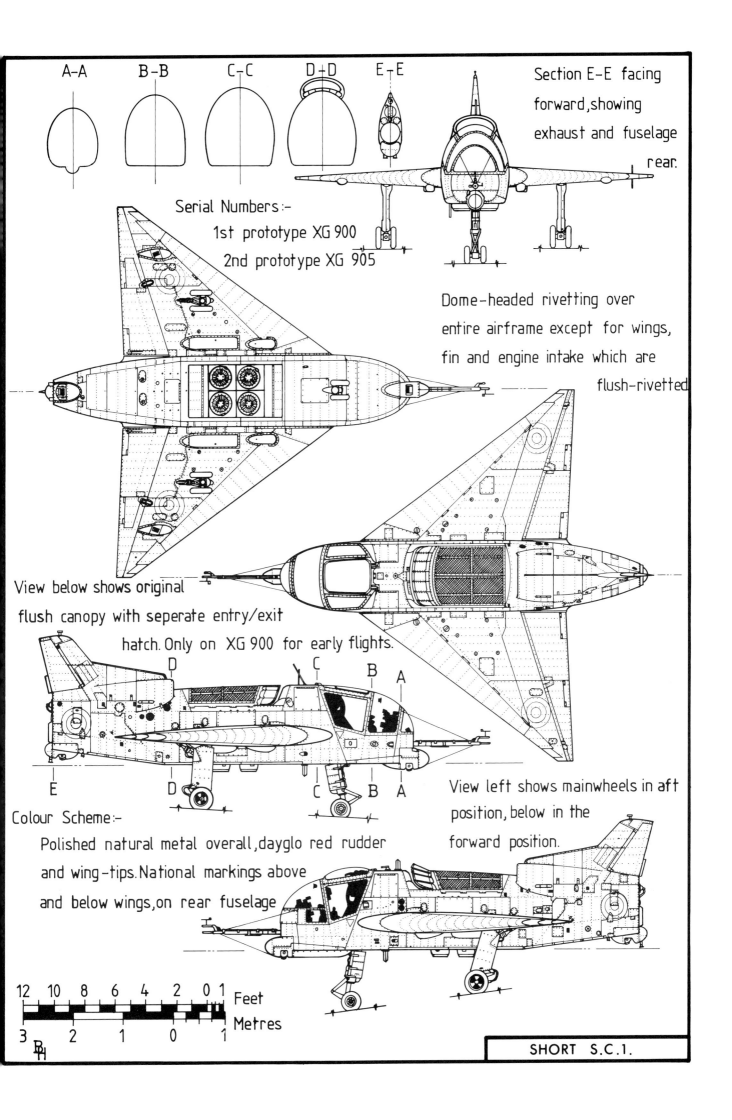

A-A    B-B    C-C    D-D    E-E

Section E-E facing forward, showing exhaust and fuselage rear.

Serial Numbers:-
1st prototype XG 900
2nd prototype XG 905

Dome-headed rivetting over entire airframe except for wings, fin and engine intake which are flush-rivetted

View below shows original flush canopy with seperate entry/exit hatch. Only on XG 900 for early flights.

D    C    B    A

D    C    B    A

E

View left shows mainwheels in aft position, below in the forward position.

Colour Scheme:-
Polished natural metal overall, dayglo red rudder and wing-tips. National markings above and below wings, on rear fuselage

12  10  8  6  4  2  0  1    Feet
                            Metres
3        2      1      0      1

SHORT  S.C.1.

*Miles Student in the test programme and as yet unpainted. The long slim tail boom carries the unusual tailplane and fin assembly. (Pilot Press Ltd.)*

# MILES M.100 'STUDENT'

| Manufacturer | F.G. Miles Ltd. |
|---|---|
| Specification | No Specification – Private Venture |
| Role | Primary Trainer Prototype |
| First Flight Date | 14th May 1957 |
| | Serial (variously): G–35–4; XS 941; G–APLK |

The design was a private venture project by F.G.Miles to produce a competitor to the Hunting Jet Provost for use by the Royal Air Force as a basic trainer. However, due to the need to concentrate on more lucrative work, the financial constraints led to delays, such that the Jet Provost was actually in service with the RAF even before the Miles design had flown!

## DEVELOPMENT HISTORY

The design and construction of the aircraft was started in 1955 at the company's factory at Shoreham, to where they had moved from their earlier site at Woodley, and it received the company designation of M.100. 'Student'. Due to the delays described above, it was not completed until early 1957.

Flight trials commenced at Shoreham, despite it having only a very small grass runway, with the first flight on 14th May 1957 being flown by George Miles himself, one of the designers and who, with his brother, owned the company. Proposed as a military trainer, it carried the first of its three registration numbers XS 941.

Trials were generally successful but, having been so far behind the aircraft it was supposed to be competing against, there was no further official interest in the project.

Its performance was not startling, due to the very low powered engine, and it was therefore changed to an engine giving some 20% increase in thrust. The aircraft flew in this MK. 2 guise on 22 April 1964. The design always had the facility for carrying armament on underwing pylons, and the aircraft took part in gunnery trials flying from Boscombe Down. Its armament was two .303 machine-guns housed with their ammunition in underwing pods. Although capable of carrying alternative loads of rocket projectiles or bombs, these were not fitted during the trials.

Several variants, including a Naval trainer and one for use in civilian flying schools, were proposed to try to gain interest to enable the aircraft to be put into production but nothing was to become of them. These more advanced aircraft were to be known as the M.100 'Centurion'. Although primarily a two-seat trainer, the space behind the seats could be adapted to enable a maximum of four people to be carried. However, an agreement was reached with South Africa for the aircraft to be built under licence there, for use by the armed forces either in the trainer or counter-insurgency role. The sole prototype was dismantled and crated for the journey, when the British government embargoed the export. It was, therefore, kept in storage in its crate at Shoreham from October 1965.

The Ministry of Defence funded a research programme into aircraft noise reduction in early 1974, and for some reason it was decided to use the Miles Student. (This seems a little odd as, with its tiny engine, the aircraft was a very quiet one!). It was therefore reassembled, now having the serial G–35–4, and checked out before being modified at Dunsfold. It successfully completed the six-month trials programme at Hatfield before being returned to Shoreham.

There it was to remain, until purchased by Aces High, based at North Weald, where it was re-assembled yet again, with yet another registratlon, this time a civilian one, G–APLK. However, its career was very brief as it crashed soon after its first flight, tearing off one of its wings, although luckily the accident was not a fatal one. At the time of writing, it is still at North Weald awaiting a decision as to its future.

# CONSTRUCTION

The design was kept very simple for both economy and ease of production. The fuselage construction was broken down into three major sub-assemblies: the nose and cockpit, centre-section and tail-boom. The structure was of light alloy throughout and featured a side-by-side seating arrangement in the roomy cockpit. The aircraft sat very low on the ground and access was via a 'car-type' door on each side, the door sill being only 18" from the ground. The instrument panel carried only one set of instruments shared by both pilots, but was not laid out in the standard 'T' arrangement as required by the Services. Each pilot had a 'pistol-grip' type control column, and shared the centrally mounted throttle quadrant, which again would not have met Service requirements. Visibility all round was good, despite some rather heavy canopy framing. All windows were fixed and, to leave the aircraft in an emergency, the crew jettisoned the entry doors and literally fell out the side of the aircraft. The aircraft could not have accommodated ejection seats without major redesign.

There was a short pointed nose in front of the cockpit within which the nosewheel bay was accommodated. The oleo retracted rearwards into the bay, and was steerable through ± 22°, and could be unlocked to allow free castoring. Retraction and extension was pneumatically powered.

The NACA-type engine intake was set in the roof of the cabin, the engine being mounted in the top of the fuselage centre-section, and was accessible for servicing by removing the whole of the cowling. This could be done by one man standing on the ground. One of the 'selling points' was that all servicing could be done without the need for any steps or gantries, except for actual engine removal. The floor of the engine bay acted as a firewall, isolating it from the rest of the airframe. The engine was electrically started and the only ancillary system driven by it was the electric generator.

The wing was shoulder mounted and attached to the fuselage at two strengthened frames at the forward and aft end of the centre-section, and had a symmetrical NACA 23015 section, with a root thickness/chord ratio of 15% and aspect ratio of 5.9:1. The leading and trailing edge sweep angles were 18°25' and 6°15' respectively. It was of two-spar construction with multiple ribs. Two flexible fuel tanks were situated in each inner wing structure, one forward and the other aft of the mainspar. These were filled from panels in each wing root and fed to a single collector tank containing a booster pump. From here, it was fed to the engine via a recuperator for negative-g flight. Internal fuel capacity was 100 gallons, but with two tips tanks this was increased to 140 gallons. The flying controls were hinged to the rear auxiliary spar and comprised ailerons outboard and plain, pneumatically-operated flaps inboard these having three selectable positions, up, 20° and fully down 50°. The ailerons had no trim tabs.

The fuselage centre-section below the wing attachment points was occupied by the narrow track main undercarriage, which had a novel folding-action upwards and inwards into the fuselage when retracting. The retraction and extension were by double action rams which were pneumatically powered. The toe-operated disc brakes fitted to each mainwheel were operated hydraulically through a simple closed circuit system, as on a car. Unusual air brakes were fitted aft of the mainwheel bays. These were hinged at their upper edges, rotating outwards about this hinge to present a perforated panel at 90° to the airflow (looking much like a wedge of cheese!)

## DATA

### DIMENSIONS
| | |
|---|---|
| Span | 29'2" |
| Length | 31'6" |
| Height | 6'3" |
| Track | 7'0" |
| Wheelbase | 10'5" |

### AREAS
| | |
|---|---|
| Wing (gross) | 144.0 sq ft |

### WEIGHTS
| | |
|---|---|
| Empty | 2,400 lbs |
| Loaded | 3,600 |
| Max. Overload | 3,900 lbs |
| Wing loading | 25 lbs/sq ft |

### PERFORMANCE
| | |
|---|---|
| $V_{dive}$ | 400 kts |
| $V_{max}$ | 259 kts at 20,000 ft |
| Cruise | 226 kts at 10,000 ft |
| Vstall | 59 kts |
| Take-off distance to 50' | 2,220 ft |
| Landing distance from 50" | 1,920 ft |
| Initial Climb Rate | 1,780 ft/min |
| Time to 10,000 ft | 6.8 mins |
| to 20,000 ft | 17.4 mins |
| Range at 20,000 ft | 385 nm at 198 kts |
| | 540 nm (with 300 lbs, fuel in tip tanks) |
| Duration | 2.25 hours |
| Design Load Factor | 10g at 3,600 lbs |
| Rate of roll | 120°/sec |

### REFERENCES
| | |
|---|---|
| F G Miles | —Archives |
| Miles Student | —Brochure |

The aircraft with its wingtip tanks fitted. Engine intake channel has yet to receive its distinctive strakes on each side. (Pilot Press Ltd.)

The cylindrical tail boom carried no internal equipment and served only as a mounting for the tailplane. This was constructed about a single mainspar just aft of mid-chord to which the elevators were hinged. The remaining structure comprised an auxiliary leading edge spar and multiple ribs. It was set at a dihedral angle of 11°, with a leading edge sweep of 14°. Each elevator had a trim tab stretching over approximately 75% of its trailing edge. Twin fins and rudders were mounted at the tailplane tips. Each fin was mounted vertically and had leading and trailing edge sweeps of 40° and 21° respectively. The rudders were hinged to the mid-chord mainspar, had no trim tabs but had horn balances at the tips. All flying control surfaces were manually operated.

The pneumatic system operated from engine compressor bleed air at a nominal 40 psi. and fed the undercarriage, air brakes and flaps. It had two reservoirs which were able to operate the entire system through three complete cycles. There was also an emergency accumulator fitted behind the instrument panel for one lowering of the undercarriage. The only other system was the electrical one, which was 28 volt d.c. supplied from an engine driven generator, charging a 25 amp.hr. battery, with an external power socket low on the left side of the fuselage note. An inverter supplied a.c. power to the flight instruments.

## POWER PLANT
One Turbomeca Marbore 2 axial flow turbojet with a Sea Level Static Thrust of 883 lbs. Later replaced by a Marbore 6F with a Sea Level Static Thrust of 1,055 lbs. Alternative engines proposed included the Lycoming ATI.70–2 and ATI.70–3, and the Garrett 1004.

Miles Student in its military guise as XS941. Note prominent intake strakes now fitted, and lack of nose probe. (Pilot Press Ltd.)

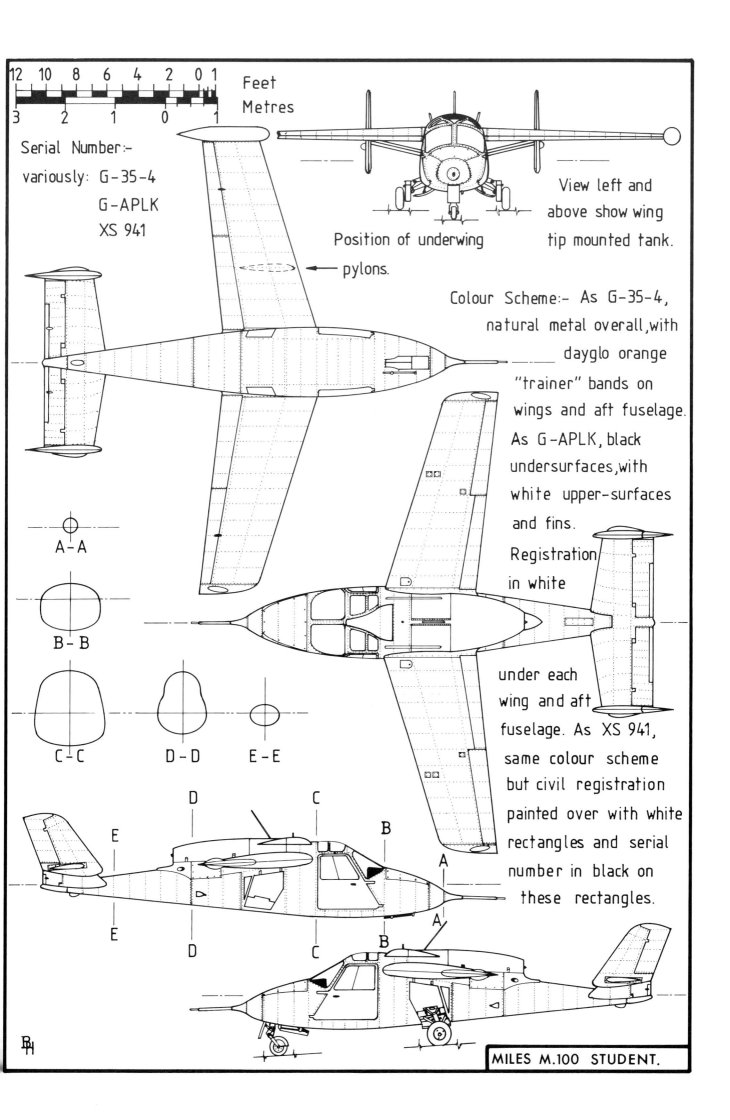

Feet
Metres

Serial Number:-
variously: G-35-4
G-APLK
XS 941

View left and
above show wing
tip mounted tank.

Position of underwing
← pylons.

Colour Scheme:- As G-35-4,
natural metal overall,with
dayglo orange
"trainer" bands on
wings and aft fuselage.
As G-APLK, black
undersurfaces,with
white upper-surfaces
and fins.
Registration
in white

A-A

B-B

C-C          D-D          E-E

under each
wing and aft
fuselage. As XS 941,
same colour scheme
but civil registration
painted over with white
rectangles and serial
number in black on
these rectangles.

E        D        C        B
                          A

E        D        C        B
                          A

B
H

MILES M.100 STUDENT.

*Saunders-Roe SR.53 XD145 during ground trials before its first flight. Its very clean, uncluttered lines are well illustrated. Dummy missiles are yet to be attached to the wingtips. (Crown Copyright)*

# SAUNDERS-ROE S.R.53

| | |
|---|---|
| **Manufacturer** | **Saunders-Roe Ltd.** |
| **Specification** | **E.R.138D.** |
| **Role** | **Single-Seat Interceptor** |
| **First Flight Date** | **XD 145 – 16th May 1957** |
| | **XD 151 – 8th December 1957.** |

The S.R.53 was designed as a mixed power plant single-seat interceptor, and could have been so used if it had entered production but, in many ways, this role was ill-conceived. It would have resulted in a Mach 2 aircraft flashing around the sky, with its target having to be acquired visually by its pilot, space being available in the small nose for only a gun-ranging radar whose range was measured in yards, and then having to fire its missiles at a range measured in miles, provided that the controlling ground radar operator had been able to position the aircraft successfully! Getting the pilot to a position where he could attempt visually to acquire his target would have been no mean task with an aircraft possessing a performance which was far in excess of anything in service and, even if the controller had been successful, it would have been extremely difficult to pick up the target at 40,000 feet at these speeds, let alone at the altitudes that this aircraft was capable of achieving. In the event, the aircraft was superseded in this role, even before it had flown, by the later, and much more capable, S.R.177. It was therefore relegated to a proof-of-concept research prototype, and for missile launching trails at high Mach numbers.

## DEVELOPMENT HISTORY

On 21st February 1952, the Ministry invited tenders from various firms for an aircraft to meet Specification F.124T, which called for a small, simple, rocket-propelled interceptor which, on completion of its mission, glided back to its base or any suitable landing site. It was to have a jettisonable cabin for pilot escape, and to be armed with 50 unguided rocket projectiles in a retractable stowage. Saunders-Roe were not even among the firms to be circulated. The company had for some time been investigating a similar type of project, although they had come to the conclusion that an aircraft with some form of 'get-you-home' power plant was a more viable proposition.

After strong representation, on 27th February the Ministry lent a copy of the Specification to Saunders-Roe who were asked to submit a tender by 24th March 1952. However, having already done virtually all of the ground work, they submitted their brochure within four days! The arguments put forward by the firm for a mixed power plant configuration bore fruit, and the Specification was changed to request this on 9th May 1952.

Saunders-Roe were awarded the contract and an Instruction to Proceed on 30th October. On 2nd December, the Specification was changed yet again to O.R.301 Issue 2, calling for the armament to be changed, substituting the carriage of two Blue Jay (Firestreak) guided missiles under the wings in place of the unguided missiles. The jettisonable cabin requirement was deleted and the pilot was provided with a normal ejection seat instead. The design gradually crystallised into the S.R.53, and the official Specification was re-written around it and became F.138D. A contract for the construction of three prototypes was awarded on 8th May 1953, and the serials XD 145, 151 and 153 were allocated but, on 15th January 1954, the third prototype was cancelled.

In line with the then current policy of ordering more than one design to fulfil any specification to allow a 'fly-off' comparison, plus the fact that this new design was so radically different and with a vastly superior performance to anything so far flown, Avro were also awarded a contract to build two prototypes and a full-scale test airframe to Specification F.137D. of their design, the Avro 720. This was also powered by the Viper turbojet, but had an Armstrong Siddeley liquid oxygen/kerosene rocket motor in place of the HTP/kerosene-fuelled Spectre.

The original target date for the first flight was July 1954, but it soon became obvious that this was optimistic, partly due to the complexity of the project, and partly because the company was committed to other contracts for its livelihood and lacked the facilities and manpower to speed the construction of the radically new aircraft.

The use of High Test Peroxide as a fuel caused its own new problems, as it had never been used before (remember that the design was intended for operational use at normal squadron level and not as a cosseted research tool). Particular problems centred around the bag fuel tanks for its storage, and these had not been fully solved by the time the first prototype was ready; this caused it to fly initially with only two HTP tanks.

During tests of a rear fuselage section fitted with a rocket motor at de Havilland, trailing edge damage was caused to both the elevator and rudder. Their structures were changed to a honeycomb sandwich type of construction to help alleviate this problem, but this acoustic damage directly resulted in the complete redesign and lengthening of the rear fuselage, of the P.177, by then in the design stage. A Supermarine Swift was also allocated to investigate further the problems of acoustic damage to airframes.

The S.R.53 could not be tested at the manufacturer's base as they did not have an airfield! Hurn Airport, Bournemouth, was chosen, being just across the Solent and the nearest suitable airfield to the company's works. The runways and taxi-ways were tested for their suitability for the aircraft's high pressure tyres, an HTP storage was constructed, and radio aids installed. However, the initial trials were to be made from Boscombe Down, with its special test facilities and much longer runways, before transferring to Hurn. In the event, all flights were made from the former airfield and Hurn was never used.

After protracted ground tests, the first prototype XD 145 finally got airborne on 16th May 1957, some three years later than originally planned. The only externally obvious modifications due to the flight tests were the airbrakes. These were found to be very powerful but their use caused severe rudder and tailplane buffet. Therefore, they were extensively perforated to alleviate this problem but, in consequence, they became much less effective throughout the speed range.

The first flights were made 'clean' but, subsequently, dummy Firestreak missiles were carried on the wingtips. To record the rocket plume, these were fitted with cameras but, later, special pods were fitted to each wingtip, housing trace recorders and colour film cine cameras. The one on the left with a single rear-mounted camera, and that on the right additionally with a forward inward-facing camera, recorded the reading on the six fuselage-mounted pressure gauges just forward of the wing root. (Note that the instrument pods were fitted directly to the wing in place of the wingtip fairings, and not on the standard launch shoes for the missiles.)

There were also special problems for the pilot during the circuit and landing phase of flight, due to the lack of thrust from the Viper turbojet. With the leading edge droop, and only 10° trailing edge flap extended, the pilot was committed to land as there was insufficient thrust to overcome drag. No more than 10° flap was used for any of the landings during the whole programme. Slow speed flight was investigated down to buffet, but no stalling trials were completed. It was painfully obvious that a more powerful turbojet was needed, if only as a 'get-you-home' aid.

The second prototype, XD 151, joined the programme, flying on 8th December 1957. This had the full complement of five HTP tanks (the first prototype being subsequently brought up to this standard). It was also wired for full missile firing trials and, to record these, a forward-facing camera was mounted in a fairing on the nose in front of the cockpit windscreen. It, too, had the perforated airbrakes.

Trials continued with the two aircraft, until 5th June 1958 when the second prototype was destroyed in an accident on take-off, killing the pilot, although this was caused by a concrete pole crushing the canopy rather than by any fault in the aircraft itself. The cause of the accident was never fully established, with all aircraft systems appearing serviceable, although several theories have been put forward. Not including this sortie, the aircraft had completed 11 flights, with 31 on the other aircraft. Subsequent to the accident, XD 145 continued to fly a further 14 sorties and the test programme came to an end in October 1959.

At the end of its flying career, the aircraft was sent to the Rocket Propulsion Establishment at Westcott for further ground research and, on completion of these, was stored amongst other early rocket equipment. Despite reports in other publications, to my knowledge it was still in storage there as late as 1972, although nominally it was the property of the RAF Museum.

In 1978, it was finally taken out of storage and transferred to Brize Norton on 13th November, where it was completely refurbished by the Brize Norton Aviation Society, a task which took three years to complete. Due to deterioration, and no suitable spares, the mainwheels were converted from nosewheels intended for a Lightning, and the nosewheel came from an HS.125 Dominie. Dummy

*Saunders-Roe SR.53 XD151 second prototype at Farnborough. Just discernible against the rather cluttered background is the cine camera fairing on the nose for recording missile firing trials. The large blade aerial on the upper fuselage is in fact an El Al Britannia's propellor blade! (Westland Aerospace)*

Firestreaks were obtained from RAF Binbrook and painted to represent those originally carried by the S.R.53. The project was completed in 1981 and was handed over to the Cosford Aerospace Museum on 30th November of that year, where it is now on display. Fortunately the red-painted instrument pods survived and are also on display at the museum.

# CONSTRUCTION

The fuselage was constructed, inverted, in its jig and, being of such compact size, was unusual in being built in one piece with no constructional breaks. It was rotated upright only when completed, ready for wing attachment. Its general layout had a pointed nose section of circular cross-section, changing to a 'figure-eight' section aft of the cockpit, with the centre fuselage upper lobe containing the turbojet and tailpipe, and the lower the rocket fuel and motor. The structure was a conventional semi-monocoque frame and stringer construction, with single skinning, except for the centre fuselage in the region of the HTP tanks, which had double skinning. The entire airframe was manufactured from aluminium alloy, except for some castings in the control circuit and the pilot's windscreen frame, which were of magnesium.

A long pitot boom was mounted at the tip of the pointed nose and, just aft of the flare into the fuselage proper, Frame 1 formed a solid bulkhead being the forward end of the nosewheel bay, the aft end being also a solid bulkhead, acting as the forward end of the cockpit pressure zone. The nosewheel oleo was hinged to the aft bulkhead,

retracting forwards, and the bay was enclosed by a single door hinged to the right. The nosewheel was non-steerable, but fully castoring, and was fitted with a single wheel and high-pressure tyre of 17.65" diameter. The aircraft was manoeuvred on the ground by means of differential braking. Within the wheelbay were the pilot's oxygen, and the nitrogen system, charging valves, together with the pitot static system drain. Level with the aft end of the bay, on the left side of the fuselage, was a servicing panel for the 28 volts d.c. electric ground supply socket. Above this, was a large panel giving access to a nose compartment containing instrumentation.

On the second prototype a semi-circular section, flat-fronted, fairing containing a forward facing cine camera for recording the proposed weapon launching trials was mounted on the nose at the aircraft's centreline, forward of the windscreen.

The pressurised cockpit occupied the whole depth of the fuselage, whose canopy was fitted with a semi-circular windscreen arch, flat centre windscreen panel and curved quarter-lights. The left quarter-light was more heavily framed, as it was hinged inwards at its upper edge to act as a direct-vision panel for bad weather landings. The main windscreen and quarter-lights were hot air de-iced through a duct at their front end. Access to the cockpit was via a ladder hooked into two holes on the left side of the fuselage, the canopy being a large hatch hinged on its right side with a perspex transparency permanently fixed at its centre, blending into the windscreen arch and centre fuselage. The whole hatch was jettisonable in an emergency, either alone, or automatically with the activation of the Martin-Baker Mk.3 ejection seat.

# SAUNDERS ROE S.R.53

Electrics were fed from a nominal 28 volt d.c. battery and three 115 volt a.c. systems. An auxiliary power unit was fitted just aft of the cockpit pressure bulkhead, exhausting from the upper right side of the fuselage.

The Viper turbojet occupied the entire upper part of the centre fuselage, and was fed by two small 'elephant's-ear' intakes just aft of the cockpit canopy each side. It was started by compressed air from a Ground Power Unit, and as well as providing thrust, it was also a source of bleed air for cockpit conditioning and pressurisation, and provided electrical and hydraulic power. There were eight rows of slots for boundary layer bleed in front of each intake, exhausting through louvres below the intake lip on each side. Access for servicing and removal of the engine was via two large doors hinged upwards along the centreline. A strong horizontal forged alloy 'gunwale' extended aft from the cockpit sill on each side, to which were attached the turbojet mounting platforms. The jetpipe extended aft in the upper fuselage lobe and exhausted beneath the fin. The tail fairing was attached by quick release fasteners to allow removal for servicing. On each side of the rear fuselage were the rectangular airbrakes, with a maximum opening angle of 70°. Initially they were plain panels, but due to severe rudder and tailplane buffet when deployed, were subsequently extensively perforated.

The lower fuselage, below the turbojet engine, was entirely occupied by fuel tanks. At the forward end, kerosene for the jet was housed in a compartment built onto the aft face of the cockpit pressure bulkhead. The lower part of Frame 12 was a solid bulkhead, as were the lower halves of Frames 13, 14, 15, 16 and 17. These separated each of the five

HTP tanks, the centre one, No. 3, also acting as the collector tank for feed to the rocket motor. (Due to problems with the bag tanks, the first prototype initially flew with only two HTP tanks fitted, but was later modified to have all five. The second prototype had all five from the start.) The rocket motor was mounted to Frame 18 and the entire lower fuselage fairing around it could be removed for servicing. On the lower centreline, all six fuel tanks were accessible through rectangular panels. A large vent pipe and mast was fitted to the access door below the collector tank. There was also a large circular access panel in the lower skin level with the wing trailing edge.

The wing panels were bolted to the fuselage via four forged alloy attachments at Frames 13, 14, 15 and 16, thus allowing easy removal. The wing was of multi-web construction with four mainspars. It had a chord at the aircraft centreline of 16'6", and a tip chord of 5'1.75". The aerofoil was an RAE 102 symmetrical section with a 6% thickness/chord ratio, a leading edge sweep of 42°6' and a quarter chord sweep of 34°12'. It had 5° anhedral and an incidence of +2° to the fuselage datum. The full span leading edge droop was hinged to the front spar, with three selectable positions; 0°, 9° and 30°. The main undercarriage bay was between Spars 2 and 3 with a single undercarriage rib at approximately mid-span between the front and rear spars. The undercarriage retracted inwards and was stressed for a 10.5 ft./sec. touchdown descent rate at normal landing weight. The undercarriage bay was faired by two doors, one attached to the oleo and the other hinged at the wing root. Maxaret anti-skid brakes were fitted and the wheels had high pressure 22.6" diameter tyres.

There was a second, solid, rib outboard of the

*Although not a very clear photograph, it shows the jet and rocket orifice layout and the size of the rocket plume. Dummy Firestreak missiles are now in place. (Royal Aeronautical Society)*

undercarriage rib forming a bulkhead for the integral tank containing additional rocket motor kerosene which surrounded the undercarriage bay between the fore and aft mainspars in each wing panel. The wing ended in a tip rib, to which could be fitted either a fairing, the instrumentation pods or a sole plate for the missile launch shoes.

To the rear mainspar were hinged the plain trailing edge flaps inboard and the ailerons outboard. Each flap had two hinge points and were selectable in stages to a maximum of 35°. The flaps and leading edge droop (together with the air brakes) were electrically controlled and hydraulically operated. The ailerons were power-boosted, with manual reversion, were mass-balanced, and had a range of movement of ± 11°, and were fitted with geared balance tabs, the left tab also being used for trimming.

The fin had a thickness/chord ratio of 7% and a leading edge sweep of 41°21' and was constructed around two spars, the mainspar being attached to the fuselage at Frame 24 which comprised two ring-type alloy forgings. The rudder, of honeycomb construction, was hinged to the rear auxiliary spar, and was manually operated. It had a geared balance tab at its trailing edge base and, above this, a small spoiler tab controlled by the autostabiliser. The balance tab was also used for trimming. Fin area was able to be kept relatively small due to the end-plate effect of the tailplane.

The tailplane was pivoted to the top of the fin mainspar, being moved by an hydraulic jack, accessible through panels on either side of the fin forward of the mainspar. It had a chord at the centreline of 7'5.5", an RAE 102 symmetrical section, a thickness/chord ratio of 6%, with a leading edge sweep of 42°30', and a quarter-chord sweep of 34°24'. There were no cut-outs in the skin which was continuous from tip to tip, and the construction, like the wing, was of multi-web type. The tailplane was fully powered with trimming override, and had a range of movement of +3° to –10°, with neutral at +2° to the aircraft datum.

A constant chord elevator was hinged to the aft spar at five points, and was also of honeycomb construction. Its range of movement was +6° to –20° and was power assisted, with manual reversion. Feel was provided at low speed by a 'q' feel system, which progressively was phased out as speed increased to be replaced by spring feel at high speed, a local sensing device allowing elevator blow-back to prevent overstressing the airframe.

For the intended stalling trials, it had been realised that the high-mounted tailplane might be blanked by the turbulent wing-wake, thus being ineffective and preventing recovery from a 'deep stall'. It was intended to fit two solid fuel rocket motors at the rear of the fuselage, firing vertically downwards relative to the aircraft datum, to pitch the nose down and thus effect a recovery from this condition. These rockets were never fitted as stalling trials were not carried out.

**POWER PLANT**
One Armstrong Siddeley A.S.V.8 Viper 101 axial flow turbojet developing a Sea Level Static Thrust of 1,640 lbs., plus one de Havilland D.Spe.1A Spectre rocket engine with a Sea Level Thrust of 7,000 lbs. (The engine was designed to achieve 8,000 lbs thrust, but was unable to do so). When operating 'hot' i.e. burning both HTP and kerosene, it was fully variable between 2,000 and 7,000 lbs., thrust. When operating 'cold' i.e. using only HTP, it was fully variable between 300 and a maximum of 3,500 lbs.

The first prototype as preserved at Cosford. The nosewheel is castored through 180°. Just visible under the tail of the aircraft are the two camera and instrument pods carried at times in place of the missiles. (Ron Moulton)

# DATA

## DIMENSIONS

| | |
|---|---|
| Span (without missiles) | 25'1.25" |
| Span (including missiles) | 28'1" |
| Span (with instrument pods) | 27'0" |
| Length (including nose probe) | 46'4.5" (as measured) |
| Height | 10'10" |
| Fuselage length | 39'1.25" |
| Tailplane Span | 12'0" |
| Undercarriage Track | 14'0" |
| Wheelbase | 17'0" |

## AREAS

| | |
|---|---|
| Wing (gross) | 271.3 sq ft |
| Tailplane (gross) | 56.07 sq ft |
| Fin and Rudder (net) | 26.5 sq ft |

## FUEL CAPACITIES

| | |
|---|---|
| Kerosene for turbojet | 500 lbs |
| Kerosene and HTP for rocket | 10,500 lbs |

## WEIGHTS

| | |
|---|---|
| Tare Weight | 6,650 lbs |
| Zero Fuel | 7,400 lbs |
| All Up Weight | 18,400 lbs |
| Overload | 20,238 lbs (Maximum tested) |

## DESIGN PERFORMANCE

| | |
|---|---|
| Maximum Take-off weight | 21,000 lbs |
| Maximum Dive Speed | 525 kts, below 41,000 ft Mach 2.0 above 41,000 ft |
| Load Factor | 4.8g below 40,000 ft, and 6.9g above |

## TAKE-OFF PERFORMANCE

| | |
|---|---|
| Weight at start of roll | 18,400 lbs |
| Unstick speed | 155 kts |
| Ground Roll | 800 yards. (15° flap) |
| Take-off to 50' | 1,075 yards |

## CLIMB

| | |
|---|---|
| Rate of Climb at Sea Level | 12,000 ft/min |
| at 50,000 ft | 39,000 ft/min |
| Time from brakes off to 50,000 ft | 3.01 mins |
| Time from brakes off to 60,000 ft | 3.3 mins |

(Note for ex-fighter pilots of that era, the above climb performance produces a time of 17.4 seconds to climb from 50,000 to 60,000 ft.! Some four years later, in what was then the front line RAF fighter, the Hunter, the author coaxed one up to an indicated 56,000 ft., and took over 25 minutes!)

| | |
|---|---|
| Maximum projected ceiling | 130,000 ft |

## MAXIMUM LEVEL SPEED

Limited solely by fuel available

| | |
|---|---|
| 40,000 ft | 1.4 Mach |
| 50,000 | 1.76 Mach |
| 60,000 ft | 2.1 Mach |

## TURNING PERFORMANCE

| | |
|---|---|
| 50,000 ft Minimum Radius | 2,700 yds at 0.96 Mach |
| 60,000 ft Minimum Radius | 4,700 yds at 1.15 Mach |

## SUPERSONIC PERFORMANCE

Acceleration Time from 0.9 to 1.4 Mach at 50,000 ft: 33 secs
Maximum Duration at 1.4 Mach at 50,000 ft: 1.6 mins
Acceleration Time from 0.9 to 1.4 Mach at 60,000 ft: 21 secs
Maximum Duration at 1.4 Mach at 60,000 ft: 2.0 mins

## PERFORMANCE ON VIPER TURBOJET ALONE

| | |
|---|---|
| Rate of Climb at Sea Level | 420 ft/min (at Take-Off weight) |
| Rate of Climb at 5,000 ft | 100 ft min (at Take-Off weight) |
| Level flight ceiling | 10,000 ft (drift-down with rocket fuel exhausted) |

Maximum speed at 10,000 ft
after drift-down — 170-180 kts

## ENDURANCE

i) Climb to 60,000 ft; cruise level for 7.02 mins; combat at 0.95 Mach for 2.0 mins; glide 30.0 mins; stand off at 5,000 ft, for 6.0 mins—Total Flight Time: 48.32 mins.

ii) Climb to 50,000 ft; cruise level for 10.0 mins; combat at 0.95 Mach for 2.0 mins; glide 28.0 mins; stand off at 5,000 ft, for 6.2—Total Flight Time: 49.21 mins.

Operational Sortie Performance:
(Long Warning time—14 mins)
Start of Roll to 50,000 ft—3.01 mins
Turn 180° and accelerate from 0.9 to 1.6 Mach—1.22 mins.
(Turn radius 3,200 yds.)
Intercept completed after a total of 4.6 mins from take-off.
Turn 180° and accelerate from 0.9 to 1.3 Mach—1.3 mins.
(Turn radius—2,800 yds.)
With two solid booster rockets for take-off
 Start of Roll to 50,000 ft—2.2 mins
 Accelerate from 0.9 to 1.4 Mach—0.55 mins
Turn 180° and accelerate from 1.4 to 1.8 Mach—1.4 mins.
(Turn radius—5,000 yds.)

## FLIGHT TESTS

During the Flight Test programme, until it was halted after a total of 56 flights, the maximum altitude achieved was 55,500 ft., with a maximum speed of 1.33 Mach at 49,000 ft. The maximum sortie radius from base was only 60 miles during any flight.

Total flying time for both prototypes was only 22 hrs. 20 mins. The first prototype completed 31 sorties before the crash of the second prototype and 14 after. The second prototype completed only 11 sorties.

## PERFORMANCE SUMMARY (REPORT FT/21/R/84)

Due to the overall performance characteristics of the S.R.53, ie rapid change of weight, Mach No., altitude, etc., much of the data was of a dynamic nature as opposed to the small quantity of data obtained under more satisfactory static conditions.

There was no detectable variation in drag characteristics due to the presence of either the instrumentation pods or dummy Firestreak missiles. Measured drag values were slightly less than predicted during the climb to 50,000, at which point the predicted and actual values coincided.

## STABILITY AND CONTROL SUMMARY (REPORT FT/21/R83 'Satisfactory positive longitudinal

stability characteristics throughout the speed range tested, reducing slightly above the transonic speed range. The autostabiliser was effective at low speeds and reduced any tendency to dutch roll, (the aircraft could be safely flown without it being used). The autostabiliser's effectiveness decreased with increasing EAS. and altitude. The ailerons produced an exceptional rate of roll at all speeds. Directional stability was satisfactory up to maximum speed achieved during flight testing.

The elevator and ailerons had manual reversion, and the aircraft could be safely flown in this mode to approximately 0.85-0.9 Mach at which speed the aircraft became uncontrollable due to the high control forces.'

## REFERENCES

| | |
|---|---|
| Cosford Aerospace Museum | —The Aircraft |
| Saunders-Roe S.R.53 | —Report No. T.P. 130 |
| Saunders-Roe S.R.53 | —Report No. T.P. 361 |
| Saunders-Roe S.R.53 | —Report FT/21/R/83 |
| Saunders-Roe S.R.53 | —Report FT/21/R/84 |
| British Hovercraft Corporation | —Photographic Archives |

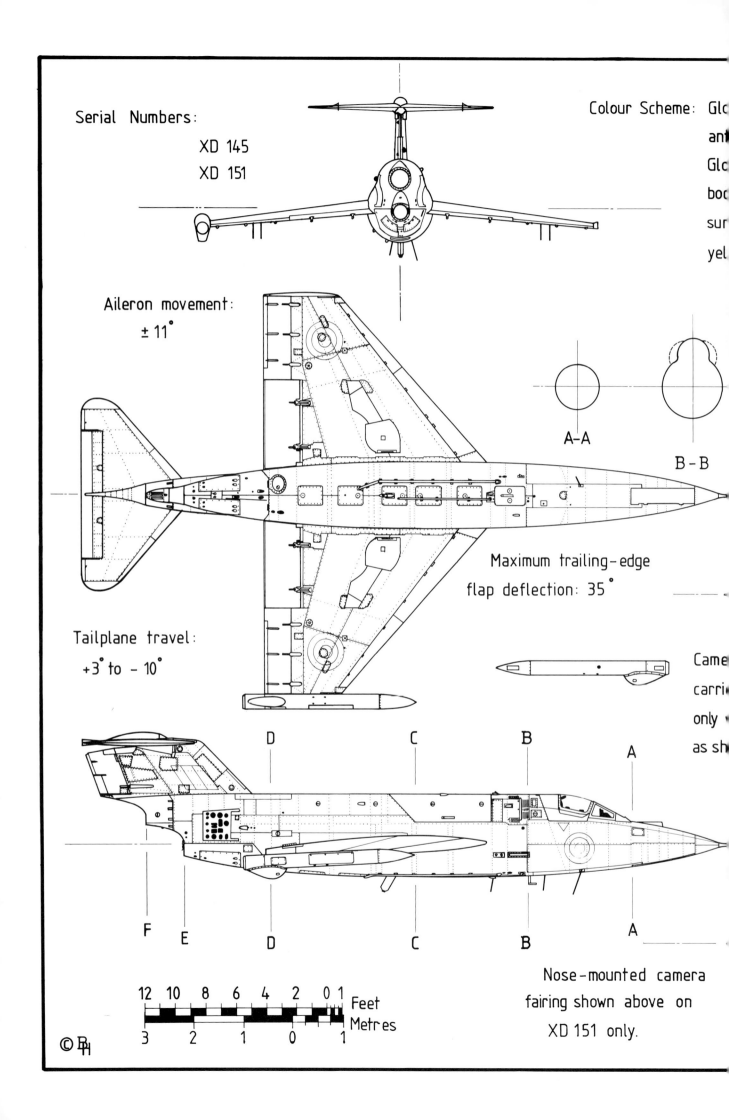

Serial Numbers:

XD 145

XD 151

Colour Scheme: Glo

an

Glo

bod

sur

yel

Aileron movement:
± 11°

A-A

B-B

Maximum trailing-edge
flap deflection: 35°

Tailplane travel:
+3° to - 10°

Came
carri
only
as sh

D          C          B          A

F     E     D          C          B          A

Nose-mounted camera
fairing shown above on
XD 151 only.

12  10   8    6    4    2    0  1   Feet
                                    Metres
 3        2         1        0         1

© PH

overall, matt black
anel and cockpit interior.
mera pods and missile
lue missile control
"fire" panels,
s.

Maximum leading-edge
droop: 30°

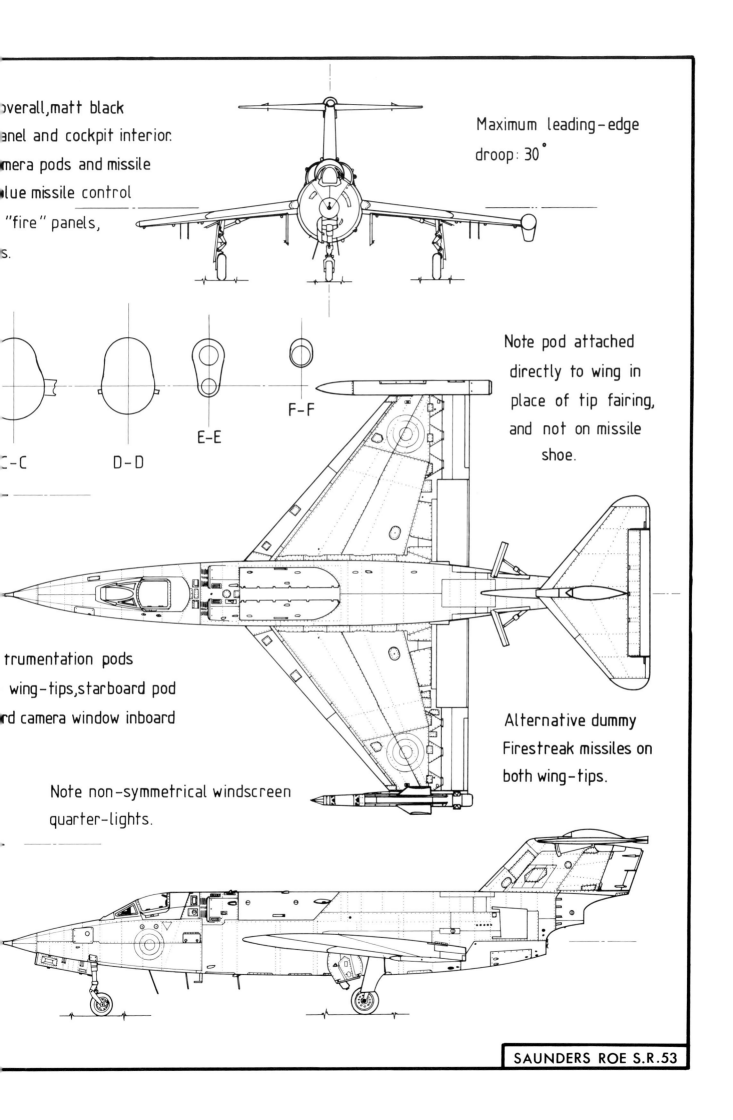

Note pod attached
directly to wing in
place of tip fairing,
and not on missile
shoe.

F-F

E-E

C-C          D-D

trumentation pods
wing-tips, starboard pod
rd camera window inboard

Alternative dummy
Firestreak missiles on
both wing-tips.

Note non-symmetrical windscreen
quarter-lights.

SAUNDERS ROE S.R.53

*Wooden mock-up Saunders-Roe SR.177 showing good nose, intake and forward fuselage structure detail, together with the large ventral engine bay access door. (Westland Aerospace)*

# SAUNDERS-ROE P.177

| Manufacturer | Saunders-Roe Ltd |
|---|---|
| Specification | F.177.D |
| Role | Single-Seat Interceptor |
| First Flight Date | Planned for Spring 1958. |

Early in the design stage of the S.R.53, it became apparent that, in its planned form, it would not have made a very effective interceptor, for the reasons explained in the chapter on that aircraft. Saunders-Roe were also concerned about the imbalance between the thrust of the turbojet compared to that of the rocket, the jet alone only being capable of getting the aircraft back to base at the end of the sortie. This effectively relegated the S.R.53 project to that of an experimental, proof-of-concept, prototype, even before it flew.

To get the utmost from the design potential, it was felt that the turbojet/rocket capability should be better balanced, with the turbojet powerful enough to sustain the specified cruising requirements, and the rocket used only for take-off, climb, turning and acceleration.

A much larger, and more sophisticated, design was started, retaining the same basic overall aerodynamic layout but allowing the carriage of a much enhanced radar for target detection, and with a considerably greater fuel capacity, giving the aircraft longer endurance for maximum operational flexibility. This new design eventually evolved into the P.177, planned to be used by both the Royal Air Force and Royal Navy, with the maximum possible commonality.

The overall layout was similar to the S.R.53, with mid-mounted delta wings and tailplane, the latter set at the top of the broad fin. Initially, the power plant layout was the same, ie. with the jet above the rocket and fed by intakes behind the cockpit; however this was changed early in the design stage to have the rocket at the top and the turbojet engine fed through a 'chin' intake just behind and below the radome.

## DEVELOPMENT HISTORY

Despite the S.R.53 having not yet flown, the Ministry of Supply held discussions with both Avro and Saunders-Roe regarding the higher-performance, more capable, interceptor which was to follow on. Both companies were going for an aircraft where the turbojet contributed a much more balanced thrust with that of the rocket, rather than being a 'get-you-home' source of power, as on the S.R.53, and both having a much better performance radar to complement the proposed armament.

Initially, the Saunders-Roe proposal was based very closely on the S.R.53 layout, but this was soon revised and the whole airframe was totally redesigned. The wing area was increased, and blown flaps introduced, so that one basic design could be suitable for both RAF and Naval use, the Royal Air Force stipulating that no compromise of their version would be tolerated to enable it to meet Naval requirements. So impressed were the MoS. with their submission, that the requirement was not put out for tender and the contract was awarded to the company, with the Specification virtually being written around their design. A contract was awarded in May 1955, with the requirements to be O.R.337 and N.A.47 for the RAF and Navy respectively. In September of the same year, a full-scale engineering mock-up was ordered, together with an Instruction to Proceed with the manufacture of the prototypes, with the first flight planned for mid-1957. Due to other commitments and the sheer complexity of the programme, this target soon became unrealistic and, as early as April 1956, it was agreed that to allow for their completion by January 1958, the first five aircraft should be aerodynamic shells, with no radar or weapons systems installed.

On 4th September 1956, a contract was issued for the completion of an initial batch of 27 aircraft, nine for basic development and nine each for RAF and Naval development trials. Those for the RAF were designated P.177.R and for the Navy P.177.N. Any 'overseas' variants were to be designated P.177.K.

It was clear from the outset that Saunders-Roe did not have the capability for building more than the initial development batch of prototypes at their Cowes factory. Therefore, the work was to be transferred to other companies who had more capacity. The detail design and manufacture of the wings was to be done by Marshall's at Cambridge, and Armstrong Whitworth at Coventry was given the job of 'productionising' the design and final assembly of the production aircraft. The firm of F.G.Miles designed and manufactured the cockpit canopy. Initial plans called for 150 aircraft for the RAF and 150 for the Navy. With the emerging West German interest, there was the possibility of a further 600+ being needed.

The Defence White Paper of April 1957 put a stop to all of this, as it did with many other promising designs. The requirement for the Royal Air Force was immediately cancelled, but work on the other 18 aircraft for the Navy was continued and the first prototype was to be completed in Naval configuration. There were still plans for the production of 150 aircraft, and German interest was still strong. However, somehow the Germans had been persuaded that their version should be fitted with a Rolls-Royce R.A.24R turbojet in place of the de Havilland Gyron Junior.

In August 1957, the Defence Minister, after seemingly no consultation with the Navy, cancelled their programme as well. Soon it was obvious that Germany would not support the programme with no orders for the home airforces, and they too cancelled in December 1957. After the cancellation of the Navy contract, the Ministry of Supply agreed to fund continuation of the first five aircraft until December 1957 to a new Specification F.177D. To expedite manufacture, these were to be built without the arrester hook, catapult spools and hold-back attachment. The aircraft then under construction was serialed XL905–907 and XL920, 921. This contract was also terminated on 24th December of that year.

The five almost completed airframes, plus their jigs, were put into storage in the hope of resurrection but after some brief Japanese interest in the purchase of these and the S.R.53 for trials purposes, they were all finally scrapped in 1958.

# CONSTRUCTION

The airframe was manufactured from light alloy, with only certain high-stress components being made from steel. The fuselage broke down into forward, centre and aft sections for manufacture and transportation, with radome and rocket engine cowling attached fore and aft respectively.

The ogival, pointed radome was of circular cross-section, housing the scanner for the A.I.23 Airpass radar and hinged to allow access to the radar equipment mounted aft of the scanner. Aft of Frame 3, which was in line with the engine intake lip, back to Frame 22, the fuselage was effectively horizontally divided into two, with the upper part being of a totally different type of construction to the lower.

The forward fuselage was of conventional frame and stringer construction, the floor of the cockpit forming the upper wall of the intake duct. Aft of the cockpit, virtually the whole upper fuselage comprised the forward equipment bay, accessed from each side via large rectangular doors, hinged on their top edges. The entire upper fuselage, from the radome back to the transport joint, was pressurised. Under the nose was the semi-circular intake, with a fixed conical centre-body. The first 15" of the intake lip formed a sliding cowl, driven by a hydraulic motor and three jacks, being extended forward by 6" for engine pressure recovery at low forward speeds, the system being activated by undercarriage extension and retraction. The lower part of the intake splitter slid forward with the intake. Between the lower part of the nosecone and centre-body, and around the mid part of the cone, was a boundary layer bleed duct, which split into two, exhausting through louvres either side of the fuselage. Although occupying the entire lower half of the fuselage, the engine intake duct bifurcated either side of the nosewheel well, with the nosewheel retracting forwards into the bay. The nosewheel was fitted with a 19" diameter tyre for the RAF and a larger, 22.5" diameter tyre, for the Navy version. Immediately aft of the nosewheel bay, within the intake duct, was a debris guard to prevent foreign object ingestion by the engine, comprising two semi-circular metal grills which lay flush with the wall of the intake duct splitter when not in use, and which were pivoted out and back by a hydraulic jack to cover each half of the duct whenever the undercarriage was extended. A panel in the lower fuselage skin allowed removal of any debris. The twin ducts converged aft of this guard before entering the engine bay.

In addition to the main equipment bay doors, on the left side of the lower fuselage were panels to the hydraulics, and an automatic disconnection panel for telebrief, radar elecrical plug and cooling air supply. Each side of the nose were panels containing radar and electrical equipment. On the right side,

opposite the hydraulic servicing panel, were those for replenishing the liquid oxygen and for access to the fire extinguisher bottle.

The cockpit had a vee-shaped windscreen with two large optically flat main panels, and two smaller quarter-lights. The main panels were hot-air demisted, and the left one was also electrically heated over part of its surface to act as a clear vision 'panel'. The clamshell canopy was heavily framed and, although it provided adequate visibility for the pilot, there was obviously a large blind spot to the rear, hardly ideal for a fighter aircraft! Any production versions may therefore have had a one-piece blown canopy for better all-round visibility.

The centre fuselage was virtually of constant cross-section for its entire length, its upper half being occupied by seven fuel tanks, each separated by solid metal bulkheads. Along the spine area was

*Rear view of the wooden Saunders-Roe SR.177 mock-up, showing details of the rocket engine installation, fin structure and airbrake panel. Close study reveals that the mock-up has the extended jetpipe redesign required after acoustic damage to the fin and tailplane of the SR.53 was revealed.*
*(Westland Aerospace)*

a 2'0" wide channel section accommodating the flying control runs, in the skin of which were large tank access panels. A solid floor to the tank bays was provided by a metal plate mounted horizontally across the fuselage for the whole length of the centre-section, together with a substantial keel beam. The flat fuselage sides were of conventional construction down to the lower longeron, but with a double skin (the remainder of the structure having a normal single skin) with doors along each side for servicing the engine accessories and systems. The entire lower centre fuselage was occupied by two large engine bay doors, through which the engine could be serviced or removed. Set into these doors, forward and on the left, were the ground starter and kerosene refuelling points, and in the forward end of the right-hand door was a large NACA-type intake for the auxiliary power unit, exhausting through another duct at the aft end. Immediately aft of the engine bay doors were the main undercarriage bays, each with two doors, the aft one of which was sequenced closed after undercarriage extension. The mainwheel oleos retracted aft and inwards so that, when retracted, the wheels lay at approximately 45° to the vertical. Even so, there was not quite enough room, so the aft doors had small bulges to accommodate the wheels in the bay. The wheels were fitted with 31" diameter tyres and had Maxaret anti-skid brakes fitted.

On the Naval variant, on each side where the lower longeron was joined to Bulkhead 3, was fitted a catapult hook, and on the lower centreline at Bulkhead 8, a catapult hold-back fitting. Also for this variant, the undercarriage was stressed to accept a much higher vertical velocity on touchdown.

Aft of the transport joint the structure was quite conventional, with access doors on each side for the aft equipment bay. Sloping forward from the top of Frame 20 to attach at the lower longeron at Frame 17 was a massive fin mainspar frame. Originally, the lower fuselage structure finished at this latter frame, with a long fairing above extending aft to the rocket exhaust. However, the S.R.53 had revealed acoustic fatigue problems with this layout, damage being caused to both the aft fuselage and elevator skins. Consequently the lower fuselage was redesigned, with the afterburner jetpipe extended aft by 3'6". To the aft-most fuselage frame, at the top were attached the three rocket engine mounts, and below, at the end of the lower longeron were the arrester hook attachments. The detachable rocket motor fairing was the major external difference between the two versions. That on the RAF version was a simple, open ended cone, fastened to the upper part of the fuselage by six quick release catches. On the Naval variant, however, a side 'skirt' extended down the fuselage to level with the arrester hook attachments. The hook itself was of the 'A' type which, when

retracted, lay along the edge of the fairing skirt, passing either side of the turbojet afterburner nozzle, and the rocket motor chamber, with the hook part level with the topline of the fuselage at the base of the rudder. Forward of the fairing on each side were large access doors to the rocket motor accessories bay. On the right side was the HTP refuelling point. Either side of the jetpipe, and hinged to Frame 18, were the large square, fully variable airbrakes, with a maximum opening angle of 70°. (There is a possibility that these would have later been perforated surfaces, in the light of experience with the S.R.53.)

The engine was mounted at -3° to the fuselage datum; however, the jetpipe bent so that the afterburner jetpipe and nozzle were at +0.5° to the datum. On the Naval version only, part of the pre-afterburner jet efflux was deflected downwards through a duct to exhaust under the fuselage between the mainwheel oleos. (An artist's impression shows two small ducts, venting through each mainwheel bay opening. However, there does not appear to be sufficient room for this, so one duct exhausting on the aircraft's centreline has been depicted in the drawings.) It is also unclear whether this system would have been fitted to the prototypes or whether it was to be subject to later development. The fully variable convergent/divergent afterburner nozzle exhausted below the Spectre rocket engine, which was mounted at -3.5° to the fuselage datum imparting some upthrust to its exhaust efflux. The entire fairing around it could be detached using quick-release fasteners for servicing and engine removal.

Early in the design stage, to allow maximum commonality and to satisfy both the RAF and Naval requirements, the original wing design was enlarged and given a flap blowing system. The wings were of modified delta planform with a basic 6% thickness/chord ratio and a symmetrical section. They were of multi-web construction, built around four massive spars, had a root chord at the aircraft's centreline of 18'0", and were set at +3.5° incidence to the fuselage datum, with 5° anhedral. The four spars were bolted to the fuselage on forged alloy stub spars at Bulkheads 2, 3, 4 and 5, each having a two-pin attachment, allowing easy removal of the whole surface after control runs, etc. had been disconnected. Like the fuselage, the wing was of all alloy construction and had a leading edge sweep angle of 40°10', a quarter-chord sweep of 32°10' and an extended tip chord of 6'0", giving an aspect ratio of 2.27:1.

Hinged to the front spar were leading edge flaps, operating in conjunction with those on the trailing edge which were hinged to the rear spar inboard of the ailerons. Like the ailerons, these were of honeycomb construction and were provided with an engine bleed-air system to increase lift, and therefore reduce approach speeds. The ailerons were hinged at three points, operated by large jacks housed within streamlined fairings under the wings, acting at the centre hinge point. There were no trim tabs on the ailerons, lateral trim being effected by spring-bias.

The tips of the wings ended in standard sole plates to enable the missile launch shoes to be attached. (For some reason the Naval shoes were slightly larger than for those to be carried by the RAF version, increasing overall wingspan by 2".) Armament was to be two Blue Jay Mk.4 missiles (Red Top), although Firestreaks could also be carried. No internal armament was planned for the aircraft. A wing hard-point was provided for the carriage of external stores, the pylon being plumbed for the fitting of drop tanks.

Fin attachment to the fuselage was at the previously described massive diagonal fin mainspar frame, with a forward attachment point at Frame 14. It was built around two spars, with standard rib construction, all from light alloy, having a leading edge sweep angle of 47°. Despite the very high design speeds for the aircraft, fin area was able to be kept relatively small while still giving adequate directional stability, due to the end-plate effect of the tailplane mounted at the tip. Large panels in each side provided access to the rudder and tailplane control runs operating jacks. The rudder was of constant chord, and like the wing control surfaces was of honeycomb construction, with a clear navigation light mounted at its tip. A pitot head projected forward from the fin tip.

The slab tailplane, with no separate elevators, was mounted at the tip of the fin and was of multi-spar and rib construction being pivoted at approximately mid-chord, with a leading edge sweep of 39°. On the Naval version only, a constant chord trailing edge trimming flap of honeycomb construction was fitted. This surface was locked except during the approach phase, when the wing flaps were lowered and their blowing system became operative. Then the flap was unlocked and deflected upwards to give a countering nose up trim change to that occurring from the flap blowing system.

### Cockpit layout: Prototypes. XL 905, 906, 907, 920, 921

The pilot had a Martin-Baker Mk.4. ejection seat, with a seat-pan mounted combined canopy and seat jettison handle. He had normal, adjustable rudder pedals, but an unusual control column. This slid fore and aft in a tube fitted below the main instrument panel for pitch control, and was pivoted left and right for roll control. The centre part of the main instrument panel contained the standard six flight instruments plus a TACAN indicator, with three engine indicators mounted above. To the left of the main panel were the accelerometer, under-carriage, leading edge droop, flap and flap blow, and arrester hook controls. To the right were the turbojet engine indicators. On the left cockpit wall were mounted the identical throttles, the one for

the turbojet above that for the rocket. The upper lever incorporated the relight button and the lower the press-to-transmit and airbrake switches. On the left console were the jet and rocket controls, autostabiliser, TACAN and trim switches, with the central warning panel mounted at the forward end on a sloping panel with the brake pressure gauge. Between the pilot's legs, below the control column, were standby trim, and anti-spin parachute stream and jettison switches. At the front of the right console were the undercarriage, flap, leading edge, arrester hook and canopy position indicators. Aft were the turbojet, then rocket fuel indicators, outboard of which were the rocket chamber pressure and coolant outlet temperature gauges, and behind these the environmental controls, oxygen, cabin pressure selector.

### Cockpit layout: subsequent to first five Prototypes

Differences immediately noticeable were the fitting of the radar scope and controller, and in the main instrument panel. The large, circular A.I.23 display was mounted centrally, immediately above the main instrument panel, which was changed to the standard O.R.946 layout comprising large, circular, attitude and plan-position indicators, and vertical tape altitude and horizontal strip speed displays. To the right were standby artificial horizon, airspeed indicator and altimeter. To the left was a cleaned-up 'take-off and landing' controls panel. The shape of the turbojet throttle handle was unchanged, except in that it now had the press-to-transmit button and airbrake switches in its end. The rocket lever now ended in a simple knob. The left console was generally cleaned-up, with mounted on it from the rear, controls for the IFF., and TACAN, autostabilisation, trims, UHF radio and central warning panel. Hinged to the rear of the left cockpit wall, to be swung forward when needed, was a quadrant on top of which was mounted the A.I.23 radar multi-function control column. The right console was similar to that on the prototypes, but was again reorganised. The turbojet indicators were now all on the combined rocket and turbine panel outboard of the fuel quantity indicators. The pilot's multi-service connector was, unusually, on the right side of the seat-pan.

### FUEL SYSTEM

Being of the 'cold' variety, the rocket engine fuel was kerosene and High Test Peroxide, (HTP.), and thus the power plants required the carriage of only two types of fuel. The turbojet was supplied from two fuselage tanks, the forward one wrapped around the lower part of the engine intake duct, and the aft one was No. 6 in the line of tanks, which occupied the entire upper part of the centre fuselage. There were also integral tanks in either wing panel, together with the provision of two underwing drop tanks. (Illustrations show these to be carried only by the Naval version, annotated as a 'difference'; however, with identical wings, they could also have been carried by the RAF version, if so required). Provision was made, again only on the Naval variant, for a flight-refuelling probe, mounted on the left side of the fuselage immediately below the forward equipment bay door.

## ARMAMENT

To reduce delays to the flight test programme, in April 1956 it was agreed that the first five prototypes were to be 'aerodynamic shells' with no radar or weapons system fitted. Dummy missiles were to be carried for aerodynamic trials. The sole armament planned for the interceptor version was to be two Red Top missiles. Initially, these were planned to be carried side-by-side piggy-back fashion on the upper fuselage at approximately wing mid-root chord, but after wind tunnel tests this was changed to being carried on launch shoes fitted to the wing tips, as on the SR.53.

## PROPOSED VARIANTS

The P.177 was officially designated as a long-range strike fighter/high altitude interceptor. The differing roles could be attained by varying the 'mix' of fuel capacities, so that more tankage could be devoted to fuel for the turbojet. In fact, one variant had the rocket motor removed entirely and was powered solely by an advanced afterburner Avon.

For the variant proposed for the German Air Force, the Gyron Junior was to be replaced by a Rolls-Royce R.A.24R Avon.

## RAF/NAVY DIFFERENCES SUMMARY

The primary external differences for the Naval version were to be:

i)   More highly stressed undercarriage to cope with greater descent rates at touchdown.
ii)  Larger diameter nosewheel tyre.
iii) Jet deflection.
iv)  Arrester hook and altered rear fuselage fairing.
v)   Catapult hooks and Hold Back fitting.
vi)  Tailplane trim flap.
vii) In-flight refuelling probe.
ix)  Wing span increased by 2".
x)   Normal carriage of underwing tanks.

## POWER PLANT

One de Havilland DGJ.10R Gyron Junior axial flow turbojet developing a Sea Level Static Thrust of 10,000 lbs., and 14,000 lbs., thrust with a 2,000°K afterburner. In addition, one de Havilland D.Spe.5A Spectre rocket engine fully controllable between 2,000 and 8,000 lbs thrust, when burning both kerosene and High Test Peroxide, and with a maximum thrust of approximately 3,500 lbs when operating 'cold' and using only HTP.

Alternative of one Rolls-Royce R.A.24R Avon axial flow turbojet with a Sea Level Static Thrust of 11,250 lbs., dry and 14,430 lbs., thrust with afterburner.

# DATA

## DIMENSIONS

|  | P.177R | P.177N |
|---|---|---|
| Span (over missiles) | 30'3.25" | 30'5.25" |
| Length | 50'6" | 50'6" |
| Height | 14'3.5" | 14'3.5" |
| Fuselage length | 48'1" | 48'1" |
| Tailplane Span | 13'3" | 13'3" |
| Undercarriage Track | 6'11" | 6'11" |
| Wheelbase | 16'0" | 16'0" |

## AREAS

| | |
|---|---|
| Wing (gross) | 327.0 sq ft |
| Flap (gross) | 30.25 sq ft |
| Tailplane (gross) | 65.0 sq ft |

## FUEL CAPACITIES

|  | P177R | P.177N |
|---|---|---|
| Internal HTP for rocket | 600 gallons | 600 gallons |
| Internal kerosene for rocket | 120 gallons | 110 gallons |
| Internal kerosene for turbojet | 570 gallons | 580 gallons |
| Total Internal Fuel | 1,290 gallons | |

Capacity of proposed underwing drop tanks unknown.

## WEIGHTS

|  | P.177R | P.177N |
|---|---|---|
| Zero Fuel | 14,533 lbs | 14,810 lbs |
| All Up Weight | 25,786 lbs | 27,348 lbs |
| Overload | 28,174 lbs | — |
| Combat | 17,050 lbs | 17,560 lbs |

## ESTIMATED PERFORMANCE

Although capable of higher performance, the maximum speed was limited to Mach 2.35 due to the light alloy construction.

Absolute ceiling 86,000 ft
Acceleration at 80,000 ft Mach 1.4 to 2.0–66 secs
Acceleration at 80,000 ft in a 5 mile radius turn Mach 0.9 to 1.6–70 secs. (For a comparison a Lightning required a 15 mile radius turn without loss of speed and level acceleration time from Mach 0.9 to 1.6–200 secs, at much lower altitude).

## PERFORMANCE WITH FUEL FOR THE SPECIFIED MISSION

|  | P.177R | P.177N |
|---|---|---|
| Time to 10,000 ft | — | 1.22 mins |
| Time to 22,000 ft | 2.12 mins | — |
| Time to 50,000 ft | 3.06 mins | 2.55 mins |
| Level accel, Mach 0.9 to 1.6 at 50,000 ft | 0.97 mins | 0.72 mins |
| Total Time to 60,000 ft | 4.35 mins | 3.65 mins |

## PERFORMANCE WITH FULL ROCKET FUEL

|  | P.177R | P.177N |
|---|---|---|
| Time to 50,000 ft | 2.36 mins | 2.2 mins |
| Level accel, Mach 0.9 to 1.6 at 50,000 ft | 0.93 mins | 0.69 |
| Total Time to 60,000 ft | 3.59 mins | 3.26 mins |

## REFERENCES

| | |
|---|---|
| Saunders-Roe P.177 | —Report No.T.P.244 |
| Saunders-Roe P.177 | —Report No.T.P.354 |
| British Hovercraft Corporation | —Photographic Archives |

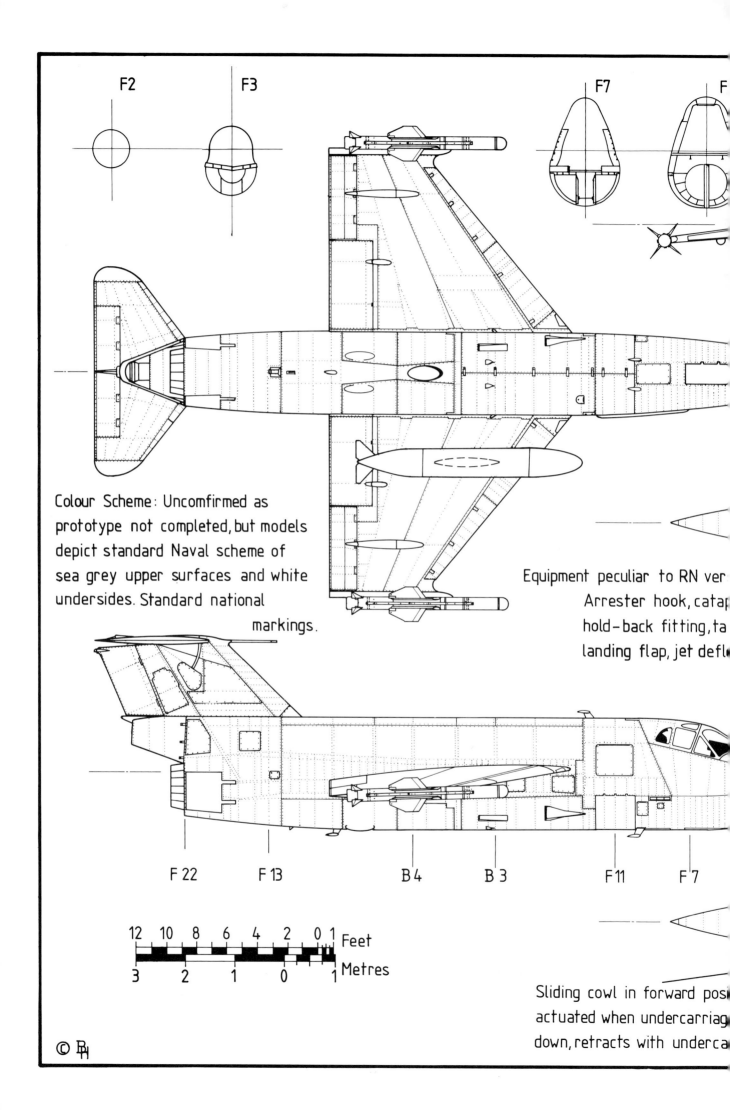

F2    F3    F7    F

Colour Scheme: Uncomfirmed as
prototype not completed, but models
depict standard Naval scheme of
sea grey upper surfaces and white
undersides. Standard national
markings.

Equipment peculiar to RN ver
Arrester hook, catar
hold-back fitting, ta
landing flap, jet defl

F 22    F 13    B 4    B 3    F 11    F 7

12  10  8  6  4  2  0 1  Feet
3     2     1     0     1  Metres

Sliding cowl in forward posi
actuated when undercarriag
down, retracts with underca

© PH

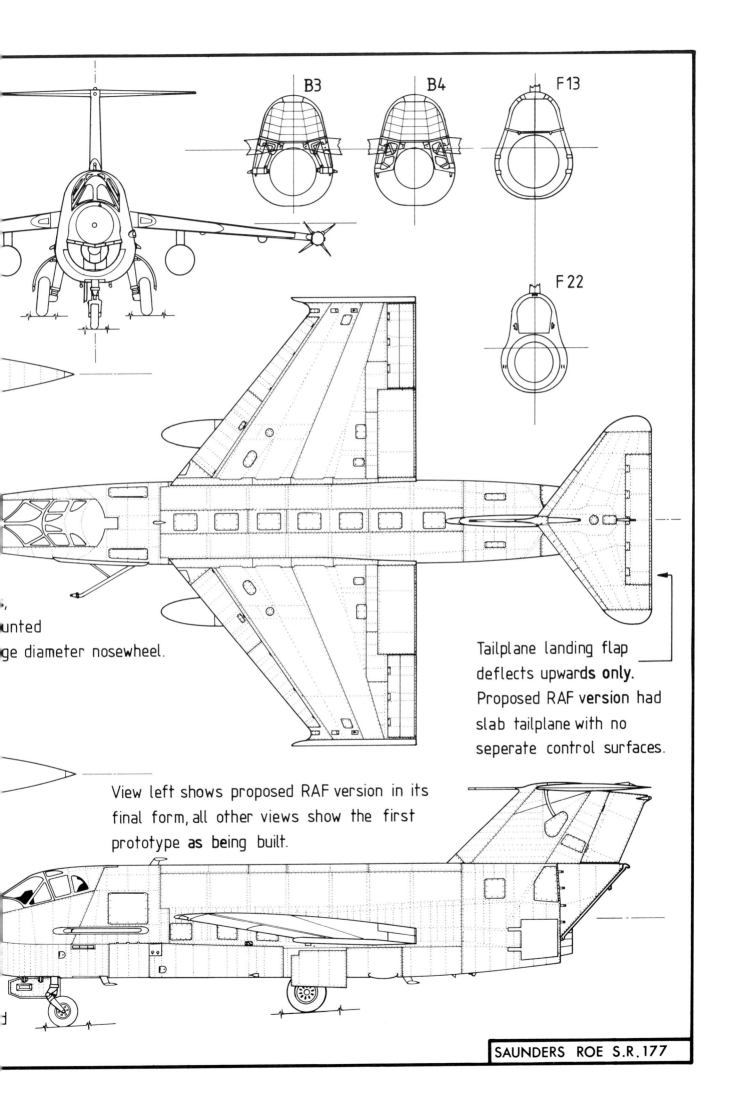

B3

B4

F13

F22

unted

ge diameter nosewheel.

Tailplane landing flap
deflects upwards **only**.
Proposed RAF **version** had
slab tailplane with no
seperate control surfaces.

View left shows proposed RAF version in its
final form, all other views show the first
prototype **as be**ing built.

SAUNDERS ROE S.R.177

*Hawker P.1121 final mock-up showing good detail of the ventral intake and its boundary layer bleed. It appears to have a single piece, unframed curved windscreen which was later to be redesigned with two bracing frames. (British Aerospace (Kingston))*

# HAWKER P.1121

| Manufacturer | Hawker Aircraft Company Ltd |
|---|---|
| Specification | Private Venture – Specification Allocated |
| Role | Interceptor/Ground Attack Prototype |
| First Flight Date | Planned for April 1958 |

The P.1121 was one of the most promising designs of its time but, with no official backing forthcoming, the cost of development was too great for the company to bear alone so, sadly it was not to be.

## DEVELOPMENT HISTORY

Early in 1954, OR.323 was circulated to the industry, detailing the requirements thought necessary for the next generation of fighters after the Hunter and Swift. Hawker responded with a proposal designated P.1103, with preliminary design work starting on 24th March 1954. After investigating many layouts and engines, by January 1955 it was decided to develop a two-seater fighter with a single engine, ventral intake and a large radar.

At about this time, OR.329 (Specification F.155T) was issued and the design was further adapted to enable it to meet this new Specification; the

company was able to issue the brochure on 5th October 1955. The forward fuselage was redesigned to enable it to accommodate a 40" diameter radar antenna. It was to be powered by a single de Havilland Gyron engine, plus two wing-mounted rocket motors. The armament was to be two of the enormous Vickers Red Dean missiles.

In April 1956, the company was informed that their tender had not been successful (the Fairey submission having won the contract) but it was decided to continue the detailed design and to construct a prototype at the company's own expense. Shortly after, the Air Staff intimated to Hawker's that there might be a requirement for a long-range interceptor with a secondary ground attack role, and suggested that the P.1103 might be adapted. A study of the strike version was started, designated P.1116, which showed that the optimum design favoured a much smaller, less swept wing. However, this change would have negated a considerable amount of the design work already completed and, therefore, there was a complete re-appraisal of the project to see if more of the P.1103 structure could be used. The new design study, for a single-seat strike aircraft using much of the P.1103 structure, was started on 28th May 1956 and was designated P.1121.

Unfortunately, the situation in Britain at the time was, to put it mildly, in a state of flux! Air staff opinion was changing and moving away from any more interceptors and it was felt that effort should concentrate on the strike version at the expense of the interceptor. At the same time, the Central Fighter Establishment was advocating strongly that priority be given to the interceptor, with the strike role being secondary! The proposed engine was coming under review with the need to improve low level range. Discussions were held with Bristol Siddeley for use of the Olympus 21R engine, which had a much better specific fuel consumption, and with Rolls-Royce for use of the Conway engine. Meanwhile, de Havilland had offered a de-rated Gyron, but this did not show the promised improvement in sfc. By August 1956, matters were even more complicated with the information that the Olympus was about to be axed, and the Gyron was put on hold to 'await further evaluation of its application to certain aircraft'!

Despite all this, construction continued and, by July 1956, the main members of the centre fuselage jig had been erected at Kingston. Dowty, who was designing the undercarriage, had raised doubts as to the aircraft's stability during ground manoeuvring with the very narrow-track undercarriage, but their design changes were over-ruled on the grounds of complication and weight.

Meanwhile, the Air Staff confirmed that full priority should be given to the strike version, but would it be possible to consider a second crew-member? One month later, they still encouraged the project to go ahead at full speed but said that there would be no funds forthcoming for it, due to a financial squeeze! Despite this conflicting infor-mation and gloomy predictions, on 31st August 1956 Hawker's Board took the bold decision to continue development of the P.1121 in its current form, as a general purpose strike fighter with priority being given to the interceptor performance with the low level role as secondary. An internal company specification was drafted to form the basis of the design and construction of a single prototype, which was to be only a bare aerodynamic shell with the minimum of built-in equipment. Construction was to be state-of-art, in the hope that it would be rapid and trouble-free, and a target date for first flight was set at April 1958. The prototype was still to be powered by the Gyron, with the possibility of the Conway for the low-level role.

At Kingston, manufacture of the ground test rigs for the fuel, cabin conditioning and flying control systems was proceeding to plan, and problems were being resolved in relation to the hydraulic system and the temperatures likely to be encountered at 2.5 Mach. A full-scale mock-up was completed for the Board's inspection on 24th January 1957, the prototype's construction given the go-ahead, and trials of a model in the RAE low-speed tunnel were satisfactorily completed the following month.

On 4th April 1957, the infamous Government White Paper was released which appeared to sound the death-knell for the British aircraft industry, in that no fighters were required after the P.1b, and no bombers after the V-force! However, as the P.1121 was being built at the company's own expense, they decided, much to their credit, to continue with it anyway.

By the summer of 1957, the first major problem arose. A Gyron was running at Hatfield behind a static test version of the intake, and it became immediately apparent that the combination was far from satisfactory, with the engine surging well below maximum rpm. Several intake modifications were tried but, if anything, they made matters worse, with the engine even more prone to surging. Therefore, the intake was returned to Kingston for more extensive modifications, including removal of the internal bullet fairing, the top inlets being improved, and internal vanes being fitted. Also, a bell-mouthed extension was attached to the sharp intake lips. A later standard of Gyron was removed from the Sperrin test aircraft and run behind the modified intake. There was some improvement, but the engine was still very prone to surge unless the top inlets were open. The tests terminated abruptly when a loose rivet from the intake damaged the engine compressor. Bristol Siddeley had meanwhile requested that they might test an Olympus engine with the intake, which had been de-modified back to its sharp-lipped shape, and it was duly delivered there in October. The engine ran perfectly, right up to full throttle. The Gyron was obviously just too sensitive.

Despite these problems, de Havilland agreed to continue development of the flight engine but, at Hawker's the decision was reluctantly taken to continue development at a much reduced rate of expenditure, and the prototype was moved to the corner of the experimental shop, with manufac-turing effort being reduced to about one-fifth rate. Meanwhile, the design office started investigating in detail as to how far a two-seater version of the P.1121 could be made to satisfy OR.339 – the requirement that was eventually to produce the TSR.2.

Several alternative versions were proposed by this stage, including the standard single-seat inter-ceptor, the single-seat strike aircraft, a two-seat aircraft, a single-seat naval interceptor with wing-fold at the roots, a much lengthened two-seater strike aircraft and, finally, a twin-engined two-seat version. None were pursued beyond the initial design stage. There was some brief interest from the Germans who sought information on the project and the US Navy showed interest in a low altitude strike fighter version, but neither came to anything, nor did a short awakening of interest by the Ministry of Supply in March 1959 in using the P.1121 as a test-bed for the Olympus engine intended for the TSR.2.

During the summer of 1959, the company tried to

*Hawker P.1121 mock-up clearly shows the Hunter ancestry in its wing planform. The sharp dihedral on the tailplane is well emphasized, as is the intake scoop faired into the dorsal spine for aft fuselage cooling. (British Aerospace (Kingston))*

urge completion of the prototype so that knowledge obtained from flight at speeds between 2.0 Mach and 3.0 Mach would not be lost, and on an aircraft available within the year! They stated that they were willing to fund the project themselves until September of that year in the hope of forthcoming support, but could not afford to complete the project alone. No support materialised, and the P.1121 project officially ceased on 30th September 1959.

(*Note*: Some accounts have stated that in 1959 there was a virtually complete Mach 2.0 aircraft just sitting in the hangar and that Hawker's Board would not spend another million pounds on getting it airborne. Unfortunately, this was a long way from the truth. A complete systems installation mock-up had been completed but the prototype was far from completion. The centre and forward fuselage shells aft of the nosecone had been completed, minus the intake, but none of the fuselage aft of the transport joint behind the mainwheel wells had even been started. The structure of the left wing was complete, but only skinned on the upper surface, and there are rumours of one tailplane skin, possibly at Cranfield. On inspection, no wiring looms, pipes or any form of equipment had been installed at all. The aircraft was obviously a long way from being ready to fly!)

Fortunately, what there was of the first prototype was not scrapped, but eventually found its way to the Institute of Technology, Cranfield, where it was used as an instructional airframe. It was then transported to the RAF Museum reserve collection.

## CONSTRUCTION

The fuselage construction was conventional, using heavy gauge light alloy skin riveted to closely spaced frames and stringers. Steel was used only for highly-stressed parts. It was divided into three major sub-assemblies: the forward section comprising the nosecone and radio bay, cockpit and forward equipment bay. The centre-section housed the engine, intake, main undercarriage bays and forward fuselage fuel tanks. The rear section housed the jetpipe and afterburner nozzle, aft fuel tanks, fin and tailplane attachments. (The rear fuselage on the prototype was manufactured from light alloy, but it was intended to be from sheet titanium with steel fittings on production machines.)

A pitot boom was mounted at the very tip of the circular section pointed nosecone, which was attached to the forward fuselage proper by quick-release fasteners. The portion of the structure forward of the cockpit's front pressure bulkhead was occupied by the radio bay. Large access panels were also in the lower skin, giving access to the controls under the cockpit floor. The unusually large and roomy cockpit had the standard OR.946 main instrument panel layout. The side consoles appeared to be similar in layout to the Hunter, and the sub-panel in front of the control column between the pilot's legs was identical, containing the engine starter button and various electrical switches. The pilot had a Martin-Baker Mk.4 ejection seat.

The cockpit windscreen had an optically flat centre panel and two single curvature side quarter-lights. The canopy was of the clamshell type, hinging at its aft end, constructed of light alloy with large oval side windows and a smaller one in the top for limited upwards vision; visibility aft was virtually non-existent. It was jettisoned in an emergency to allow ejection. The cockpit was heated and pressurised by engine bleed-air to a maximum differential of 5.5 psi.

On each side of the lower forward fuselage was a rectangular panel, which were in fact retractable inlets for two ram-air turbines, the one on the right serving the hydraulics and that on the left electrics. The actual turbines were fitted in the equipment bay immediately behind the cockpit aft pressure bulkhead, exhausting through louvres on each side of the fuselage. (The retractable inlets had been tested earlier mounted in a Hunter gun-pack.) The cockpit faired elegantly into a spine running the whole length of the fuselage aft to the jetpipe orifice where it terminated in a fairing containing a 15' diameter ring-slot braking parachute. The spine doubled in width at approximately mid-centre section where it incorporated an intake for engine bay and jetpipe cooling and ventilation.

The centre-section was built around four massive frames to which were fitted the wing spar attachments. The upper part of the forward section accommodated five lightweight nylon bag-type fuel tanks. On either side of these were large rectangular bays with doors in the skin. On the prototype, these were to house electrical equipment and test instrumentation but, on the operational version, were the stowage for the internal armament of fifty 2" unguided rocket projectiles.

The large semi-circular, variable geometry, ventral intake had sharp lips which were swept back in planform 45°, with a sharp-edged centre splitter plate. It was of the two-dimensional ramp, compression type, actuated by two automatic control systems governed by two shock position sensors mounted in the intake. (On the prototype this was to be pilot-controlled.) The first automatic system sensed the oblique shock-wave position and actuated the variable angle centre wedge to maintain the shock-wave just ahead of the intake lips. This was necessary for high-pressure recovery and minimum spillage drag. The second system sensed the normal shock-wave position and regulated the amount of air spillage through four large rectangular doors in the lower fuselage sides just under the wing root leading edges, thus avoiding conditions known to induce intake 'buzz'. The intake wedge geometry was altered by means of two small hydraulic rams supplied by the hydraulic system and, in the event of a failure, from an accumulator.

Boundary layer from the front fuselage was bled off via a slot in the upper lip of the intake, and that

from the splitter wedge via slots on the wedge face just aft of the intake lip. Both exhausted through a long bleed vent on either side of the fuselage below the armament bays. Two rows of suction relief doors were fitted aft of the intake lips, spring-loaded closed and opening by suction during high engine demand at low speeds and high incidences. (These were obviously the subject of some development, the operational version of the aircraft showing only one row of three doors each side in

## DATA

### DIMENSIONS

| | |
|---|---|
| Span | 37'0" |
| Length | 66'6" |
| | 69'1" (overall including nose probe) |
| Height | 15'4" |
| Tailplane Span | 19'3" |
| Track | 6'11" |
| Wheelbase | 15'2" |
| Static Ground Angle | 5°30' |
| Tail Down Angle | 11°30' |

### AREAS

| | |
|---|---|
| Wing (gross) | 474 sq ft |
| Wing (net) | 380 sq ft |
| Tailplane (gross) | 115 sq ft |
| Tailplane (net) | 74 sq ft |
| Fin and Rudder (net) | 75 sq ft |
| Ailerons (each) | 18.8 sq ft |

### WEIGHTS

| | |
|---|---|
| Max All-Up Weight | 42,000 lbs (Normal) |
| | 48,000 lbs (Overload) |
| Landing Weight | 31,200 lbs |
| Combat Weight | 35,000 lbs (Representative) |

### LOADING

| | |
|---|---|
| At Max All Up Weight | 88.6 lbs/sq ft (Normal) |
| | 101 lbs/sq ft (Overload) |
| Landing | 65.8 lbs/sq ft |
| Combat | 73.8 lbs/sq ft |

### PERFORMANCE

| | |
|---|---|
| $V_{max}$ at Sea Level | 1.3 Mach (design limit) |
| $V_{max}$ at 36,000 ft | 2.35 Mach (design limit) |
| $V_{max}$ at 50,000 ft | 2.25 Mach |
| Ceiling (Thrust limit) | 58,000 ft |
| Ceiling (Zoom climb) | 70,000 ft |

Endurance 30 mins (Test flight to Mach 2.0, normal fuel)
Endurance 3 hours (Test flight to Mach 0.9, overload fuel)

Acceleration at tropopause 0.9 Mach to 2.35 Mach – 3.6 mins

### REFERENCES

| | |
|---|---|
| British Aerospace (Kingston) | —Archives |
| British Aerospace (Kingston) | —Photographic Archives |
| Hawker Aircraft Ltd | —Drawing No. E.230456 |
| | —Drawing No. E.231379 |
| | —Drawing No. G.232460 |
| Dowty Equipment Ltd | —Drawing No. 08642.P./08642.S |
| | —Drawing No. 08312Y |
| RAF Museum | —Brochure |
| | —The Aircraft |

place of the two rows of four doors.) The intake duct curved upwards over the nosewheel bay.

A reinforced frame sloped aft from just in line with the suction relief doors at the bottom up behind the side armament bays, to which was hinged the nosewheel oleo, retracting aft into its bay. Designed by Dowty, the oleo was of the levered-suspension type with a liquid spring shock absorber. The wheel was fitted with a 26" diameter tyre inflated to 170 psi., pressure, and was steerable through ±55°. A ventral airbrake was fitted just aft of the nosewheel bay, which together with the two mounted high on the aft fuselage opened through an angle of 70°. Airbrake action was fully variable by the pilot. In the event that the airbrakes were extended when the undercarriage was selected down, the ventral airbrake retracted to a maximum opening angle of 30°, or was limited to this angle if selected while the undercarriage was down, the other two surfaces opening to the full 70°. At the aft end of the centre-section were the forward halves of the main undercarriage bays, low down on each side. The oleos were pivoted on massive steel forgings attached to the main fuselage frames, and were laterally articulated using a liquid spring capsule shock absorber. The oleos retracted aft into the rear fuselage. Each half of the bays was faired by its own door, the rear one being sequenced closed after undercarriage extension. Each wheel was fitted with a 33" diameter tyre inflated to a pressure of 170 psi., and the gear was stressed to accept a rate of descent of 16 ft./sec. The engine bay occupied the whole of the remainder of the centre-section, and was divided into three zones by fireproof bulkheads, with each zone having its own ventilation and cooling air supply from the ram intake in the dorsal spine. During ground running, compressor bleed air ensured an adequate supply of air to each zone, and each zone could be fed independently with fire extinguishant from bottles housed in the mainwheel bays.

The rear fuselage had area-rule bulging in planform and could be detached at the transport joint for removal of the engine. After jacking up the fuselage level and the aft end removed, the engine could be withdrawn rearwards onto its transportation trolly sliding aft on two integral rails in the centre fuselage. The rear fuel tanks were wrapped around the jetpipe just aft of the mainwheel bays, bringing total capacity in the fuselage to 1,055 gallons. The complete fuel system was filled through a single pressure-refuelling point in the left mainwheel bay. The jetpipe ended in the afterburner section which had a variable convergent/divergent nozzle.

The wings were mid-mounted on the fuselage, and were constructed around four main spars with a very thick gauge, (0.3"), light alloy skin. Each panel was attached to the fuselage at the four main fuselage frames, and was manufactured primarily from light alloy, except for the steel forgings at the roots of the spars. The wing was set at an incidence of +1°30' to the fuselage datum with a 2° anhedral angle, and an aspect ratio of 2.89:1. It had a Hawker symmetrical section with a thickness/chord ratio at the root of 5.1% and at the tip 3.8%. Chord at the centreline was 18'0", with a leading edge sweep angle of 40°36', giving a quarter-chord sweep of 36°. Wind tunnel tests had indicated the possible need for dog-tooth leading edge extensions outboard, but this was subject to flight test verification. 210 gallons of fuel were carried in the inboard section of each wing in integral tanks between the mainspars, and there were also two hard points under each wing, at Stn. 87" and 153", able to carry weapons or 300 gallon drop tanks inboard and 150 gallon tanks outboard. (The prototype could carry the tanks, but was not wired for weapons.) Drop tank fuel sequencing was unusual in that the fuel in the inboard tanks was used first then that in the outboard ones.

Lateral control was by outboard ailerons hinged to the aft-most spar, with plain flaps mounted inboard, construction of both ailerons and flaps being of light alloy skins bonded to a honeycomb core, giving low weight and torsional stiffness. Each aileron was operated through a range of ±20° via six hydraulic jacks equally spaced along its span, half being powered by different systems and, in the event of one system failing, the other was capable of satisfying all demands. Aileron trim was achieved by varying the datum of the spring-feel units. The plain flaps were selectable in stages to a maximum of 80°, and had a cut-out section at the inboard end to clear the undercarriage doors.

The fin was based on a light alloy two-spar structure, with a Hawker symmetrical section, having a leading edge and quarter-chord sweep angle of 63°24' and 56°24' respectively. The thickness/chord ratio was 5% at the root and 3.5% at the tip. The rudder was of similar construction to the ailerons, hinged to the aft spar, and was powered by two hydraulic jacks, with a movement range of ±25°. The control units for the rudder jacks incorporated input from the autostabiliser and autopilot, trimming being by varying the datum of the 'q'-feel units.

Longitudinal control was by an all-moving, light alloy, slab tailplane mounted low on the rear fuselage to give satisfactory static stability throughout the flight envelope. It was built around a single mainspar, with its heavy gauge skin milled from the solid, the upper and lower surfaces riveted to the spar and stringers. It was of symmetrical section, with a leading edge sweep of 41°, quarter-chord sweep of 37°, aspect ratio of 3.23:1 a thickness/chord ratio varying from 5% at the root to 3.5% at the tip and a 10° dihedral angle. The two halves were connected across the fuselage by a 7" diameter steel tube passing under the jetpipe. Operation was via two tandem-cylinder hydraulic jacks with a movement range of +5° to −20°. Artificial feel was via a non-linear spring acting with continually variable control column gearing, with an override to ensure the correct gear being selected with undercarriage down. Trim was by varying the datum of the feel unit.

## HYDRAULIC SYSTEM
There were three independent engine-driven systems, each with its own accumulator and cooler, operating at 4,000 psi. Two systems supplied the flying control exclusively, with the third serving the undercarriage, flaps, airbrakes, wheel brakes, nose-wheel steering, rocket-launcher doors, intake wedge and afterburner nozzle.

## ELECTRICAL SYSTEM
The prototype only had a d.c. electrical system, the supply being from two engine-driven 6KW generators and emergency supply from the ram-air turbine mounted in the forward fuselage. Later aircraft were to have a 200 volt, 400 cycles/sec., three-phase a.c. supply driven by two alternators, with the d.c. system being fed from a 24 volt battery, charged via a transformer by the a.c. system. A three-axis autostabiliser was fitted for improved weapon aiming, with the autopilot actuating the flying control via the autostabiliser. (The latter was not to be fitted on the prototype.) UHF radio, with I.F.F. and ILS were to be fitted.

## WEAPONS
No functional weapons were to be fitted to the prototype, although dummies could be carried for aerodynamic research. However, both the proposed interceptor and strike versions were to carry an internal armament consisting of fifty 2″ unguided rocket projectiles housed in bays either side of the forward fuselage. The bay doors were hinged at their rear edges and opened momentarily during launch. Alternatively, a 30 mm. Aden cannon could be housed in each bay. The interceptor could carry either a Firestreak or Red Top missile on its inboard pylons, with an A.I.23 radar in the fuselage nosecone, while on the strike version a tactical-strike weapon could be carried on a modified left inboard pylon, with two cameras mounted in the fuselage nosecone. However, it was recognised that this pylon could be better occupied by another drop tank to improve range, so the production variant had the tactical weapon mounted in a slight recess under the centre fuselage. (*Note*: The tactical weapon shown in the accompanying drawings is not representative of the actual shape.)

## POWER PLANT
*Prototype.* One de Havilland Gyron P.S.26–6 axial flow turbojet developing a Sea Level Static Thrust of 17,400 lbs., dry and 23,800 lbs., with an 1,800°K afterburner.

*Production Variants*

*Either. a)* One de Havilland Gyron P.S.26–3 axial turbojet developing a Sea Level Static Thrust of 20,000 lbs, dry and 27,000 lbs, with a 2,000°-K afterburner.

*b)* One Rolls-Royce Conway R.Co.11R axial flow turbojet developing a Sea Level Static Thrust of 15,800 lbs, dry and 25,700 lbs, with a 2,000°K afterburner.

*c)* One Bristol Siddeley Olympus B.01.21R axial flow turbojet developing a Sea Level Static Thrust of 17,270 lbs, dry and 29,000 lbs, with a 2,000°K afterburner.

*Hawker P.1121 first prototype fuselage under construction. Apart from one wing, this is about as much of the structure as was actually completed, and surprisingly still survives. The systems installation mock-up can be seen immediately behind the prototype's fuselage. (British Aerospace (Kingston))*

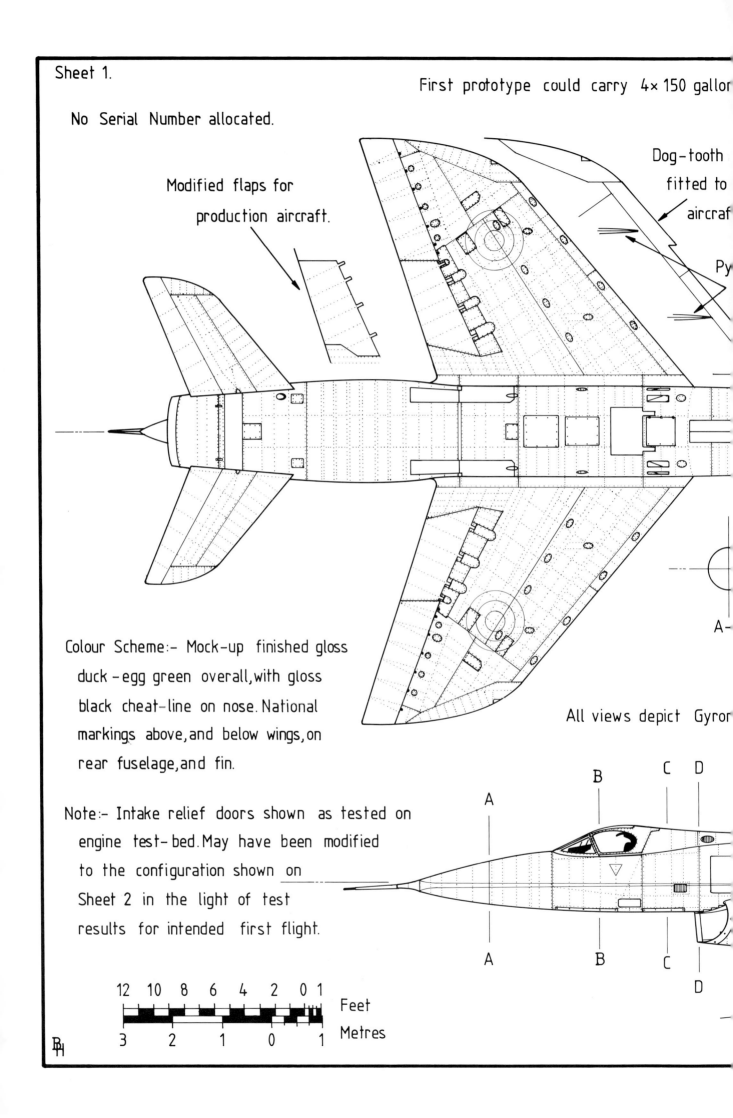

Sheet 1.

No Serial Number allocated.

First prototype could carry 4× 150 gallor

Modified flaps for
production aircraft.

Dog-tooth
fitted to
aircraf

Py

A-

Colour Scheme:- Mock-up finished gloss
duck-egg green overall, with gloss
black cheat-line on nose. National
markings above, and below wings, on
rear fuselage, and fin.

All views depict Gyror

Note:- Intake relief doors shown as tested on
engine test-bed. May have been modified
to the configuration shown on
Sheet 2 in the light of test
results for intended first flight.

B      C  D

A

A      B      C

D

```
 12  10  8   6   4   2   0 1
  |  |  |  |  |  |  |  |  |  |  |  |  |     Feet

  3       2       1       0       1     Metres
```

PH

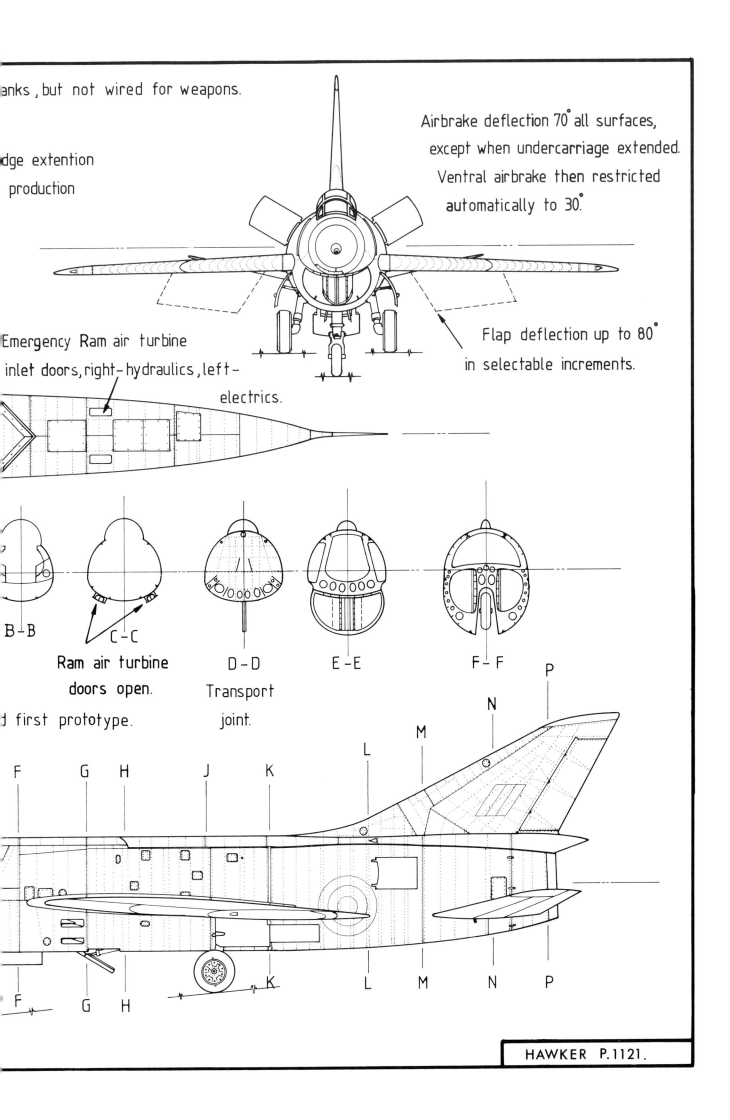

anks, but not wired for weapons.

dge extention

production

Airbrake deflection 70° all surfaces,
except when undercarriage extended.
Ventral airbrake then restricted
automatically to 30°.

Emergency Ram air turbine
inlet doors, right-hydraulics, left-
electrics.

Flap deflection up to 80°
in selectable increments.

B-B

C-C

Ram air turbine
doors open.

d first prototype.

D-D

Transport
joint.

E-E

F-F

F  G  H      J  K        L      M    N    P

F    G   H          K        L      M      N      P

HAWKER P.1121.

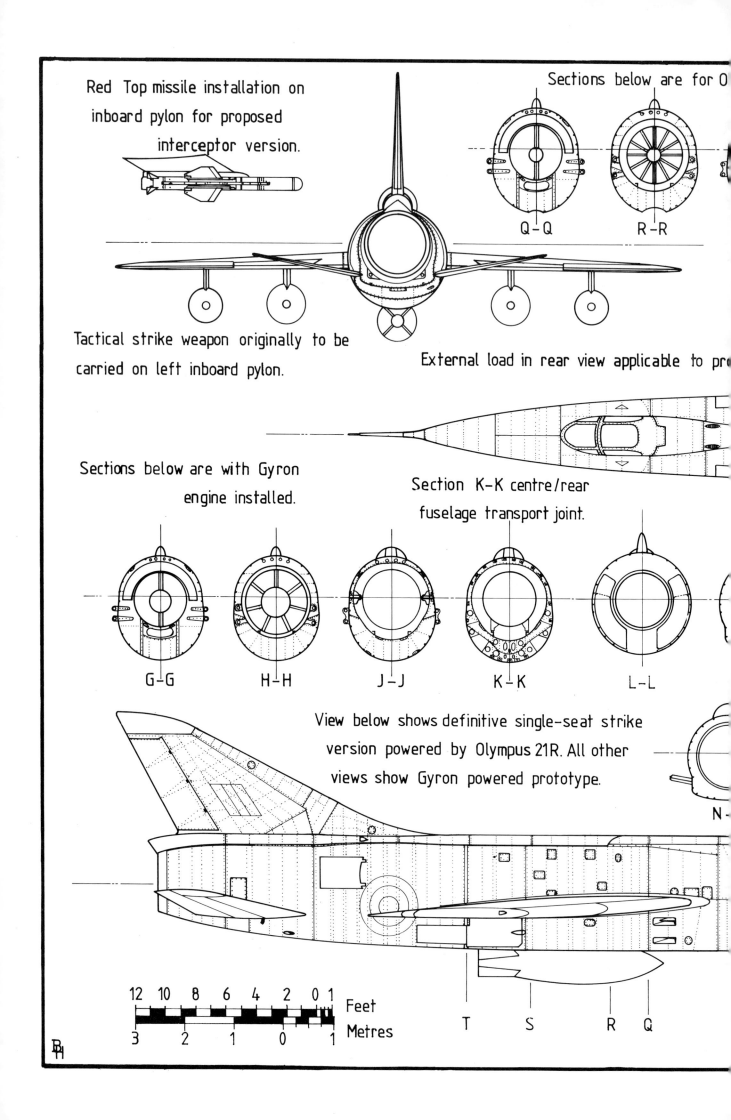

Red Top missile installation on
inboard pylon for proposed
interceptor version.

Sections below are for O

Q–Q          R–R

Tactical strike weapon originally to be
carried on left inboard pylon.

External load in rear view applicable to pr

Sections below are with Gyron
engine installed.

Section K–K centre/rear
fuselage transport joint.

G–G          H–H          J–J          K–K          L–L

View below shows definitive single-seat strike
version powered by Olympus 21R. All other
views show Gyron powered prototype.

N –

12  10  8  6  4  2  0 1   Feet
3      2      1      0      1   Metres

T          S          R    Q

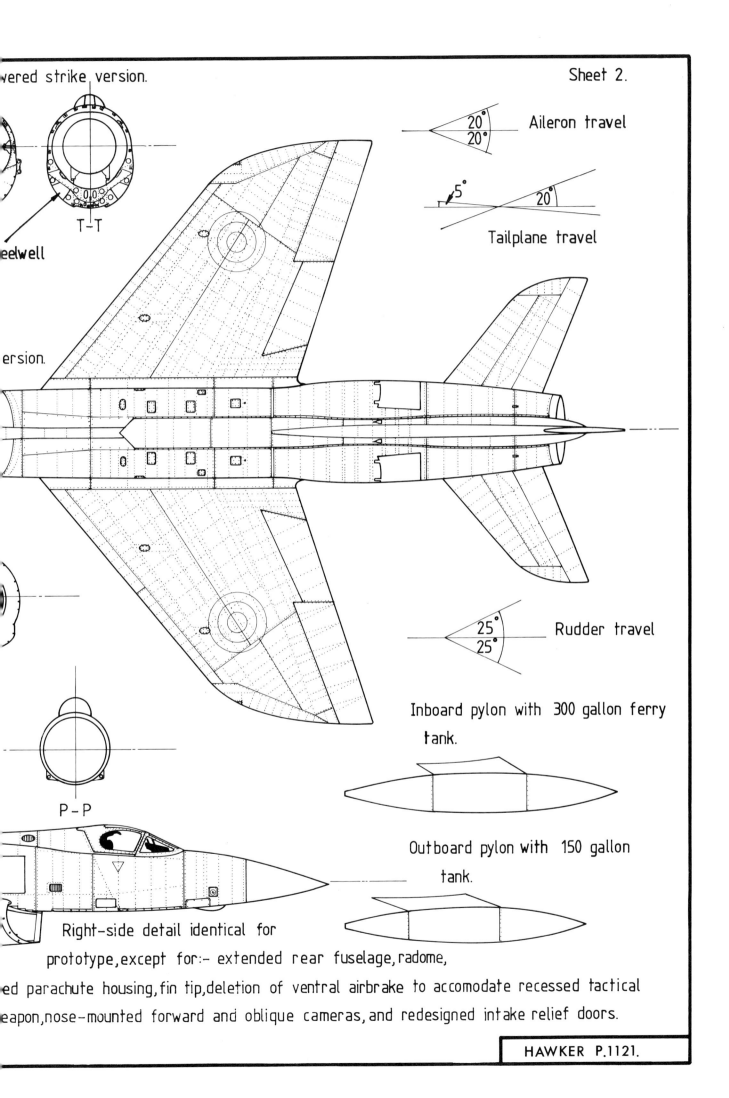

vered strike version.

Sheet 2.

T-T

eelwell

ersion.

Aileron travel
20°
20°

Tailplane travel
5°
20°

Rudder travel
25°
25°

Inboard pylon with 300 gallon ferry
tank.

Outboard pylon with 150 gallon
tank.

P – P

Right-side detail identical for

prototype, except for:- extended rear fuselage, radome,

ed parachute housing, fin tip, deletion of ventral airbrake to accomodate recessed tactical

eapon, nose-mounted forward and oblique cameras, and redesigned intake relief doors.

HAWKER P.1121.

Handley Page HP.115, XP841 three-quarters view showing the fabric-covered elevon control surfaces and jet orifice. This angle emphasizes the fine blend of the wing and forward fuselage. (Handley Page Ltd.)

# HANDLEY PAGE 115

| Manufacturer | Handley Page Ltd |
|---|---|
| Specification | ER.197.D. |
| Role | Research Prototype |
| First Flight Date | XP 841 – 17th August 1961 |

When the Concorde design was being finalised, there were several unknowns regarding the aerodynamics of the slender delta wing planform chosen, and therefore it was decided to build two different experimental prototypes to investigate various areas, especially those at low speed and high incidences. A scale 'ogee' wing was to be fitted to a modified Fairey Delta 2, primarily for the higher-speed end of the envelope, but this conversion was both lengthy and costly, so a cheap, quickly-produced research glider was authorised to investigate slender delta aerodynamics in general as well as those problems directly relevant to Concorde. Originally, it was planned to build a second, powered, version, but the requirement was quickly altered resulting in the HP.115 from the beginning being constructed as a powered aircraft. The aircraft was to be used not only to confirm the

wind tunnel data, but also to establish the stability derivatives of a slender delta planform.

From the initial calculations, wind tunnel tests, and simulation, serious misgivings were felt with regard to the flight characteristics of the design, especially in the lateral stability qualities and, under certain conditions of flight, particularly turbulence and cross-wind landings, indications were that it would be, at best, a very unpleasant aircraft to fly.

Therefore, it was with some trepidation that the flight trials were approached. In the event, the fears were groundless and, within certain limitations the aircraft could be flown exactly the same as any other aircraft of more conventional design.

## DEVELOPMENT HISTORY

Late in 1958, it was decided that a small, cheaply-produced glider should be built to investigate the low-speed handling characteristics of the slender delta planform. Several companies were approached and the proposal from Handley Page was felt to be of the right size. A powered aircraft was preferred but, despite the complexities of a towed launch and the output of the glider being less due to its shorter flying time, it was felt that this was still a better compromise, as it would be built sooner and show any possible problems earlier.

Preliminary discussions had been made with Handley Page, due to their experience in research into highly-swept wing planforms, and they had produced a provisional design brochure, already with their designation HP.115 on 8th January. The proposal was for a small, 20 foot span aircraft, constructed either from wood or metal, with provision for various planforms to be explored. Provision was made for the fitment of either a Scorpion or Super Sprite rocket motor under the centre-section, with the possibility of a jet-powered version later. The pilot sat in a large blister fairing in the nose and had an ejection seat for emergency egress. The fin was a clipped delta shape and the fixed undercarriage was from a Percival Prentice (maingear) and a Miles Aerovan (nosegear).

The requirements were discussed on 23rd January 1959 and tenders requested from various companies for both a glider, and a powered version of the research prototype. A Specification X.197.T was raised on 4th March 1959, and proposals from Bristol, Fairey, Handley Page and Miles were received for a quarter-scale model of the proposed Supersonic Transport.

That from Handley Page was considered to meet most closely the requirement and they were therefore awarded the contract. It was decided, however, that the jet-powered version should be developed instead of the previously proposed glider version. Development would take longer, but the machine would in the end be a more useful and productive research tool. A new specification ER.197.D. was raised to cover this change.

The aircraft was constructed at the Handley Page works at Radlett and, on completion, was transported by road to RAE Bedford where, after protracted taxi-ing trials which were more to do with the added caution and the desire to learn as much about the radical new design, than anything to do with the aircraft itself, the first flight was achieved on 17th August 1961. It immediately became apparent that the previously-held beliefs regarding the poor flying characteristics were groundless. It proved to be a pilot's aircraft and was liked by everyone who flew it.

Longitudinal handling was very good, with control responses precise, even in turbulence. The minimum speed achieved in the air was 60 kts.IAS corresponding to a Coefficient of Lift (CL)=0.8, at which speed the incidence was some 30°. At this slow speed, the aircraft remained perfectly controllable, as there had not been achieved any limiting factor to the minimum speed. No higher incidences were tested, as their use would have been purely academic in the research programme relevant to the Concorde.

The aircraft was very 'stiff' directionally, and the roll due to rudder very large. As speed decreased lateral control deteriorated, especially in any turbulence or yaw, and dutch roll damping decreased, eventually becoming neutral. Even further reduction in speed produced the characteristic divergent dutch roll, with oscillations as large as ±30°. Recovery from this condition could be made immediately, and at will, by instinctive, large, lateral control movements, or by reducing the angle of incidence.

The better than anticipated handling characteristics were due in no small way to the excellent control quality, and the aircraft's response to their movement. At an early stage, careful attention was paid to their design and, in anticipation of problems, three hinge positions, three tab gearings and three spring rates were provided for. In the event, the first chosen proved ideal and no changes were needed. It has been expressed that in some ways this had been a pity, as much valuable data could have been obtained by varying the combination to achieve satisfactory handling characteristics.

Landing speeds were in the region of 120 kts., (CL = 0.2), the minimum touchdown speed being in the region of 90 kts, (CL=0.35), limited by the aircraft's geometry allowing a maximum ground angle of 14°.

Trials progressed satisfactorily until 20th November 1964 when the aircraft suffered a crash landing. After a 'roller' landing, while climbing out, a marked jolt was felt through the airframe, and it was confirmed by visual inspection from both the control tower, and another aircraft, that the left wheel together with the whole leg fairing was cocked 70°–80° to left. The wheel was also hanging about 3" lower than the right, and the entire left undercarriage assembly appeared to be loose. After burning off fuel to reduce weight and the risk of fire, a landing was made keeping the left wing up as long as possible. The aircraft touched down smoothly, but as speed reduced the pilot was unable to stop the left wing touching the ground, causing the aircraft to skid off the runway, turning through nearly 200° before coming to rest.

After repair the trials programme resumed, until grounded for three months in early 1966 for the fitment of microphones to investigate vortex noise, and strain gauges. It flew again on 18th May 1966. It was then grounded again in September of the same year for the installation of a wingtip mounted parachute and pressure plotting transducers, flying again on 22nd February 1967.

The HP.115 completed its research programme in the summer of 1972 and was stored at RAE Bedford until it made its final flight on 31st January 1974, on a delivery flight to RAF Colerne for preservation in the collection at that RAF station. Thus ended a long and very productive test career. Apart from a few display, familiarisation and assessment flights, most of the flights were devoted to research. In addition to the tasks already described were study of wing vortex noise and pressure fluctuation, vortex evolution and breakdown, and effects of refraction

*Handley Page HP.115 front view showing details of the highly swept wing top surface and engine installation. The detachable wooden leading edges are well delineated. (Handley Page Ltd.)*

by the primary vortex. The total number of flights made was 933, with total hours being 475, thus using less than half of the designed 1,000 hours fatigue life.

In addition to coming to the end of its useful research life and its relevance to current developments, one of the prime reasons for the cessation of flying was that maintenance of the engines was becoming an increasing problem. Not only were they operating for most of their life at, or near, full power, which caused higher than normal wear, also the smoke used for visualising the vortex caused contamination of the compressor. This had to be washed after each flight when smoke had been used, but was not 100% successful, and a slow deterioration in compressor performance ensued. Also, the original pilot's gauge for monitoring the jetpipe temperature did not have a sufficiently open scale at 'the top end' for close monitoring of the jpt., so that under conditions where this and not rpm was the limiting factor, the engine limits could be easily exceeded. This resulted in engine No. 2002 having its overhaul life reduced from 100 to 60 hours. A new jpt. gauge was fitted allowing monitoring tolerances of only 1° to 2°. Engine No. 1949 replaced the original one in the Autumn of 1965, but had to be rejected after only 32 hours running time.

It was not considered economic to re-engine the aircraft with another version of the Viper, or even a completely new type, and therefore the HP.115 was grounded. Apart from the undercarriage accident, the aircraft had an excellent serviceability record, and its productivity was considered exceptional for a research aircraft.

After a relatively short stay at Colerne, it was transported by road to the RAF Museum at Cosford on 8th October 1975. From there, its final move, again by road, was to RNAS Yeovilton, where it is currently preserved as part of the Concorde exhibition.

## CONSTRUCTION

The airframe was originally planned to be constructed from wood, for speed and cost reasons. This was rejected at an early stage for several reasons, including the lack of workmen skilled in this material, and also that wood would have produced a significantly heavier airframe. As well as the normal '1.5 safety factor', an additional heavy stressing factor was added due to the lack of knowledge with this type of structure and its aerodynamic characteristics. There was also to be no structural test specimen, and therefore the design was 'over-built' for safety. Despite this also affecting the structure when constructed from metal, the resulting airframe was significantly lighter.

Construction was virtually entirely from light alloy, from the lightest and most easily worked materials available, with the exception of the detachable, sharp wing leading edge which was constructed from fabric-covered wood, and the control surfaces.

The shape was dictated by the need to have a good production of the characteristic slender delta vortex flow. This needed a clean wing with as few protuberances as possible, especially along the upper surfaces. Thus the pilot's 'nacelle' was as small as practicable, and underslung to retain a smooth dorsal line. Originally the engine was also to be similarly placed, but structural complication and fear of ingestion problems militated against this. Two strong keel members ran aft of the nose nacelle to join it to the aft fuselage at the jet orifice to transmit longitudinal load and provide anchor points for the engine nacelle and fin structure. They were covered by a plain 'box-section' light alloy fairing, on which were mounted two radio aerials. Various access panels were provided in this fairing, and at the aft end was a substantial tail bumper. Maximum ground angle was limited to 14° with the resulting geometry with the mainwheels.

All instrumentation, batteries, and equipment were carried within the nose nacelle. About the only gesture towards sophistication was the provision of a Martin-Baker Mk.4.VHP lightweight ejection seat for the pilot, allowing escape at very low speeds and at zero height.

Systems were kept to a minimum and were very simple. Electrical supply for the instruments and recording equipment was from two ground charged 24 volt accumulators and, with the exception of the turn and slip indicator, the gyro flight instruments were suction-driven from two venturis below the nose. A long instrumentation boom, with pitot head and pitch and yaw vanes was mounted on a framework beneath the nose. The nosecone was detachable for the installation of ballast weights. Differential wheelbraking was provided by pilot-operated close circuit hydraulic motors.

Pneumatically-operated airbrakes were fitted, one ventilated panel under each wing undersurface just in front of the main undercarriage. These were fully variable in operation, with a maximum opening angle of 76°, and were operated from a ground-charged system at 3,300 psi. With the very low performance, and high drag characteristics of the design, they were superfluous to their usual purpose, ie., slowing the aircraft down, but could be used for varying the drag for investigation of flight characteristics at various Lift/Drag ratios.

The wing was constructed around multiple spars parallel to the centreline, a forward mainspar and several lateral frames. It had a symmetrical, biconvex, circular arc section of 6% thickness/chord ratio, with a sharp leading edge for clean vortex generation. Chord at the centreline was 40'0", and gross area 432.5 sq ft. Sweep angles were 74°42' on the leading edge, 0° at the trailing edge, and dihedral 0°. The resultant Aspect Ratio was 0.92. A small compartment was provided in the leading edge, immediately forward of each control surface, for lateral ballast weights.

The leading edge forward of the mainspar was of fabric-covered wooden construction and was readily detachable to allow the substitution of various shaped leading edges. Four wing planforms were provided for in the original design, these being:

a)   A Delta with pointed wingtips.
b)   A Cropped Delta with streamwise tips.
c)   An Ogee shape with fixed triangular l/e extensions.
d)   An Ogee shape with cambered l/e.

In the event, the original wing planform, the second configuration above, was retained throughout the aircraft's life, no other configuration being tested.

The wing-mounted flying controls were manually operated, being fabric-covered elevons, hinged to the rear of the wing with a movement range of +29° to –34°. Spring tabs were fitted, movement range being ±12°, and geared/trim tabs with a trimming range +9° to –3°. Originally, separate outboard ailerons and inboard elevators were proposed, but worry about the blanking of the inner surfaces by the wing-vortex necessitated the change to the single surface on each wing.

Fuel was carried in the centre fuselage and inner wing panels, in three tanks with a total capacity of 140 gallons. Gravity refuelling was via a panel in the top of the fuselage just forward of the jet intake.

The undercarriage was fixed, and comprised mainwheel oleos taken from the Piston Provost, fitted with 16" diameter wheels, modified to accept a vertical velocity of 12ft/sec at touchdown. Similarly, the fully castoring nosewheel oleo was that of the Jet Provost, fitted with a 14" wheel.

To show the surface pattern generated over the wing upper surfaces, kaolin and red ink was injected into the airflow via six holes in the wing surfaces. Later, to enable the wing vortex to be seen and photographed and to determine the point of vortex-burst, coloured-smoke generators were bolted beneath the inner wing leading edges, first to the left side, then both. These had a curved pipe leading up around the leading edges, to the top surfaces. An alloy shield was fitted to each wing to protect the wooden leading edges.

The engine was mounted in a nacelle atop the rear wing centre-section at an angle of 6°30' to aircraft datum, but extreme aft end of the jetpipe, just forward of the actual orifice was angled upwards at 3° to the datum to align the resultant thrust through the centre of gravity. Multiple access panels allowed servicing and removal. Severe engine problems were encountered due to the majority of each sortie needing to be at constant take-off rating, causing excessive wear to the

## DATA

### DIMENSIONS

| | |
|---|---|
| Span | 20'0" |
| Length | 46'6" (excluding noseprobe) |
| Length | 50'4" (including noseprobe) |
| Length | 42'0" (fuselage only) |
| Height | 12'9" (static) |
| Height | 7'11" (fin tip above aircraft datum) |
| Wheelbase | 18'7" |
| Track | 10'6" |

### AREAS

| | |
|---|---|
| Wing (gross) | 432.5 sq ft |
| Elevons | 34.1 sq ft (each surface) |
| Fin and Rudder (gross) | 31.3 sq ft |
| Rudder (aft of hinge) | 8.0 sq ft |
| Dive Brakes | 15.0 sq ft |

### WEIGHTS

| | |
|---|---|
| Maximum permissible | 5,600 lbs |
| Normal loaded | 5,050 lbs |
| Fuel | 1,170 lbs |

### REFERENCES

| | |
|---|---|
| Handley Page Association | —Archives |
| Handley Page Association | —Photographic Archives |
| RAE Farnborough | —Library |
| RNAS Yeovilton | —The Aircraft |

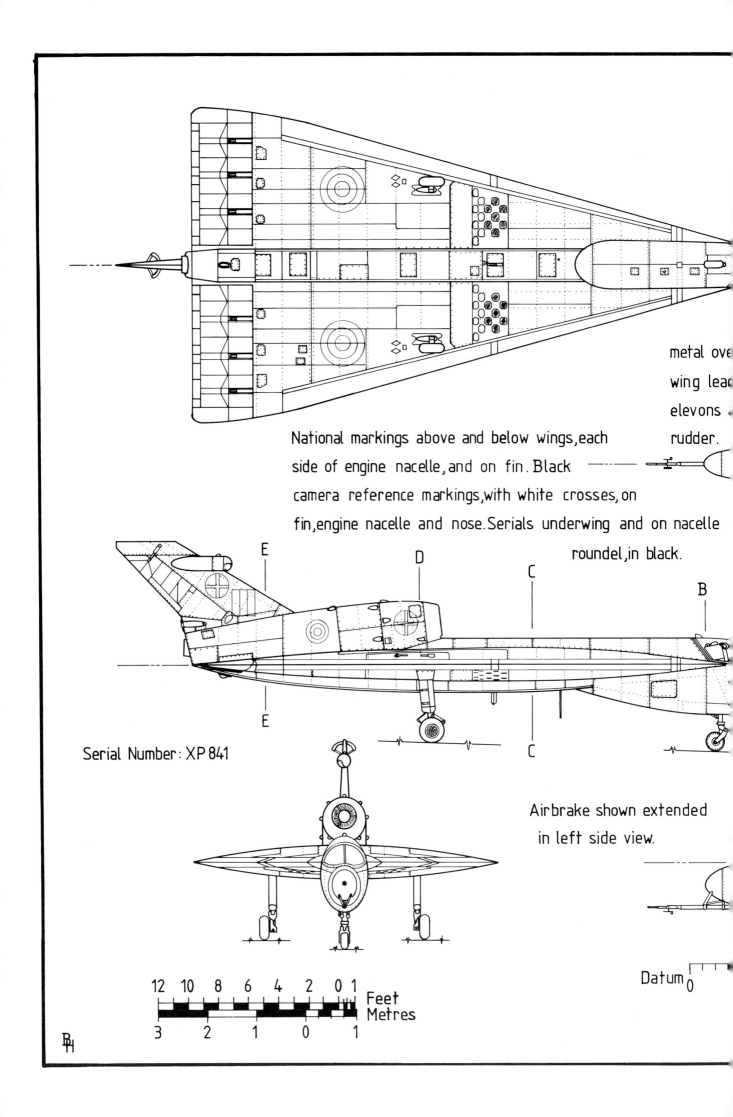

metal ove[r]
wing lea[d]
elevons [and]
rudder.

National markings above and below wings, each
side of engine nacelle, and on fin. Black
camera reference markings, with white crosses, on
fin, engine nacelle and nose. Serials underwing and on nacelle
roundel, in black.

E

D

C

B

E

C

Serial Number: XP 841

Airbrake shown extended
in left side view.

Datum₀

12  10  8   6   4   2   0 1
Feet
Metres
3    2    1    0    1

Datum 0

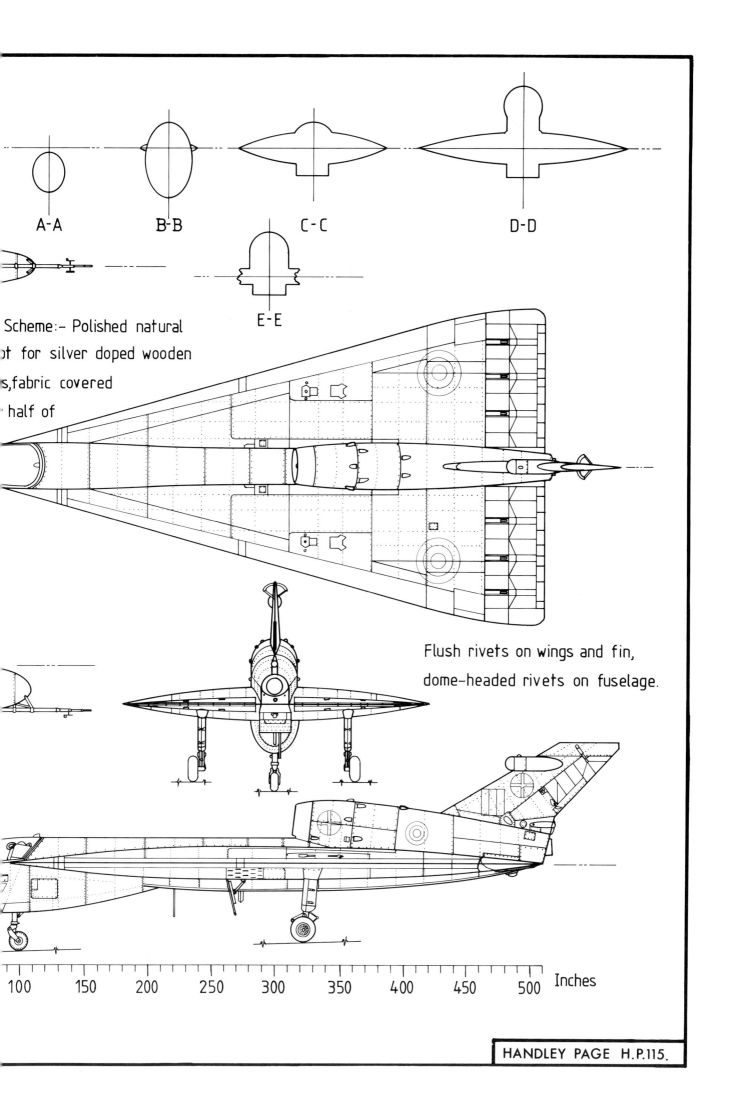

A-A  B-B  C-C  D-D

E-E

Scheme:– Polished natural
ot for silver doped wooden
s, fabric covered
half of

Flush rivets on wings and fin,
dome-headed rivets on fuselage.

100  150  200  250  300  350  400  450  500  Inches

HANDLEY PAGE H.P.115.

engine. There were also flame-out problems due to the disturbed airflow into the intake at low speeds and very high incidences.

The fin was constructed around a centreline spar, attached to a strengthened frame at Fuselage Stn. 460, with a forward drag member. A substantial 'bullet' fairing was fitted near to the tip leading edge, which contained a cine camera for recording the vortices. Root chord was 7'3.5", and tip chord 3'10.8". Leading edge sweep was 60°, giving a gross area external to the fuselage, (including the rudder), of 31.3 sq ft. The inset rudder was hinged to the rear of the spar, with a movement range (parallel to plane of wing) of ±25°, and of ±36°30' (perpendicular to hinge line). A trim tab was provided, as was a large external horn mass-balance at the rudder's tip. As with the elevons, the rudder was manually operated. Thus, all the engine had to do was push the aircraft through the sky, which was fortuitous bearing in mind the limited thrust available! A streamlined fairing containing an anti-spin/braking parachute was mounted between the base of the rudder and the engine exhaust cone.

## SPECIFICATION
The basic performance requirements laid down in the specification were:

a) Maximum dive 250 kts EAS.
b) Loading 5g.
c) Distance to 50 ft, not to exceed 4,000 ft, at a speed not less than 120 kts at maximum all-up weight for take-off.
d) The same distance not to be exceeded from 50 ft, at 120 kts during landing.
e) Endurance after climb to 10,000 ft, to not be less than 30 minutes, plus allowance for descent, baulked landing, a circuit and final landing.
f) To be capable of a 2g pullout at 175 kts, and to perform a 2g turn at the same speed.
g) Spinning and aerobatics were not intended but the aircraft must be capable of recovery from such manoeuvres.

## POWER PLANT
When the aircraft was built the Armstrong Siddeley Viper Mk.11 was not available, so a modified Viper A.S.V.8, Mk 102 axial flow turbojet was fitted to Specification D.Eng.R.D.2399 and designated Viper A.S.V.9. Only two of these engines were built, Nos.1949 and 2002, developing a Static Thrust at Sea Level of 1,850 lbs.

*A dramatic view of the nose and underside showing the very wide undercarriage track compared to the overall wingspan. (Handley Page Ltd.)*

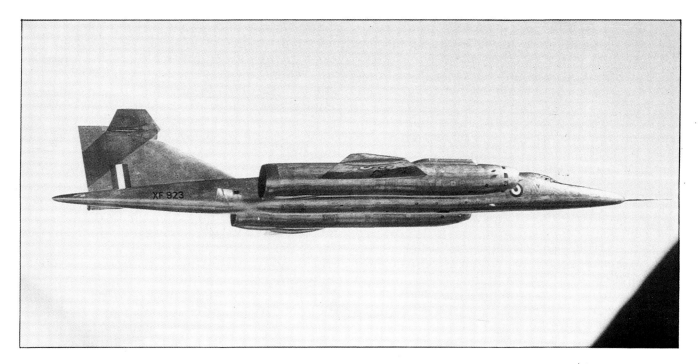

*Bristol 188 in-flight view reveals the extremely long, slim fuselage and engine nacelles and the dominant large fin for directional stability at high Mach numbers. (Royal Aeronautical Society)*

# BRISTOL TYPE 188

| Manufacturer | Bristol Aeroplane Company Ltd |
|---|---|
| Specification | ER.134D |
| Role | Research Prototype |
| First Flight Date | XF 923 – 14th April 1962 |
| | XF 926 – 29th April 1963 |

When the contract for the Type 188 was signed in October 1958, it was thought that it would be the fastest aircraft in the world except for the North American X–15, but unlike the latter it would be able to be operated like a normal aircraft. However for several reasons the machine was a failure and, with a short and unspectacular research life, it never reached anywhere near its specification's requirements. Its only real distinction was that it was the last aircraft to carry the Bristol name; from then on, their aircraft carried the BAC title.

## DEVELOPMENT HISTORY

In response to current Operational Requirements, aircraft were being called for which were capable of operating for long periods at very high altitudes and speeds. Realizing how little knowledge there was at that time of the effects on an airframe of long soaking at the temperatures achieved at these high speeds, and in the use of the materials demanded for withstanding them, it was felt prudent to construct a research aircraft to investigate the problems. Specification ER.134D was raised for an aircraft capable of sustaining a speed of 2.75 Mach for a long enough period to record the kinetic

heating effects at the stagnation point of 250°C. These temperatures required a material such as steel to be used, and therefore the specification also called for the design to be manufactured from this material.

The Specification was finalized in 1954 and, having received tenders from several companies, Bristol Aeroplane Company (as it was then) was awarded a contract to built two prototypes with an additional static test airframe. (The original specification covered six prototypes, three to be used for armament research, but this requirement was cancelled, as were the three additional prototypes, before Bristol was awarded the contract). As it was to be used for propulsion research, as well as structural and dynamic research, the design had to be capable of easily accommodating other engines.

The first problem to be tackled was that of finding a suitable material and, after close liaison with Firth Vickers, a metal was finally chosen based on a grade known as F.V.520 which was capable of withstanding a maximum surface temperature of 500°C. Many new techniques had to be mastered, as stainless steel was a notoriously difficult material with which to work. One big breakthrough was the development by Bristol of a technique known as 'puddle-welding'. This was controlled fusion of the material from an arc whose electrode was surrounded by the inert gas argon. Other problems were the manufacture of large enough sheets with the required standard of flatness and thickness tolerances. All of these difficulties contributed to the lengthy con-

229

struction time of the airframes. The manufacture of several major components – tailplane, fin, rudder, outer wings including ailerons and cockpit canopy – was sub-contracted to Armstrong Whitworth, who conducted their own research into this field.

The choice of power plant also caused design changes. The original idea was to fit Rolls-Royce Avon R.A.24R engines, which were destined for the Avro 730 supersonic bomber (designed to meet OR.330) and which had a similar wing and engine configuration. However, this bomber was cancelled in 1957, as was its engine. At about the same time, the Saunders-Roe SR.177, which was to be powered by the de Havilland PS.50 engine with afterburner, was also cancelled. About a dozen of these engines were under construction and the Ministry insisted that this engine be used on the Type 188. (This did not bode well for the programme, as it meant that a new engine was to be tested on a new airframe, which is not ideal.)

While construction of the three airframes was under way, wind tunnel tests of models were also carried out, as were tests on free-flight model rockets launched from RAE Aberporth. The first airframe for static testing was finally delivered to Farnborough in May 1960. The first prototype, XF 923, was completed and rolled out for ground tests on 26th April 1961, but engine runs revealed problems with both the variable intake and afterburner system. These took the whole of the rest of the year to resolve, so the aircraft could not start taxi-ing trials until February 1962! It was finally ready for its first flight which was made on 14th April 1962, taking off from Filton and landing at Boscombe Down. The short flight was not uneventful, as shortly after take-off a hydraulic pipe sheared, and there were also some radio problems. After repairs, the aircraft embarked on the investigation of its low speed handling.

The flight envelope was gradually expanded and Mach 1 was passed without any undue aircraft handling problems, and it was returned to Filton on 15th November having been flown only 19 times in the six-month programme. However, the engine characteristics left much to be desired and were continuing to hamper the programme badly.

The second prototype, XF 926, made its maiden flight on 29th April 1963, and joined the test programme. By now, it was becoming obvious that the engine surge problems were not going to be resolved. The surging reached a peak at supersonic speeds causing the aircraft to become almost uncontrollable in both pitch and yaw. Also, the fuel consumption was so much greater than predicted, that the aircraft's fuel supply was insufficient to achieve any worthwhile long flights at high Mach number. The highest speed achieved was only 1.9 Mach, and this was able to be sustained for only two minutes before fuel constraints required a deceleration and recovery to base.

Without a major redesign of the engine inlets,

and change to another engine, the aircraft would never reach its design objective. This was considered too expensive and, by this time, the need for research information into high Mach flight at high altitude was not so urgent. (It was originally required for basic research for the development of a Mach 2.5 bomber flying at 60,000 feet. By 1964, bombers were expected to fly some 59,900 feet lower!)

The research programme was therefore terminated in 1964, with some 40 hours having been completed in 78 flights. The aircraft had proved a very expensive failure although in one area the aircraft proved valuable, however indirectly. It was one of the first aircraft to be fitted with telemetry in Britain, so that the flight test results could be studied in real-time as they were happening, rather than having to be studied and reduced after flight. This speeded up a programme no end, as each test result could be analysed immediately and, if satisfactory, the pilot could be instructed as to whether it was safe to move on to the next test point.

Both aircraft were sent to Shoeburyness to act as gunnery targets to investigate damage to 'modern' airframes. They were struck off charge on 7th November 1966. Luckily the second prototype was rescued and, after refurbishment, was put on display at the RAF Museum, Cosford, where it remains to this day.

# CONSTRUCTION

The fuselage was of minimal cross sectional area, which was determined by the size of the pilot's ejection seat! Maximum depth was only 4'11.5", and maximum width 3'9" and, being over 70' long, it was virtually like a flying pencil. The structure was entirely manufactured from welded steel sheet attached to closely spaced frames. The long pointed nose had an instrument and pitot probe fixed at its end mounting yaw and pitch vanes and temperature sensors. The equipment bay in front of the cockpit windscreen, accessible through a large hatch in the top of the nosecone, was within the pressurised cockpit zone and contained a TACAN transmitter, the standby radio, various recorders and ballast weights. Air conditioning problems were to plague the programme throughout, with cooling proving a major headache, especially for the pilot! He wore an air-ventilated suit to keep cool, as well as an anti-'g' suit, had a Martin-Baker Mk.4R seat, and sat under a sliding canopy which was primarily of metal with four heavily framed, small flat transparencies giving limited lateral and downward vision, but none rearwards. The knife-edged windscreen was raked at 65° and comprised two reasonably large main panels and two smaller side panels. In fact, the cockpit hardly broke the fuselage line.

Behind the cockpit was a large equipment bay divided roughly in half by a sloping floor mounted

*Bristol 188 after landing showing the braking parachute (fitted in an auxiliary housing attached to the rear fuselage). No explanation can be found as to why this was fitted rather than using the internally mounted chute in the rear of the tailcone. (Royal Aeronautical Society)*

perpendicular to the cockpit aft pressure bulkhead. Within the upper part of the bay was further test instrumentation, including telemetry main and emergency batteries, main radio and emergency hydraulic pump, the emergency air bottle for the lowering of the undercarriage, and the pilot's oxygen bottle, the latter two being replenished through the nosewheel bay which occupied the lower half of the bay. A turbo-generator was mounted at the aft end and exhausted through a large rectangular vent in the bottom of the fuselage. The nosewheel oleo was fully castoring and had twin wheels attached on a live axle. It retracted forwards into its bay, and each wheel was fitted with an 18″ diameter high pressure tyre. Consideration was given to refrigerating the bay, but it was found sufficient to have it vented by careful air leaks.

A further equipment bay was contained in the centre of the fuselage at approximately mid wing-chord, and incorporated the main undercarriage bay in its aft end and, at this point, the top line of the fuselage was gently waisted to comply with area-ruling. This bay contained further instrumentation, rate gyros, the master reference gyro, hydraulic accumulators, anti-skid control unit and various electrical panels. All of the equipment was mounted forwards of the wing rear spar attachment frame, which formed the forward end of the undercarriage bay. (This spar was also the fuselage datum zero.) The main undercarriage oleos were hinged just within the engine nacelle profile, and retracted inwards. The wheels were hinged at the bottom of the oleo so that, during retraction, they rotated until they were at 90° to the leg, and therefore when fully retracted they lay vertically within the fuselage. Even so, the fairing doors had a slight bulge in them to accommodate the wheels, which were fitted with Maxaret anti-skid brakes and had 34″ diameter tyres inflated to 220 psi., pressure.

Forward and aft of this central bay were the large fuel tanks. They acted as heat-sinks for cooling various items of equipment. The forward tank, divided by bulkheads into three bays to prevent surging, had a capacity of 630 gallons (4,420 lbs) and

the aft tank, divided by a bulkhead into two bays, contained 370 gallons (2,580 lbs). They were both pressure refuelled through a panel in the rear fuselage.

Four panel airbrakes were mounted approximately in line with the fin root leading edge. These were of a novel design: the forward pair were hinged at their top edges and the aft pair at their bottom edges, so that they folded outwards from the fuselage, each presenting a perforated panel to the airflow. Their design was determined by the need to reduce the hinge moment required during the very rapid actuation specified at high Mach numbers. They were actuated by twin hydraulic jacks and were linked by tie rods.

Aft of the airbrakes was yet another instrumentation bay, housing, among other items, the aircraft autostabiliser, and it was accessible through a hatch in the bottom of the fuselage. In this area of the fuselage, the frames were heavily reinforced to accommodate the fin attachments. The very end of

## DATA

**DIMENSIONAL**

| | |
|---|---|
| Span | 35′1″ |
| Length | 77′8″ (overall, including nose probe) |
| | 71′0″ (fuselage only) |
| Height | 13′11.5″ |
| Tailplane Span | 15′6″ |
| Nacelle Length | 30′8″ (excluding variable centre-body) |
| Track | 9′6″ |
| Wheelbase | 20′6″ |
| Static Ground Angle | −1° |

**AREAS**

| | |
|---|---|
| Wing (gross) | 396.25 sq ft |
| Fin and Rudder (net) | 76.87 sq ft |
| Rudder | 19.7 sq ft |
| Tailplane (gross) | 71.25 sq ft |

**WEIGHTS**
No Data

**PERFORMANCE**

| | |
|---|---|
| $V_{max}$ | 1.9 Mach (maximum achieved) |

**REFERENCES**
RAF Museum, Cosford —The aircraft
BAe Filton —Archives
'Flight' —3rd May 1962

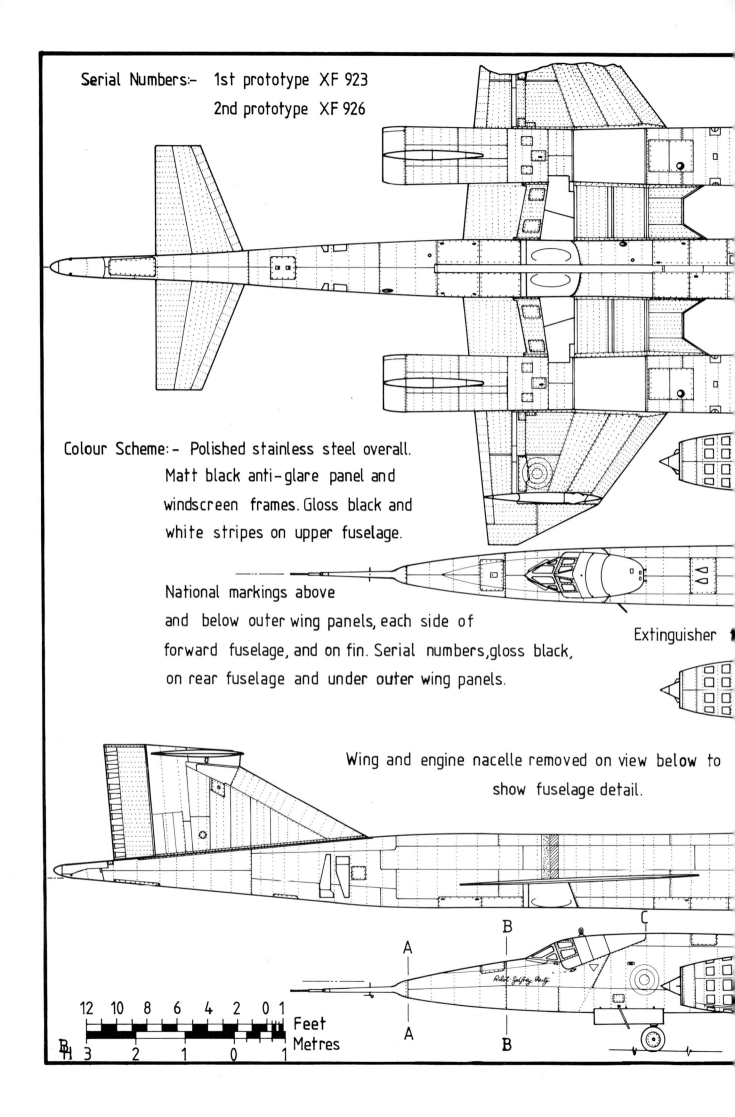

Serial Numbers:– 1st prototype XF 923

2nd prototype XF 926

Colour Scheme:- Polished stainless steel overall.
Matt black anti-glare panel and
windscreen frames. Gloss black and
white stripes on upper fuselage.

National markings above
and below outer wing panels, each side of
forward fuselage, and on fin. Serial numbers, gloss black,
on rear fuselage and under outer wing panels.

Extinguisher

Wing and engine nacelle removed on view below to
show fuselage detail.

12 10 8 6 4 2 0 1

3 2 1 0 1

Feet

Metres

A

A

B

B

C

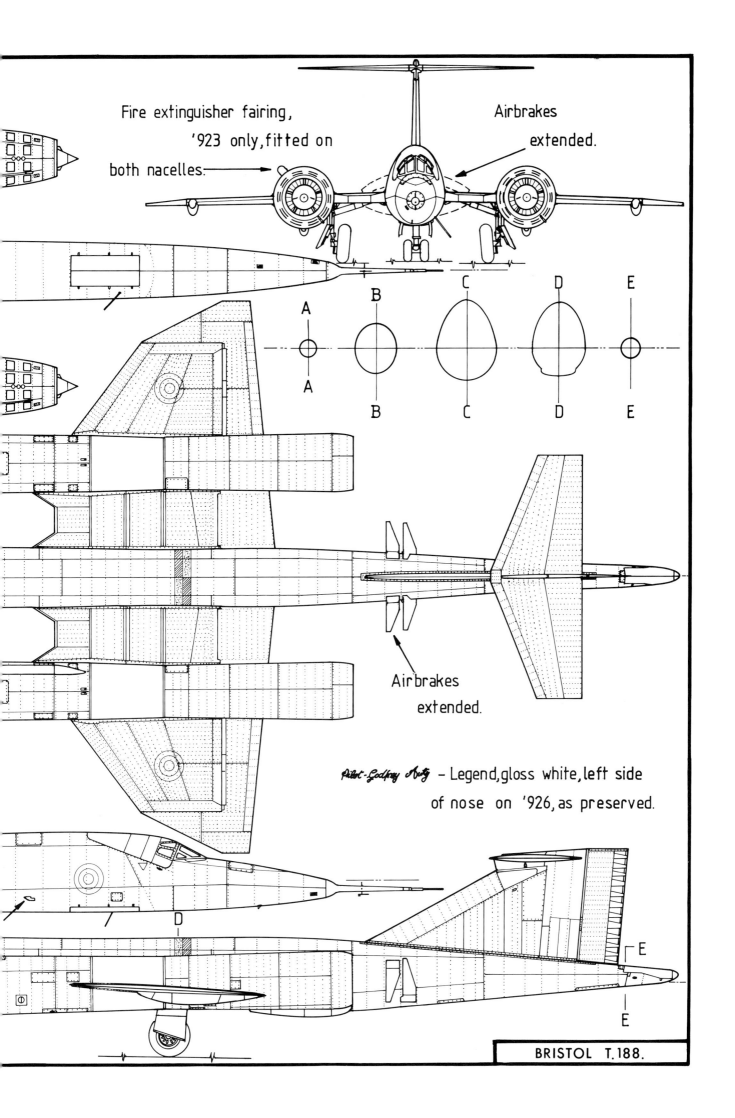

Fire extinguisher fairing,
'923 only, fitted on
both nacelles:→

Airbrakes
extended.

A
A

B
B

C
C

D
D

E
E

Airbrakes
extended.

*Pilot-Godfrey Auty* – Legend, gloss white, left side
of nose on '926, as preserved.

D

E
E

BRISTOL T.188.

the tailcone, poking out aft of the fin and rudder, contained a 16' diameter anti-spin and braking parachute deployed by a drogue gun and bullet.

The massive fin was mounted to strong attachment points on the fuselage. It had to be exceptionally strong to enable it to cope with the resulting yaw following a possible engine failure at maximum design speed. Its construction was around multiple near-vertical spars, with the only ribs being to form the leading edge profile. Its centreline chord was 21'0", (!), reducing to 8'5" at the tip. The leading edge sweep was 65°, and the trailing edge 5°45'. It had a full length rudder, with no trim tab, hinged to the rearmost spar, with its power control unit in the fuselage at its base.

The all-moving slab tailplane was mounted at the fin's tip, pivoted at its aft spar and actuated by its power control unit mounted within the fin, accessible through a large panel on the left side. Like the fin, it was of multi-spar construction, with ribs only at the leading edge and over the rear of the tailplane and trailing edge. Its trailing edge had zero sweep, but that at the leading edge was 23°20'. Its thickness/chord ratio was 4.5% and was of symmetrical section, with a centreline and tip chord of 6'0" and 3'0" respectively.

The wing was mounted just below mid point on the fuselage at an incidence of 2°30', and of bi-convex section with a root thickness/chord ratio of 4%. The main torsion box was made up from multiple spars, with very closely spaced ribs forwards to make the leading edge profile, and aft to the rear auxiliary spar. No fuel was contained in the wings. The whole trailing edge was swept forwards 6° but the leading edge varied across its span. Inboard of the engine nacelles the sweep was zero, with a large fillet into the fuselage and nacelle; outboard of the nacelle the sweep was 38°. The wing structure itself finished at Stn. 179.5"; outboard of this the large aileron horn balances formed what were in effect moving wingtip control surfaces. Their leading edge, unlike the wing's, had a rounded profile and was swept 64°. Overall the aspect ratio was 3.106:1, with the wing having a centreline and tip chord (at Stn. 179.5" of 14'5" and

7'6" respectively). The ailerons had a small tip chord of 22" and occupied the whole of the trailing edge outboard of the engine nacelles, with plain flaps inboard. The flaps could be selected in stages down to a maximum of 50°.

All of the control surface movements available were gradually reduced with airspeed. Below 0.3 Mach, the movements were ±12°30' for the ailerons and ±25° for the rudder. Above this speed, they progressively reduced to ±4°48' on the ailerons and ±1°30' on the rudder. The tailplane was slightly different in that the gearing had coarse and fine ratios. In coarse ratio its range was +4° and −15°, and in fine ratio +1°15' and −10°30'.

The engine nacelles were mounted with their centrelines at Wing Stn. 87". They were long, waisted tubes, attachment to the wing structure being unusual. The multiple wing spars were attached to three centrifugally cast stainless steel barrels, each 2'6" long, by pin lug attachments. (At the time these were the largest components ever produced by this method.) The engine intakes were set well forward of the wing leading edge and were of circular section with a retracting centre-body to control the shock-wave. A row of ten suction-relief doors were sited all round the nacelle just aft of the sharp intake lip. These were spring-loaded closed, being opened by suction at high power settings and low speeds. Aft of these was a second row of ten doors which were spill doors to alleviate ram-air drag. Control of the spill valves was from a system which sensed the position of the normal shock-wave inside the intake, which if it moved forwards was sensed, and the spill valves opened. On XF 923 only, two long fairings were attached to the top right side of the nacelles, each containing fire extinguisher equipment. At the aft end, the convergent/divergent afterburner nozzles were completely enclosed by the nacelle tailcones.

## POWER PLANT
Two de Havilland Gyron Junior PS.50/DG.J.10R axial flow turbojets with a Sea Level Static Thrust of 10,000 lbs, dry, and 14,000 lbs, with afterburner.

*Bristol 188 second prototype as preserved at Cosford, offers close inspection of the long nose and cockpit, and the engine nacelles, which were almost the same diameter as the fuselage. (Ron Moulton)*

*Hunting 126 during testing at RAE Bedford, showing carrying tufting on both wings, forward fuselage, aft fuselage and fin. The long-stroke undercarriage and tail bumper are also evident. (Pilot Press Ltd)*

# HUNTING 126

| | |
|---|---|
| **Manufacturer** | **Hunting Aircraft Ltd** |
| **Specification** | **ER.189D** |
| **Role** | **Research Prototype** |
| **First Flight Date** | **XN 714 – 26th March 1963** |
| | **XN 719 – Not Flown** |

The aircraft was developed in response to a Ministry specification calling for an aircraft to investigate the principle of using the engine's exhaust gases as a 'jet flap' to improve take-off and landing performance. This was the first full-scale test vehicle, to prove the principle of the jet-flap, which had been the subject of investigation for some years by the aircraft industry and the National Gas Turbine Establishment.

## DEVELOPMENT HISTORY
After an extensive period of wind tunnel research with models, it was decided that a full-scale research machine should be built to verify further the results. Specification ER.189D was raised to cover the construction of two prototypes, and the contract awarded to Hunting Aircraft, Luton, without putting it out to tender to other firms. One reason for choosing Hunting was the company's extensive experience of hot-gas ducting, gained during research with helicopters with tip-driven rotors.

The original idea was for all of the aircraft's propulsion to be obtained from the thin sheet of exhaust gases blowing downwards from the wing trailing edge. However, later research showed that a dramatic improvement in the Coefficient of Lift was obtained by blowing relatively cold air through several nozzles, around a radiused trailing edge, with the lower slit blowing forwards. However, on the actual aircraft the sheet was blown only over the upper surface, and not at all on the lower.

The design posed many new engineering

*Hunting 126 demonstrates the pronounced nose-down attitude in flight. The high seating position of the pilot, and small wing area are prominent features. (Pilot Press Ltd.)*

problems associated with moving relatively large volumes of hot exhaust gases through the fuselage and wing structures. However, it was possible still to manufacture the structure from normal light alloy, by efficient duct insulation and the use of a heat-reflective shield around the inside of the fuselage and wings. The flaps posed particular problems, in that only the upper surfaces were to be subjected to the hot gases, the bottom surfaces remaining relatively cool with normal airflow over them. This was overcome by a method of construction which allowed differential expansion, thus preventing local warping and allowing the correct profile to be maintained.

Construction of the first prototype was completed at Luton, and the aircraft rolled-out in August 1962 for limited taxi-ing trials, before being dismantled and taken by road the relatively short distance to RAE Bedford, arriving there on 12th December. As the runways were deliberately not cleared of ice and snow, for other trials purposes, the aircraft did not recommence taxi-ing trials until 19th March 1963. During these, several short hops were made, but the proceedings were brought to an abrupt halt by the anti-spin parachute streaming successfully, but failing to jettison. When this problem had been solved, the first flight was successfully made on 26th March 1963. As a precaution, zero flap was used for

take-off but, despite this, the aircraft was airborne after only about 600 yards. General handling characteristics were satisfactory, but the aircraft was found to fly around in an unusually nose-down attitude. The flight lasted about 18 minutes.

Contractor's clearance trials continued through the next months, until the aircraft was taken to Boscombe Down on 13th October 1964 for blower tunnel tests. After returning to RAE Bedford, it became part of the Aerodynamics Flight's fleet and continued research into high-lift flight. The Americans had shown some interest, so when it came to the end of its programme, it was dismantled and transported by air on 3rd April 1969 for tests in the large NASA wind tunnel. It was not flown while in America and it returned from there on 12th June 1970 but, on arrival, it was never un-crated.

It was returned to Bedford for temporary storage, and was struck off charge in June 1972. It was allocated to the RAF Museum, Cosford, arriving there on 30th April 1974, where it is still preserved.

Construction of the second prototype, XN 719, reached an advanced stage, but it was never completed and eventually scrapped at Luton.

(During its many moves, much material seems to have been mislaid and, when researching this particular machine, none had arrived at Cosford, nor could any be readily traced at RAE. Thus, as will be seen later, there is no detail of weights, areas or performance. I hope these will come to light at some later date.)

## CONSTRUCTION
Despite the problems of hot ducting, the structure was surprisingly conventional and was of stressed skin light alloy throughout. The fuselage frames were suitably strengthened at the points to which the wing, undercarriage and engine were mounted. The fuselage was of unusual depth compared to its width, and it was fitted with a fixed undercarriage, comprising a nosewheel oleo fitted with twin wheels having 15″ diameter tyres, with a single shock absorber and braced by a drag strut. The pilot sat very high under a large bubble canopy giving exceptional vision, the cockpit being situated immediately above the engine. The cockpit was unpressurised, as the performance of the aircraft was such that it was not required; however the pilot was provided with a normal oxygen system. He sat on a Martin-Baker VHA.Mk.4 ejection seat. The aircraft nose sloped down sharply from in front of the curved, three-piece windscreen to the single circulator intake which had an unusually fat, rounded lip. A long instrumentation boom was fixed just aft of the upper part of the lip, being a combined pitot-head, and mounting yaw and pitch vanes.

The engine was mounted immediately below the cockpit, unusually far forward in the airframe. Access to it and its accessories was through multiple large panels around the fuselage. To remove it, the whole nosecone could be removed and the engine drawn forwards. Subsequent to the first flights, a large, flat duct was fitted each side of the nose in line with the windscreen. The engine was started from an external air unit.

The fuel was carried in three flexible bag tanks, one immediately aft of the cockpit, and the other two, one above the other, in the fuselage just aft of the rear auxiliary spar attachment frame. A recuperator was fitted to ensure a continuing supply during negative–g conditions.

The main, fixed, undercarriage was fitted under the fuselage centre-section in line with the wing trailing edge. Each oleo had two diagonal struts hinged to the bottom of the fuselage. Each single wheel had a 24″ diameter tyre. The struts were fitted with streamlined fairings, although some early flights were made without them fitted. The two jetpipes exhausted low down on either side of the fuselage just aft of the mainwheel oleos.

Extensive instrumentation was carried, including an automatic observer, and temperature monitoring equipment for many parts of the airframe, and this was all housed in the aft fuselage. A large tail skid was affixed under the very rear of the fuselage.

The fin had a large dorsal fairing forward of its root leading edge, and was built around three main and two auxiliary spars. The tailplane was mounted about ¾ up the fin and on the leading edge in line with this a cine camera could be mounted for recording airflow patterns during tufting trials, these being affixed to the right wing. An anti-spin parachute was housed in a container at the fin's tip. The rudder was hinged to the rearmost spar at two points, was manually operated and had a trim/balance tab over most of its trailing edge length.

The variable incidence tailplane was of two-spar construction, hinged at the rear spar, and operated by a hydraulic powered flying control unit acting at its forward spar. The elevators were linked directly to the tailplane so that the effective camber of the tail varied directly with the incidence.

The wing was mounted high on the fuselage, was built around two spars and was attached to the fuselage frames by pin joints. Each wing panel was supported by a single strut from the bottom of the fuselage, attaching to the wing at approximately mid semi-span. The attachment points of the wing and strut were designed to allow the wing to be set at a dihedral angle of either 4° or 8° (No record can be found as to whether both angles were tested; the aircraft as preserved had the 8° dihedral angle.) The undersurface of the wings was covered with a multitude of access panels. Each aileron was attached to the wing's rear spar by five hinges, and cooling air was passed through the aileron structure via slots in the leading and trailing edges. The inboard flaps were of similar construction; in fact, the ailerons were really just extensions of the flaps, both being capable of being lowered at the same

## DATA
**DIMENSIONS**

| | |
|---|---|
| Span | 45′4″ (with 4° dihedral) |
| | 45′0″ (with 8° dihedral) |
| Length | 50′2″ (including probe) |
| | 44′3″ (without probe) |
| Height | 15′6″ |
| Tailplane Span | 11′10″ |
| Track | 11′8″ |
| Wheelbase | 14′10.6″ |

**AREAS**
No Data

**WEIGHTS**
No Data

**PERFORMANCE**
No Data

**REFERENCES**
RAF Museum, Cosford —The aircraft
RAE Farnborough      —Library Archives
Aviation Bookshop    —Archives

A-A

B - B

Serial Number: XN 714.

Plan and Side views shown
with 4° and 8° wing dihedral
respectively.

First flown without large exhaust ducts
on either side of fuselage
below windscreen
quarter-lights.

Colour Scheme: Glos
black
referenc
white cro
canopy. Na
jet exhaust
exhausts. He
aileron

E

D

C

B

A

F

E

D

C

B

A

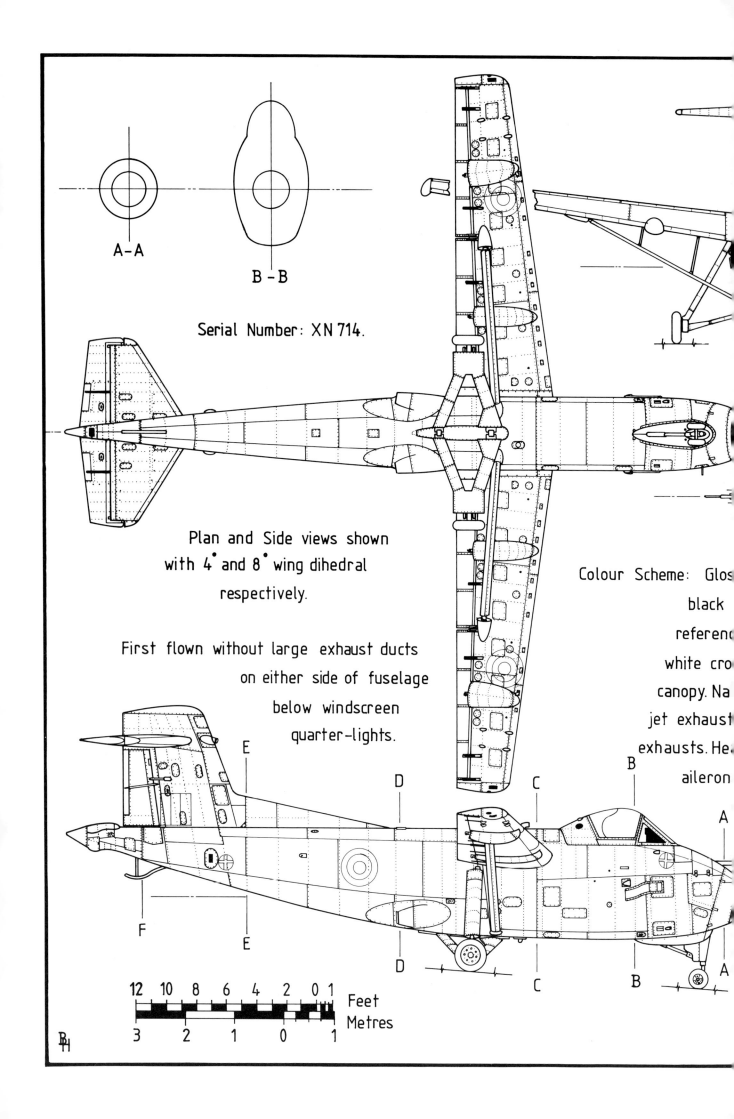

12  10  8  6  4  2  0 1    Feet
                            Metres
3      2     1    0    1

Missing detail on wing identical
to that shown on opposite
wing.

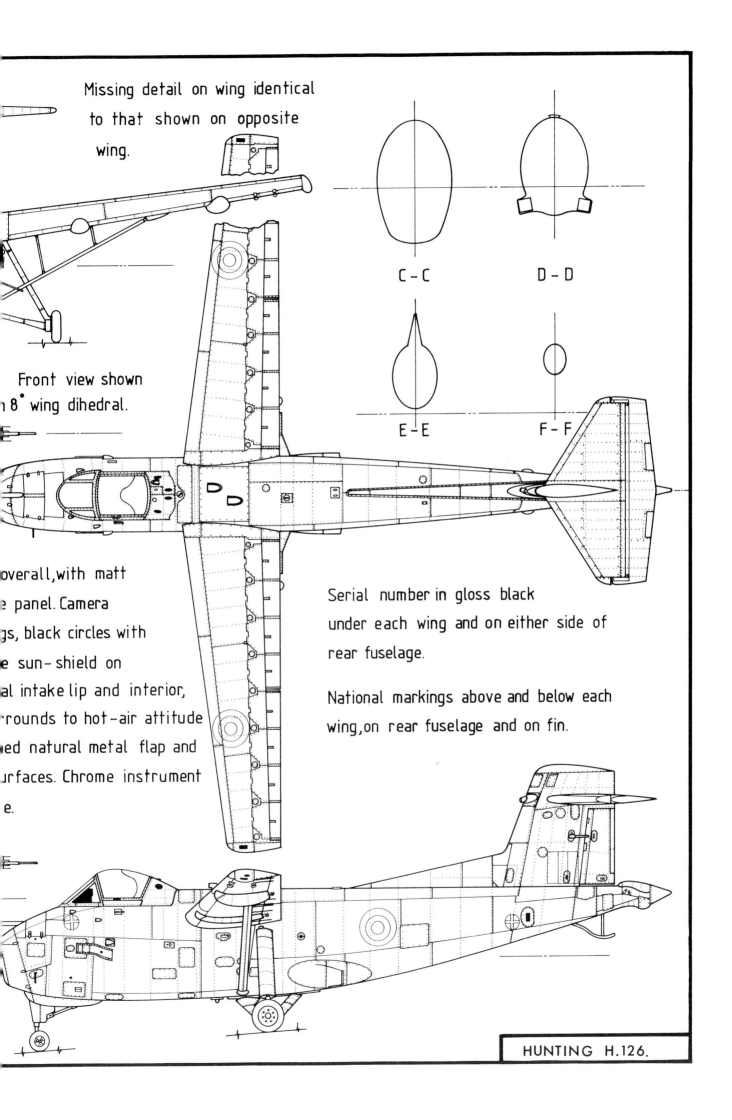

Front view shown
n 8° wing dihedral.

C – C          D – D

E – E          F – F

overall,with matt
e panel. Camera
gs, black circles with
e sun-shield on
al intake lip and interior,
rrounds to hot-air attitude
ed natural metal flap and
urfaces. Chrome instrument
e.

Serial number in gloss black
under each wing and on either side of
rear fuselage.

National markings above and below each
wing, on rear fuselage and on fin.

HUNTING H.126.

time. Each aileron and flap surface had its own operating jack mounted under the wing and covered by individual, large fairings. All the wing control surfaces were of relatively small chord, and served only as deflectors for the exhaust sheet which followed the upper surface as it was deflected downwards.

To supplement the conventional control surfaces at low speeds, engine bleed also fed 'puffer' nozzles on the underside of the wingtips for roll control, on each side of the rear fuselage for yaw, and in the underside of the very aft end of the tailcone for pitch. Only those nozzles at the rear for pitch and yaw were directly connected to the pilot's control column; those for roll control were completely independent and were autostabiliser controlled.

The engine provided power for both lift and thrust, the greater part of the efflux being ducted to the wings with only a small proportion going through the low-set normal exhaust orifices. These were set very low on the fuselage so that, when power was increased, the pitch-down moment imparted by the jet-flap was counteracted by the pitch up due to low thrust line, thus keeping the trim change to a minimum. The engine's exhaust efflux discharged directly into a 90° cascade which turned the major part of the exhaust upwards through a vertical distribution manifold, looking like, and colloquially known as, 'the dustbin'. From the top of this, three pipes fed into each wing panel discharging into the eight 'fishtails' above the wing and into the roll nozzle at the tip. The rearmost pipe fed the inner three fishtails on the flap, the middle pipe the next three (one for the outboard end of the flap and two for the aileron), and the foremost pipe the last two fishtails serving the aileron and the roll nozzle. An additional pipe led to the rear of the fuselage to eventually bifurcate for the pitch and roll nozzles. A separate duct led from the base of the cascade to bifurcate into separate ducts leading to the normal jet orifices. Provision was made for these two ducts to have thrust spoilers controllable by the pilot.

The hydraulic power for the tailplane, ailerons, flaps and wheel brakes was from two independent systems, with an emergency accumulator providing limited time operation of these controls. A totally separate accumulator fed the wheel brakes in an emergency. The a.c. electrical system was fed by two inverters, one acting as a standby, operating only in the event of the other failing.

## POWER PLANT
One Bristol Siddeley B.E.26 Orpheus 805 axial flow turbojet engine with a Sea Level Static Thrust of 4,850 lbs.

*Hunting 126 banking away allowing details of the jet flap slot to be seen, as well as the control nozzles for pitch and yaw on the rear fuselage. (Pilot Press Ltd.)*

*BAC.221 during its maiden flight with landing gear extended. Note engine duct fairing 'bump' at wing root, standard F.D.2 canopy and early aft fairing, and original fin. (Pilot Press Ltd.)*

# B.A.C. TYPE 221

| | |
|---|---|
| **Manufacturer** | **British Aircraft Corporation** |
| **Specification** | **ER.193D** |
| **Role** | **Research Prototype** |
| **First Flight Date** | **WG 774 – 1st May 1964** |

The BAC.221 looked very much like a flying scale model of the Concorde, but it was designed for basic research into the behaviour of slender delta wings. The nature of these wings was such that their behaviour could not reliably be predicted solely from model tests in the wind tunnel, as their precise characteristics varied so much with Reynolds number, more so than 'conventional' wings. Therefore, the wind tunnel predictions had to be verified by flying an actual aircraft. Rather than build a completely new aircraft, it was proposed that a minimal modification of a FD.2 would be the most cost effective scheme.

## DEVELOPMENT HISTORY

During 1958, Fairey Aviation and the RAE discussed the possible extension of the FD.2 programme to cover investigation of the behaviour of other delta shapes, by the fitting of an 'ogee' wing, and in September of that year the company submitted a proposal for an ogival wing integrated with the fuselage, this being the layout of an SST project being investigated at the time by Hawker Siddeley. The span of the proposed aircraft was reduced slightly from that of the FD.2, and had curved up wing tips, square sectioned dorsal intakes at about

30% chord, and a three foot fuselage stretch. The wing leading edge root was right at the fuselage nose and had to be drooped with the nose. However, this proposal was rejected due to centre of gravity problems with the movement of the centre of pressure at supersonic speeds, and the dorsal intakes seemed to swallow the leading edge vortex which provided much of the wing's lift at low speeds.

When Westland Aircraft took over Fairey Aviation, the proposed development of the FD.2 was given to Hunting Aircraft Ltd., Luton, and Specification ER.193D raised to cover the work. However, after only a very brief period the whole programme was taken over by Bristol Aircraft, Filton, during a general redistribution of workload in the then new British Aircraft Corporation.

Two proposals were put forward by the company:

a) Fit the optimum wing with a 6' fuselage stretch and much taller undercarriage.
b) Carry out a minimum conversion with the same fuselage and undercarriage.

The second proposal was rejected as too much of a compromise due to its inability to produce a 'slender' shape and because it had insufficient fuel capacity. So the full modification was chosen, but to be done at absolutely minimum cost! WG 774 was flown to Filton on 5th September 1960 and, after final detailed design work was completed, metal was cut in April 1961. The conversion took longer than at first thought and was not completed until 7th July 1963.

To keep expenditure to a minimum, several short

BAC.221 planview shows underside detail. Note large main undercarriage bay fairing bulges and how they fair into the engine intakes. Also obvious is the unusual application of the serial number to only one wing. (Pilot Press Ltd.)

cuts were taken which in the end cost the programme a lot of time. One was a deliberate policy not to build any systems ground test rigs. This meant that everything had to be made to flight specification and installed on the actual aircraft before it was tested. Consequently, a further ten months from completion date were to pass with system checks and ground runs before the aircraft actually managed to get airborne on its maiden flight, which was from Filton on 1st May 1964.

In the light of the subsequent series of manufacturer's trials, the fin was extended by 8" to improve directional stability, an anti-spin parachute was added, and some equipment changes were made. New systems included provision for a fully variable droop on the nose, for research into take-off and landing performance of aircraft with slender delta wings and a fully adjustable autostabisation system to vary effective stability characteristics.

The aircraft was finally delivered to RAE Bedford for use by Aero Flight on 20th May 1966. By this time, design and construction of the Concorde was well under way, so once again the research aircraft supposedly most relevant to a design had arrived too late to have any real influence!

The BAC.221 joined the slender-delta research programme already under way at Bedford with the HP.115. The wing was not an exact scale representation of that on Concorde; although generally similar in planform, it lacked the other aircraft's twist, camber, droop and thickness/chord ratio. The droop on Concorde's wing was only for cruise efficiency, which was not really relevant on the BAC.221. As a result, due to this dissimilarity, it could not investigate the likely high-speed characteristics of the wing, plus the flying control layout was also entirely different. It therefore spent much of its time researching into the approach and landing phase of flight, and helped in the development of a suitable auto-throttle system for approach speed stability.

It had inherited the FD.2's reliability and efficiency, and just got on with its research job with little or no fuss, and was thought to be an 'unremarkable' aircraft, this being meant as a compliment from its pilots. The research programmes continued until June 1973, when the aircraft was retired.

It went first for exhibition at the Museum of Flight, East Fortune, near Edinburgh, and subsequently became part of the Concorde Display at the Fleet Air Arm Museum, Yeovilton, where it remains until the present day.

## CONSTRUCTION

The fuselage was a stretched version of that on the FD.2, and was accomplished by inserting a 6'0" plug

# B.A.C. TYPE 221

into the forward end of the centre-section. On the FD.2, the fuselage station numbers were taken from a datum at the wing trailing edge. The fuselage was cut at Frame 194, a strong 'spectacle' shaped frame at the forward end of the centre-section between the intake ducts and the fuselage fuel tank, and the additional section inserted. In addition the whole fuselage forward to the nose joint had to be modified to accommodate the much longer nose-wheel undercarriage, additional fuel and instrumentation. The remainder of the fuselage structure remained much as before, other than for thickening of the skin panels over the centre-section to absorb increased loads from the wing and fin. Equipment in the nose-bay was much as before, other than for the substitution of a UHF radio for the earlier VHF variety, with its characteristic blade aerial fitted below the nose. A standby VHF transmitter was mounted in the same place as the original main VHF radio, with its adjacent whip-aerial.

The aircraft first flew with the original FD.2 cockpit canopy, but with an identically-shaped windscreen which was now gold-film heated rather than the earlier hot-air sandwich type. Early on in the programme, a new canopy was fitted which was a full Perspex moulding giving the pilot much better visibility. It was also of the frangible variety enabling an ejection to be made through it if necessary. The same modified Martin-Baker Mk.3 FDV seat was fitted.

The nosewheel undercarriage oleo was based closely on that from the Gannet, with the axle fitting modified to accept the original FD.2 live axle and twin wheels. It had two long drag braces, joined by a cross-member, to which the single retraction jack was attached. The original FD.2 forward under-carriage doors were slightly shortened, and two others added to fair the aft end of the much longer retraction bay. These aft pair of doors were sequenced shut after nosewheel extension. The forward ones still had to be opened before the nose could be drooped so, as in its earlier guise, the aircraft could sometimes be seen with its under-carriage up, nose-gear forward doors open, and its nose drooped.

The main instrumentation bay was sited in the top of the forward part of the undercarriage bay containing, among other items, the auto-observer panel and the Hussenot recorder. Inverters and transducers for the crash recorder were mounted in the aft end of the bay. Two hydraulic tanks were carried under a streamlined fairing aft of the cockpit canopy. The shape of this was slightly altered when the Perspex canopy was fitted. The remainder of the new fuselage section was occupied by a bag-type fuel tank. The autostabilisation bay was sited below the fuel collector tank.

The fin structure remained as before for the initial flights, except for the addition of a bullet

fairing at its tip, which contained a cine camera for recording airflow patterns when the right wing was tufted. A Lateral Thrust Unit, colloquially known as a 'bonker', was fitted at the fin tip. This was a very short duration miniature rocket motor, for flutter investigation. Early trials revealed a slight lack of directional stability brought about by the longer nose, so an extra 8" was added to the fin tip. This caused the rudder to be inset, and the bullet fairing now reached back to the trailing edge of the fin tip, rather than terminating at the rudder hinge line as before.

The engine installation remained as before, except for the addition of fire-suppression bottles and modifications to the control linkages. Fuel was carried in two integral wings tanks within the main torsion box and two reserve tanks in the forward part of the wing outboard of the undercarriage bays. Total capacity was 505 gallons (3,540lbs.) with 15.75 gallons (110lbs.) unusable. Supply to the afterburner was automatically cut off when the fuel in the collector tank reached a pre-determined level.

The wing was constructed in two halves which were attached to the fuselage at the same points as the earlier FD.2. The leading edge of the wing had a straight middle portion swept at 65°, which curved forwards to blend smoothly into the nose-chine and aft to the streamwise tips. Further sets of 'bonkers' were fitted above and below each wing tip, and provision was made for the attachment of drogues. Construction was similar to that on the FD.2, i.e. basically around three mainspars and several formers parallel to the longitudinal and lateral axes of the aircraft. The wing had a sharp leading edge (in contrast to the FD.2's rounded one), a thickness/chord ratio of 4.5%, and was set at 0° incidence to the fuselage datum. The aspect ratio was 1.22:1. The long, tapering chine stopped just short of the tip of the nosecone and, to ensure no

## DATA
**DIMENSIONS**

| | |
|---|---|
| Span | 25'0" |
| Length | 57'7.5" (including nose probe) |
| Height | 13'9" |
| | 14'4" (with extended fin tip) |
| Track | 10'8" |
| Wheelbase | 18'2.5" |

**AREAS**
Wing (gross)  504.0 sq ft

**WEIGHTS**
No Data

**PERFORMANCE**
$V_{max}$  1.6 Mach

**REFERENCES**

| | |
|---|---|
| FAA Museum, Yeovilton | —The aircraft |
| 'Flight' | —23rd July 1964 |
| RAE Farnborough | —Library Archives |

243

Serial Number: WG 774

F-F    E-E    D-D

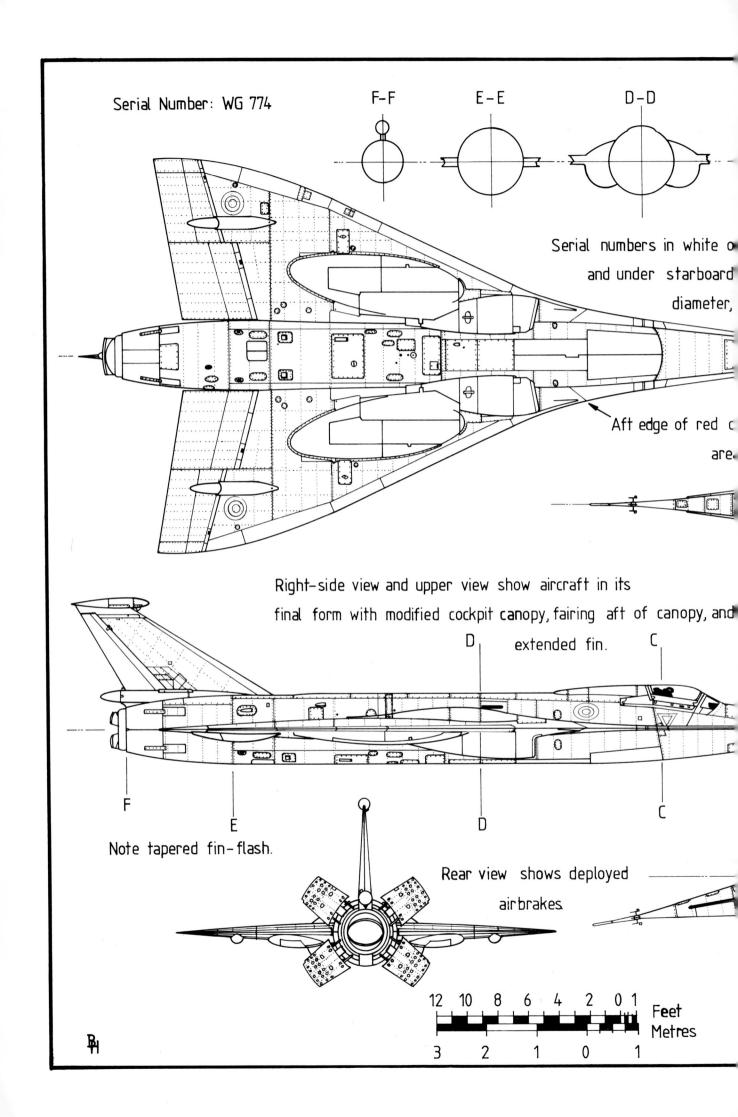

Serial numbers in white o
and under starboard
diameter,

Aft edge of red c
are

Right-side view and upper view show aircraft in its
final form with modified cockpit canopy, fairing aft of canopy, and
extended fin.

D    C

F

E    D    C

Note tapered fin-flash.

Rear view shows deployed
airbrakes.

12 10 8 6 4 2 0 1    Feet
Metres
3    2    1    0    1

ℜℌ

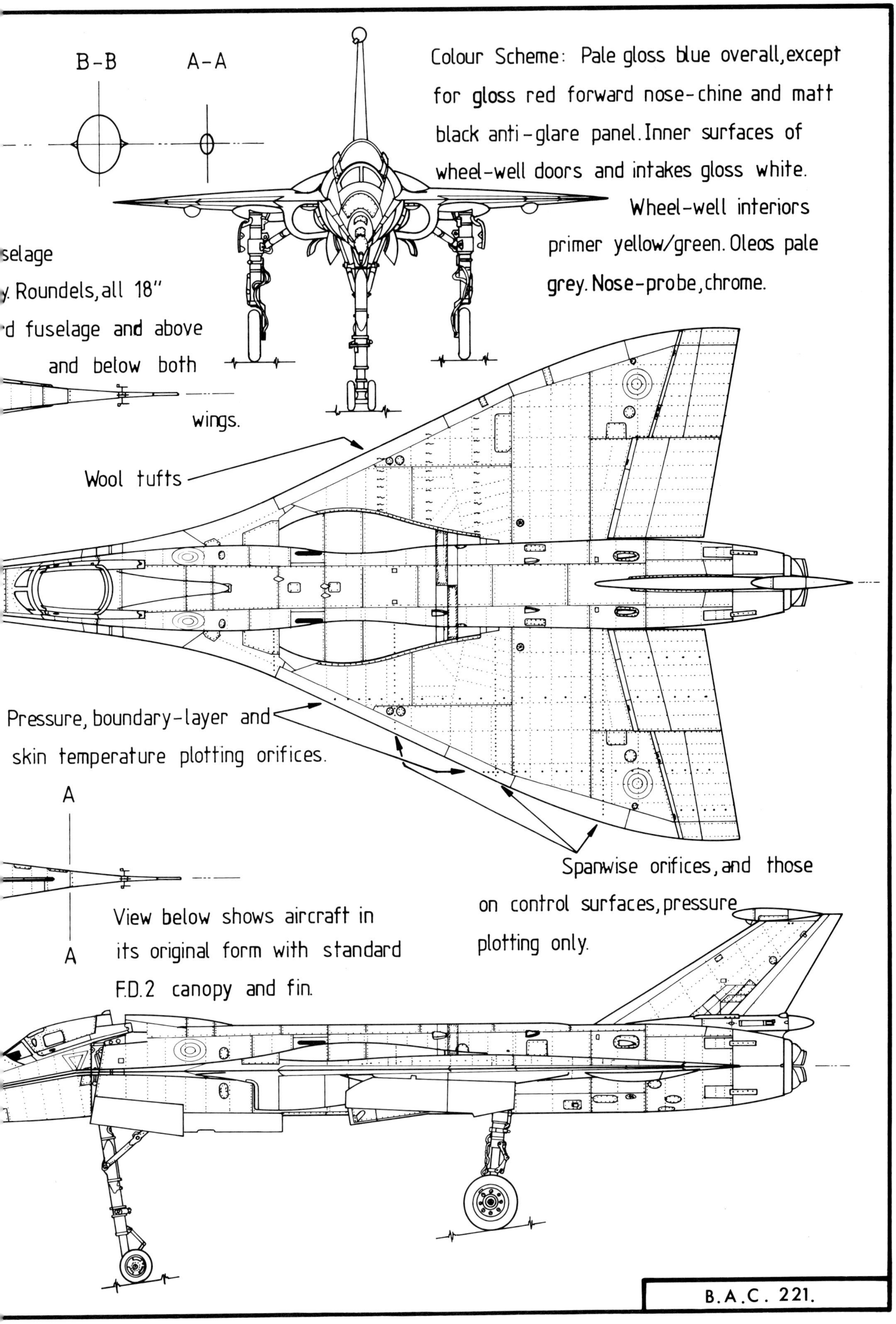

B-B          A-A

Colour Scheme: Pale gloss blue overall, except
for gloss red forward nose-chine and matt
black anti-glare panel. Inner surfaces of
wheel-well doors and intakes gloss white.
        Wheel-well interiors
primer yellow/green. Oleos pale
grey. Nose-probe, chrome.

selage
. Roundels, all 18"
d fuselage and above
    and below both
        wings.

Wool tufts

Pressure, boundary-layer and
skin temperature plotting orifices.

A
|
|
A

View below shows aircraft in
its original form with standard
F.D.2 canopy and fin.

Spanwise orifices, and those
on control surfaces, pressure
plotting only.

B.A.C. 221.

interruption to the vortex attachment when the nose was lowered, had an ingenious system of small sliding plates at the join to maintain the chine's profile. The wing was constructed to much tighter tolerances than had been used on the FD.2's wing, and great care had been taken to maintain a clean profile to the upper surfaces. However, the lower surfaces were broken by bulges for the intakes, undercarriage bays and large streamlined fairings for the aileron hydraulic operating-jacks.

Wool tufting was attached to the upper surface of the right wing, and the left wing's upper surface was extensively drilled for pressure plotting. There were two chord-wise rows on the left elevator and aileron, and two chord-wise rows on the wing itself; the latter were for pressure, boundary layer and temperature plotting. Three span-wise rows and those on the control surfaces were for pressure plotting only.

The main undercarriage oleos were basically those from the Lightning, with a universal joint at the top allowing the leg to rotate through 90° while retracting forwards, so that the wheels lay horizontally in their bays. The normal Lightning brake drums were reduced in thickness to save weight, and the tyre pressures were reduced to 180 psi. Despite the very slim wheels, the bay doors formed part of a large underwing fairing bulge to allow the undercarriage to be accommodated in the wing. This bulge faired into that which formed the engine intake.

The intakes were fixed inlets optimised for a speed just short of optimum design speed, about 1.6 Mach. (It had been decided earlier not to opt for variable-geometry intakes due to cost and complication.) They could not be located as before, due to the need for a continuous leading edge to the fuselage chine. Therefore they had to be mounted below the wing, just aft of the leading edge, with their ducts curving sharply upwards into additional bulges above the wing so that they entered the fuselage symmetrically before reaching the engine's compressor. The intakes had rounded lips, and were swept forwards slightly in planview. Pen-nib fairings were attached to the outer edge of the intake lips to eliminate excess air spillage when throttling back. Intake 'buzz' was cured by the addition of internal bulges at the intake inner and top walls, these bulges incorporating boundary layer bleed ducts.

The layout of the flying control surfaces were as for the FD.2, with elevators inboard and ailerons outboard. The elevator operating jacks were in an identical location to those in the FD.2, being just in the fuselage. The surfaces themselves were much wider in chord than on the FD.2. Rudder control was via push/pull rods, and the pilot's pedals were fitted with stops, limiting travel within three pre-selected ranges dependent on airspeed. Both the aileron and elevator operating jacks had inputs from the autostabilisation system, but there was little basic change to the elevator system other than the much larger surface chord and a changed gear ratio. All of the control surfaces were fitted with strain gauges to measure hinge moments.

Two independent hydraulic systems were fitted operating at 3,000 psi. but were considerably changed from the previous systems. No. 1 system fed one side of the tandem control jacks on the elevators, rudder and ailerons. No. 2 system fed the other side of the control jacks, undercarriage, airbrakes, nose-droop, wheel brakes and nose oleo shimmy damper. In an emergency, No. 1 system could be served by pressure from a drop-out ram air turbine. In this situation, accumulators fed the undercarriage for emergency lowering, and wheel braking.

## POWER PLANT
One Rolls-Royce Avon RA.28R axial flow turbojet, (Avon No. 4037), with a Sea Level Static Thrust of 10,150 lbs., dry and 14,000 lbs., with afterburner.

*BAC.221 just at the point of touchdown, with taller fin and redesigned camera bullet fairing. The exceptionally long-stroke undercarriage is noteworthy as is the relatively small elevator deflection to hold the touchdown attitude. (Pilot Press Ltd.)*

*Planview of the BAC TSR.2 in flight, showing the long slender nose and close-coupled wing and taileron. Flaps are still in the take-off position (British Aerospace (Warton))*

# B.A.C. TSR.2

| Manufacturer | British Aircraft Corporation |
|---|---|
| Specification | RB.192D |
| Role | Tactical Strike/Reconnaissance Bomber |
| First Flight Date | XR 219 – 27th September 1964 |
| | XR 220 – Not Flown |
| | XR 221 – Not Flown |

The TSR.2 will probably go down in history as the most controversial, 'political', aircraft ever built in Britain. Its very ordering and construction was to be used as a political tool to enforce the start of the 'rationalisation' of the aircraft industry, with many historic companies disappearing with the various mergers. It was one of the first programmes to be developed as a complete weapons system, which was to cause many an outcry when costs were debated, as every piece of equipment remotely associated with the aircraft was included in the programme's cost, which inevitably made the unit cost look exaggeratedly high. New ground was being broken at virtually every stage, as new technology and skills had to be developed. What had originally started as simply a 'Canberra replacement', became a very sophisticated, multi-role aircraft. The aircraft's final cancellation had nothing to do with its ability to meet its design requirements, and everything to do with political doctrine

and dogma. Even the way in which it was cancelled caused controversy, the announcement being made as part of a 'normal' Budget speech by the then Chancellor of the Exchequer, thus even limiting debate in Parliament. Finally, to ensure that the programme could never be resurrected by any future change of government, orders were given to destroy the only flying protype, plus the other airframes and all production jigs and drawings. Aptly, it was to be described later as 'The Murder of the TSR.2'.

There has probably been more written about the TSR.2 than virtually any other British jet aircraft, and there are many excellent articles and books available which adequately cover the political aspect. However, this is outside the scope of this book, and therefore this chapter will deal solely with the aircraft itself.

## DEVELOPMENT HISTORY

Having designed and built that most successful of jet bombers, the Canberra, late in 1956 English Electric started initial design studies for its replacement for entry into service in the mid-60s. Unlike its predecessor, it was to be designed for ultra-low level attack, rather than from high level, as had been the case with the Canberra. The design developed into a large two-seat delta, twin-engined aircraft, with the company's designation of P.17 and, apart from being powered by two

*Second prototype BAC TSR.2 under construction. Note long-stroke nose undercarriage oleo, the length being virtually equivalent to when in the STOL position. The intake is minus the bullet fairing and the various ventral access panels are open. Note also the detachable tailcone awaiting installation at the rear giving a good idea of the fuselage cross-section in this area. (British Aerospace)*

Rolls-Royce RB.133 engines, it reached almost its final form as early as February 1957.

General Operational Requirement (GOR) 339 was issued to the aircraft industry in September 1957, and tenders were solicited from Blackburn, Bristol, de Havilland, English Electric, Fairey, Handley Page, Hawkers, Shorts, and Vickers Armstrong. At approximately the same time, English Electric and Short Brothers started collaborating on a joint project, which was to give the P.17D a vertical take-off capability mounted on top of a large delta 'lifting platform' powered by no less than 60 lift and ten propulsion engines! Quite understandably, this machine was a non-starter.

By mid-1958, the decision was made that a development contract would be issued only to merging firms, in the then proposed 'rationalisation' of the whole aircraft industry. The two designs most favoured were those of English Electric, the P.17A and Vickers (ex-Supermarine branch), Type 571. The latter was slightly smaller and featured an elegant pointed nose with side intakes and a shoulder-mounted, swept wing. In January 1959, the Ministry awarded the development of the aircraft to the two firms, which signalled the start of the merger of the companies, eventually to become BAC, and design contracts were awarded in June 1959. The final aircraft was to bear more resemblance to the Type 571 than to the P.17, although it retained the latter's basic delta planform. One of the first changes was the substitution of Bristol Siddeley Olympus engines for the RB.133's. Airflow patterns from the original anhedral wing were found to interfere with the flow over the tailplanes. Therefore the wing was given zero anhedral but, to improve lateral stability, its tips were given a marked downwards angle.

To satisfy the STOL requirment, there were no flying control surfaces on the wing, the entire trailing edges out to the anhedral tips being occupied by blown flaps. Pitch and roll control was, at that time, by the novel method of having a 'taileron', the horizontal tail surfaces moving in unison for pitch and differentially for roll control. Design responsibility was divided roughly on the lines of Vickers developing the forward fuselage, electronics, undercarriage and fin, and English Electric being responsible for the centre fuselage, wing and tailplane. Manufacture was split, with Weybridge building the forward and centre fuselage sections and main wing box, and Preston building the aft fuselage, fin, tailerons and wing tips. The fuselage 'joint' was between Frames 629 and 640 (measured in inches from the nose datum). Two engineers from each facility were appointed to look after the 11" gap between the two sections to ensure they fitted! Two production lines were set up for final assembly. Meanwhile the original GOR.339 had now become OR.343 to cover the specific aircraft being developed. This was again to change to Specification RB.192D for the development batch of aircraft.

While Vickers and English Electric were given the prime task of developing the complete weapons system, many sub-contractors were used for specific specialised equipment development. The 'heart' of the aircraft was its navigation/attack/ radar and its automatic flight systems. The former was entrusted to Ferranti and the latter to Elliott-Automation. With such advanced requirements for the aircraft, these electronic systems and their integration in the overall airframe were to be the major cause of the spiralling costs of the programme, and for development delays.

The initial contract was placed on 7th October 1960, to cover the construction of nine development aircraft, which were to be built on production jigs. The disadvantage of this method was that any modifications required in the light of flight tests would have to be incorporated retrospectively to many airframes which would follow closely on the production line. It was planned that the seventh development aircraft would be the first off the Preston final assembly line. Different designations existed within the company to identify who built what, known as the Type 571 for Weybridge-assembled airframes, and Type 579 for those built at Preston.

The whole project developed into a 'design by committee', with even the smallest decision having to be discussed by many people when it could have been the decision of one man. Such was the rapid development of aviation in that period, that these delays enabled the Air Ministry to demand changes to meet new roles and requirements, which led to further delays when redesign was needed. However, the basic aerodynamic design had been finalised early on, and actually changed little, except for the relocation of the wing by approximately three inches relative to the fuselage datum in March 1960.

The enormity of the development programme was now being fully realised, especially in the field of electronics development. Inevitably, costs spiralled and caused an in-depth review by the Treasury. This lead to the RAF being asked to downgrade their requirements and, as an interim measure, allow less sophisticated electronics and systems to be fitted, but this was refused.

Free flight model tests were conducted early in 1962, and on 22nd February of that year the first flight trials of the Olympus 22R engine commenced, with the engine mounted beneath a Vulcan test-bed.

On 28th June 1963, the contract was amended to include the construction of a further eleven pre-production aircraft, to be further amended nine months later to cover an initial batch of 30 production machines. Engine development was now running into trouble, with shaft resonance present at certain engine rpm. This eventually caused the engine to explode under the Vulcan, causing extensive damage. This engine problem was not to be solved until after the first prototype's maiden flight. Meanwhile, the first prototype had been completed at Weybridge by early 1964 and, after vibration tests, was disassembled and transported by road to Boscombe Down to ready it for flight trails.

All of these problems further delayed the first flight, and fuelled the anti-TSR 2 lobby. Eventually the decision was taken that flight trials could commence, with the calculated risk of using non-flightworthy engines at much reduced power for the initial flights. After high speed taxiing trials, and some initial problems with the deployment of the braking parachutes, a brief first flight with undercarriage locked down was made on 27th September 1964, the aircraft being airborne for only 14 minutes. However, on landing, another serious problem manifested itself, in that rapid airframe vibration was experienced at a frequency close to that of the human eyeball so that the pilot could not see the cockpit instruments. This was eventually traced to an afterburner fuel pump oscillation due to a change of spring. Due to the lack of any flight-cleared engines, the second flight was not to be made for a further three months, which lead to speculation, of course, that the first flight had revealed something terribly wrong!

When the aircraft finally got airborne again, the flights were plagued by undercarriage sequencing problems during retraction and extension. One flight ended in a most delicate landing, with the main undercarriage bogeys rotated the wrong way with the leading wheel down rather than the trailing one. (There had earlier been some intimation of the undercarriage problems to come, even before the first flight. While under systems tests with the aircraft on jacks, there were difficulties in sequencing and retraction. On one occasion while retracting the undercarriage, a large chunk of metal broke off and was shot through the hangar wall like a bullet leaving a substantial hole, fortunately causing no injuries.) The problem was eventually solved by a drag link being attached from the oleo leg to the rear axle attachment. The first 'clean' flight was made, when the aircraft also went supersonic for the first time, during the delivery flight to Warton on 22nd February 1965.

The second prototype, XR 220, had by this time arrived at Boscombe Down, but suffered an accident while still attached to its transporter. The lorry jack-knifed and ended up virtually on top of the now inverted fuselage, only just missing the Lightning T.4 chase plane in the process. However, such was the strength of the airframe that there was more damage to the concrete than to it, and subsequent checks revealed that there had been no alteration to the structural rigging at all! Although completely ready for flight after reassembly, it was destined never to fly, and was towed to the far side of Boscombe Down to await its fate.

In Parliament, a Labour government had been elected and, true to their earlier promise, they cancelled the whole programme, but only announced it as an integral part of their first Budget speech on 6th April 1965. Thus, in line with the constitutional rules, a full debate was denied on the matter, debate being allowed only on the Budget itself. This meant that the last flight of XR 219 had already been made, on 31st March. At the time of cancellation, three aircraft were ready for flight, the first, second and third prototypes – XR 219/220/221, with 17 more at an advanced stage of construction, comprising 6 further development aircraft (serials XR 222–227), 11 pre-production aircraft (serials XS 660–670), and a further 30 production airframes (serials XS 944-973) at various stages of construction.

A proposal was made that XR 219 should be kept flying on general research work, being flown by Aerodynamics Flight at RAE Bedford, who were enthusiastic about the idea, provided the full flight envelope had been explored and cleared. But this was turned down, and it was also ordered that all airframes on the production lines should be scrapped together with all tools, jigs and production drawings.

Preliminary indications from the brief flight trials were that the aircraft would have probably met, or exceeded, all performance requirements, after overcoming the initial teething problems.

The first prototype was sent to Shoeburyness, together with the third prototype XR 221, plus XR 223, to act as ground targets for damage assessment to 'modern' airframes. (There were rumours that XR 219 was deliberately missed when shot at!) Quite why the first and only aircraft to fly could not be preserved in a museum and another airframe substituted, can only be a subject for speculation. XR 220 eventually was dismantled and became a part of the RAF Museum's reserve collection at Henlow, later to be transferred for display at the RAF Museum, Cosford, being essentially complete but minus its engines. XR 222 was sent to the Institute of Technology, Cranfield, and subsequently transferred, becoming a part of the Imperial War Museum Collection at Duxford, but many parts of the airframe were missing. (At the time of writing a project is under way, employing several engineers who worked on the original construction, to complete the airframe externally.) All remaining airframes were officially scrapped, but there are rumours that sufficient parts still exist around the various departments of Boscombe Down to construct virtually a complete airframe!

The contract for the TSR.2 was officially closed on 6th July 1965. As a result, the RAF never received an aircraft capable of the performance and attack capability that it badly needed. Even now despite the excellent Tornado, there has never been an aircraft to match the performance and versatility of the TSR.2.

XR 219 had flown only 24 flights during its brief life, totalling only 13 hrs 5 mins. The shortest flight being only 8 minutes (No 3), and the longest 1 hr 10 mins.

Projects in the design stage at the time of cancellation included a two-seat pilot-trainer version with a raised rear seat for the instructor. The crew were to be seated under a single-piece transparency and, apart from the aft fairing bulge, the remainder of the structure was standard. It was calculated that this large raised cockpit fairing would have limited top speed to about Mach 1.6.

# CONSTRUCTION

At the design speed, the aircraft was operating very near to the limits in temperature for normal light alloys and, therefore, special aluminium/lithium alloys had to be developed for most of the structure, and heat-treated titanium alloy had to be used around the engine bays; this had a strength/weight ratio approximately double that of heat-resistant steel. Extensive use was made of integrally-machined and chemically-etched skin and stringer panels in both the fuselage and wing.

The aircraft was built in five major components – the forward fuselage including the radome, cockpits and main electronics bay, a forward centre-section containing fuel and the engine intakes, main centre section housing the strengthened frames for wing attachment, and aft fuselage with fin and tailerons, plus the main wing box. The two wing panels were spliced together before being offered up to the fuselage as one component.

The nosecone of the aircraft was formed by a straight-sided 30° cone which housed the 19" forward-looking radar dish and, to satisfy the specification for the pilot's downward and forward vision, its topline coincided with his sight-line. The whole aircraft nose had its datum at –7°30' to the aircraft's horizontal datum which, together with the aircraft's pitch attitude being slightly nose-down while in flight, gave the pilot an exceptional forward and sideways view. A pitot boom extended forward of the cone apex, which was fitted at –6° to the aircraft horizontal datum. Fuselage Station O was in fact 4" aft of the cone apex, it having been extended after the original fuselage design had been finalised.

The pilot and navigator sat in tandem cockpits, the vertical aft pressure bulkhead being at Stn. 207, each having an individual clamshell canopy. The optical quality produced by tinting, certainly on the first prototype, caused adverse comment. Each canopy could be jettisoned individually or as an automatic part of the ejection sequence. Entry was normally from the right side, where the external locking handles and a single external jettison control were also fitted. The windscreen comprised a flat central panel and curved quarter-lights, all of which were heated by gold-film. Thought had been given to a vee-shaped screen but this was found to cause too many reflections. The central windscreen was made from high temperature alumino silicate, and was set at an angle of 36° to the horizontal, to enable it to withstand a birdstrike at transonic speeds at low level.

Both pilot and navigator were provided with moving map displays, which were driven by a

BAC TSR.2 XR219 during an early test flight with its undercarriage still extended. Airbrake panels appear to be slightly open, (evident in virtually all the views of the aircraft in flight.) The differential taileron action to control the aircraft in roll is just discernible.
(Royal Aeronautical Society)

computer deriving position inputs from the inertial navigation systems. In addition, the pilot had a head-up display, which was the first designed to reflect directly on to the cockpit windscreen. His head-down display was designed to comply with OR.946 standard. To enable sufficient depth of panel and also to improve readability, the main instrument panel was mounted normal to the glareshield giving a no-parallax view of all instruments. His cockpit was, in general, remarkably roomy, with neat side consoles containing the ancillary controls and indicators, the coaming being dominated by a comprehensive central warning system. Unusually for a bomber, the pilot had a normal 'fighter-type' control column.

The navigator's combined instrument display provided vertical speed, altitude and airspeed information. The airspeed indicator was servo-driven from the central air data computer, and had three speed indications shown – Doppler ground speed, computed ground speed from the central navigation computer, and true airspeed from the air data computer. He also had a periscope for downwards vision, which was servo-driven in both elevation and azimuth, with the ability to rotate through a full 360°. (The aft cockpit on the prototypes was not fitted to this standard, having instrumentation for the flight test observer.)

Long-range communication was by high-powered HF radio, using the then-new notch aerials mounted at the wing root leading edges. In addition, a 3,600 channel (20 selectable by the pilot) VHF/UHF transmitter/receiver was fitted, with aerials mounted

at the fin tip and under the nosecone. IFF and ECM were also to be standard fit.

Both crew-members were provided with a Martin-Baker Mk.8VA zero-zero rocket ejection seat, which gave an exceptional degree of comfort, necessary for the aircraft's role. Each seat had a hand-operated ratchet device, enabling the selection of any desired harness tightness instantaneously, as well as allowing slackening off for comfort. For the first time ever, head and arm restraints were fitted, together with the normal harness and leg restraints. The navigator could jettison his canopy and eject at any time but, if the pilot initiated ejection, the navigator was automatically ejected first, followed closely by the pilot. Automatic harness pre-tensioning was accomplished ballistically, together with the head and arm restraint, to ensure the correct posture for safe ejection.

Forward of Stn. 207, low down on each side of the nose were 7'8" bays for the fitting of sideways-looking radar scanners, and on the left side of the nose just below the cockpit sills was a retractable flight refuelling probe housing (not on XR 219). Three large avionics bay doors formed part of the lower fuselage skin. These were not just panel covers for the bays, but acted as equipment 'trays' with the avionics boxes actually mounted on them. They had to be supported on special cradles for servicing, each weighing some 250 lbs.

The main avionics bay occupied the whole width of the fuselage aft of the cockpits, between Frames 207 and 280. The bay was both air-conditioned and pressurised, and accessed via a large single door on

*The second prototype BAC TSR.2 XR220 as now preserved at Cosford. The rectangular intake relief doors are open and main intakes blanked off. (Crown Copyright RAF Cosford)*

each side. The rearwards retracting nosewheel was hinged to the aft face of Frame 280, and was fitted with hydraulic steering. When retracted, it was faired by four doors, the larger rear pair closing after gear extension. It was fitted with two wheels mounted on a live axle, their track being 1'9", each with a 32.75" diameter, low pressure tyre. The oleo was capable of being hydraulically extended or shortened with a locking mechanism. It was normally locked in the shortened position, but could be extended by 42", to allow an increased ground incidence, to give the aircraft STOL capabilities by increasing available lift from the wing.

Apart from various components and systems in the lower part, including the auxiliary power unit, the whole of the remainder of the fuselage structure back to Frame 468.5 was occupied by the forward fuselage fuel tanks, access being via eight rectangular panels in the top skin. The auxiliary power unit comprised a Cumulus turbo-compressor, providing pneumatic air bleed for engine starting and cockpit/avionic cooling, plus an electrical and hydraulic supply. It was started by a hydraulic motor fed from a pressure accumulator, which could be recharged by the pilot with a handpump.

Each side, the semi-circular, variable geometry intakes were fitted, each with two rectangular auxiliary doors, hinged at their aft edges, for increased mass-flow to the engine compressors at take-off, the intake lips being electrically de-iced. The half-cone, centre-bodies were actuated by a hydraulic jack, which was manually controlled on the prototypes, but was eventually intended to be programmed automatically for optimum airflow to the engines, dependent on speed.

The centre fuselage aft from Frame 468.5 to FR. 724 was occupied by the engine and weapons bays, with a cut-out at the top to accept the wing structure. The engine centrelines were only 49" apart to minimise asymmetric thrust in the event of one failing. After removal of the fuselage tailcone, they were withdrawn through the aft end of the fuselage for servicing. The main undercarriage was hinged to Fr. 629, retracting into its bay outboard of the intake ducting. All main members of the undercarriage were manufactured from forged and machined ultra-high tensile steel, and were designed with long-stroke oleos to enable them to cope with undulating, semi-prepared surfaces. The oleos had 'soft' characteristics over most of their travel, stiffening towards the limit of stroke. The main legs

252

retracted forwards into their bays with a complicated sequencing which rotated the twin, tandem-wheel, bogies through 180° before entering their bay. (It was this rotation mechanism which gave all of the initial sequencing problems.) Each bay was enclosed by one large forward door, which opened only during undercarriage extension or retraction, and a smaller aft door which remained open when the undercarriage was down. The wheels were each fitted with 44.5″ diameter, low pressure tyres, and incorporated axle-mounted Maxaret brakes which were each fitted with an electric fan for cooling.

The aft fuselage section contained the four petal airbrake panels, the aft fuselage tanks, and the two jetpipes, with their fully variable afterburner nozzles. Cooling air for the afterburner section was via a scoop in the leading edge of the fin. The fuselage frame at Stn. 892 was a massive forged component, to which were mounted the taileron and fin spigots. The tailcone aft of sloping Fr. 932 was attached to the main fuselage by eight quick-release fasteners and was detachable for engine removal, and housed the braking parachute container in the upper 'pen-nib' fairing between the engine jetpipes.

The thin wing was of delta planform, with a subtle variation of contour especially at the root and tip, resulting in it having linear derivatives over the whole flight envelope. This, together with its relatively small area, resulted in the desired low gust response needed for sustained low level/high speed flight. It was built around a forward mainspar and aft auxiliary spar, to which were hinged the trailing edge flaps. Between the two were multiple spars and four intermediate spars, with the thick-gauged integrally-machined skins riveted to the structure. The wing was built in two sections and then joined at the centreline by a heavy gauge splicing frame, to be attached to the fuselage as one complete unit. The entire wing structure between the spars formed an integral fuel tank.

It possessed a hybrid aerofoil section with a cambered leading edge. The leading edge, trailing edge and quarter-chord sweep angles were 58°19′, 2°29′ and 50°48′ respectively. It had zero incidence to the aircraft datum and zero dihedral angle out to Wing Stn. 182 (measured in inches from the centreline), where the wingtips were abutted, having an anhedral angle of 30°. The chord at the centreline was 33′6.8″, at Wing Stn. 48 (equivalent to the wing root), 27′3.1″, at Stn. 182 9′7.8″ and, at the projected tip 4′3.35″, thus giving the overall wing an aspect ratio of 1.96:1.

Leading edge fairings and a triangular extension of the inboard structure completed the structure of the wing. These contained fuel pipelines and large HF notch aerials at the leading edge root. The wing tips were of conventional construction for their forward 50% and housed the navigation lights, and

ILS aerials. The trailing edges of the tips were of honeycomb construction, to which were fitted ECM aerials. At the 'root' of the tips, fuel jettison pipes were fitted protruding slightly aft of the trailing edges.

(*Author's note*: The side views on the drawings of the wing give the impression of slight wing droop due to the double curvature on the under surfaces of the wing root. This shape reflects the slight drooping of the root leading edge profile. The wing leading edge is straight and has zero anhedral out to the tip abutment rib.)

The whole of the inboard wing trailing edges were occupied by the plain blown flaps. Their structure was conventional, but from materials to insulate effectively from the hot air bleed ducts. The flap

## DATA

### DIMENSIONS

| | |
|---|---|
| Span | 37′1.6″ |
| Length | 89′0.46″ (overall including noseprobe) |
| | 80′7″ (fuselage including noseprobe) |
| Height | 23′9.25″ (ground static) |
| Tailplane Span | 26′8.34″ |
| Track | 13′4″ |
| Wheelbase | 28′11.5″ |
| Ground Static Angle | 0° (relative to datum, nosewheel normal) |
| | 7° (relative to datum, nosewheel extended) |

### AREAS

| | |
|---|---|
| Wing (gross) | 700.0 sq ft |
| Fin (net) | 60.0 sq ft |
| Taileron (net) | 74.4 sq ft (each) |
| Elevator | 39.85 sq ft (each) |

### WEIGHTS

| | |
|---|---|
| Normal Loaded | 95,900 lbs |
| Max. Overload | 105,000 lbs |
| Max. Landing | 57,200 lbs |

### PERFORMANCE

| | |
|---|---|
| $V_{max}$ | 2.05 Mach (at 36,000 ft) |
| $V_{max}$ | 725 kts (Sea Level) |
| $V_{Dive}$ | 800 kts |
| Sea Level Cruise | 0.9 to 1.1 Mach |
| Initial Rate of Climb | 50,000 ft/min (plus) |
| Service Ceiling | 55,000 ft |
| Radius of Action | 1,000 miles (internal fuel) |
| | 1,500 miles (with underwing tanks) |
| Ferry Range | 2,870 miles (internal fuel) |
| | 3,700 miles (underwing tanks) |
| Take-Off roll (ISA) | 2,400′ (at 95,900 lbs) |
| | 1,600′ (at 80,000 lbs) |

### REFERENCES

| | |
|---|---|
| RAF Museum, Cosford | —The aircraft |
| Imperial War Museum, Duxford | —The aircraft |
| Supermarine Archives | —Drawing 57100/11B and 11C |
| | —Drawing 57100G.A. |
| | —Technical Manuals (XR219–227) |
| Martin Baker | —Archives |
| British Aerospace Weybridge | —Photographic Archives |
| Boscombe Down | —Library |
| 'Air Enthusiast' | —Volume 14 |
| 'Flight International' | —31st October 1963 |
| | —9th April 1964 |

trailing edges were also of honeycomb construction. Flap actuators, four to each surface, were fitted with streamlined fairings each individually shaped to give optimum airflow to the flap surfaces. Four hard-points were provided for the carriage of underwing stores at Wing Stns. 120 and 155, the inboard pylons being plumbed for the carriage of fuel drop-tanks.

The flight control surfaces comprised three slab surfaces, all fully powered, and having three axis/three channel autostabilisation. The horizontal tail surfaces moved in unison or differentially to provide both pitch and roll control, and were referred to as tailerons. These were of symmetrical RAE. 104 section, and were set low to avoid the wing vortices, thus avoiding pitch-up problems. They were of conventional multiple spar and rib construction with honeycomb trailing edges, and were hinged at approximately 50% root chord on plain spigot bearings made from p.t.f.e-based materials, which minimised friction and break-out forces. Although normally acting as slab surfaces, a small 'elevator' was hinged to the aft spar. This was actuated by a single jack, housed in a streamlined bulge in the upper and lower surfaces. It was needed because, when the blown flaps were lowered, the centre of lift was well aft of the centre of gravity, requiring excessive taileron deflection to trim the aircraft at low speed. The elevator was, therefore, unlocked whenever the flaps were lowered, deflecting upwards only, to trim the aircraft in pitch.

The complete horizontal surface was set at an anhedral angle of 4°, with leading and trailing edge sweep angles of 60° and 10° respectively. Chord at the root was 15'0" and at the tip 1'6.4".

The fin was also a single slab surface with no trim tabs, and was pivoted on a similar bearing to the tailerons. Directional trimming was by offsetting the fin datum relative to the centreline to cope with any asymmetric forces.

Structure was again conventional, with multiple spars and ribs, with a honeycomb trailing edge. It was of RAE. 104 symmetrical section, with a leading and trailing edge sweep angle of 54° and 20° respectively. Its root chord was 14'3" and that of the tip 3'2.25". The tip comprised a dielectric fairing containing a UHF aerial. None of the wing, or tail surface leading edges were anti-iced.

## SYSTEMS

### Fuel
The fuel was carried internally in integral tanks in the fuselage and wing, which were treated with special sealant to withstand the high operating temperatures. The whole system had been tested on a full-scale rig at Warton, which was fully manoeuvrable through virtually the entire pitch and roll attitudes normally to be experienced by the aircraft.

The entire wing structure inboard of the tip abutment and between the main and auxiliary spars formed two integral tanks (divided only by the central structural splicing frame), and contained 1,474 gallons. Fuel in the fuselage was carried in two pairs of tanks, the forward ones occupying virtually the entire volume aft of the main avionics bay back to the centre-section transport joint. No 1 tank contained 1,132 gallons and No.2, 1,023 gallons. No. 3 tank situated aft of the wing cut-out and above the engine bay contained 991 gallons, and the No.4, above and between the engine tailpipes, contained 909 gallons which, together with a further 59 gallons in forward and aft collector boxes, brought the total internal capacity to 5,588 gallons.

For long range missions, the internal fuel could be supplemented by in-flight refuelling through a retractable probe mounted on the left side of the fuselage nose just below the pilot's cockpit sill. In addition, two 450 gallon drop tanks could be carried on the inboard pylons. There was also provision for the fitting of a 600 gallon non-jettisonable tank in the weapon bay, and a 1,000 gallon ventral drop tank under the fuselage, bringing the total possible capacity to 8,188 gallons. Fuel jettison vents were mounted at the trailing edge of each wing surface, just outboard of the wing tip abutment.

### Hydraulics
To combat the high temperatures, the hydraulic system used DP.47 Silicodyne H fluid operating at 4,000 psi. The majority of hydraulic pipes and couplings were manufactured from either stainless steel or titanium, varying in diameter from 0.5" to 2.5", with silicone rubber fluid-tight seals. Four independent systems were provided, two solely for flight controls operation and two for the general services – flaps, undercarriage, nosewheel operation, airbrakes and intake cones. The general services hydraulic systems could be used to serve the flight controls in the event of battle damage or an emergency.

### Air conditioning and pressurisation
Conditioning and pressurising were provided for both the crew and avionic compartments, the equipment comprising two air-cycle boot-strap cold-air units, one being permanently on standby and automatically brought on line in the event of failure of the other. The system was unusual in that it utilised fuel-cooled heat exchangers, and the mass flow to the cockpit could be varied as well as the temperature. However, provision was also made for crew ventilated suits, as well as anti-g suits.

### Electrics
Solid-rotor, air-cooled alternators, with no rotating windings, were used, together with solid-state voltage regulators. Each alternator was driven by a Plessey constant-speed drive unit, supplying 30–55 kVA. at 400 cps. output for the two main a.c.generating circuits. Another solid-rotor alternator, with

its associated regulator, driven by a hydraulic motor, provided a constant frequency supply for a third, emergency circuit.

## Avionics

The design of the complicated avionic suite was entrusted to several firms, dependent on their proven expertise. The central digital computers were supplied by Elliott Automation, as was the autopilot. The inertial reference system comprised three gyros and four gimbals and, together with the forward-looking radar, were developed by Ferranti. As well as serving the navigation/attack system, the forward-looking radar provided terrain-following data for fully automatic or manual flight at, and below, 200'. Two 7'6" sideways-looking radar antennae, developed by EMI, were mounted on the lower fuselage nose. One system was used for navigation, for the updating of the Doppler/inertial fixes. The other was for aerial reconnaissance purposes. Line scan, also supplied by EMI, was to be recorded on board, or transmitted to base for 'real time' data by a television link, and carried in the dedicated weapons bay-mounted pannier. Doppler equipment was supplied by Decca and the air data system by Smiths Instruments. The navigational computer could be pre-programmed by tape before flight, but could be modified by the crew if so required during flight.

## Weapons

The 20'6"×3'0"×3'3" weapons bay in the fuselage centre section was designed to accommodate a maximum of two tactical weapons, or 6×1,000 lbs conventional bombs. Externally, two tactical weapons could be carried on the inner wing pylons only, or each pylon could accommodate a 1,000 lbs conventional load. Alternatively, 4 × air-surface missiles, or 4×37 missile rocket packs, could be carried.

In place of weapons, a reconnaissance pannier could be fitted, carrying three vertical cameras, Line scan, sideways-looking radar, a data link radio transmitter and aerial. Three F.9 cameras were to be carried in the fuselage nose, to give the aircraft a limited permanent reconnaissance capability, comprising an oblique one on each side of the fuselage aft of the main avionics bay and a forward-looking camera in a retractable under-belly installation below it.

No weapons carriage capability, other than that of fitting dummies, was provided on the first prototype.

## POWER PLANT

Two Bristol Siddeley Olympus 22R. Mk320 twin-spool, axial flow turbojets each developing a Sea Level Static Thrust of 19.600 lbs., dry and 30,610 lbs., thrust with fully variable afterburner and water injection.

*Thankfully preserved despite orders to destroy, XR220 (see also page 248) can be studied closely in the RAF Museum at Cosford, Staffordshire. XR222, less complete, can be seen in the Imperial War Museum Collection at Duxford, Cambs. (Ron Moulton).*

# Selected Further Reading

## BOOKS

*Armstrong Whitworth Aircraft Since 1913*, Oliver Tapper (Putnam, 1988)

*Avro Aircraft Since 1908*, Aubrey Joseph Jackson (Putnam, 1989)

*English Electric/British Aircraft Corporation Lightning*, Bryan Philpott (Patrick Stephens Ltd., 1984)

*English Electric P1 Lightning*, Roland Beamont (Ian Allan, 1985)

*Fairey Aircraft Since 1915*, H.A. Taylor (Putnam, 1974)

*Fighter Test Pilot: From Hurricane to Tornado*, Roland Beamont (Patrick Stephens Ltd., 1988)

*Gloster Aircraft Since 1917*, Derek N. James (Putnam, 1987)

*Handley Page Aircraft Since 1907*, C.H. Barnes (Putnam, 1976)

*Hawker Aircraft Since 1920*, Francis K. Mason (Putnam, 1971)

*Hawker Hunter: Biography of a Thoroughbred*, Francis K. Mason (Patrick Stephens Ltd., 1985)

*Interceptor: Royal Air Force Multi-gun Single-seat Fighters*, James Goulding (Ian Allan, 1986)

*Miles Aircraft Since 1925*, Don Lambert Brown (Putnam, 1970)

*Project Cancelled: Disaster of Britain's Abandoned Aircraft Projects*, Derek Wood (Jane's Publishing Co., 1986)

*Supermarine Aircraft Since 1914*, C. Andrews & E. Morgan (Putnam, 1987)

*Three Centuries to Concorde*, Charles Burnet (Mechanical Engineering Publications, 1979)

## MAGAZINES AND JOURNALS

*The Aeroplane Magazine*
   18 December 1953
    2 August 1957
   11 September 1959

*Aeroplane Monthly*
   November 1973
   July 1980
   August 1983
   December 1983
   October 1988

*Air Enthusiast*
   Nos. 10, 13 and 15

*Aircraft Illustrated*
   April 1985

*Aviation Week*
   26 August 1957

*Flight*
   26 April 1957
   19 July 1957
    4 April 1963
   12 September 1963

*Flight International*
   2 August 1957

*Royal Aeronautical Society Journal*
   May 1965

# INDEX